The Future of Academic Freedom

CRITICAL UNIVERSITY STUDIES
Jeffrey J. Williams and Christopher Newfield, Series Editors

The Future of Academic Freedom

Henry Reichman

Foreword by Joan Wallach Scott

 JOHNS HOPKINS UNIVERSITY PRESS   BALTIMORE

© 2019 Johns Hopkins University Press
All rights reserved. Published 2019
Printed in the United States of America on acid-free paper
9 8 7 6 5 4 3 2

Johns Hopkins University Press
2715 North Charles Street
Baltimore, Maryland 21218-4363
www.press.jhu.edu

Library of Congress Cataloging-in-Publication Data

Names: Reichman, Henry, 1947– author. | Scott, Joan Wallach, author
    of foreword.
Title: The future of academic freedom / Henry Reichman ; foreword
    by Joan Wallach Scott.
Description: Baltimore : Johns Hopkins University Press, 2019. |
    Series: Critical university studies | Includes bibliographical
    references and index.
Identifiers: LCCN 2018032666 | ISBN 9781421428581 (hardcover :
    alk. paper) | ISBN 9781421428598 (electronic) | ISBN 142142858X
    (hardcover : alk. paper) | ISBN 1421428598 (electronic)
Subjects: LCSH: Academic freedom—United States. | Education,
    Higher—Political aspects—United States. | Higher education
    and state—United States.
Classification: LCC LC72.2 .R45 2019 | DDC 378.1/210973—dc23
LC record available at https://lccn.loc.gov/2018032666

A catalog record for this book is available from the British Library.

*Special discounts are available for bulk purchases of this book.
For more information, please contact Special Sales at 410-516-6936
or specialsales@press.jhu.edu.*

Johns Hopkins University Press uses environmentally friendly book
materials, including recycled text paper that is composed of at least
30 percent post-consumer waste, whenever possible.

In memory of
Reginald Zelnik

and

Judith Krug
mentors, friends, champions of free speech

Contents

Foreword

The past few years have seen increasing attention to questions of free speech and academic freedom amid a confusing outpouring of opinion about whether our campuses are hotbeds of leftist authoritarianism unfriendly to conservative thought. Much of this attention has been provoked by a concerted right-wing campaign to discredit higher education and the critical thinking it is meant to encourage. With the election of Donald J. Trump in 2016, the steady erosion of state and federal support for universities, underway for many years, has intensified. His outright disdain for so-called elites has encouraged unprecedented expressions of hatred for the work of college and university teachers; his secretary of education has defined our teaching as dangerous indoctrination; his judges are in the process of dismantling protections for unions, teachers unions among them. And the media frenzy his performances have created has only intensified the misinformation he and his minions seek to peddle.

In the face of all the fake news we've had about campus life in the twenty-first century, Henry Reichman's book comes as a welcome relief. It is an engaging, detailed, and thorough study of the meaning, history, uses, and abuses of academic freedom as it has been defined and defended by the American Association of University Professors (AAUP). Reichman has served as a vice president of the association and has led its Committee on Academic Freedom and Tenure (Committee A) for the past six years—a tumultuous time in US history. As he points out, however, the sense of peril is not new: the founding of the AAUP and its articulation of the principles of academic freedom more than a century ago were responses by embattled professors to assaults on their profession.

In this book, Reichman engages a vast theoretical, practical, and political literature that covers terrain both historical and contemporary. His approach is critical: he rejects the notion that the university is a "marketplace of ideas," insisting instead—as the AAUP founders did—on the importance of professional expertise; he embraces the idea that education exists to advance the common good, measured not in economic terms but as an enhancement of the human spirit; and he is adamant about the importance of protecting the political rights of students and faculty alike to protest inequality and injustice on campus and in the larger society.

His arguments on these issues are nuanced, and they will be of enormous help to those who want to formulate positions on matters ranging from the free speech rights of controversial speakers to the value of collective bargaining for college and university teachers. He offers important statistics to illustrate his points, whether about the corporatization of the academy or the incidences of left-wing student protest. (One set of figures should put to rest the claim that the Right is always the victim of the Left in these protests. Attacks on faculty and students who deplore Israel's treatment of Palestinians far outnumber protests against the likes of provocateurs Ann Coulter and Milo Yiannopoulos.) The wisdom in these pages is distilled from years of thinking—Reichman embodies the careful and committed approach of AAUP leaders over the years, but he brings to it his own experience as a student protester at Columbia University in 1968, as a faculty leader at California State University, East Bay, and, most recently, as chair of AAUP's Committee A.

These references to his experiences, as well as the detailed discussion of a number of Committee A investigations, make the text a lively read. One gets to think with him about some tricky issues: What are the limits of the "heckler's veto"—the silencing of speech by protesters? What is the difference between free speech and academic freedom? Does the university have the right to prohibit certain forms of speech it deems contrary to its mission? What should the administrative response be to faculty targeted for online harassment? In the process, the reader becomes familiar with what might be called the logic of AAUP reasoning—a complex process, based on careful examination of context, precedent, possible effects, and the consideration of what have come to be fundamental principles of due process and fair practice.

The title of the book implies a serious and disturbing question: Can the special freedom claimed for the academic mission survive the attacks upon it? What is the future of academic freedom? Reichman's answer is not reassuring. His chapters introduce us to the changes that have undermined the status and influence of higher education in the United States: dramatic cuts in funding at the state and federal levels; the substitution of contingent for tenured faculty; the denial of faculty participation in university decision-making; the administrative embrace of corporate thinking that attends to bottom lines, defines students as paying customers, and calculates its response to difficult issues (student protests, curriculum changes, donor mandates) in terms of risk and reputation (how will this affect the "brand"?); and the increasing interference by trustees and politicians in the operations of the academy. The current controversies are only the latest stage in a long, slow decline that has been marked by AAUP resistance all along the way. Reichman cites again and again the association's recommendations, critical reports, amicus curiae briefs, and lots more. These have not stopped what sometimes feels like a relentless bulldozer destroying everything in its wake, and yet they have provided the grounds for resistance, the tools for organizing.

Reichman's answer to the question his title implies is not exactly yes; instead, it's an urgent call to stop the destruction. Academic freedom is never guaranteed, he reminds us; it is "an imperiled gain that must repeatedly be won anew." Without concerted action on the part of a too-often complacent, apathetic, or overworked faculty, "powerful forces in our society today . . . would not only restrict the faculty's academic freedom but also . . . transform our institutions of higher education into engines of profit instead of sources of enlightenment." Reichman's book is a call for action. If there is to be a future for academic freedom, indeed for higher education as we've known and practiced it, a robust and outspoken defense is called for. I leave him with the last word: "A century ago, the AAUP issued the 1915 *Declaration of Principles on Academic Freedom and Academic Tenure.* These principles helped build what became the largest and most successful system of higher education in the world. One hundred years later, US institutions of higher learning urgently need a renewed commitment from faculty, students, and community allies to reclaim the possibilities threatened by academic capitalism."

If reading this book doesn't rally the forces, I don't know what will.

Joan Wallach Scott

Preface

> It is evident that any restriction of academic freedom acts in such a
> way as to hamper the dissemination of knowledge among people and
> thereby impedes rational judgment and action.
>
> —Albert Einstein (AAUP member, 1935–55)

In 2012, I was elected an officer of the American Association of University Professors (AAUP) and became chair of its Committee A on Academic Freedom and Tenure, thus commencing an adventure that has yet to end. In the years since I have found myself in the thick of an escalating and protracted battle in defense of professional principles and values established more than a century ago. My work has brought me to college and university campuses in all regions of the country. I have listened to the concerns of hundreds of faculty members, tenured and "adjunct," in research and teaching institutions, at public and private institutions, and in community colleges. I have met with college and university presidents, provosts, deans, and other administrators, and even with a few trustees. I have led two AAUP investigations of serious violations of academic freedom—at the University of Illinois and the University of Missouri—and helped write extensive reports on academic freedom and electronic communications, student media, and the "assault on science." I have been, in short, not just a scholar but an advocate and activist.[1]

As part of my work I have written regularly about academic freedom and related issues in higher education, mainly for AAUP publications and most prolifically online at the AAUP's *Academe* blog, where I have posted hundreds of entries since 2013. In the main these writings have been interventions in debates and controversies embroiling the academic world. This book is based on some of the more substantial of these pieces, in most cases recast here in significantly expanded and often greatly modified form. Taken as a whole, the book aims to bring to discussions of academic freedom some of the practical lessons I have learned working for the AAUP.

What do we speak about when we speak of academic freedom? As Louis Menand has written, "Academic freedom is not just a nice job perk. It is the philosophical key to the whole enterprise of higher education."[2] Since the AAUP's 1915 *Declaration of Principles on Academic Freedom and Academic Tenure* and especially since the 1940 joint *Statement of Principles on Academic Freedom and Tenure* by the AAUP and the Association of American Colleges, "the AAUP definition of academic freedom has become the standard formulation."[3] According to these foundational texts, academic freedom encompasses three fundamental freedoms to which college and university faculty members should be entitled: freedom in research and in the publication of the results, freedom in the classroom in discussions of their subjects, and freedom to speak or write freely as "citizens, members of a learned profession, and officers of an educational institution" on matters of public or institutional concern.[4] The institution of tenure—indefinite appointment following a suitable probationary period, with dismissal permitted only for "cause" and after appropriate due process procedures—derives from the need to protect academic freedom, which can exist "only to the extent that its exercise is institutionally supported and guaranteed."[5] To defend academic freedom, the AAUP sometimes functions, in Sheila Slaughter's words, "as an extralegal body that attempts to enforce the Statement of Principles through investigating violations and censuring universities that deviate from the Principles. The investigative reports it produces serve as a body of extralegal case law."[6]

Especially in the wake of the 2016 election, academic freedom has come under renewed assault, and there is growing interest among faculty and university administrators in understanding the challenges of the current environment and in the principles that underpin higher education's past success. But if it is still the case, as Neil Gross has suggested, that "most professors simply have not given all that much thought to the concept," then practical education about the importance of academic freedom is of the highest priority.[7] To adequately defend it, we need to better understand its meaning, the nature of the hazards it faces, and its relation to freedom of expression more generally.

One basic assumption underpins the arguments in the pages that follow. This is that, as Jack Schuster has put it, "whatever the venues and boundaries of postsecondary education, the faculty reside at the very core of the enterprise. . . . The extent to which higher education is effective (or not) in accomplishing its missions turns on the quality of the faculty." Or, as former University of Virginia president Teresa Sullivan has written, "Without the faculty, no part of the institution's mission can be met."[8] The faculty "are the appointees, but not in any proper sense the employees" of those who manage their institutions, the AAUP's founders famously declared. Yet today the central role of the faculty is more precarious than ever. As University of Wisconsin professor Chuck Rybak has written, among hostile politicians, trustees, and administrators "the level of obsession with faculty, with bringing talented, humble, and hardworking people to heel—the people most responsible for delivering the university's mission—approaches pathology."[9] To be sure, "higher education is nothing if not resilient."[10] But if higher education is to adapt and survive, the faculty and its allies must retake center stage in defense of academic freedom and shared governance.

Each of the chapters in this book may stand on its own, but taken together I hope they convey a unified basic argument: that academic freedom is threatened today from multiple directions and that challenges to it are central to the present crisis in higher education. More specifically, I argue, among other things, that academic freedom is closely related but not identical to freedom of speech; that new social media pose unique challenges to academic freedom;

that the influence of market-oriented business practices and of outside donors may also endanger academic freedom; that the expressive rights of students must be upheld as part of the defense of academic freedom; and that recent controversies over outside speakers on campus have been exaggerated and pose less of a challenge to academic freedom than do more ominous developments like the decades-long expansion of contingent faculty employment, legislative and trustee intrusion into academic affairs, and the targeted harassment of individual faculty members.

Chapter 1 looks back over a century of the AAUP's history to consider what sorts of challenges to academic freedom might be expected in coming years, thereby offering an introductory overview of the book's themes.[11] Chapter 2 reviews recent theoretical writings on academic freedom in order to reinforce justifications for it as a contribution to promoting what the AAUP's founders called "the common good."[12] Chapter 3 explores academic freedom's oft-disputed claim to protect a faculty member's statements as a citizen, what the AAUP calls "extramural utterances," while chapter 4 extends that discussion to consider the impact of electronic media on faculty rights.[13] Chapter 5, published for the first time here, considers the impact on and implications for academic freedom of higher education's increasing reliance on private external funding. Chapter 6 looks at online education, rebutting claims that it will somehow cure higher education's "cost disease."[14] Chapters 7 and 8 consider the academic freedom of students, with a lengthy look in the latter at recent controversies involving invited speakers.[15] Chapter 9 recounts the history of the AAUP's gradual embrace of collective bargaining, exploring some of the implications of that move for its defense of academic freedom.[16] Chapter 10 concludes the book with a sober assessment of the prospects for academic freedom and higher education more generally under the presidency of Donald J. Trump.[17]

The opinions expressed in these pages reflect my close engagement with the history, policies, and practical work of the AAUP, and therefore in many respects they parallel that organization's perspective. In the end, however, the views expressed here are my own and not necessarily official positions of the AAUP.

I am grateful for the support and comradeship of the current and former members of the AAUP's Committee A. That so many brilliant and passionate scholars assemble twice each year to discuss, debate, and enforce principles first enunciated a century ago, and that they do so with such penetrating intelligence, is itself a testament to the power of academic freedom and the necessity of the AAUP.

Since 2012, AAUP president Rudy Fichtenbaum has been an unwavering partner in leadership from whom I have learned more than I can describe. This book could not have been completed without the dedicated efforts of the AAUP's amazing national staff, especially the association's incomparable executive director Julie Schmid; former associate general secretary Martin Snyder; Greg Scholtz, Anita Levy, Hans-Joerg Tiede, and the late and legendary Jordan Kurland of the Department of Academic Freedom, Tenure, and Governance; general counsel Risa Lieberwitz, and Aaron Nisenson and Nancy Long of the legal staff; and Gwen Bradley and Mike Ferguson (a highly skilled and sensitive editor) of the Department of External Relations. Michael Meranze bombards me regularly with useful reading suggestions; his ideas and those of his colleague in arms Chris Newfield will be found throughout these pages. My former colleagues at the California State University and in the California Faculty Association first inspired my defense of our profession, and I continue to learn from so many of them about how to be a principled professor, most notably Dee Andrews, Bob Cherny, Jennifer Eagan, Steven Filling, Susan Gubernat, Susan Meisenhelder, Bill Reuter, Judith Stanley, Lillian Taiz, and Marshelle Thobaben.

Becoming chair of Committee A allowed me to get to know Joan Wallach Scott, whose work as both a historian and fighter for academic freedom I had long admired from afar. She is now my most valued reader. I am grateful beyond measure for her unwavering support of this project and for her friendship.

The book is dedicated to the memory of Reginald Zelnik, a truly great historian and Free Speech Movement activist who guided and supported my academic career until his untimely passing, and of Judith Krug, founding director of the American Library Association's Office for Intellectual Freedom, who years ago rescued an unemployed scholar and turned him into a civil libertarian. I wish they could read this book, which is inconceivable without their years of guidance, wisdom, and support.

Finally, my beloved wife and life partner, Susan Hutcher, makes it all possible simply by always being there for me

Chapter One

Does Academic Freedom Have a Future?

On September 7, 2016, Nathaniel Bork, a part-time philosophy instructor at the Community College of Aurora near Denver, drafted a letter to the school's accrediting agency. He was concerned about a new curriculum imposed on the faculty, which he believed was watered down and not appropriate for a college course, but first he submitted the draft to the school's administration to ensure that his letter did not contain factual inaccuracies. Two days later an administrator visited his class, and on September 13 he was summarily dismissed from his position. The college would claim that a routine, coincidentally timed classroom observation revealed instructional deficiencies so severe that they necessitated Bork's immediate removal, but an American Association of University Professors (AAUP) investigating team concluded that such a rationale "strains credulity." He had, the investigation pointed out, previously received numerous stellar evaluations from peers and students alike. As a part-time adjunct off the tenure track, Bork had no access to a grievance procedure. Indeed, the AAUP investigation found "a total lack of due-process protections" for the school's part-time adjuncts, who constitute 80 percent of its faculty.[1]

Two weeks before Christmas in 2015, fourteen tenured and nine tenure-track faculty members at the College of Saint Rose in New York received notice that their employment had been terminated as part of an "academic program prioritization" process that eliminated twenty-seven academic programs. An AAUP investigating team concluded that the process was "entirely inconsistent" with recommended standards for program discontinuance, that the college "acted in disregard of normative standards of academic governance," and that "the faculty ha[d] repeatedly been left out of deliberations or had its reasoned objections ignored," all of which "rendered tenure virtually meaningless and thus severely undermined academic freedom."[2]

In June 2017, Johnny Williams, a tenured professor in sociology at Trinity College in Hartford, Connecticut, posted an online response to a police shooting. "It is past time for the racially oppressed to do what people who believe themselves to be 'white' will not do, put [an] end to the vectors of their destructive mythology of whiteness and their white supremacy system," he wrote, adding a hashtag that some interpreted as advocating violence. The post was quickly picked up by Campus Reform, a right-wing website that "monitors" faculty expression, and spread to other outlets, and within hours Williams and his family had received multiple death threats. The harassment grew so severe, extending to others at the college, that Trinity administrators felt compelled to close the campus for a half day. Two Republican legislators called on Trinity "to immediately, and permanently, remove Mr. Williams from the ranks of the school's faculty." Trinity quickly placed Williams on involuntary leave, failing even to speak to him in advance. Only after the campus AAUP chapter and other faculty members, supported by the national AAUP, exerted pressure did the school acknowledge that a faculty member's expression as a citizen is protected by academic freedom.[3]

The experiences of Bork, the St. Rose faculty, and Williams typify some of the challenges to academic freedom that college and university faculties face in today's environment. Insofar as such cases are increasing in frequency, they do not bode well for academic freedom's future. Nevertheless, prognostications about the future of academic freedom are best informed by the lessons of its past. And if there is any lesson to be learned from the more than one-hundred-year history of the AAUP, it is that academic freedom can never be taken for granted.

While academic freedom is one of the foundations of greatness in the American higher education system,[4] it has always been—and always will be—contested and vulnerable. The AAUP in 1915 first defined the fundamental principles of academic freedom, including the freedom to teach, conduct research, and speak as a citizen without institutional restraint. The subsequent 1940 *Statement of Principles on Academic Freedom and Tenure*, formulated jointly by the AAUP and the Association of American Colleges (now the Association of American Colleges and Universities), with its expansive 1970 interpretive comments, further enshrined these principles and has gained such extensive support that it is now viewed as standard in colleges and universities across the country.[5] Embraced by the American Federation of Teachers and the National Education Association and endorsed by nearly 250 educational associations and scholarly organizations, the *Statement* or its principles can be found in thousands of faculty handbooks, collective bargaining agreements, and institutional policies. Today, few American colleges or universities fail to claim to embrace some version of academic freedom, albeit not always in the manner that the AAUP has defined and defended it for more than a century. Even the enemies of academic freedom are often compelled to disguise their assaults on it by employing the language of academic freedom itself.[6]

Nevertheless, it is difficult not to recognize that, in key respects, the present situation is painfully reminiscent of that faced a century ago by the AAUP's founders. In 1915, only a handful of prominent full professors at elite institutions held an appointment carrying indefinite tenure. In 1940, tenure policies at most institutions were inadequate, if they existed at all. By the 1960s and 1970s, however, the tenure system had become an established norm in American higher education, and today only a small minority of American four-year colleges and universities fail to recognize the need for some sort of tenure scheme linked to the protection of academic freedom. But if most colleges and universities now provide tenure protections, they provide them for an ever-shrinking segment of the faculty. At present, only about one-third or less of all those who teach in higher education are included in the tenure system—certainly more than were in that position in 1915 or even, perhaps, as late as

1940, but a much smaller percentage than a few decades ago.[7] As of 2017, some 40 percent of 1.6 million postsecondary teaching positions were part-time, with only a handful tenured; another 14 percent were graduate student employees.[8] It is not only the explosion of part-time appointments that is to blame. Since 1993, a majority of new full-time appointments have also been off the tenure track. As Jack Schuster has written, "Tenure is being slowly—or perhaps not so slowly—but surely *circumvented*, in a sense made less and less relevant."[9] If, as the AAUP has argued, tenure provides the most reliable protection for academic freedom—especially if its protections can be enforced by the provisions of a collective bargaining agreement— then academic freedom today may be as endangered as it has been at almost any moment since the AAUP's inception.

The AAUP was created in the context of the expanding economic and social inequality and concentration of corporate power associated with the Gilded Age. Conditions today are eerily similar. Economic inequality has reached a level not seen since the 1920s or earlier.[10] The expanding influence of wealth on politics, society, and culture cannot be ignored. Moreover, if those who founded the AAUP were justly concerned, as are we, about the untoward influence of corporate and business interests on higher learning, today's universities—and many smaller colleges too—now function increasingly like business enterprises themselves. Governance at these institutions is progressively more hierarchical, and the focus is more and more on "the bottom line." What Sheila Slaughter and Gary Rhoades have labeled "academic capitalism" has increasingly subordinated higher education's dedication to the public good. As a consequence, "market behaviors have come to permeate almost *all* aspects of colleges and universities, from research to instruction."[11] The great philosopher and AAUP founding president John Dewey and his colleagues might have found much in our current system of higher education that is new and improved, especially with respect to its greater accessibility, but they would surely recognize the profound dangers posed by these trends.[12]

Academic capitalism—or, as many term it, "corporatization"[13]—has greatly impacted academic work and the ability of the faculty to unite in defense of professional norms, including academic freedom. As Rhoades notes, "At the core of the growth categories of academic employment is deep job insecurity and an almost total lack of due process, which fundamentally compromises academic freedom."[14] But it is not simply that the faculty is now divided between those on the tenure track and those with contingent, often part-time appointments. Disciplinary divisions—between professional and academic, STEM (science, technology, engineering, and math) and humanities—have expanded as well. Faculty work is also increasingly segmented, with an expanding bifurcation between teaching and research, and growing tension over the emergence of new nonfaculty academic professions that also claim expertise in teaching and learning, especially as instruction has incorporated new technologies.[15] At the same time, academic capitalism's stress on measuring, assessment, and quantification has yielded what David Graeber colorfully called "the bullshitization of academic life: that is, the degree to which those involved in teaching and academic management spend more and more of their time involved in tasks which they secretly—or not so secretly—believe to be entirely pointless."[16] Although countertrends cannot be ignored, Jack Schuster and Martin Finkelstein may not be far off the mark when they conclude that "centrifugal pressures on academic life, often market-driven, that increasingly differentiate among faculty, render the concept of *the* faculty more and more hollow."[17]

Defending and Expanding Tenure

In important respects the challenges confronting today's professoriate remain fundamentally similar to those faced by our predecessors. First and foremost among those challenges is the search for ways to protect academic freedom in a world where a growing majority of teachers are employed in what are essentially "at-will" positions. The solution forged by Dewey and his colleagues was the tenure system, under which, after an appropriate probationary period, a faculty member may be dismissed only for cause and after a hearing by a body of colleagues or in response to extreme financial exigency.[18] While some claim that this system is outdated, it remains critical to the defense of academic freedom. The point, however, is not simply to "defend" tenure, especially if such defense is understood as limited to those already blessed with this increasingly infrequent status. The point, instead, is to expand considerably its reach, much as the AAUP's founders did a century ago.

And their success provides encouragement. Can non-tenure-track positions be converted to tenure-track ones? Of course they can; as Hans-Joerg Tiede has documented for the 1930s, a period also marked by "the prevalence of contingent faculty," our predecessors did it.[19] There is a rightful place in the academy for some temporary part-time appointments, but compelling allegedly "adjunct" faculty to cobble together the semblance of a career from a series of part-time jobs is not only an unconscionable abuse of those colleagues but also an ominous threat to the academic freedom of all faculty members and, indeed, to the integrity and quality of higher education in general.[20]

It is important also to stress that the explosive growth of hiring off the tenure track presents an obstacle not only to academic freedom, shared governance, and the economic security of the faculty but to student success as well. As early as 1986, AAUP's Committee A wrote in a report entitled *On Full-Time Non-tenure-track Appointments*, "We question whether the intellectual mission of a college or university is well served when the institution asserts that certain basic courses are indispensable for a liberal education but then assigns responsibility for those courses to faculty members who are deemed replaceable and unnecessary to the institution."[21] Indeed, some research has demonstrated that excessive reliance on faculty with contingent appointments adversely affects graduation rates, "with the largest impact on students being felt at the public master's level institutions."[22] According to a study sponsored by the Delta Cost Project, colleges and universities with higher shares of students at risk of noncompletion also have higher shares of contingent faculty.[23]

"If there is any issue that has been talked about with more deep ignorance and unthinking," wrote Wisconsin professor Chuck Rybak, "it's the concept of tenure."[24] Tenure is not a "perk"; it is *earned*, not merely granted. For Rybak, "tenure is a source of pride . . . because it signifies nearly *two decades* of my life: the study, training, job searches, students and their triumphs, individual and book publications, teaching awards, community work, institutional work, and so on."[25] Most importantly, tenure is first and foremost about the protection of academic freedom, not job security. As AAUP president and University of Chicago physiologist A. J. Carlson put it in 1938, "Tenure in academic ranks is a sine qua non for academic freedom. . . . Without tenure, freedom is at the mercy of the administrator, and the myopic or dictatorial administrators will foster a faculty full of fear and assiduous in apple polishing rather than in teaching or research."[26]

Tenure, it should also be noted, was never defined by the AAUP or others as a protection only for research, as some now claim.[27] As the AAUP's Committee on Contingency and the Profession insisted in its 2010 report *Tenure and Teaching-Intensive Appointments*, "Tenure was not designed as a merit badge for research-intensive faculty or as a fence to exclude those with teaching-intensive commitments."[28] Hence, proposals for a "teaching-intensive" tenure track, such as that offered by Michael Bérubé and Jennifer Ruth, are not so much innovations as reaffirmations of tenure's fundamental premises, and they could provide one possible route for reversing the baleful trend toward contingency of the past few decades.[29]

In other words, even as college and university faculties must champion as aggressively as possible the academic freedom rights of all who teach and research, including part-time "adjuncts," we must continue to insist, in the words of the 1940 *Statement*, that "after the expiration of a probationary period, teachers or investigators should have permanent or continuous tenure, and their service should be terminated only for adequate cause . . . or under extraordinary circumstances because of financial exigencies." There is no more

critical task in the defense of academic freedom today than a renewed fight to make the overwhelming majority of faculty appointments once again full-time and probationary for tenure.[30]

Threats to Academic Freedom

In its first hundred years, the AAUP became justly renowned for
its defense of individual faculty members whose academic freedom
was violated, an activity that the association is committed to continuing and, where feasible, expanding. But, as Geoffrey Stone has pointed
out, "the real threat to academic freedom comes not from the isolated
incident that arises out of a highly particularized dispute, but from
efforts to impose a pall of orthodoxy that would broadly silence all
dissent."[31] This clearly is the lesson of the AAUP's failures during
World War I and the Red Scare of the 1950s. More encouraging, however, has been the association's more recent willingness to stand up to
the national security state, for example, in its 2003 report *Academic
Freedom and National Security in a Time of Crisis*.[32]

It must also be stressed that threats to academic freedom cannot
always be identified politically with the "Right" or the "Left." It is not
only that those terms are notoriously imprecise, encompassing both
opponents and supporters of the rights of their adversaries. Facile
notions that "both sides do it" miss an important point. Threats often
arise from neither the Left nor the Right. Attacks on academic freedom are most dangerous when they come from entrenched power.
On college and university campuses that means the administration,
the trustees, and (at public institutions) politicians. It matters less for
academic freedom if these forces can be labeled "Right" or "Left"—
although sometimes that is clearly both possible and necessary—than
that they have the power to implement policy and take action. As the
late conservative intellectual Peter Augustine Lawler put it, "The most
pervasive trend opposing higher education in America is compla-
cently bipartisan. It is facilitated by administrators academic and
otherwise, foundations, bureaucrats, and experts."[33] Both "rightists"
and "leftists" among faculty, students, alumni, and donors are well

within their rights to make demands on the institution, including even to call on the institution to discipline dissenting faculty or students. However, it is the obligation of the institution and its leadership to resist such calls and to defend academic freedom.

The Power of Money

From where might future efforts to impose a "pall of orthodoxy" emerge? What broad threats to academic freedom can be observed on the horizon? First, and most visible, is once again the expanding and corrupting influence of money.[34] The need for resources has always posed challenges to the principles of academic freedom. How much sway should donors, granting agencies, and governments have in how colleges and universities make use of the resources they provide? When must an institution and its faculty simply say "no" to offers of funding that carry constraining conditions? These questions are at least as old as the AAUP itself.[35] But as colleges and universities grow increasingly dependent on outside largesse, concerns about the abuse of external influence are mounting. Take the University of Michigan as an example. There a former pension manager barred by the Securities and Exchange Commission convinced his former colleague, who was in charge of the school's endowment, to invest $95 million into funds he represented. In addition, executives at some of the nation's top investment firms donated hundreds of millions of dollars to the university, while its endowment invested as much as $4 billion in those companies' funds. One donation of real estate property was ultimately resold to a representative of the donor for less than one-third of its appraised value, netting less than $2 million, while the donor claimed a charitable tax deduction of $33 million on the deal. "Michigan walked away with $1.94 million . . . for allowing someone else to try to take millions out of the U.S. Treasury," opined one tax specialist.[36]

As one study argued, "Endowment management is now a form of financial-academic capitalism in which universities engage in market activities to generate profit in order to secure advantage over competitor institutions by amassing wealth." Such an approach is a "contributing factor to the steep and persistent stratification that characterizes higher education in the U.S." For example, a 2010 decision by Michigan's Board of Regents to cut the spending rate from its nearly $11 billion endowment kept more than $30 million a year inside the endowment rather than doing more to help keep tuition low, hire more faculty, and update classrooms, an independent analysis by the *Detroit Free Press* found.[37]

The recent proliferation of externally funded "centers" catering to the needs of business or other outside forces, often with transparently political agendas, is another troubling illustration. To be sure, donors have every right to request that their donations be used for goals they support. It is the responsibility of the university, however, to ensure that those goals do not conflict with basic principles of institutional autonomy, academic freedom, and shared governance. In 1914, Harvard president Abbot Lawrence Lowell turned down a $10,000,000 bequest that was conditioned on the firing of a controversial professor.[38] Indeed, on the issue of outside interference in the university—whether from government or private interests—the AAUP's view is essentially that propounded in 1957 by US Supreme Court justice Felix Frankfurter, who identified "four essential freedoms of a university—to determine for itself on academic grounds who may teach, what may be taught, how it shall be taught, and who may be admitted to study."[39] (For more on the impact of outside donors on academic freedom, see chap. 5.)

Research universities not only seek arrangements with private interests to fund activities once supported by the government but may also themselves seek to become more "entrepreneurial," claiming the right to control what has historically been the faculty's intellectual property, hence restricting the faculty's academic freedom to control the results of research. In 1993, for example, the University of California, Berkeley, in negotiations open to neither the university community nor the public, granted the biotech firm Novartis "exclusive license to commercial research" conducted by members of its Department of Plant and Microbial Biology, even if Novartis did not fund that research, including projects supported by public agencies like the National Institutes of Health or the National Science Foundation. The agreement was unprecedented and highly controversial—a committee of the California legislature held a hearing on the deal—and it raised profound questions about academic freedom and shared governance.[40]

As Jacob Rooksby has put it, "Higher education and intellectual property have a long and complicated relationship." Until relatively recently, research universities have been treated as a public good where unfettered investigation pushes new boundaries with results readily available to the public. Valuable patents and copyrights have typically been held by individual faculty members. But increasingly—especially after the 1980 passage of the Bayh-Dole Act, which encouraged technology transfer—"much of what can be assigned as intellectual property in higher education is being claimed by its institutions, with the interests of the public being harmed in the process."[41] In its 2011 decision in the case of *Stanford v. Roche*, the US Supreme Court ruled that a faculty member's rights to patents and other intellectual property belong to that faculty member unless specifically signed over to the university.[42] In response, some research universities (e.g., the University of California and the University of Chicago) now compel faculty members to sign over these rights in advance, as either a condition of university support for research or a condition of employment itself. Sometimes they even falsely claim that *Stanford v. Roche* requires them to do so. In short, they have begun to act as if they were corporate businesses whose employees produce works made for hire. Yet "patent enforcement reconciles awkwardly with the public good," and "university success with licensing patents already has proven to be uncertain."[43]

Defunding Public Higher Education

Even before the 2008 economic crisis, public colleges and universities faced strained financial conditions stemming from a decades-old trend of state disinvestment. Across the country government support for higher education has been declining even as the demand for higher education, by percentage of the population—and, in particular, by percentage of the traditional college-age population—has increased.[44] Analysis from the Delta Cost Project shows that between 2003 and 2013 state support for public research universities declined by 28 percent on a per-student basis. In 1980, states contributed 54 percent of total higher education spending. By 2014, this had dropped to 37 percent. At the University of California, Santa Barbara, state support fell from 54.1 to 23.4 percent, Michigan State University saw its support go from 45 to 17.8 percent, and at the University of Virginia support declined from 36.9 to 14.4 percent. Nationwide the cuts have totaled at least $500 billion.[45] According to a report by the State Higher Education Executive Officers (SHEEO), in 1992 tuition accounted for slightly less than three-tenths of the total educational revenue for public colleges and universities. But by 2017, tuition supplied nearly half of the total revenue, with tuition revenue exceeding public appropriations in twenty-eight states.[46]

Since the 2008 economic crisis, the decline has been especially steep. In 2017, only five states spent more per student than in 2008, with the average state spending $1,448, or 16 percent, less per student in 2017.[47] Since 2008, SHEEO reports, per-student appropriations for public higher education have fallen by around one-sixth in Texas, Georgia, and North Carolina; by more than one-fifth in Florida and Mississippi; by more than one-fourth in South Carolina; by about one-third in Nevada and Alabama; and by more than two-fifths in Arizona and Louisiana. There hasn't been much of a recovery either. Across the country, state allocations for higher education grew by just 1.3 percent from 2017 to 2018. In fiscal year 2018, nearly one-third of the fifty states decreased higher education funding.[48]

This dramatic decline has correlated with changes in the ethnic and racial composition of the student body. The National Center for Educational Statistics calculates that children of color became the majority of K–12 students for the first time in 2014. By June 2025, such students will constitute the majority of high school graduates, and soon after 2030 minorities—who represented just 30 percent of postsecondary students as recently as 2000 and constitute almost 40 percent now—are expected to become the majority on college campuses.[49] As the California Faculty Association, an AAUP affiliate that represents 28,000 faculty members in the California State University (CSU) system, reports, in 1985, 63 percent of that system's student body identified as white, and 27 percent identified with another ethnic group. By 2015, the pattern had essentially reversed, with 26 percent of students identifying as white and 62 percent of students identifying as belonging to another ethnic group. But CSU's state funding actually fell by 2.9 percent in constant dollars over the same period, even though the system gained more than 150,000 additional full-time-equivalent students. State funding and tuition increases combined have only increased CSU funds by 41.5 percent in real dollars since 1985, a considerable lag behind the 64 percent increase in students. As one faculty member put it, "As the student body of the CSU became darker, funding became lighter."[50]

The implications of this phenomenon for academic freedom and shared governance are multiple and profound. First, the decline in public support has accelerated trends toward privatization and academic capitalism. Foremost, there is the privatization of cost. Perceived less and less as a public good, education is increasingly seen as a commodity to be paid for by its consumer, the student, via higher tuition and fees, financed often through federally guaranteed student loans at interest rates well above market.[51] Moreover, the more students are viewed as "customers" and "consumers," the greater the pressures to accommodate their immediate desires, however narrow and shortsighted these may be—and not just the desires of any students, but those of the students most capable of paying.

In a disquieting number of cases, difficult financial straits have afforded college and university administrators specious justifications for assaulting the academic freedom of their faculties, as at the College of St. Rose. Administrators (and some legislators) have sought to justify faculty layoffs and the discontinuance of controversial programs not by claiming exigency but simply by making ill-defined assertions of "distress"—sometimes on grounds that are unproven, if not demonstrably bogus. In recent years, the AAUP has censured several institutions, including the University of Southern Maine, Felician College in New Jersey, and National Louis University in Chicago, for such actions.[52] At the last school, the administration, by means of layoffs and program closures, almost overnight transformed the university's once-vibrant faculty from a group dominated by tenured and tenure-track professors to one consisting overwhelmingly of part-time, underpaid, and, by this point, terribly frightened "adjuncts."

Perhaps the most dramatic example of how financial conditions may negatively affect the academic freedom of the faculty can be found in Wisconsin, where in 2015 legislators and Governor Scott Walker cut funding for the University of Wisconsin system by $250 million over two years. This followed two-year cuts of $250 million in 2011 and $100 million in 2013. In addition to these draconian cuts, in 2015 the state also approved provisions to remove the protections of tenure from Wisconsin law, increase the power of administrators, degrade the long-standing university system of shared governance, and authorize the board of regents to terminate faculty appointments for reasons of "program discontinuance, curtailment, modification, or redirection." This move marked a profound departure from the former policy, which allowed termination of appointments only for just cause after due notice and hearing or in the event of a fiscal emergency.[53] (For subsequent events indicating that fears about the implications of these changes have not been unfounded, see chap. 10.)

Nevertheless, despite dominant narratives emphasizing higher education's individual "return on investment," public support for state funding of higher education remains remarkably high. According to a survey by researchers at Columbia University's Teacher's College, most Americans continue to support government funding and to recognize that colleges and universities play many roles beyond helping graduates obtain a good job. More than three-quarters of respondents (76%) said public spending on higher education has been an excellent or good investment, with nearly half viewing public spending as an excellent investment. More than four-fifths of respondents (83%) said higher education institutions contributed to scientific advances that benefit American society. Approximately three-quarters of respondents said higher education institutions contributed to graduates' personal enrichment and growth (76%), to national prosperity and development (73%), and to advancing graduates' wealth and success (72%). Three-fifths (61%) of respondents supported increasing government spending on postsecondary education.[54]

Legislative and Board Interference

The Wisconsin situation speaks as well to another ongoing challenge to academic freedom: the increasing tendency of legislatures and governing boards to interfere in decisions more appropriately made at the campus level, including ones that should normally be the responsibility of the faculty. The 1966 *Statement on Government of Colleges and Universities*, jointly formulated by the AAUP, the American Council on Education, and the Association of Governing Boards of Universities and Colleges, declares, "The governing board of an institution of higher education, while maintaining a general overview, entrusts the conduct of administration to the administrative officers—the president and the deans—and the conduct of teaching and research to the faculty. The board should undertake appropriate self-limitation." The statement affirms that "when ignorance or ill will threatens the institution or any part of it, the governing board must be available for support."[55]

Unfortunately, too many boards, legislative bodies, and governors ignore this wise guidance.[56] At the University of Iowa a search for a new president was hijacked by a group of trustees beholden to the governor, who rigged the search to hire a largely unqualified businessman with no experience in higher education, much to the dismay of both faculty and lower-level administrators.[57] The Board of Curators of the University of Missouri similarly hired businessman Tim Wolfe to run the Missouri system, despite his complete lack of higher education credentials, with disastrous results. Wolfe was forced to resign amid not only widely publicized racial unrest but also pervasive discontent among faculty members, deans, and students.[58] When a graduate student instructor at the University of Nebraska was harassed after a video was circulated of her aggressively confronting a recruiter for the conservative group Turning Point USA, three members of the state legislature publicly campaigned not only for her removal but also for a de facto purge of the English Department, leading an AAUP investigation to conclude that "the heavy hand of political pressure" played a major role in the instructor's suspension and summary dismissal.[59]

And then there is North Carolina, where legislators and members of the University of North Carolina (UNC) Board of Governors launched a series of assaults on privately funded centers on poverty and civil rights, as well as on individual faculty members—with either tacit acceptance by or minimal resistance from university administrators. Gene Nichol, Boyd Tinsley Professor of Law at the UNC School of Law and a principal target of such attacks, was "on at least a half-dozen occasions between 2012 and 2015" informed by his dean of "threats he had received from leaders of the North Carolina General Assembly or the governor's office concerning my publications. The proffered legislative coercion was straightforward, unambiguous and direct." When Nichol failed to cease writing op-ed pieces critical of the state's Republican leadership, a private entity funded by the governor's budget director filed a series of public records requests demanding all of his "emails, phone call records, text messages, appointment calendars and correspondence."[60]

"Republican leaders had said, very explicitly, for almost three years, that unless I stopped publishing articles" in the local media, Nichol wrote, the Poverty Center that he headed would be closed. "I didn't stop writing. In February, 2015, they made good on that persistent promise."[61] The impact of such actions extended well beyond the law school. A former UNC system faculty senate chair concluded, "We've now reached a point where the Board of Governors is acting in ways that interfere with faculty prerogative on curriculum, on research, and on service."[62] In 2014, religion and politics scholar Omid Safi left UNC for a position at Duke. He told the campus newspaper that his decision was a response to political censorship by the UNC administration:

> I study the intersection of religion and politics and no one at UNC had ever objected to anything I had to say about human rights violations in Iran, in Saudi Arabia, in Turkey, in Israel, in any other country. When I started to write about the North Carolina human rights violations and injustices, and the ways that the Republican state legislature was characterizing things like the Moral Monday movement as "outside agitators," I was told in no uncertain terms that while people in the UNC administration individually agreed, . . . they were afraid that these kind of comments would lead the GOP to cut UNC's budget. . . . So ironically, although Duke is an elite, private, privileged school, I found it easier to do this kind of political truth-telling at Duke than I did at Carolina.[63]

Nichol concluded that "governing boards stacked with political operatives and potential high-dollar donors are not great candidates for the protection of core values of academic freedom and independence. Nor are the chancellors, provosts, and presidents that they choose to employ. University academic independence has disappeared in North Carolina. It was easily surrendered. It won't readily return."[64]

A related baleful development has been the growing tendency to view college and university presidents as equivalent to corporate CEOs, supported almost without question by compliant boards that regularly approve ever more astronomical executive salaries.[65] So, for example, when faculty members at the University of Southern California called for the resignation of that institution's president—whose salary exceeded $3.1 million—in the wake of a series of embarrassing scandals involving sexual harassment and administrative misbehavior, it took only an hour for the board chair—who once called himself the president's "servant"—to voice unconditional support for the besieged executive, who resigned several days later anyway.[66] The increasingly common practice of conducting presidential searches in secret, with little to no input from faculty or students, has been decried by the AAUP and others.[67]

With respect to small liberal arts colleges, Pomona College professor John Seery commented acidly that college presidents more often than not "don't know what they are talking about, and yet they talk as if they do. As a class of professional liars, they shouldn't be trusted with the truth-seeking institutions with which they've been entrusted. They are to promote the college as a place of teaching. But they are not teachers."[68] Canadian writer and professor Ron Srigley has also offered a penetrating critique of the "all-administrative university":

> Regardless of one's thoughts about education or the direction the university should take, the assumption that a single, corporate-minded CEO surrounded by staffers and other administrators, not colleagues, is better positioned to understand and serve the institution's interests is a rather extraordinary one. Though there's been some decline in recent years, universities still tend to be full of a lot of very smart people who genuinely love their students and know their fields of study. They used to run the place quite well. The fact that we've sidelined them in preference of a small, quite differently motivated group of corporate wannabes is something that stretches one's credulity.[69]

These trends threaten not only shared governance and the faculty's academic freedom but also the very ability of higher education to fulfill its mission of serving what the AAUP's founders called "the common good," which provides the foundational rationale for academic freedom. As Christopher Newfield has concluded, once powerful engines for creating the middle class, colleges and universities have more and more become vehicles for creating and sustaining "the increasingly unequal society we have right now" and have hastened the "transition from a large, culturally dominant middle class to a smaller, more insecure one."[70]

One other way in which state legislatures have sometimes constrained academic freedom has been through the imposition on public—and sometimes private—institutions of so-called campus carry laws, which mandate colleges and universities to permit students and staff to carry concealed weapons. As a November 2015 statement opposing such laws, issued jointly by the AAUP, the American Federation of Teachers, the Association of American Colleges and Universities, and the Association of Governing Boards of Universities and Colleges, stated, "College campuses are marketplaces of ideas, and a rigorous academic exchange of ideas may be chilled by the presence of weapons. Students and faculty members will not be comfortable discussing controversial subjects if they think there might be a gun in the room."[71] In November 2017, the AAUP filed an amicus curiae brief challenging such a law in Texas. The brief declared,

> The decision whether to permit or exclude handguns in a given classroom is, at bottom, a decision about educational policy and pedagogical strategy. It predictably affects not only the choice of course materials, but how a professor can and should interact with her students—how far she should press a student or a class to wrestle with unsettling ideas, how trenchantly and forthrightly she can evaluate student work. Permitting handguns in the classroom also affects the extent to which faculty can or should prompt students to challenge each other. The Law and Policy thus implicate concerns at the very core of academic freedom: They compel faculty to alter their pedagogical choices, deprive them of the decision to exclude guns from their classrooms, and censor their protected speech.[72]

On August 16, 2018, however, a panel of the US Court of Appeals for the Fifth Circuit ruled that the three University of Texas professors who filed suit in the case could not prove "a subjective chill" on their academic freedom because "none of the cited evidence alleges a certainty that a license-holder will illegally brandish a firearm in a classroom." In the end, the court ruled, "whether concealed-carrying students pose certain harm . . . turns on their independent decision-making. Because [the professors fail] to allege certainty as to how these students will exercise their future judgment, the alleged harm is not certainly impending."[73]

Civility, Social Media, and Harassment

Our era is one in which it has become increasingly difficult to take certain positions without becoming subject to a flood of abuse. Moreover, as Timothy Reese Cain has pointed out, "It is not just truly heterodox perspectives but also opinions that even a vocal minority oppose that can cause significant disruption."[74] Controversies about race, the Israeli-Palestinian conflict, gender, sexual orientation, religion, or terrorism may roil campus conversations in ways that lead to efforts that chill freedom. Ironically, one such effort has been the spread of calls for "civility." For example, in 2014, as the University of California, Berkeley, was preparing to commemorate the fiftieth anniversary of the Free Speech Movement, Chancellor Nicholas Dirks informed the campus that "we can only exercise our right to free speech insofar as we feel safe and respected in doing so, and this in turn requires that people treat each other with civility. Simply put, courteousness and respect in words and deeds are basic preconditions to any meaningful exchange of ideas. In this sense, free speech and civility are two sides of a single coin—the coin of open, democratic society." In response, UCLA professor Michael Meranze wrote, "Ultimately the call for civility is a demand that you not express anger; and if it was enforced it would suggest that there is nothing to be angry about in the world." Greg Lukianoff of the Foundation for Individual Rights in Education cited John Stuart Mill to argue that "calls for civility are often a tool to enforce conformity. A fierce and angry defense of the values of the dominant class might be hailed as righteous rage, but even a milder, dissenting opinion is easily labeled uncivil." Free Speech Movement veterans also voiced their opposition.[75]

The celebrated case of Steven Salaita at the University of Illinois at Urbana-Champaign (UIUC) was another prominent example.[76] Professor Salaita was hired to a tenured position and was set to begin his employment in August 2014 when the administration and trustees became aware of a series of highly controversial tweets he had produced concerning the Israeli-Palestinian conflict. Because his appointment was still formally subject to trustee approval, it was withdrawn at the last minute. From the beginning the AAUP treated this as a case of "summary dismissal" and denial of appropriate due process. For the association the issue was never the content of Salaita's message. One may consider the contents of his tweets to be juvenile, irresponsible, or repulsive and still defend Salaita's right as a faculty member to produce them.

In a remarkable statement defending the decision to dismiss Salaita, the UIUC chancellor declared, "What we cannot and will not tolerate at the University of Illinois are personal and disrespectful words or actions that demean and abuse either viewpoints themselves or those who express them." The university's trustees further claimed that disrespectful speech "is not an acceptable form of civil argument" and that "it has no place . . . in our democracy."

These remarks have been subject to such withering criticism— and have since been all but formally disavowed by the university's trustees—that most of it need not be repeated. But three fundamental points should be stressed. First, while "civility" may be an admirable and desirable value to encourage, its use as a criterion for disciplinary action is necessarily vague and ill-defined. It is not a transparent or self-evident concept, and it does not provide an objective standard for judgment. Second, the standard of "civility" inevitably conflates the tone of a statement with its content. In many cases that the AAUP has investigated over the years unacceptable emotive qualities have been ascribed to ideas a teacher has endorsed and then employed by critics to discredit those ideas themselves or to discipline the instructor who advocated them. Third, and perhaps most importantly, whether it is a matter of First Amendment rights or the principles of academic freedom, the dangers to democracy of attempting to bar emotionally provocative speech should be obvious. As the US Supreme Court put it in a 1971 case that struck down punishment because of a speaker's use of an offensive expletive, "We cannot sanction the view that the Constitution, while solicitous of the cognitive content of individual speech, has little or no regard for that emotive function which practically speaking may often be the more important element of the overall message sought to be communicated."[77]

In the Salaita case, as in others, the rapidly expanding use of social media seemingly intensified the controversy. In a distressing trend, college and university administrators, as well as politicians and journalists, may treat faculty emails, Facebook posts, or Twitter messages as somehow exempt from the full protections of academic freedom and, arguably, the First Amendment. As the AAUP stated initially in 2004 and has repeated frequently ever since, "Academic freedom, free inquiry, and freedom of expression within the academic community may be limited to no greater extent in electronic format than they are in print."[78]

Tweets may be reminiscent of slogans, chants, and agitational speeches that in previous times might have gotten a faculty member in trouble. Take, for example, the 1971 case of Angela Davis, then a philosophy instructor at UCLA, whose contract was not renewed by the University of California Board of Regents because of the allegedly "unscholarly" and "irresponsible" content of her political speeches off campus. In that case, University Regent William Coblentz dissented from the board's decision, noting that "in this day and age when the decibel level of political debate . . . has reached the heights it has, it is unrealistic and disingenuous to demand as a condition of employment that the professor address political rallies in the muted cadences of scholarly exchanges. Professors are products of their times even as the rest of us."[79] Twitter is also a product of our time, and when professors tweet, they also do not necessarily communicate in "the muted cadences of scholarly exchanges."

Sometimes administrators have couched their censorious actions in rhetoric about combating cyberbullying, which undoubtedly is a problem among some students but hardly one that justifies the surveillance and censorship of faculty and student expression. Of course, there needs to be a distinction between emotional expression and threats of violence. Nothing in either US First Amendment law or AAUP case history prevents a college or university administration from responding to genuine threats of violence or true harassment—against individuals or groups—including threats made via social media.[80]

As the case of Johnny Williams illustrates, targeted harassment and threats of violence directed against members of the faculty and others in the university community pose a rapidly expanding threat to academic freedom. A January 2018 survey of more than five hundred chief academic officers found that 59 percent believe that academics are being "unfairly attacked," mainly by conservative websites and politicians. Twenty-nine percent said that those attacks included professors at their own institutions. Another 36 percent said they fear that professors at their institutions could become targets of campaigns against their ideas.[81]

As the AAUP, the Association of American Colleges and Universities, and the American Federation of Teachers declared in a September 2017 joint statement,

> These campaigns of harassment endanger more than the faculty member concerned. They pose a profound and ominous challenge to higher education's most fundamental values. The right of faculty members to speak or write as citizens, free from institutional censorship or discipline, has long been recognized as a core principle of academic freedom. While colleges and universities must make efforts to provide learning environments that are welcoming, diverse, and safe for all members of the university community and their guests, these efforts cannot and need not come at the expense of the right to free expression of all on campus and the academic freedom of the faculty.[82]

(For more on social media and harassment, see chap. 4.)

Academic Freedom and Freedom of Expression

The atmosphere for academic freedom on a given campus is inextricably linked to the broader atmosphere for freedom of expression. As Walter Metzger put it in his seminal history of American academic freedom, "The connections between free speech and academic freedom are many and subtle," adding, however, that "the

advance of the one has not automatically produced a comparable advance of the other."[83] Although academic freedom may be
limited by professional standards in ways that freedom of speech is
not, it is difficult to imagine the faculty's academic freedom thriving
where the freedom of expression of students and others is restricted.
Today the words of the AAUP's 1994 report *On Freedom of Expression and Campus Speech Codes* are more pertinent than ever: "On a
campus that is free and open, no idea can be banned or forbidden.
No viewpoint or message may be deemed so hateful or disturbing
that it may not be expressed. . . . An institution of higher learning
fails to fulfill its mission if it asserts the power to proscribe ideas—
and racial or ethnic slurs, sexist epithets, or homophobic insults
almost always express ideas, however repugnant. Indeed, by proscribing any ideas, a university sets an example that profoundly disserves
its academic mission."[84]

Connected to censorship through the banning of allegedly offensive utterances is the mounting invocation of "hostile learning
environments." Such environments may be defined not just by impermissible disrespect or abuse but by the mere creation of discomfort.
Colleges and universities have traditionally been places designed, in
part, to make people uncomfortable. Education can and should be
joyful, but it should also be challenging, difficult, and sometimes un-
settling. Yet increasingly we hear that the faculty's right to academic
freedom must be limited by the "right" of students not to be "offended"
or unduly disturbed by material or ideas they encounter in and out of
class. To be sure, colleges and universities must protect their students
from genuine threats, and the freedom of students to question and to
dissent is as important as their instructors' freedom to do so. But
current demands that syllabi include mandatory "trigger warnings" and
that the university community adhere to some arbitrary standard of
"civil" discourse—products, I would argue, of the consumerist culture
of the market—are out of place and threaten not only academic freedom but also the academy's fundamental purpose and mission. As
the AAUP declared in its 2014 statement *On Trigger Warnings*, "The

presumption that students need to be protected rather than challenged in a classroom is at once infantilizing and anti-intellectual."[85]

Concerns about hostile learning environments and trigger warnings raise the question of what some call student academic freedom. Recent years have seen an upsurge in student activism, especially among minority students, many of whom seek "safe spaces" free of racist and other forms of abuse, and who sometimes have tried to silence those—administrators, faculty, or fellow students—who they perceive as threats to their safety and even their comfort, or whose response to their demands they deem inadequate. Many in the media and even in the civil liberties community have derided these efforts as evidence of oversensitivity and even intolerance, and some have gone so far as to argue that they pose the main threat to free speech on campus and even in the country as a whole.

It is certainly true that student rights include the right to upset other students. But in many ways equally if not more important is the right of the offended students to express their grievances as forcefully as they can without undue disruption of the institution's mission. As Geoffrey Stone put it, "Toleration does not imply acceptance or agreement. The freedom to speak does not give one the right not to be condemned and despised for one's speech."[86] The real question is whether and how to act on such demands. Indeed, the issue is often less one of free expression than one of communication, environment, and values.[87] (For more on student academic freedom, see chaps. 7 and 8.)

A Call to Action

The founders of the AAUP, largely privileged and from elite institutions, defined for themselves and future generations the principles of academic freedom and the fundamental concerns and standards of the profession. They understood viscerally that in jointly expressing and advocating these principles there is strength. It is a tribute to the profession that the organization they founded has survived, albeit not without challenges to its reason for being.

Today, however, too many faculty members take the AAUP and, more importantly, the very existence of academic freedom for granted. Too often they regard academic freedom more as an inviolable (and frequently misunderstood) inheritance from the past than as an imperiled gain that must repeatedly be won anew. There are powerful forces in our society today that would not only restrict the faculty's academic freedom but also seek to transform our institutions of higher education into engines of profit instead of sources of enlightenment. But these forces pale before the challenge of the faculty's own apathy and indifference. Yes, faculty are overworked. But service to the profession cannot be neglected. Yes, union activism, participation in faculty governance bodies, and simple involvement can be time-consuming and tiresome. But it can also be rewarding and enjoyable. Yes, we have our divisions: humanists versus scientists, business versus education faculty, part-time versus full-time, young versus old. But if we do not overcome these differences, if more of us do not become active, all of us will suffer the consequences. As Sheila Slaughter has put it, "The difficulty of protecting academic freedom . . . should not cause us to abandon it."[88]

A century ago, the AAUP issued the 1915 *Declaration of Principles on Academic Freedom and Academic Tenure*. These principles helped build what became the largest and most successful system of higher education in the world. One hundred years later, US institutions of higher learning urgently need a renewed commitment from faculty, students, and community allies to reclaim the possibilities threatened by academic capitalism.

In 2006, the late Mary Burgan, then general secretary of the AAUP, outlined the many challenges facing today's faculty but concluded that "the moral power of faculty colleagues coming together under these challenges recalls other eras when America's academics outlasted the incursions of politics, managerial authoritarianism, or even their own inertia to preserve the academy's essential commitment to academic freedom and mutuality in governance. . . . After working with committed colleagues among the faculty and within academic administrations over the past forty years, I have confidence that their skill, cunning, and idealism will continue to animate higher education, defending it from its enemies without. And from its enemies within."[89]

The answer to the question posed in the title, then, is really quite simple: "It is up to us."

Chapter Two

How Can Academic Freedom Be Justified?

What do we mean when we use the term *academic freedom*? The concept would appear to be widely accepted, but its interpretation is often disputed. The American Association of University Professors' 1915 *Declaration of Principles on Academic Freedom and Academic Tenure* first defined three basic elements of academic freedom: freedom in the classroom, in research, and in extramural utterance. These remain central to most understandings of the concept. But the application of these standards has varied over time and often been contested. Equally contested have been the various justifications offered in support of academic freedom, including for its employment in jurisprudence. These often have dramatically different practical implications.

The variety—and richness—of such justifications is on display in several recent books that discuss academic freedom as both a theoretical and legal concept.[1] These works suggest a polar opposition between two fundamental approaches to justifying academic freedom. In one approach, academic freedom is conceived, for example, by David Bromwich in "Academic Freedom and Its Opponents," his contribution to *Who's Afraid of Academic Freedom?*, a sprawling and stimulating collection of essays edited by Akeel Bilgrami and Jonathan Cole, as "a category of political freedom. It belongs to the larger class of rights enjoyed by citizens of a free society."[2] The other approach, according to its most extreme advocate, Stanley Fish, views academic freedom as "peculiar to the academic profession and limited to the performance of its core duties." In this view, academic freedom is founded on professional autonomy and enjoys no direct link to the broader freedoms to which the citizenry as a whole may lay claim.

Bromwich and Fish expound purist versions of their respective positions, but in between lie approaches that blur the boundary between them. Most significant are those who seek to link the professional and the political—sometimes awkwardly but, I will argue, in the end persuasively—by joining professional privilege to higher education's contribution to "the common good."

Fish's *Versions of Academic Freedom* announces in the author's customarily confrontational manner "the inauguration of a new field—Academic Freedom Studies." The assertion is as false as it is arrogant; the pages and pages devoted to the subject before Fish ever weighed in are sufficient evidence of that.[3] Fish's role is to advance an interesting if flawed taxonomy of five distinct "theories" of academic freedom, conceived largely as ideal types, ranging on a continuum from the most to the least professional, with the former stressing the "academic" and the latter the "freedom."

Fish's own view, which he calls the " 'It's just a job' school" (a "school," he acknowledges, of which he may be the only member), defines academic freedom as little more than "a guild slogan that speaks to the desire of the academic profession to run its own shop." For him, academic freedom

> rests on a deflationary view of higher education. Rather than being a vocation or holy calling, higher education is a service that offers knowledge and skills to students who wish to receive them. Those who work in higher education are trained to impart that knowledge, demonstrate those skills and engage in research that adds to the body of what is known. They are not exercising First Amendment rights or forming citizens or inculcating moral values or training soldiers to fight for social justice. Their obligations and aspirations are defined by the distinctive task— the advancement of knowledge—they are trained and paid to perform, defined, that is, by contract and by the course catalog rather than by a

vision of democracy or world peace. . . . That latitude does not include the performance of other tasks, no matter how worthy they might be. According to this school, academics are not free in any special sense to do anything but their jobs.

What Fish calls the "For the common good" school "has its origin in the AAUP *Declaration of Principles* (1915), and it shares some arguments with the 'It's just a job' school, especially the argument that the academic task is distinctive." However, Fish explains, "the 'For the common good' school moves away from the severe professionalism of the 'It's just a job' school and toward an argument in which professional values are subordinated to the higher values of democracy or justice or freedom; that is, to the common good."

Fish's third school is the "Academic exceptionalism or uncommon beings" school—exemplified largely in his account by the somewhat unfortunate and unsuccessful legal arguments made by some Virginia professors who, in the case of *Urofsky v. Gilmore*, sought exemption from statutory limits on their access to pornography—which he sees as "a logical extension of the 'For the common good' school." For, he argues, "if academics are charged not merely with the task of adding to our knowledge of natural and cultural phenomena, but with the task of providing a counterweight to the force of common popular opinion, they must themselves be uncommon."[4] Fish's two final schools—the "Academic freedom as critique" school and the "Academic freedom as revolution" school—are conceived largely as products of a slippery-slope progression from the "For the common good" school and provide easy if rather uninteresting targets for Fish's hyperprofessional polemic.

There is much to be said for Fish's emphasis on academic freedom as essentially a right belonging to a profession; indeed, this is a stance that the AAUP has endorsed over the years. In a symposium on Fish's book, Yale Law School constitutional scholar and former AAUP general counsel Robert Post, a prominent theorist of Fish's "common good" theory,[5] expressed basic agreement "with the thrust of Fish's thesis." He writes, "Like Fish, I believe that academic freedom exists to protect the ability of academics to pursue their professional tasks. Academic freedom does not concern human freedom generally, but rather the autonomy of the scholarly profession. This simple premise is sufficient to cut through much of the bluster that envelops so many modern disputes about academic freedom."[6] Post, however, objects to Fish's extreme version of this thesis, beginning with his assumption that "claims of academic freedom are properly addressed to those within the scholarly profession," which "leads him to the disconcerting conclusion that academic freedom can never be justified in terms of goods that exist outside of professional scholarship." For if academic freedom can be justified only in terms of strictly academic values, then there is no basis for a constitutional or legal concept of academic freedom. Moreover, "Fish proposes criteria for distinguishing scholarship from politics in ways that fail to account for the breadth and diversity of the scholarly practices that actually characterize the modern university."[7]

This last point is crucial. One of the most striking features of Fish's book is its strenuous insistence that scholarly practice must be strictly apolitical, that there must be a clear and bright line drawn between proper academic work and any taint of political activism.[8] Fish quotes approvingly William Van Alstyne's claim that a faculty "is employed professionally to test and propose revisions in the prevailing wisdom, not to inculcate the prevailing wisdom in others."[9] But Fish's narrow academicism suggests that even, perhaps especially, proposing revisions in prevailing wisdom could prove unacceptably "political." As John K. Wilson points out, the irony is that, despite his professed concern with avoiding the political, "Fish's theory requires an obsession with politics, so that it can be sniffed out and suppressed. There are two fundamental problems with this idea. First, testing professors for the political content of their work invariably diverts attention from a focus on academic work. Second, the prohibition on politics leaves faculty with controversial ideas vulnerable to political retaliation."[10]

To be sure, academic freedom should not protect indoctrination, nor should students—or for that matter faculty—ever be compelled to embrace political, ideological, or religious positions in the name of scholarship. However, it must be asked, what norms can be applied to distinguish the inappropriately political from acceptable scholarly practice? Fish has no real answer other than his own prejudices. Sometimes Fish differentiates scholarship from politics in terms of the distinction between theory and action. Professional scholarship, he writes, is "a realm where contemplation with no end beyond itself is mandated and 'practical activities' are admitted only as the objects of that contemplation." But does this realistically describe what scholars in many fields actually do? Are there no practical activities in which they might appropriately engage? Post observes that some "academic disciplines study the world precisely in order to act on it. This is true of practical disciplines, like medicine or dentistry or nursing, which study the best ways to intervene in the world to create better outcomes. The research of academic doctors is often directed to new forms of action, like new surgical procedures. Policymaking disciplines (like environmental studies) may have a similar structure. For such disciplines, the distinction between theory and action will not divide scholarship from politics."[11]

Indeed, reading Fish's book, one is struck by his cramped notion of what constitutes faculty work in different fields. His examples of appropriate scholarship are drawn almost uniformly from literary studies, a discipline in which he has long advocated a vigorously apolitical approach. In his presentation, academic work is, well, strictly "academic," in the popular sense of lacking both practical utility and broadly meaningful import. According to Fish, literary studies, as well as law, history, philosophy, and, "yes, even politics," are simply professional activities in which knowledge is "disassembled" for dry-as-dust analysis. While that knowledge may be "reassembled by others and put to worldly uses . . . that's not the academic's job."

But in many—some might even say all—disciplines that is precisely one of the academic's jobs. In 1902, John Dewey observed how social science disciplines often "deal face-to-face with problems of life, not problems of technical theory. Hence the right and duty of academic freedom are even greater here than elsewhere."[12] Fish also seems oblivious to academic freedom issues in the hard and applied sciences. Employing Fish's approach, it would be nearly impossible to confront the complex issues involved in, say, controversy over the use of institutional review boards as prior licensing agents in human subjects research, a problem powerfully explored by Philip Hamburger in the Bilgrami/Cole collection. As Hamburger explains in his essay "IRB Licensing," "Academic studies of human subjects traditionally were uncensored, and through their radical critique of government, these studies did much to shape the establishment of government health services. Now, however, the very government department that imposes health-care regulations also imposes licensing on much of the academic study of health care. It thereby profoundly limits the studies that draw information at a personal level from doctors, nurses, administrators, patients, and their families." To be sure, the "It's just a job" school opposes government intervention in scholarship, but it is precisely because in these fields scholarship directly serves the common good and involves action, as well as thought with evident political ramifications, that an external justification for the academic freedom necessary for progress is essential.

Take another example: the AAUP in 2012 placed Louisiana State University (LSU) on its censure list after the school dismissed Ivor van Heerden, a researcher serving since 1992 in a non-tenure-track appointment. For years, his work in coastal erosion and in hurricane- and flood-related issues brought him public prominence and consistently favorable evaluations. But after van Heerden found that a main cause of flooding and resulting loss of lives after Hurricane Katrina was structural failure of the levees overseen by the US Army Corps of Engineers, university administrators moved to distance LSU from his work, which was clearly political in Fish's sense, and ultimately fired him. But in Fish's scheme van Heerden's research was never scholarly in the first place because it involved practical action from its very initiation. Hence, in Fish's conception, his dismissal, while perhaps ill-advised, did not violate his academic freedom.

In her highly engaging and personal book *Galileo's Middle Finger*, Alice Dreger recounts a number of episodes in the biosciences in which the kind of separation between scholarship and politics posited by Fish would be impossible to establish. According to Dreger, "Science and social justice require each other to be healthy, and both are critically important to human freedom. Without a just system, you cannot be free to do science, including science designed to better understand human identity; without science, and especially scientific understandings of human behaviors, you cannot know how to create a sustainably just system." Dreger's book is an extended appeal to both scientists and social activists to pay "attention to evidence in the service of the common good." In fact, as Dreger demonstrates, without such a foundation for academic freedom, professional norms themselves would become unenforceable and closed to both internal and external critique (about which more later).

In short, as Post argues, "There is no unified set of criteria that can mechanically be applied to all departments of a modern university. The criteria that attract Fish may make perfectly good sense when describing the difference between politics and scholarship in fields like English or comparative literature, but they would make hash of many other respectable academic fields."[13]

In his conclusion Fish belatedly acknowledges that "there is no 'intrinsic' form of the academy." Indeed, he adds, "there is no reason in nature for the category of academic work not to include the direct taking up of charged political questions with a view to pronouncing on them and thus prompting students to action." In other words, Fish's ivory tower version of academic work is precisely that: his personal preference, based on a foundation "no firmer than its self-assertion."

But another literary scholar, Stefan Collini, in his eloquent and incisive *What Are Universities For?*, offers a more nuanced and vibrant picture of the academy that allows plenty of space for the kind of disinterested scholarship favored by Fish but still succeeds in justifying on external grounds both the university and, by implication, academic freedom, thereby providing a useful basis for defending the "common good" approach.

Curiously, Fish's litany of flawed external justifications for academic freedom and the academic enterprise itself—promoting democracy, inculcating values, preparing fighters for social justice— omits the most common justification for higher education offered today by university administrators and politicians alike: its economic utility. Collini, however, focuses on this justification. He begins with the essential proposition that "higher education is a public good, not simply a set of private benefits for those who happen to participate in it." Yet he also acknowledges "one of the great strengths of the university and one of the keys to its remarkable longevity: while serving other needs, it also simultaneously provides a supportive setting for the human mind's restless pursuit of fuller understanding." In fact, "subjects which were initially introduced for broadly practical purposes have outlived those purposes and gone on to establish themselves as scholarly disciplines in their own right." Collini adds, "It is sometimes said that in universities knowledge is pursued 'for its own sake,' but that may misdescribe the variety of purposes for which different kinds of understanding may be sought."

Like Fish, Collini strains to avoid any instrumentalist vision of the contemporary university. Addressing the increasingly intense pressure for universities to justify their existence in terms of economic improvement, he writes,

> A society does not educate the next generation in order for them to contribute to its economy. It educates them in order that they should extend and deepen their understanding of themselves and the world, acquiring, in the course of this form of growing up, kinds of knowledge and skill which will be useful in their eventual employment, but which will no more be the sum of their education than that employment will be the sum of their lives. . . . If we find ourselves saying that what is

valuable about learning to play the violin well is that it helps us develop the manual dexterity that will be useful for typing, then we are stuck in a traffic-jam of carts in front of horses.

Collini makes the perceptive observation that universities often appeal quite differently to their government funders than they do to alumni. Unlike governments, alumni are assumed to be open to appeals to intellect and curiosity. They respond to requests for donations "because they precisely want to support something that they feel has more intrinsic and lasting value" than material improvement and economic activity. For these reasons Collini vigorously champions the university not as the sort of scholastic ivory tower that Fish would embrace but as a distinctive "public good," serving the entire society in multiple ways, including the political. Although his focus is on his native Britain, he marshals in support of this position a marvelous quotation from John Adams, the second US president, that should perhaps become a slogan: "The whole people must take upon themselves the education of the whole people, and must be willing to bear the expense of it."[14]

One important distinction that Fish draws between his own views and those of the "common good" school concerns the value of shared governance to academic freedom. Because Fish "conceives of the academy as a guild," he "recognizes as natural the desire of guild members to regulate their own affairs." Yet he dismisses the faculty's aspiration to have a say in the university's governance (and not just its curriculum and scholarly standards) as a mere "desire for power" with no true relevance to the protection of academic freedom. According to Fish, "The production of good scholarship does not depend on the political organization of the university within which scholarly inquiry is conducted; no matter what the lines and direction of authority might be, scholarly work can flourish."

Fish concedes sympathy with a line of reasoning that would privilege faculty expertise in strictly educational decisions. But at the same time he throws up his hands in despair at ever determining which decisions are truly educational and which administrative;

indeed, his attempt to clearly distinguish the two parallels his equally artificial severance of the "academic" from the "political." Still, he seems convinced that many decisions are in fact merely bureaucratic, and where these are concerned faculty need have no say at all. The point, however, is that precisely because the distinction between educational and administrative decision-making is not always obvious, the faculty need to be involved to some degree in virtually all aspects of governance. For example, while few faculty members are expert in architecture and design, building construction may have important implications for an institution's educational mission. At my own university a new building was recently constructed that was composed exclusively of faculty offices. Departments whose classes are offered on the other side of campus were relocated there, but their classroom assignments remained largely unchanged. The potentially harmful impact of this move on student-faculty interaction and thereby on the broader educational experience should be obvious.

Hence, Collini argues more broadly that as "organizations for the maintenance, extension, and transmission of intellectual enquiry" universities are "a collective enterprise and one which transcends the needs or interests of the present generation, let alone of the individual scholar. This enterprise requires, among other things, active citizenship on the part of the long-term inhabitants of the scholarly republic." Of course, where faculty responsibilities end and administrative prerogatives begin may not always be well defined and will vary according to the size, purpose, and history of a given institution. And it is certainly true that shared governance may be "cumbersome and awkward at best."[15] Nonetheless, a dedication not only to scholarship but also to academic freedom and to the broader "common good" demands shared governance.[16]

In both Fish's extreme version and the "common good" approach, efforts to define academic freedom on professional grounds must confront internal contradictions. These are highlighted in useful contributions to the Bilgrami/Cole collection by Bromwich, Joan W. Scott, and Michelle Moody-Adams. Bromwich, in "Academic Freedom and Its Opponents," is the most critical of the professional approach, urging readers "to resist the narrower and more profession-centered definitions of academic freedom that have arisen in recent years— above all, the view that academic freedom can be practiced only rela- tive to a disciplinary consensus. Such a tacit redefinition plucks freedom from the conscience of the individual scholar and lodges it in an official locus of oversight, a professional corporate body." In Bromwich's view, founding academic freedom on professional ex- pertise as determined by disciplinary and professional bodies means that faculty are effectively licensed "by the previous and ever-to-be- renewed consensus of experts in the field. Knowledge turns into the name of something commanded by administrators and produced by professors."

This is a powerful argument, and it must be acknowledged that reliance on disciplinary standards and credentialed expertise in the determination of what is acceptable academic work will tend to priv- ilege the status quo and disadvantage the iconoclastic and the novel. But the problem, as Post has repeatedly argued, is that "the market- place of ideas . . . is radically incompatible" with academic freedom's professional task. "The point of the professional ideal of academic freedom is to ensure that universities are organized to advance their mission of producing expert, disciplinary knowledge," he ar- gues in the Bilgrami/Cole collection. "But if, as the theory of the marketplace of ideas holds, 'the First Amendment recognizes no such thing as a "false" idea,' then it cannot sustain, or even tolerate, the disciplinary practices necessary to sustain the truth claims to which the ideal of expert knowledge aspires." For instance, it is per- fectly acceptable under the First Amendment for a politician, preacher, or an average citizen today to declare evolution a Satanic "theory," but such a declaration would be wholly unacceptable com- ing from a college biology instructor, in class or, arguably, out of class as well.[17]

Scott, in "Knowledge, Power, and Academic Freedom," her contri- bution to the Bilgrami/Cole collection, identifies the contradiction well: "Disciplinary communities provide the consensus necessary to justify academic freedom as a special freedom for faculty," she writes. "But the inseparable other side of this regulatory and enabling authority is that it can suppress innovative thinking in the name of defending immutable standards. Paradoxically, the very institutions that are meant to legitimize faculty autonomy can also function to undermine it." Or, as Moody-Adams puts it in "What's So Special about Academic Freedom?," her essay in the collection, "Many critics argue that far from being a defense against the coercive force of external orthodoxies, academic freedom more often insulates the academy's internal orthodoxies from critical scrutiny."

Can this paradox be resolved? Scott doesn't think so, but she sees the very essence and desirability of academic freedom in its mediation of these sorts of tensions, which are inherent to modern scholarship. She points out that the theory of academic freedom emerged in the early twentieth century as an attempt to address "a tension at the heart of the modern university: that between corporate power and intellectual inquiry, between instrumental knowledge production and open-ended inquiry."[18]

The founding and first years of the AAUP provide important experience in this regard. The organization has sometimes been accused of straying from a studied position of political neutrality that should supposedly permeate the spirit of both "objective" inquiry and academic freedom. But the AAUP's founders, as Hans-Joerg Tiede's fastidiously researched book on these years, *University Reform*, demonstrates convincingly, were actually not at first chiefly concerned with academic freedom, which they saw as both an instrument of and a precondition for professional autonomy, their true goal. Their concern was not only to identify means and methods of insulating the scholarly enterprise from corporate power but also, as Tiede shows especially in the case of John Dewey, to unleash scholarship to challenge that power and its growing influence in the polity.[19]

"It is precisely because the tensions evident a century ago continue to trouble the relationships among faculty, administrators, and boards of trustees," writes Scott, "because the value of critical thinking is regularly under siege in the disciplines, the universities, and the nation; and because the[se] tensions . . . are not susceptible to final resolution" that we need academic freedom, which is "an ideal that we reach for, even as its attainment never seems quite complete."

Moody-Adams addresses the problem from a slightly different angle. She argues that "freedom of speech and academic freedom must, indeed, be justified on very different grounds. Yet the two kinds of freedom raise similar questions about how to distinguish offensive expression that deserves protection from harmful expression that might not." Still, she admits, "democratic values and the values of academic life are sometimes in conflict."

Academic freedom must be acknowledged, Moody-Adams argues, to be an "exclusionary" concept. "Communities of academic inquiry are constituted by exclusionary practices governing membership, and standards of argument and inquiry evolve as shared understandings that are internal to these exclusive 'communities of the competent.'" But this leads critics to conclude that academics merely prohibit views that threaten their power. In other words, challenges to academic freedom are often constituted as claims against the very authority of the academy to reject certain judgments and ideas and to impose disciplinary standards. Can we "provide a compelling counterweight to unsympathetic critics who treat the academy's claims to authority as the mere monopoly of an arrogant and self-righteous professional guild?" Moody-Adams asks. Yes, she concludes, but that "reply must start from an idea that informed the 1915 founding of the AAUP: the idea that academic freedom must be seen as a public trust, rooted in the belief that those to whom its rights and privileges are granted can be safely accorded a wide-ranging freedom to regulate themselves."

Both Scott and Moody-Adams point to the emergence of feminist approaches in a variety of disciplines as examples of how, as Moody-Adams puts it, "structures that might impede" recognition of dissident or innovative scholarship "ultimately protect their rights and privileges . . . when (and if) they make their way into the academy."

Conflicts over what is legitimate scholarship and what may be excluded from the scholarly consensus are central to Dreger's book, which recounts in chilling detail how various dissident voices in science have been silenced by both the often stodgy and weak-willed conservatism of the academy and the crusading zeal of external activists. Yet what becomes clear from Dreger's accounts of her tussles with those who would mute dissenting voices on controversial topics like transsexual identity and in fields as different as anthropology and endocrinology is that iconoclastic views may be marginalized most readily not when disciplinary standards are enforced but when they are disregarded.

As Keith Whittington has emphasized, "Modern academic disciplines make progress by systematically screening out ideas and arguments that cannot survive careful scrutiny. In this way they insist not on homogeneity but on expertise." But, he adds, "if a community of scholars is not to become lethargic, and if the advancement of knowledge is to proceed, scholars cannot become complacent in their studies and blind to their deficiencies and biases."[20]

For some theorists of academic freedom, efforts to ground the concept in professional autonomy, even where that is tempered by commitment to the "common good," are inherently and irreparably flawed. Academic freedom, they argue, is nothing if it does not protect critical thought. In a widely read 2006 exchange with Post, Judith Butler argued that unless the very questioning of professional norms is protected by academic freedom, the concept will be hollow.[21] And she suspected that most academic norms, or at least those that she alleged underpin Post's conception of academic freedom, are excessively resistant to challenge, much less change. Not surprisingly, Fish criticizes Butler's approach, which he treats as the prime exemplar of the "Academic freedom as critique" school. Butler assumes, he writes, that norms are "rigid and block change, whereas in fact they are engines of change."

Here Fish is more right than wrong, although his account underestimates the power of tradition and, frankly, fear of the new and different in academia. He and Butler renew the debate in the

Bilgrami/Cole collection by offering diametrically opposed views of the movement for an academic boycott of Israel. Fish, in "Academic Freedom and the Boycott of Israeli Universities," opposes the boycott as a violation of academic freedom, a position shared (if on a somewhat different foundation) by the AAUP. Butler supports the boycott. The debate over academic boycotts lies beyond the scope of this book.[22] What is relevant here is Butler's contention that "academic freedom is a conditional right," that "academic freedom is a good under those conditions when it does not conflict with greater goods."

To be sure, it is undeniable that under authoritarian, nondemocratic conditions academic freedom in any sense of the term will be imperiled if not entirely restricted. And the fight to restore it may well be subordinated to more encompassing aspirations. But that is not because academic freedom is a "lesser" good than others but because it is one essential element of the pursuit of a broader "common good." While Butler recognizes the tension that Scott identified as inherent to the practice of academic freedom, her approach neither accepts that tension (as does Scott) nor resolves it; instead, she reduces the tension to what must in the end be a personal choice. For if academic freedom is to be subordinated to "greater goods," what and who determine which goods are greater? For Butler, clearly the emancipation of the Palestinians from Israeli domination is such a greater good, even if she casts this as simply a struggle to maintain the economic conditions essential to facilitate academic freedom in Palestinian educational institutions. I find that contention arguable, but the larger point is, why stop with Palestine? Why not prevent scholars from engaging with any country that fails to meet some intangible standard of "freedom"? More importantly, why not restrict academic freedom for the sake of other "greater goods," for example, the "good" of enforcing "civility" and protecting students from presumptive "dangers"? Once we step down the path of trying to rank academic freedom in a hierarchy of "goods" or "freedoms," the entire concept is essentially lost.[23]

Those who understand academic freedom as part of a broader category of political freedom have generally sought to ground that freedom in First Amendment jurisprudence. While the Supreme Court has declared academic freedom "a special concern of the First Amendment," as Walter Metzger has demonstrated, the constitutional approach to academic freedom differs significantly from the professional version formulated by the AAUP in ways that render protections of individual faculty members less than fully adequate. According to Metzger's account, "The centerpiece in the constitutional definition of academic freedom is not institutional neutrality, the pivot of the professional definition, but institutional autonomy, long seen by the organized profession as a lesser good and potentially as a serious threat."[24] In his contribution to the Bilgrami/Cole collection, Post goes further, arguing that as a constitutional doctrine the concept is "incoherent because courts lack an adequate theory of why the Constitution should protect academic freedom."

This incoherence poses a challenge to the viability of the "common good" justification advocated by Post. Under the Fish "It's just a job" approach, it doesn't much matter what the courts say, so long as they recognize narrowly professional prerogatives, although Fish's book includes an extensive, if confused, discussion of academic freedom jurisprudence. But the "common good" approach demands external validation that the courts could conceivably supply. The "marketplace of ideas" conception most associated with the First Amendment, however, provides no support for academic freedom or indeed for professional and expert speech more generally.

Post's solution, elaborated with admirable thoroughness in *Democracy, Expertise, and Academic Freedom*, rests on the linked concepts of "democratic legitimation" and "democratic competence." The argument, greatly simplified, goes something like this: in a democracy decisions must be made in ways that are responsive to public opinion. Hence, "First Amendment coverage should extend to all efforts deemed normatively necessary for influencing public opinion." This legitimation of decision-making, however, will only be successful if public opinion is informed by expert knowledge. Indeed, "reliable expert knowledge is necessary not only for intelligent self-governance, but also for the very value of democratic legitimation." Post calls this necessity "democratic competence." But such competence conflicts with legitimation. Under the First Amendment all opinions are equally valid. Under the First Amendment the expert judgment of, say, a doctor is just an opinion. But it is an opinion that can be regulated. Post offers this example:

> Consider a dentist who wishes to advise her patients to remove their dental amalgams and who is prohibited from doing so by local regulation. Imagine that the dentist charges that the regulation violates the First Amendment. The question of whether the regulation blocks the transmission of knowledge and hence triggers First Amendment coverage depends upon whether dental amalgams actually endanger the health of patients. How can a court answer this question? It must necessarily apply the disciplinary knowledge of medical experts. It follows that First Amendment coverage depends upon the application of the very disciplinary practices that government regulation seeks to control. A court will have no option but to apply the authoritative methods and truths of medical science in order to determine whether prohibiting the dentist's advice triggers First Amendment review. It follows that the value of democratic competence can be judicially protected only if courts incorporate and apply the disciplinary methods by which expert knowledge is defined. This is the kernel of truth at the core of the new institutional approach to the First Amendment.

He thus concludes, "When courts protect the circulation of expert knowledge, they also extend constitutional recognition to the disciplinary practices and methods that create such knowledge. In effect this immunizes such practices and methods from unrestricted political manipulation."

Post's concept of democratic competence comes as close as possible to resolving, at least in the legal arena, the tension between academic freedom's narrowly professional foundation and its justification through appeal to a democratic "common good." But it is at least questionable whether the courts will resolve the "incoherence" of academic freedom jurisprudence in the manner Post recommends. A study by Michael LeRoy suggests they may not. After reviewing 210 court cases generating 339 decisions, LeRoy found that 73 percent of cases brought by faculty on First Amendment grounds were unsuccessful. On this basis he concludes that "First Amendment jurisprudence does not protect the most controversial ideas expressed by faculty in higher education." As a result, he urges "professors to be more realistic about the limits of First Amendment protection" and counsels them to "think more deeply about strategies to preserve academic freedom. Courts are not suited for this task."[25]

Whether or not LeRoy's conclusions are valid, it is clear that the First Amendment may not always be the best vehicle for defending academic freedom. For one thing, although Post labors hard to craft a constitutional theory to protect the academic freedom of individual scholars, Philip Lee points out that in the courts "First Amendment protections exist to protect academic institutions, not the academics themselves." In July 2018, state attorneys representing the University of Texas declared, "The right to academic freedom, if it exists, belongs to the institution, not the individual professor." Almost immediately the campus president issued a clarification that referenced a system policy according to which faculty members are free to conduct and publish research and to discuss their subjects in the classroom. But the attorneys fired back that this was "a workplace policy" and not a protection provided by the First Amendment.[26]

Lee therefore argues that "while constitutional law is still the proper mechanism for defending institutional rights from government interference, contract law should be the primary mechanism for protecting professorial academic freedom."[27] Under Lee's approach AAUP policies would be enforceable under contract law if specifically covered by either collective bargaining agreements or institutional employment contracts. This is, of course, a route that the AAUP has been urging for years and one that ultimately provides the best assurance that academic freedom will enjoy legal protection.[28]

At the same time, if it is questionable whether the courts will embrace Post's jurisprudence of "democratic competence," it is at least equally questionable whether faculty will be in a position to win the kinds of contractual protections that Lee recommends. That is because the state of academic freedom today is at the least imperiled. Fredrik deBoer, for one, finds "a pervasive sense of fear" to be "endemic on many campuses."[29] A 2010 survey of 24,000 undergraduate students and 9,000 campus professionals (academic administrators, faculty, and student affairs professionals combined) at twenty three colleges and universities found only 16.7 percent of faculty members strongly agreeing that "it is safe to hold unpopular opinions on campus." (The figure for students was 35.6%.)[30] DeBoer attributes this in part to an employment situation in which "openings for full-time faculty members are few and adjuncts fill the gaps," putting all leverage in the hands of institutions. "With so many underemployed PhDs, controversial faculty can be swiftly replaced. The difficulty of obtaining a new job, meanwhile, compels employees to keep their mouths shut."

Michael Bérubé and Jennifer Ruth also make this argument in their brief but powerful book *The Humanities, Higher Education, and Academic Freedom*. It is not simply that faculty without tenure are easily replaced but that professionalism itself has been undermined. "With the erosion of the professionalism once institutionalized by the tenure system," they contend, "the university community has not blossomed into a vibrant democracy but reverted to the kind of demeaning and resentful culture typical of patronage systems." Indeed, there can be little question that deprofessionalization and loss of academic freedom go hand in hand. Recognition of academic freedom as founded on professional autonomy should make that clear.

But there is another factor at play that relates to academic freedom's link to broader societal freedoms. In "Academic Freedom: A Pilot Study of Faculty Views," a summary in the Bilgrami/Cole collection of a survey of Columbia University faculty members, Jonathan R. Cole, Stephen Cole, and Christopher C. Weiss report some disturbing data. Based on responses to a series of hypothetical scenarios involving issues of academic freedom, they found a "deep commitment" to academic freedom among only about half of the respondents in a reputedly quite liberal faculty. "Other norms that the faculty valued trumped the academic freedom value in a significant proportion of the cases," they report. "In percentage terms, 62 percent of the responses indicated a strong commitment to academic freedom when we looked at the scenarios in their totality." The authors suggest that "if an erosion of the norms of academic freedom and free inquiry has taken place at American universities and colleges, it may well be the result of abridgements of the freedom of speech that we have seen on university campuses over the past several decades."

The extent of such abridgement is well documented in Greg Lukianoff's frightening book *Unlearning Liberty*. Lukianoff is executive director of the Foundation for Individual Rights in Education (FIRE), known for its vigorous stance against "political correctness." Although many view FIRE as a conservative group, Lukianoff himself is a self-proclaimed liberal Democrat and professed atheist. Whatever his politics, however, his book should serve as a clarion call to all concerned about the health of our colleges and universities. Lukianoff is not directly concerned with academic freedom, although a chapter dedicated to assaults on faculty free speech is certainly bracing. His fear is that restriction of student rights has "made us all just a little bit dumber."

Lukianoff begins with these statements: "Colleges and universities were built on the recognition that you have to leave knowledge open to continuous debate, experimentation, critical examination, and discussion. Ideas that don't hold up to this scrutiny should be discarded. It is a ruthless and tough system in which ideas that once gave us great comfort can be quickly relegated to the dustbin of history. It isn't concerned with your feelings or your ego, as it has a much more important job: discerning what is true and wise." To accomplish that task, "colleges are supposed to provide at least as much, if not more, freedom of speech and thought as society at large, not the other way around. Campus administrators have been successful in convincing students that the primary goal of the university is to make students feel comfortable. Unfortunately, comfortable minds are often not thinking ones."

No doubt many will find such a blanket indictment a bit extreme and perhaps unfair; aren't violations of student free expression relatively rare? After reading Lukianoff, it is difficult to sustain that judgment. In chapter after chapter he documents how campus administrations, often with the acquiescence and even cooperation of students, work to limit expression through unconstitutional speech codes and harassment policies, heavy-handed orientation and residence hall training programs, free speech zones, and denial of due process. Although Lukianoff does identify several faculty culprits, one of the strengths of his book is his refusal to pin the blame, as many conservatives do, on supposedly weak-kneed liberal faculty members. Instead, his target is "administrators who present themselves as benign philosopher-kings." To be sure, "many professors have played an unforgivable role in propagating speech codes and seriously undermining the philosophy of free speech, and of course some professors engage in questionable pedagogy." However, Lukianoff repeatedly stresses that "the actual regimes of censorship on campus are put in place primarily by the ever-growing army of administrators."[31]

Administrative bloat is, in Lukianoff's opinion, a major driver of campus censorship. "The rise in cost is related to the decline in rights on campuses in important ways," he argues. "Most importantly, the increase in tuition and overall cost is disproportionately funding an increase in both the cost and the size of campus bureaucracy, and this expanding bureaucracy has primary responsibility for writing and enforcing speech codes, creating speech zones, and policing students' lives in ways that students from the 1960s would never have accepted."

Pomona College political scientist John Seery has phrased it more colorfully. He says, "The most unabashed forms of politically correct scripting on campus—the hunt to root out microaggressions and supposedly traumatizing speech—originate from the bloated administrative wing of campus. . . . The people ventriloquizing students, through relentless sensitivity campaigns, about safe spaces, hate speech, structural oppression, and diversity imperatives are the deans and deanlets of residential life (as one of my colleagues puts it, the 'Residential Life Industrial Complex')."[32]

With respect to the academic freedom of faculty, Lukianoff embraces the "common good" school's justification of such freedom. Citing Post, he sees "education's role in serving the proper functioning of democracy as the primary reason for the existence of academic freedom." Hence, "by propagating speech codes, universities are lying to their students about what their rights are and misinforming them about how speech relates to the functioning of democracies, thus undermining the very reason for academic freedom."

Students, of course, do not have academic freedom per se.[33] As Moody-Adams puts it, "Students must be free to learn, free to speak about what they learn, and free to disagree with their instructors in appropriate ways and contexts. But there is neither a moral nor a legal imperative to extend the full range of rights and privileges of academic freedom to all who may want it." But Lukianoff's work suggests that the state of student expressive rights is intimately linked to that of faculty academic freedom. Moreover, insofar as university administrations have abandoned the defense of academic freedom—or simply pay lip service to the principle—faculty members who wish to defend their own freedom as scholars will need to join with students in opposing restrictions on their freedom to speak. (For more on student free speech and academic freedom, see chaps. 7 and 8.)

The picture drawn by Lukianoff and others of the state of freedom on campus is sobering at the least. But as the books considered here demonstrate, discussion and reflection on that freedom remain vigorous and engaged. The essays in the Bilgrami/Cole collection testify to the rich variety of thought-provoking perspectives to be found on the topic. Fish's book offers a sobering corrective to some more extreme notions of academic freedom, but its cramped

conception of the distinction between the "academic" and the "political" fails to offer a meaningful justification for academic freedom.
In the end the most persuasive arguments are ones, like those offered
by Post and Scott, that embrace the internal tensions and paradoxes
of academic freedom by rooting it in professional autonomy, but
linking that autonomy to broader expressive rights in the service of
a common good that provides the necessary justification for professional autonomy. Now if only we could convert the theoretical vigor
and intellectual engagement of these works into more practical organized actions in defense of that common good. For academic freedom is hardly a mere "academic" concern.

Chapter Three

Can Faculty Speak Freely as Citizens?

At the height of the Pullman railroad strike of 1894, Edward Bemis, a professor at the University of Chicago, delivered a speech critical of the railroad companies. Chicago's president, William Rainey Harper, was not pleased. "Your speech has caused me a great deal of annoyance," he wrote to Bemis. "It is hardly safe for me to venture into any of the Chicago clubs. I am pounced upon from all sides. I propose that during the remainder of your connection with the University you exercise very great care in public utterance about questions that are agitating the minds of the people." At the end of the academic year, Bemis was dismissed from his position.[1]

Founded in 1885 by Leland and Jane Stanford in memory of their only child, Leland Stanford Jr., who died at age 15, Stanford University was initially governed by a board consisting only of its two founders. After Leland Stanford's death in 1893, Jane Stanford assumed sole control of the institution. In 1898, Professor H. H. Powers, a political scientist, delivered a speech on religion that she found heretical. She demanded his removal, and since all faculty members were at the time on annual appointment, her order was followed. In 1901, Edward Ross, an economist whose support of trade unions and free silver and opposition to Chinese immigration irked Mrs. Stanford, was also forced to resign, although he and his supporters raised a good deal of fuss, and the case has, in Hans-Joerg Tiede's words, "reached iconic status" in the historiography of academic freedom.[2] "A professor of the Leland Stanford Junior University . . . should prize the opportunities given him to distinguish himself among his students," Mrs. Stanford wrote of Ross. A scholar should not step "out of his sphere, to associate himself with the political demagogues of this city, exciting their evil passions."[3]

These early cases, especially that of Ross, have often been cited as giving impetus to the formation of the American Association of University Professors in 1915.[4] They—and a long series of cases that have followed—also exemplify what Matthew Finkin and Robert Post have called "the most theoretically problematic aspect of academic freedom," the freedom of faculty members to speak as citizens without institutional restraint, commonly referred to as freedom of "extramural utterance."[5]

The 1915 *Declaration* was markedly ambivalent about the nature and extent of this freedom:

> In their extramural utterances, it is obvious that academic teachers are under a peculiar obligation to avoid hasty or unverified or exaggerated statements, and to refrain from intemperate or sensational modes of expression. But, subject to these restraints, it is not, in this committee's opinion, desirable that scholars should be debarred from giving expression to their judgments upon controversial questions, or that their freedom of speech, outside the university, should be limited to questions falling within their own specialties. It is clearly not proper that they should be prohibited from lending their active support to organized movements which they believe to be in the public interest. And, speaking broadly, it may be said in the words of a nonacademic body already once quoted in a publication of this Association, that "it is neither possible nor desirable to deprive a college professor of the political rights vouchsafed to every citizen." . . .
>
> It is, it will be seen, in no sense the contention of this committee that academic freedom implies that individual teachers should be exempt from all restraints as to the matter or manner of their utterances, either within or without the university. Such restraints as are necessary should in the main, your committee holds, be self-imposed, or enforced by the public opinion of the profession. But there may, undoubtedly, arise occasional cases in which the aberrations of individuals may require to be checked by definite disciplinary action.

What the *Declaration* did maintain, however, was that such disciplinary action "cannot with safety be taken by bodies not composed of members of the academic profession."[6]

The 1940 *Statement* was less ambiguous but still open to conflicting readings, famously declaring that "college and university teachers are citizens, members of a learned profession, and officers of an educational institution. When they speak or write as citizens, they should be free from institutional censorship or discipline, but their special position in the community imposes special obligations. As scholars and educational officers, they should remember that the public may judge their profession and their institution by their utterances. Hence they should at all times be accurate, should exercise appropriate restraint, should show respect for the opinions of others, and should make every effort to indicate that they are not speaking for the institution."[7] Finally, in 1970 the AAUP and the Association of American Colleges and Universities (AAC&U) developed an interpretation of this provision, which declared that extramural speech should not be subject to discipline unless it bears on professional competence, a judgment reserved for the faculty.

But when does such speech bear on professional competence, and what consequence do the "special obligations" of "accuracy," "appropriate restraint," and "respect for the opinions of others" retain? Should extramural expression unrelated to a faculty member's expertise or to "matters of public interest or concern" be protected— in short, does academic freedom protect any speech not made in one's capacity as a faculty member? Did the 1970 interpretation mark a rejection of the 1915 and 1940 principles, with their implicit sense that "there are no rights without corresponding duties"?[8] These questions have gained enhanced relevance now that in the era of electronic media faculty extramural expression has become far more accessible and instantly available on a large scale (on academic freedom in the era of electronic communication, see chap. 4). Lively debate over when expression by faculty members as private citizens should merit institutional sanction continues.

That debate was central to the case of Joy Karega, an assistant professor of rhetoric and composition at Oberlin College, who in November 2016 was dismissed from her position by the college's board on the recommendation (albeit a divided one) of a faculty review body.[9] Karega had posted on Facebook demonstrably anti-semitic messages, which were roundly condemned. In response to that case a writer for the *Federalist* criticized the AAUP, arguing that its "conflicting guidance leads up to events at Oberlin College." He claimed that in cases involving extramural expression "the AAUP's 1940 *Statement of Principles on Academic Freedom and Tenure* and the 1970 'Interpretive Comments' contain conflicting positions as to what protections and duties professors possess." The 1970 interpretation, the argument went, "creates an additional, hard-to-satisfy standard for judging whether such speech impacts a faculty member's fitness for employment. This newer standard gobbles up the obligations in the 1940 *Statement*."[10]

In fact, there is no real conflict here. The 1940 *Statement* was issued jointly by the AAUP and the Association of American Colleges (AAC), now the AAC&U. Both organizations also developed the 1970 comments. A 1938 draft of the *Statement* had included, at the conclusion of the paragraph defining extramural expression, this sentence: "The judgment of what constitutes fulfillment of these obligations should rest with the individual." As Hans-Joerg Tiede has pointed out, had that sentence survived, it would have rendered institutional sanctions all but impossible to impose.[11] But the AAC membership rejected it, and the sentence was deleted. However, in November 1940 the two groups issued a clarifying interpretation concerning extramural expression. Acknowledging that the *Statement* released earlier that year called attention to "the special obligations of faculty members arising from their position in the community: to be accurate, to exercise appropriate restraint, to show respect for the opinions of others, and to make every effort to indicate that they are not speaking for the institution," the November 1940 joint interpretation added this important caveat:

If the administration of a college or university feels that a teacher has not observed the admonitions of paragraph 3 of the section on Academic Freedom and believes that the extramural utterances of the teacher have been such as to raise grave doubts concerning the teacher's fitness for his or her position, it may proceed to file charges under paragraph 4 of the section on Academic Tenure. In pressing such charges, the administration should remember that teachers are citizens and should be accorded the freedom of citizens. In such cases the administration must assume full responsibility, and the American Association of University Professors and the Association of American Colleges are free to make an investigation.[12]

Hence, almost immediately after adoption of the 1940 *Statement*, the two organizations were already indicating what is now commonly accepted: that the fundamental issue is "fitness for position," that "teachers are citizens" with "the freedom of citizens," and that the AAUP is free to investigate and ultimately, if deemed appropriate, censure institutions that violate such freedoms.

Like the First Amendment to the US Constitution, which guarantees the freedoms of citizens, the 1940 *Statement* can only be understood in the context of subsequent interpretation and jurisprudence, in the case of the *Statement* the various investigative reports and interpretive statements issued over the years by the AAUP. Here a brief historical digression will be helpful. In 1960, Leo Koch, a young, untenured biology professor at the University of Illinois at Urbana-Champaign (UIUC), published a letter to the editor in the university newspaper that readers interpreted as an endorsement of premarital sex.[13] While today few, if any, would even raise an eyebrow over the totally tame and by today's standards uncontroversial content of Koch's letter, at the time and under pressure from a local cleric, the university administration and much of the faculty were outraged. A faculty senate committee wrote, "In his role as citizen, the faculty member has the same freedoms as other citizens, without institutional censorship or discipline, although he should be mindful that accuracy, forthrightness, and dignity befit his association with the University and his position as a man of learning." The committee concluded that "Professor Koch's letter did constitute a breach of academic and professional responsibility. The letter is not a reasoned, detached document marshaling evidence or reason in support of a view held by the writer. It is rather an impassioned message." Although the committee recommended a reprimand, Koch was fired.

The AAUP investigated. As John Wilson put it, the question facing the association "was not whether Koch would be condemned for his impassioned views but whether he deserved to be punished with the loss of his job. The question was whether the 'dignity' required by the gentleman scientist model was merely a moral guide for faculty, or an enforceable job requirement."[14] The investigation was led by the esteemed Yale Law School First Amendment scholar Thomas Emerson. Under Emerson's leadership, the investigating committee concluded that "the notion of academic responsibility, when the faculty member is speaking as a citizen, is intended to be an admonition rather than a standard for the application of discipline." Indeed, Emerson went so far as to suggest that only expression violating the law could be punished. This view did not, however, win the support of the majority of Committee A, which nonetheless still condemned the Koch dismissal as "outrageously severe and completely unwarranted" and criticized violations of due process in the case.[15]

If Committee A would not go as far as Emerson did, in October 1964, responding to criticism and calls to amend the 1940 *Statement* so that enforcement of "standards of academic responsibility . . . would constitute a solely self-governing function of the academic profession," the committee issued the *Statement on Extramural Utterances*, which to this day remains the foundation of the AAUP's position.[16] That statement declared,

> The controlling principle is that a faculty member's expression of opinion as a citizen cannot constitute grounds for dismissal unless it clearly demonstrates the faculty member's unfitness to serve. Extramural utterances rarely bear upon the faculty member's fitness for continuing

service. Moreover, a final decision should take into account the faculty member's entire record as a teacher and scholar. In the absence of weighty evidence of unfitness, the administration should not prefer charges; and if it is not clearly proved in the hearing that the faculty member is unfit to continue, the faculty committee should make a finding in favor of the faculty member concerned.[17]

In 1970, both the AAUP and AAC&U agreed to enshrine this formulation into the interpretive comments offered to the 1940 *Statement*. Since then, the AAUP has consistently held to this principle in its conduct of investigations and its decisions on censure and has considered the 1940 "special obligations" as largely hortatory, although consistent violation of these obligations may still lead to a judgment of unfitness.[18]

Did adoption of the *Statement on Extramural Utterances* and its subsequent incorporation into the 1970 interpretive comments deviate from the 1940 *Statement*? Few thought so at the time. The *Statement* was not submitted to the AAUP Council for approval, indicating that as solely a Committee A document it simply clarified existing policy. Future AAUP president, Committee A chair, and constitutional scholar William Van Alstyne characterized the 1964 *Statement* as a "strict construction" of the 1940 *Statement*, acknowledging nonetheless that it had to a great extent "disarmed" the admonitions of that statement.[19]

In 1971, an AAUP investigating committee in the case of the dismissal of Angela Davis from a lecturer position at UCLA expanded on the fitness principle:

What is required by the concept "fitness for one's position?" Most obviously, it means the capability and the willingness to carry out the duties of the position. First among these, for most academic personnel, are the duties of a competent and responsible teacher. . . . Depending on his discipline, rank, or assignment, and the practices of the institution, a faculty member's position may involve other responsibilities, in research, in advising students, in sharing departmental chores or administrative duties, and the like. To meet the AAUP's standard of unfitness, then, the faculty member's shortcoming must be shown to bear some identified relation to his capacity or willingness to perform the responsibilities, broadly conceived, to his students, to his colleagues, to his discipline, or to the functions of his institution, that pertain to his assignment. Thus, under the quoted principles, institutional sanctions imposed for extramural utterances can be a violation of academic freedom even when the utterances themselves fall short of the standards of the profession; for it is central to that freedom that the faculty member, when speaking as a citizen, "should be free from institutional censorship or discipline" except insofar as his behavior is shown, on the whole record, to be incompatible with fitness for his position.

The Davis report added,

> At some stage in a contested argument over academic responsibility and fitness to teach, appeal must be made to someone's judgment in applying what are necessarily somewhat imprecise standards for the limits of propriety of extramural controversy. The judgment to be made is how far the condemned polemics fall below a professionally tolerable norm, and about the gravity, the frequency, and other circumstances of the incidents along with other evidence bearing on the speaker's overall academic responsibility.
>
> It is entirely possible, even likely, that the balance might be struck differently on the same evidence by leaders of the academic community and by members of a governing board, especially where political and other public controversy is involved. . . . In the light of these considerations, the wisdom of the AAUP procedural standards—which require careful exchange of views between faculty committees, administrations, and governing boards in disciplinary actions of the present kind—is apparent.[20]

How does this relate to the Karega case? It should be noted that initially Committee A did place that case on its agenda, but in the end neither the committee nor the AAUP executive director decided to take action. Why? Here it may be useful to compare the Karega case with another case in which charges of antisemitism played a critical part, the celebrated case of Steven Salaita at UIUC.[21] That case resulted in the placement of the UIUC administration on the AAUP's censured list, as well as in an $875,000 settlement for Professor Salaita. But before doing so, one additional comment is necessary. Faculty members who speak as citizens often speak about topics far from their academic specialty. Physicists or engineers, for example, may express controversial views on political or social issues that have no bearing at all on their fitness to teach or conduct research in physics or engineering. In such cases, it would be extremely rare for anyone to question a teacher's fitness on the simple grounds of their personal views. Indeed, in two cases—at Northwestern University and at California State University, Long Beach—engineering professors publicly advocated Holocaust denial but retained their positions without challenge so long as they did not inject those views into the classroom.[22]

Things are often quite different in the social sciences. In Salaita's case his academic study of indigenous peoples can be said to be at least indirectly related to his views on the Israeli-Palestinian conflict expressed in his tweets. Karega was hired to teach "social justice writing," and her posts can be judged to concern that subject. Salaita, however, was tenured; Karega was still in a probationary position. (It may also be argued that Karega's Facebook posts were more demonstrably antisemitic and offensive than Salaita's tweets, but the issue addressed here is not content. Indeed, I will stipulate that in both cases the remarks were offensive precisely because this doesn't really matter.) As a tenured faculty member, Salaita was entitled to much more generous consideration than Karega, whose academic fitness for permanent employment was still to be determined.

Nonetheless, a strong case can be made that Karega did not deserve to be dismissed. Before the faculty committee rendered its recommendation, Steven Lubet, Williams Memorial Professor of Law at Northwestern University, who comments often about issues of antisemitism, opined that "suspending Karega is wrong, or at least ill-advised." He added, "I am wary of disciplining any professor for extra-academic writing or social media posts, no matter how obnoxious, so long as they are not reflected in her teaching or interactions with students. I work at a university where Arthur Butz—one of the nation's premier Holocaust deniers—has been teaching electrical engineering for decades. As far as anyone can tell, he respects the line between his deeply offensive prejudices, which he does not express on campus, and his teaching assignments. Perhaps Karega could do the same (although perhaps not)."[23] Writing in *Commentary*, Jonathan Marks of Ursinus College, who publishes frequently in conservative publications, agreed. He wrote,

> I oppose firing academics over constitutionally protected hate speech, whether it is directed against blacks, Muslims, women, homosexuals, or Jews. I share the view of old fashioned liberals that, at least at colleges and universities, we run little risk in giving wide latitude to rotten and even unhinged ideas. If we limit ourselves to firing only people whose terrible ideas undermine their ability to teach, conduct research, and serve on committees, we will probably be rid of most Karegas anyhow. To do more, in the hope of firing every last one of them, is the equivalent of demolishing student speech protections in order to catch the last racist bathroom graffiti artist. Disgusting and unhinged views will always be with us. Our dedication to the protection of speech and academic freedom cannot be contingent on the elimination of such views.

Echoing the AAUP's position, Marks added, "People can hold absurd views in one area and be capable of Nobel-caliber work in another. We should be very reluctant to fire teachers over offenses that have not somehow manifested themselves in scholarship, teaching, or service, or that do not directly implicate their fitness."[24]

Why then did the AAUP not investigate Karega's dismissal? The 1970 interpretive comments notwithstanding, did the association, in effect, adopt the view that "professors would do well to acknowledge that the privileges of academic freedom they enjoy do not grant them unregulated speech protections, but instead are combined with the duties to be accurate, respectful, and restrained?"[25]

The answer lies in a final distinction between the Salaita case and that of Karega. Steven Salaita was provided with no due process. Although he should have enjoyed the protections of tenure, the university administration at the time used the flimsy excuse that his appointment had yet to be approved formally by the trustees to summarily dismiss him without any faculty input and without a hearing. They undoubtedly did so, of course, because had they waited to begin formal disciplinary procedures the overwhelming likelihood is that Salaita would still be a member of the UIUC faculty. In the case of Karega, however, while the Oberlin administration's initial response was somewhat muddled and confused, in the end, as Marks pointed out, her case "was reviewed by an elected faculty committee, a plurality of which voted for dismissal. She was represented by counsel and permitted to present evidence in her favor."[26]

It is not the AAUP's role to function as some sort of court of appeal to review the substance of faculty decisions, especially when the institutional processes pursued hew closely to AAUP guidelines. It is not up to the AAUP to decide which faculty members should be granted tenure, which should be dismissed, or which should be disciplined and how severely they should be punished. That is the responsibility of the faculty and administration at the institution concerned, acting within the parameters defined by the 1940 *Statement* and derivative AAUP policies. While there were faculty members who would not have recommended Karega's dismissal, the fact that a duly constituted faculty committee did in the end so recommend suggests that the AAUP's procedural standards were essentially followed. Therefore, the AAUP's decision not to investigate Karega's dismissal should not be construed as implying endorsement of Oberlin's decision or certainly of the *Federalist*'s cramped reading of the 1940 *Statement*.

To be sure, however, not all faculty committees are truly representative, and not all disciplinary proceedings are fair. The case of Ward Churchill in Colorado some years ago is one example of how a handpicked and biased "faculty committee" can serve as a useful tool for the violation of genuine due process rights, as an exhaustive report prepared by the AAUP's Colorado Conference demonstrated.[27] And it is certainly conceivable that even an appropriately constituted faculty review body can be swayed by political or other passions to render decisions that amount to genuine violations of academic freedom. That was certainly an issue in the Leo Koch case and was also sadly the case in more than a few instances during the Red Scare of the 1950s. In that light the AAUP and faculty in general must remain vigilant and resist the temptation to, as Marks writes, dismiss colleagues "merely for [their] loathsome opinions."

One further question remains concerning the academic freedom right of extramural utterance. How can such a right be justified, given that such expression may be only peripherally or not at all related to a faculty member's teaching or research? Some have argued that freedom of extramural expression is an extension of the ordinary citizen's personal liberty or that it is a right distinct from, but closely related to, academic freedom. Hence, for instance, Judith Butler has argued that "academic freedom and freedom of expression are not the same." Nevertheless, "the wall between academic freedom and freedom of expression is porous."[28] But as desirable as it would be for such protection to extend to all employment relations, in the United States under the First Amendment the vast majority of private employees may be disciplined or even dismissed without a hearing for voicing their political or social views in or outside the workplace, unless their rights are protected under a contract, usually one negotiated by a union, and even then such protections generally fall short of those supported for faculty members by the AAUP. Even in the public sphere US courts have permitted extensive regulation of government employee speech out of deference to "the mission and functions of the employer."[29]

As the 1915 *Declaration* put it, "It is, in short, not the absolute freedom of utterance of the individual scholar, but the absolute freedom of thought, of inquiry, of discussion and of teaching, of the academic profession that is asserted by this declaration of principles."[30] In this light, extending protection of extramural expression to individual faculty speaking "outside the walls" of the institution and outside of their disciplinary expertise is critical for several reasons. In 1916, AAUP founder Arthur Lovejoy argued in an exchange with then AAUP president John Wigmore that restricting freedom of extramural expression to subjects related to a faculty member's academic specialization would "make it possible for trustees who wished to eliminate from an institution an economist of whose economic views they disapproved, to dismiss him because of an allegation of disagreement between their views and his own on political science or on the theory of evolution." Concluded Lovejoy, "in order effectually to protect the investigator *within* his special province, you must protect him outside of it also."[31]

Faculty members are unlikely to believe that an institution that would curtail their expression as citizens will adequately defend their expression as teachers or researchers. As Finkin and Post argue, "If faculty experience their institutions as repressive, they will be vulnerable to forms of self-censorship and self-restraint that are inconsistent with the confidence necessary for research and teaching." Hence, they conclude, freedom of extramural expression may be best "conceptualized as a prophylactic protection for freedom of research and freedom of teaching."[32]

"There is no clear divide between extramural speech and the core scholarly work of academics, and policies designed to restrict the former will inevitably affect the latter," adds Keith Whittington, the William Nelson Cromwell Professor of Politics at Princeton University. Indeed, he suggests, "the presence of unorthodox, controversial, and even wild-eyed professors on the faculty should be regarded as a sign of institutional health. The far larger threat to the reputation of a university should be the stifling docility of 'cautious mediocrity' or the unimaginative regimentation of ideological conformity."[33]

Chapter Four

Can I Tweet That?

In September 2013 at the University of Kansas, a journalism professor, responding to a shooting incident at the Washington Navy Yard, tweeted a comment about gun control that many gun advocates found offensive, even threatening. He was barraged with hate messages and death threats, and several legislators called for his dismissal. Although the university publicly reaffirmed its commitment to his academic freedom, he was suspended to "avoid disruption." This incident prompted the Kansas Board of Regents in December 2013 to adopt new rules under which faculty members and other employees may be suspended or dismissed for "improper use of social media." The new policy defined social media as "any facility for online publication and commentary," a definition that covered but was "not limited to blogs, wikis, and social networking sites such as Facebook, LinkedIn, Twitter, Flickr, and YouTube."

This definition could arguably also include any message that appears electronically, including email messages and even online periodicals and books. The policy defined "improper use of social media" in extremely broad terms, including communications made "pursuant to . . . official duties" that are "contrary to the best interest of the university," as well as communication that "impairs discipline by superiors or harmony among co-workers, has a detrimental impact on close working relationships for which personal loyalty and confidence are necessary, impedes the performance of the speaker's official duties, interferes with the regular operation of the university, or otherwise adversely affects the university's ability to efficiently provide services."[1]

The American Association of University Professors, the American Civil Liberties Union, and faculty leaders in Kansas quickly condemned the new policy as "a gross violation of the fundamental principles of academic freedom." In the face of widespread criticism, the regents agreed to work with campus leaders to revise the policy, but when a faculty-administration task force recommended an entirely different approach, the idea was rejected, and the policy remains largely intact.[2]

Faculty use of social media is increasing. In a 2013 survey of eight thousand faculty members, 70 percent of those responding reported visiting a social media site within the previous month for personal use, a rate that rose to 84 percent when those who use social media sites less frequently were included. More than 55 percent said they had made professional use of social media outside the classes they teach at least monthly, and 41 percent reported having used social media in their teaching.[3] No doubt more than five years later such usage has continued to expand.

As the AAUP's 2013 report entitled *Academic Freedom and Electronic Communications* noted,

> Social media sites blur the distinction between private and public communication in new ways. Unlike blogs or websites, which are generally accessible to anyone with Internet access who goes in search of the site, social media sites offer the appearance of a space that is simultaneously private and public, one that is on a public medium (the Internet) and yet defined by the user through invitation-only entry points, such as Facebook "friend" requests, and a range of user-controlled privacy settings.
>
> The extent of the privacy of such sites, however, is at the least uncertain and limited, because it is dependent not only on the individual's privacy-setting choices and those of the members in the individual's network but also on the service provider's practices of analyzing data posted on the network. Moreover, social-media providers often modify their policies on privacy and access in ways that their users do not always fully comprehend.[4]

Concerns about online privacy have only intensified in the wake of widespread disclosures about Facebook's violations of user confidentiality. We now know that Facebook—like many other social media sites—"meticulously scrutinizes the minutiae of its users' online lives, and its tracking stretches far beyond the company's well-known targeted advertisements. Details that people often readily volunteer—age, employer, relationship status, likes and location—are just the start. Facebook tracks both its users and non-users on other sites and apps. It collects biometric facial data without users' explicit 'opt-in' consent."[5] Perhaps a greater danger is that, as one close observer of the internet pointed out, "the information and social platforms of the Internet . . . are being corrupted in the service of con men, political demagogues and thieves."[6] As University of North Carolina professor and media activist Zeynep Tufekci has argued,

> In the 21st century, the capacity to spread ideas and reach an audience is no longer limited by access to expensive, centralized broadcasting infrastructure. It's limited instead by one's ability to garner and distribute attention. And right now, the flow of the world's attention is structured, to a vast and overwhelming degree, by just a few digital platforms: Facebook, Google (which owns YouTube), and, to a lesser extent, Twitter.
>
> These companies—which love to hold themselves up as monuments of free expression—have attained a scale unlike anything the world has ever seen; they've come to dominate media distribution, and they increasingly stand in for the public sphere itself. But at their core, their business is mundane: They're ad brokers. To virtually anyone who wants to pay them, they sell the capacity to precisely target our eyeballs. They use massive surveillance of our behavior, online and off, to generate increasingly accurate, automated predictions of what advertisements we are most susceptible to and what content will keep us clicking, tapping, and scrolling down a bottomless feed.[7]

Yale Law School professor Jack Balkin notes that social media offer "an implicit bargain: a seemingly, unbounded freedom to speak in exchange for the right to surveil, govern, and manipulate end-users."[8] Kate Klonick, a doctoral candidate at Yale Law, has argued that platforms like Facebook, Twitter, and Google have become the "New Governors of online speech." And while these private, self-regulating firms have been "economically and normatively motivated to reflect the democratic culture and free speech expectations of their users," the legal environment in which they operate is muddled at best. Moreover, "private platforms are increasingly making their own choices around content moderation that give preferential treatment to some users over others." Whether the self-regulatory regimes established by these companies will remain adequate and effective is thus at best an open question.[9]

The AAUP recommends that institutions of higher education work with their faculties to develop policies governing use of social media. Clearly, the Kansas approach is not what the association has in mind. The fundamental starting point when it comes to regulation of electronic communications by faculty is simple. As the AAUP stated initially in 2004 and has repeated frequently ever since, "Academic freedom, free inquiry, and freedom of expression within the academic community may be limited to no greater extent in electronic format than they are in print, save for the most unusual situation where the very nature of the medium itself might warrant unusual restrictions—and even then only to the extent that such differences demand exceptions or variations. Such obvious differences between old and new media as the vastly greater speed of digital communication, and the far wider audiences that electronic messages may reach, would not, for example, warrant any relaxation of the rigorous precepts of academic freedom."[10] Simply put, administrators cannot, without a warrant, open a letter sent to a faculty member's departmental mailbox, so arguably they should not be allowed to look at the content of that faculty member's email.

Still, how might electronic communications more broadly and, in particular, faculty participation in electronic social media be appropriately regulated? Should faculty be permitted to use such media without restriction? This chapter explores these questions with respect to all aspects of the understanding of academic freedom employed by the AAUP and most colleges and universities: freedom in research and in the publication of its results; freedom in the classroom; freedom to comment upon and dissent from university policies and practices; and lastly—and most critically—the freedom of faculty members, as citizens, to speak about matters of public concern, whether such matters are related to their professional expertise or not.[11]

Freedom in Research

The emergence of electronic media has greatly expanded access to information. Journal articles and a wide array of other published and unpublished research materials may now be available to anyone from anywhere. In some cases journals themselves have become a form of social media where published research results may be discussed and exchanged with breathtaking speed. At the same time, as Robert O'Neil has noted, "although a university does to some degree control a scholar's recourse to print materials by its management of library collections, . . . the potential for limitation or denial of access is vastly greater when the institution maintains and therefore controls the gateway to the Internet."[12]

Of course, colleges and universities are clearly entitled to limit access to their library collections, including electronic resources, but third-party vendors sometimes seek to impose restrictions on access exceeding those claimed by an institution itself, and these are rarely defined or even reviewed by faculty governance bodies. Third-party vendors may, like social media applications, also gain access to user information, especially when they offer research tools such as customized portals, saved searches, or email alerts on research topics, some of which may mimic the feel and function of social media. How these vendors employ such information and who is entitled to access it may be beyond an institution's control. While the digital world has offered great promise to make information accessible to a global community, commercial forces have locked up much research behind paywalls and ever-more-restrictive licensing agreements. Faculty members who produce research in digital form may yield control over how that research may be accessed and by whom.

The advent of social media has also raised new questions about scholarly communication. Social media and electronic communications technologies can make research in progress both more accessible and more vulnerable to intellectual property theft. "Professors who present papers at scholarly conferences often use those occasions to try out new ideas and stimulate discussion," the AAUP's report on electronic communications noted. "While they may be willing, even eager, to share unpolished or preliminary ideas with a closed group of peers, they may be less happy to have those in attendance broadcast these ideas through social media. Conference papers are often clearly labeled as 'not for circulation.' At some meetings, however, attendees at sessions have communicated to others electronically—and often instantaneously—through social media, email, or blogs, reports and comments on papers and statements made by other conference attendees. Many academic conferences have associated Twitter hash tags—at times suggested by the conference organizers. As a result, ideas and information that previously would have been controlled by the presenter and limited to a relatively small audience may quickly become accessible globally."[13]

The Electronic Classroom

According to the 1940 *Statement of Principles on Academic Freedom and Tenure*, "teachers are entitled to freedom in the classroom in discussing their subject."[14] But what constitutes a classroom? In the digital age the concept of "classroom" must be broadened to reflect how instruction increasingly occurs through media without physical boundaries and that the "classroom" must encompass all sites where learning occurs. Indeed, it should be stressed that academic freedom in the online classroom is no less critical than it is in the traditional classroom.

As early as 1998, the late historian of technology David Noble worried that "once faculty and courses go online, administrators gain much greater direct control over faculty performance and course content than ever before and the potential for administrative scrutiny, supervision, regimentation, discipline and even censorship increase[s] dramatically."[15] Today growing numbers of colleges and universities have contracted with providers of learning management systems like Blackboard to provide platforms for online or hybrid classes. While these systems boast features attractive to many instructors, as Jonathan Rees points out, they also may "restrict the freedom of the faculty to teach the way they want to and make it easier for the administration to track instructional activity of all kinds."[16]

The AAUP has also noted how "new teaching technologies and learning-management systems also allow faculty members and students to be monitored in new ways." Online teaching platforms and learning management systems—which through discussion boards and similar devices may function as de facto social media—may allow instructors to learn whether students in a class did their work and how long they spent on assignments. "Conversely, however, a college or university administration could use these systems to determine whether faculty members were spending 'adequate' time on certain activities."[17] While learning management systems make it possible for faculty members to keep electronic teaching materials separate from scholarly, political, or personal materials often found on faculty websites or personal social media pages, many instructors still frequently post course materials on websites or on social media alongside other content, some of which may be controversial and irrelevant to a given course. In addition, faculty members who consider the development of, say, a dedicated Facebook page or Twitter hashtag for a class run the risk that discussions there are likely to bleed over into topics perhaps far removed not only from the instructor's intentions but also from the purposes of the course and be accessible to nonstudents, some of whom may not have the best of intentions.

Social media may also threaten academic freedom in traditional classrooms. "None of us teach without the risk of full public exposure," says Siva Vaidhyanathan, professor of media studies at the

University of Virginia. Everything changes, he adds, once a comment is "frozen in digital form." And if that frozen comment or a stealthily recorded video from the classroom is removed from its context, "that can create a cascade of harassment and can threaten a career."[18] While class lectures, syllabi, and even an instructor's email messages to students should be considered the intellectual property of the instructor, much of what teachers distribute to students both online and in the classroom or write in email messages may legally be redistributed by students for noncommercial use under the "fair-use" principle. Moreover, copyright does not cover expression that is not reduced to "tangible" form, including extemporaneous utterances, as it might a formal lecture, a PowerPoint presentation, or written material like a syllabus.

In August 2013, the teaching duties of a tenured professor in Michigan were reassigned after a student anonymously videotaped part of a ninety-minute lecture, a heavily edited two-minute version of which—described by some as an "anti-Republican rant"—was then aired on a conservative internet site, on Fox News, and on YouTube, where it was viewed over 150,000 times.[19] In October 2013, a Wisconsin geography professor sent her students an email message explaining that they could not gain access to census data to complete a required assignment because the "Republican / Tea Party–controlled House of Representatives" had shut down the government, thus closing the Census Bureau's website. After a student posted the message on Twitter, it appeared in a local newspaper and in national conservative media, resulting in numerous complaints to the university, which sent an email message to the campus distancing the administration from the comment.[20]

In December 2016, the College Republicans at Orange Coast College in California posted a recording of an instructor of psychology talking in her human sexuality class about the results of the presidential election. The video opened midsentence with the words "white supremacist" and continued, "And a vice president that is one of the most anti-gay humans in this country." She added, "Our nation is divided, we have been assaulted, it's an act of terrorism."

The College Republicans filed a complaint and wrote on Facebook, "Did you know you're a terrorist for having supported Trump? I didn't but apparently that's what they're teaching in Orange Coast College's classrooms postelection."[21]

In California, public community colleges like Orange Coast are subject to state code, which states, "The use by any person, including a student, of any electronic listening or recording device in any classroom without the prior consent of the instructor is prohibited, except as necessary to provide reasonable auxiliary aids and academic adjustments to disabled students. Any person, other than a student, who willfully violates this section shall be guilty of a misdemeanor. Any student violating this section shall be subject to appropriate disciplinary action."[22] The student who recorded the class was suspended for two terms, but the suspension was revoked after a week.[23]

The AAUP recommends "that administrations and elected faculty bodies work jointly to establish institutional regulations that prohibit the surreptitious recording of classroom discourse or of private meetings between students and faculty members."[24] Some have wondered why such recordings differ from "a student who takes careful notes on a professor's comments and publicly reports them."[25] But recording is quite different from note taking. Recordings can be abused in ways that would be far more difficult with notes, which can be more easily disputed. To be sure, surreptitious recordings have in some cases exposed corruption and hypocrisy (albeit mostly not at universities). But at the same time, the ability to edit and doctor such recordings makes them ripe for abuse. The classroom is not a site where professors simply express their own ideas and beliefs. It is where they teach, employing a variety of discursive tactics, and where students are asked to learn, not just hear or even engage with contrary ideas. In the classroom effective instructors frequently play "devil's advocate," espousing arguments with which they disagree in order to encourage students to respond. They may also rephrase arguments made in readings or by students in order to draw out their implicit meanings in ways that might shock. Recording these out of context will often create an appearance that the arguments so phrased are the instructor's own.

Surreptitious classroom recordings endanger not only professors but also their students. Protecting the right of students to speak freely and openly in class is at least as critical as the protection of their instructors. Historian L. D. Burnett considers her classroom a "rehearsal space" where students can work through ideas. "I want my classroom to be the one place," she argues, where "students know they won't unwillingly be part of someone's snarky narrative."[26] In 2011, responding to a secret recording of a labor studies class at the University of Missouri, the AAUP observed, "When students voice their views in class, they should not have to fear that their comments will be spread all over the Internet. When faculty members rightly explore difficult topics in class, they should not have to fear for their jobs or their lives."[27]

As the AAUP first stated in the 1915 *Declaration of Principles on Academic Freedom and Academic Tenure*, "Discussions in the classroom ought not to be supposed to be utterances for the public at large. They are often designed to provoke opposition or arouse debate."[28] In the 1980s, a group called Accuracy in Academia encouraged students to record professors' classroom statements and send them to the organization to be tested for "accuracy." In response, the AAUP, along with twelve other higher education associations, declared, "The classroom is a place of learning where the professor serves as intellectual guide, and all are encouraged to seek and express the truth as they see it. The presence in the classroom of monitors for an outside organization will have a chilling effect on the academic freedom of both students and faculty members. Students may be discouraged from testing their ideas, and professors may hesitate before presenting new or possibly controversial theories that would stimulate robust intellectual discussion."[29]

University Affairs, Extramural Expression, and Social Media

Two stories illustrate problems associated with the faculty's rights to comment on university affairs. The first concerns an AAUP council member who was chair of his academic senate when that body came into conflict with a hostile administration. The senate was dissolved and new elections were held, which returned the original officeholders to power. Administrators not only rejected these results but also barred the senate from communicating them to the faculty via email. Unfortunately, when the senate chair filed suit on First Amendment grounds, he lost, the court ruling that he was speaking "pursuant to official duties" and that his access could thus be restricted on the basis of the US Supreme Court's *Garcetti* decision.[30] In a second case, a Colorado professor sent an email comparing potential budget cutbacks to the 1914 Ludlow Massacre of striking miners in that state. His email access was revoked because he allegedly had threatened violence, and while his access was soon restored, his ability to send messages to large groups was not.[31]

The right of faculty members to speak freely about internal college or university affairs is a fundamental principle of academic freedom that applies as much to electronic communications as it does to written and oral ones. This includes the right of faculty members to communicate with one another about their conditions of employment and to organize on their own behalf. Union leaders, senate officers, and other faculty representatives engaged in governance activities should have free and unfettered access to university-controlled lists of faculty members they represent, and all faculty members should be able to comment electronically on governance issues without restriction or fear of disciplinary action.

The right of faculty members to speak without institutional restriction as citizens on matters of public concern was, of course, the central issue in the controversy over the Kansas policy, and it is the central issue in a seeming avalanche of high-profile incidents involving social media, beginning with the much-publicized 2014 case of Professor Steven Salaita.[32] Professor Salaita was hired to a tenured position at the University of Illinois at Urbana-Champaign (UIUC) and was set to begin his employment when the administration and trustees became aware of a series of highly controversial comments on Twitter that he had sent concerning the Israeli-Palestinian conflict.

Because his appointment was still formally subject to trustee approval, it was withdrawn at the last minute.

The case, which resulted in a large financial settlement and placement of UIUC on the AAUP's list of administrations censured for violations of academic freedom (from which they were removed in 2017 after instituting reforms), raised significant issues about social media. One involves the very nature of Twitter as a mode of expression. For anyone who may not be familiar with it, Twitter allows people to broadcast short statements of no more than 140 characters—increased to 280 in 2017—to their "followers" and to all those following a specific subject matter "hashtag." These "tweets" may in turn be retweeted and in short order may reach tens of thousands or more individuals beyond their original audience.

What can be said in just 140 or even 280 characters? On the one hand, in a scholarly sense, not a whole lot. Academics are notoriously long-winded; our written productions tend to be cautious and constrained, hedged with all sorts of nuance and qualification. On the other hand, these brief messages can carry a lot of power; they are often emotional and almost always direct and simple—but owing to their frequent use of irony, often easily misinterpreted—in ways that scholarly communications rarely are. Twitter may indeed be considered, as the historian Natalie Z. Davis argued in a letter to the UIUC chancellor, a genre with its own set of distinctive practices and codes. Here's part of what Davis wrote:

> Some of Professor Salaita's tweets were vehement and intentionally provocative: he used strong language both to criticize the deaths from Israeli bombing and to attack anti-Semitism. The lack of "civility" in some of his tweets is linked to the genre itself: a tweet is often an answer to a tweet, and a tweet always anticipates a response. It is a form of concise communication based on give and take, on the anticipation that the respondent may respond sharply or critically to what you have said, and that the exchange will continue. Thus, in his public political life, Professor Salaita participates in a mode that always leaves space for an answer.[33]

Of course, a distinction must be made between emotional expression and threats of violence, including those made via social
media. Threats, however, need to be genuine, and even then those
who make them are entitled to legitimate due process protections.
Moreover, under current First Amendment law those alleging that a
threatening communication is exempt from free speech protection
must prove that those making the threat have "acted with either the
purpose of issuing a threat or with knowledge that the communication would be viewed as a threat," a high bar to meet.[34] And while
the language of Salaita's tweets sometimes evoked violence, none
of it amounted to a true threat to any identifiable individual or
group, at least any group accessible to Salaita. Impassioned, even
violent language or vivid metaphors are not enough to constitute a
genuine threat. Moreover, the contention—advanced by the UIUC
administration—that students would be threatened or intimidated
by Salaita's language demanded corroboration by specific evidence
that Salaita's classroom conduct evidenced behavior somehow analogous to the content or tone of the tweets. But no one produced
such evidence. In fact, just as it was observed in 1971 that Angela
Davis's subdued classroom demeanor contrasted dramatically with
her reputation as a firebrand orator, so too available evidence suggests that Salaita's classroom language and tone never resembled
that of his controversial tweets.

Targeted Online Harassment

The very nature of social media may facilitate troubling patterns
of behavior. "If it was once hard to speak, it is now hard to be heard,"
wrote Columbia Law School professor Tim Wu. "Among the newer
emerging threats is the rise of abusive online mobs who seek to
wear down targeted speakers and have them think twice about writing
critical content."[35] As Zeynep Tufekci has explained, in electronic
media "the most effective forms of censorship today involve meddling
with trust and attention, not muzzling speech itself. As a result, they
don't look much like the old forms of censorship at all. They look
like viral or coordinated harassment campaigns, which harness the

dynamics of viral outrage to impose an unbearable and disproportionate cost on the act of speaking out."[36]

Indeed, this sort of harassment directed against individual faculty
members—often in response to their own social media posts—has
in the past two years emerged as perhaps the gravest immediate menace to academic freedom. As the AAUP, the Association of American
Colleges and Universities (AAC&U), and the American Federation
of Teachers (AFT) noted in a September 2017 joint statement,

> At a variety of institutions—public and private, large and small—
> individual members of the faculty have been singled out for campaigns
> of harassment in response to remarks they have made, or are alleged to
> have made, in public speeches, on social media, or in the classroom.
> Vicious threats of violence and even death have been directed against
> individual faculty members and their families, including their children.
> A large number of those threatened have been African American.
>
> The threats are often accompanied by calls for college and university
> administrators to summarily dismiss or otherwise discipline the of-
> fending faculty member. Sometimes the threats are also directed at
> those administrators or the institutions themselves. In some cases the
> comments made by the faculty member were highly provocative or eas-
> ily misconstrued, but in other cases the allegedly offensive remarks
> were misattributed or not even made at all. In all cases, however, these
> campaigns of harassment endanger more than the faculty member con-
> cerned. They pose a profound and ominous challenge to higher educa-
> tion's most fundamental values.[37]

Two early examples of such harassment involved a prominent
and distinguished scientist, on the one hand, and a previously un-
heralded junior faculty member just coming up for tenure, on the
other. In August 2010, climate scientist Michael Mann, professor of
atmospheric science at Pennsylvania State University, was opening
mail when white powder fell from a letter. It was cornstarch, not
anthrax, but this was just one in a long series of threats Mann had
received since the late 1990s in response to his research demonstrating how global warming was producing a rising temperature curve

whose shape he likened to a hockey stick. One email said he and his collaborators "ought to be shot, quartered, and fed to the pigs along with your whole damn families."[38] At the University of Missouri in 2015, Melissa Click, an assistant professor of communication, was videotaped pushing aside the video camera of a student claiming to be a journalist and calling for "some muscle" to remove him from what was by law a public space. The video was posted to the internet, where it was widely viewed. Click quickly admitted her mistake and repeatedly apologized, but she was nonetheless subjected to a torrent of abuse, including violent threats against her and her family. Legislators demanded Click's dismissal, holding millions of dollars in university funding hostage. The university's trustees, ignoring campus policies and procedures, complied. After an investigation, the AAUP placed Missouri on its list of administrations censured for violations of academic freedom.[39]

But the floodgates really opened in the wake of the 2016 election. The experience of Johnny Williams at Trinity College was recounted in chapter 1. But quite a few others have also gained attention:

- Joshua Cuevas, an associate professor and educational psychologist at the University of North Georgia, documented his experience with a chilling months-long campaign of attacks that began after he blocked an online commenter who had directed curses and insults at his posts.[40]
- At Drexel University in Philadelphia political scientist George Ciccariello-Maher was twice suspended, allegedly for his own safety, after campaigns of harassment in response to his provocative tweets. He subsequently left the university.[41]
- Lars Maischak, a lecturer in history at California State University, Fresno, tweeted that "to save American democracy, Trump must hang." At the time, he had under thirty followers and thought his messages would never "be read by anyone but a close circle of acquaintances who would know to place them in their context." But after a Breitbart writer featured them, Maischak and the university were bombarded with tweets and

emails calling for him to be fired, deported, or killed. Maischak was placed on leave for the semester and then assigned to teach only online.[42]

- A year later another Fresno faculty member, tenured professor Randa Jarrar, prompted calls for her dismissal after she tweeted that the recently deceased Barbara Bush was "an amazing racist" and exulted, "I'm happy the witch is dead." Over two thousand people responded to her tweet before she made her account private. While university president Joseph Castro publicly called her comments "disgraceful," he acknowledged that they were protected by the First Amendment.[43]

- Kenneth Storey, a part-time lecturer at the University of Tampa, was subjected to harassment and abruptly fired after he suggested on Twitter that Hurricane Harvey was "karma" for Texas's support of the GOP. After the AAUP wrote to complain, he was allowed to resign voluntarily via a confidential settlement.[44]

- Tommy Curry, an associate professor of philosophy at Texas A&M University, became the target of online threats and racist harassment after the *American Conservative* ran a piece that took out of context four-year-old comments he made about violence against whites. One tweet directed at him depicted someone putting a gun in a monkey's mouth. Instead of defending Curry's academic freedom, the Texas A&M president publicly declared his comments "disturbing" and standing "in stark contrast to Aggie core values."[45]

- In June 2017, Sarah Bond, an assistant professor of classics at the University of Iowa, published an article endorsing the scholarly consensus that ancient artifacts were painted in different colors but have, over time, faded to their base light marble color— giving the false impression that white skin was the classical ideal. But selected quotes from her essay were posted online by the right-wing website Campus Reform, which falsely claimed she had argued that appreciation of "white marble" used in classical artwork contributes to "white supremacist ideas today."

This prompted online threats of violence, antisemitic messages (Bond is Jewish), and calls for her termination.[46]

- At a commencement speech at Hampshire College, Princeton University scholar Keeanga Yamahtta-Taylor criticized President Donald J. Trump, which led to such an onslaught of online abuse that she ended up canceling all public talks.[47]

- At Dartmouth College lecturer Mark Bray received death threats and antisemitic messages after he suggested in a televised discussion of violent responses to fascism that "it's a privileged position to be able to say that you never have to defend yourself from these kinds of monsters." In response, Dartmouth president Philip Hanlon publicly disavowed Bray's comments while failing to mount any defense of the faculty's academic freedom, prompting a protest letter signed by over 120 Dartmouth faculty members.[48]

- Laurie Rubel, professor of mathematics education at Brooklyn College, received dozens of hostile emails daily, including threats of physical and sexual assault, some referencing her religion and gender, after an article she published was "caricatured and decontextualized" by Campus Reform, Fox News, Breitbart, and others.[49]

- At the University of Nebraska, graduate student instructor Courtney Lawton and English professor Amanda Gailey were harassed after they demonstrated against the presence of a representative of Turning Point USA on campus. Lawton was relieved of her teaching duties.[50]

- Less than four hours after Manisha Sinha, a prominent historian of abolitionism at the University of Connecticut, published an op-ed piece on CNN comparing the possible impeachment of President Trump with that of Andrew Johnson, a phone caller read out her address and claimed to be on his way to kill her. She called 911. The caller was identified as a man in Texas.[51]

In this context, in spring 2017 the AAUP called on its members to report, in confidence, their own experiences of targeted harassment and intimidation. In response, over a hundred stories poured in from faculty members who "reported being singled out . . . primarily as a result of comments they had made, or were alleged to have made, in public presentations, in scholarly publications, on blogs, on social media, or in the classroom. In many cases, they reported that the triggering event occurred in the course of their normal academic duties as teachers, researchers, or concerned citizen-scholars addressing the public."[52] Of fifty incidents occurring since fall 2016, in 48 percent the targeted expression concerned race; in 34 percent, politics; and in 14 percent, gender. Teaching prompted 37 percent of the harassment; research, 18 percent; social media commentary, 29 percent; and other extramural expression, 16 percent. Females were targeted in 62 percent of the incidents reported. Some examples are offered here:

- A full professor of surgery at a large state university was targeted as a result of his public advocacy for fact-based science and, in particular, his campaign against anti-vaccination misinformation. The harasser made repeated allegations against the professor, including accusations of theft and defrauding the government. The professor had to alert patients to the harassment campaign in order to protect his professional reputation and medical practice.
- A student taking a course that included content related to fracking and climate change demanded the right to use outside sources without consideration of their scientific merit and still receive an A in the course. When the instructor responded by requiring students to use data from the Intergovernmental Panel on Climate Change to support their arguments, the student dropped the course. The student then contacted a well-known "alt-right" student publication, which published the course syllabus with the faculty member's phone number, email address, and office hours online. The instructor received threatening emails and became the subject of hateful commentary when the story went viral on Twitter. The student went unpunished by the administration.

- A faculty expert on crop science who blogs, tweets, and speaks publicly on biotechnology and genetically modified organisms was threatened on Twitter after tweeting critically about the online publication of an article on pesticides in a major news magazine, which did not identify its author as a paid corporate activist.

- The name of a Jewish professor whose research and publications focus on critical whiteness studies was posted on white supremacist websites, along with the names of other Jewish scholars in the same field. The professor was also listed under an antisemitic Twitter hashtag, along with her photograph, with the caption characterizing her as an attacker of "White identity."

- A conservative online student newspaper published an article about a faculty member's requirement that students use Modern Language Association style guidelines for assignments, including gender-inclusive language. After the right-wing website Campus Reform picked up the story, Fox News interviewed a student who complained about losing one point on a writing assignment for having failed to use such language. The original article went viral, and the professor who taught the course received hundreds of threatening emails, many of them violent and misogynistic, and dozens of telephone calls of a similar nature.[53]

It's not only faculty; students too may become targets. For example, "after American University elected the first African-American woman to lead its student body, the white supremacist leader who founded one of the largest hate sites on the internet began an online campaign to troll her and her sorority with racist taunts." Andrew Anglin, neo-Nazi founder of the Daily Stormer website, posted pictures and video of Taylor Dumpson, along with links to her Facebook account and American University's Twitter address, directing his readers to "troll storm" her with a barrage of racist and demeaning messages on social media. The university provided police protection for Dumpson, who on April 30, 2018, filed a lawsuit against Anglin and two others.[54]

At the University of Illinois at Urbana-Champaign, Tariq Khan, a graduate student in history, spoke at a November 16, 2017, anti-Trump rally and got into an altercation with a counterprotester. Edited footage of the clash captured by the pro-Trump student's friends was included in a story on the website Campus Reform about Khan "attacking conservative students." Soon the university was deluged with emails and calls demanding Khan's expulsion, with some threatening his life. Criminal accusations of assault, robbery, and property destruction filed against him by members of the campus Turning Point USA chapter were quickly dismissed, but the university's Office for Student Conflict Resolution caved to the pressure, requiring Khan to attend anger management classes, as well as placing him on conduct probation for the remainder of his studies. But that was not all. According to Khan, Turning Point members shared his contact information—thereby enabling threats against him and his family—and harassed his wife, who is not a student, at an off-campus, non-university-related event until police escorted them out. On another night, Khan's wife found a masked man in their front yard, taking pictures of their car's license plate.[55]

Professor Meredith Clark of the University of Virginia, who researches the intersections of race, media, and power, said she had "yet to see a university handle essentially a social-media crisis well, particularly one that their students are involved in." She added, "What I think is particularly dangerous about the replications of those sorts of acts on social media is that they create a model for others to copy. There are ways for people to find out about when things are being done to disrupt other campuses, and they can repeat those same behaviors, and that can cause some problems."[56]

Sociologist Tressie McMillan Cottom has described well how these attacks typically develop:

> The first clue a professor gets that her life is about to change arrives in the most bureaucratic and benign of ways: It is often an email. The email may say that a known right-wing publication is planning to run a story about your research or your teaching, and it offers you a chance to comment.

Next, the architecture of online news media takes over. A story, perhaps about your syllabus or a story you told in a lecture, is posted. A series of outraged tweets goes out. An army of social media accounts, some run by real humans and some by "bots," is pressed into service. The targeted advertising that Facebook uses to sell you the shoes you thought about buying on Amazon last week also helps the troll armies push stories about a "liberal commie" into the social media feeds of those on the right who are likely to believe and share it.

Within 24 hours, your university email is swarmed with messages from people claiming to be concerned students, concerned parents and concerned donors. Somewhere in the hundreds of emails there may be official communications from students and co-workers, but you don't have the resources to find them. You cannot do your actual job of teaching and researching because you are drowning in emails, phone calls and messages.

If you are one of the lucky ones, it stops there. Increasingly, it does not stop there. Angry consumers of this kind of culture war red meat do not live just on the internet. They live in your community. They may mail you packages, perhaps with dangerous contents in them. They may send you death threats. They may use the surveillance apparatus we built to sell internet ads and control poor people to find out where your children go to school or where your spouse works. They may threaten them, directly or indirectly.

The distance between these trolls and their targets is shrinking; increasingly, the perpetrators of this harassment have a real-life presence on campus. They organize sophisticated armies of student "journalists" to surveil and trap professors and students into being "liberal." They record and remix footage, circulating it on a vast web of social media, blogs, content farms and even in mainstream media. They capture the public's imagination, feed conservative media's obsession with the liberal academia, and they make it seem safe to hordes of on-the-ground soldiers fighting an imaginary race war to come to a campus near you to recruit.[57]

Much of this activity may be attributed to the work of well-funded private groups and media outlets. In 2003, the AAUP's Special

Committee on Academic Freedom and National Security in a Time of Crisis remarked that such groups, "parading under the banner of patriotism or acting to further a specific cause, have been monitoring academic activities and have denounced professorial departures from what these groups view as acceptable."[58] They act at times as effective blacklists. Two such groups, Canary Mission and Amcha Initiative, target alleged supporters of the Boycott, Divestment, Sanctions (BDS) movement. In spring 2018, Katherine Franke, a professor of law at Columbia University, was barred from entering Israel based on information found on those sites. Franke denied that she was in any way a leader or even currently involved in any group that advocates for BDS. How is it, she asked, that "Israel delegates to right-wing trolls the job of determining who should be admitted to Israel?"[59] There are also reports that pro-BDS students have been interrogated by the FBI, with the cooperation of their universities, on the basis of their inclusion on the Canary Mission list.[60]

In the United States by far the most significant and influential of these groups are the websites Campus Reform, College Fix, and Professor Watchlist. The last site, a project of Turning Point USA, purports to identify faculty members who "discriminate against conservative students and advance leftist propaganda in the classroom."[61] It lists names of professors with their institutional affiliations and photographs, thereby, as the AAUP noted in January 2017, "making it easy for would-be stalkers and cyberbullies to target them. Individual faculty members who have been included on such lists or singled out elsewhere have been subject to threats of physical violence, including sexual assault, through hundreds of e-mails, calls, and social media postings."[62]

Inspired by an independent action taken by faculty members at the University of Notre Dame, the AAUP in December 2016 drafted an open letter to the sponsors of Professor Watchlist and invited members and supporters to sign it. The letter concluded, "We support and stand with our colleagues whose academic freedom your list threatens. Therefore, we, the undersigned, ask that you add our names to the list." The AAUP gathered more than twelve thousand signatures.[63] Some at the time suggested that this response actually gave a rather amateurish blacklisting effort more publicity and credit than it deserved. Professor Watchlist is best ignored, it was said. That, however, conjured up memories of the too-passive approach the AAUP unfortunately took in the 1950s, when blacklists of alleged Communists resulted in the dismissals of dozens of faculty members across the country. The timidity of the AAUP at that time was disgraceful. It is a mistake the association is determined not to repeat.

Turning Point USA, it should be added, has also launched a well-funded campaign to get conservatives elected to student governments, although the campaign's success is questionable. The *Chronicle of Higher Education* identified "at least a dozen colleges that featured candidates who were either Turning Point members, were endorsed by Turning Point, or received campaign assistance" from the group. The organization's leader, 24-year-old Charlie Kirk, called the effort a "rather undercover, underground operation."[64] At one college event, in a lecture on how to "crush" opponents, Kirk argued that "the person who wins the debate is not the person with the best argument. It's the person who is . . . able to articulate a position—even if the position is a horrible one and makes no sense."[65]

From July 2016 through June 2017, Turning Point raised more than $8.2 million, up from $4.3 million in the previous fiscal year, with expenditures over $8.3 million, but its donors remain mostly anonymous. Using tax records, the *International Business Times* identified seventeen donors, including Chicago-based Republican megadonor Richard Uihlein ($275,000), the family foundation of Illinois Republican governor Bruce Rauner ($150,000), the Henry and Lynde Bradley Foundation ($20,000), and the Richard and Helen DeVos Foundation, named after the in-laws of current secretary of education Betsy DeVos ($10,000 in 2015).[66] However, Turning Point has come under harsh criticism from other conservative groups. In a May 2018 internal memorandum (later leaked and then published on the organization's website) the Young America's

Foundation blasted Turning Point for its "lack of integrity, honesty, experience, and judgment." The memo charged the group with falsifying the numbers of its members and activities, fabricating results to cover up failed efforts, recruiting "racists and Nazi sympathizers," and engaging in other "unethical activity." Sarah Ruger, director of Free Speech Initiatives for the Charles Koch Institute, labeled the Professor Watchlist "McCarthyism 2.0," adding that it "keeps [her] up at night."[67]

To be sure, efforts like Professor Watchlist are themselves protected by the First Amendment. Faculty members are therefore well advised to gird themselves before entering the public arena, especially if their views may be considered provocative by extremists. But as Professor Ciccariello-Maher declared in his resignation letter from Drexel, "We are all a single outrage campaign away from having no rights at all."[68] These campaigns of harassment endanger the collective academic freedom of the faculty. Administrators and governing boards must, therefore, "reject outside pressures to remove or discipline faculty members whose ideas or commentary may be provocative or controversial and to denounce in forceful terms these campaigns of harassment."[69] When Dana Cloud, a faculty member at Syracuse University, received threats in the wake of a provocative tweet, her provost, Kent Syverud, forcefully rejected calls for her discipline or dismissal. "No," he responded. "We are and will remain a university. Free speech is and will remain one of our key values. I can't imagine academic freedom or the genuine search for truth thriving here without free speech. Our faculty must be able to say and write things—including things that provoke some or make others uncomfortable—up to the very limits of the law."[70]

Unfortunately, too many college and university leaders have fallen short of this standard, often treating these incidents as if the main concern were institutional image. In some cases faculty members have been disciplined or had their statements denounced without any effort to explain or defend their academic freedom. But the harassers cannot be appeased by disciplinary actions, including dismissals. Although an administration is certainly free to express disapproval of a faculty member's speech, it must be kept in mind that a number of sensationalized reports of faculty members' statements or online posts have been taken out of context. Hence, reports may not correctly reflect the actual speech. Moreover, as Jonathan Rees has pointed out, "Ideas that really aren't that controversial in academic circles are becoming so as they get chewed up and regurgitated by the enemies of higher education into forms that their originators wouldn't even recognize." Rees adds, "Institutional branding concerns are not sufficient justification to violate our constitutional rights. If big donors don't want to give because someone on your faculty has controversial views, then you probably don't want their money because they don't really understand why universities exist in the first place."[71] In general, there should be an understanding that faculty members never speak on behalf of the institution, so there should be no strong compulsion to criticize their words beyond a blanket disassociation from them. As journalist David Perry has suggested, it shouldn't be too difficult for colleges and universities simply to declare, "We do not let right-wing media influence our hiring or firing decisions. That will be our only comment on the matter."[72]

To be sure, concerns about campus safety are legitimate. However, as the AAUP, the AAC&U, and the AFT jointly declared,

> Anything short of a vigorous defense of academic freedom will only further imperil safety. Concessions to the harassers send the message that such odious tactics are effective. They have a chilling effect on the entire academic community. Academic leaders are therefore obligated to recognize that attacks on the academic freedom of individual instructors pose a risk to the institution as a whole and to the very project of higher education as a public good. As the AAUP's *Statement on Government of Colleges and Universities* stressed, the protection the college or university "offers to an individual or a group is, in fact, a fundamental defense of the vested interests of society in the educational institution."[73]

Some institutions have taken positive steps to both inform and defend their faculty members. The University of Iowa's "Faculty

Support & Safety Guidance" document "is designed to assist the campus community in responding to situations in which faculty members are targeted by individuals or groups outside of the university based on the content of the faculty member's scholarship, teaching, clinical care, and/or service. . . . The targeting of scholars for their ideas or views not only harms those individuals, but also strikes at the university's academic core. Through this guide and other means, the university seeks to protect faculty against the intimidation or violence that the expression of unpopular ideas sometimes generates." The document defines policies and procedures and offers specific guidance to individual faculty members, department chairs, administrators, and communications staff.[74] The University of Illinois also developed institutional protocols after its response to an attack "wasn't as coordinated as it could've been." Vice Provost for Academic Affairs Bill Bernhard said, "It's important for the department head, the dean, and the provost to get out and express support for the faculty member, for academic freedom and the exchange of ideas. We want to make sure that these leaders know it's their responsibility to do so and provide them with ideas on how to go about addressing these situations."[75]

For individual faculty members Dana Cloud has summarized her own experience with a harassment campaign and offered some recommendations for targeted faculty members who may be under attack. These include the following:[76]

- Reverse the narrative by shifting its focus from what you said to the content of the harassment itself. Show how the harassers are the ones threatening actual violence.
- Find allies on campus.
- Gain the support of major organizations that defend academic freedom, in particular, contact the AAUP.
- Obtain signatures from academics and allies everywhere. Use social media and organizations you work with to circulate an online petition.

- Get organized. Participating in activist organizations, including faculty unions, the AAUP, disciplinary organizations, and national and international organizations, is crucial.

The Case of Professor McAdams

It will be useful to take an extended look at an unusual case in which it may be argued that it was a faculty member who encouraged harassment of another instructor through the exercise of his own freedom of extramural expression. The case is of special interest because it is one of the first—if not *the* first—cases involving the disciplining of a faculty member for social media activity to come before the courts.

Marquette University professor John McAdams maintains a personal blog, the Marquette Warrior, in which he regularly voices strong opinions on a variety of political and university issues and where he engages in sometimes pointed and even harsh criticism of colleagues. McAdams's views tend toward the political Right and are not very popular among his colleagues. In particular, he opposes gay marriage. When one of his student advisees, who also opposes gay marriage, complained that a graduate student instructor had stifled discussion of the issue—a complaint determined upon official investigation to be largely unfounded—McAdams, without speaking to either the instructor or her department, posted what some thought to be a personal attack on the graduate student instructor, Cheryl Abbate. He also circulated an audio recording of the student's confrontation with the instructor made without her knowledge or consent. The post, which named Abbate and revealed her contact information, quickly went viral, and soon Abbate was subjected to a tremendous barrage of hostile, obscene, and threatening email, phone, and social media messages. She was fearful enough to leave Marquette and transfer to another university.

McAdams claims that his blog is journalism and totally extramural and hence protected by the principles of academic freedom. As one regular contributor to the AAUP's *Academe* blog put it, "McAdams' blog is a classic example of extramural utterances." It "is not part of his teaching or his research. It is an expression of his own opinions." McAdams therefore had the right to criticize a fellow instructor, even falsely and carelessly: "Marquette is perfectly free to condemn McAdams for an alleged breach of civility, but not to punish him. And although some faculty might legitimately fear being criticized by McAdams, no one has a right to be free from criticism, or to punish McAdams for their own decision to self-censor."[77]

Another contributor saw it differently, however, in good measure because the instructor was also a student. He wrote,

> When a professor engages in extramural utterances that harm a student, . . . it would be wholly inappropriate for administration officials to ignore such consequences. . . . There are two competing claims to academic freedom here. One is the right of a professor to engage in institutional criticism of practices and outcomes that may include naming names of administrators and faculty members. The other is the right of professors to teach without hindrance, within a climate conducive to disparate pedagogies, without fear of being policed by a[nother] professor on the Internet. Professor McAdams's actions are disruptive to the academic freedom of an institution.[78]

A third AAUP member argued that academic freedom was not the issue at all. He wrote that the case "hinges primarily on McAdams' rejection of his responsibilities as a teaching member of the faculty. Academic freedom, though necessarily onstage in the dispute, does not play a leading role. We ought to conceive of this matter in terms of other principles. . . . It is one thing to snipe at administrators or to criticize one's colleagues' teaching on one's blog—though unpleasant or uncivil (circumstances depending, of course), such is and must remain protected speech—and it is something very different to publicly condemn a professional-in-training, for whose welfare one bears some responsibility."[79]

The Marquette administration summarily suspended McAdams from his teaching duties and banned him from campus. That prompted theology professor Daniel Maguire, an advocate for gay marriage, to write a letter in protest. Maguire noted in the letter that he disagrees with McAdams on many issues but still questioned how he was being treated. "My key objection is that action was taken against a professor without due process," Maguire said. "I decided to write the letter because I'm a believer in due process. I'm a long term member of the AAUP, which is really the premier of academic freedom and integrity."[80] Gregory Scholtz, associate secretary and director of the AAUP's Department of Academic Freedom, Tenure, and Governance, also wrote the Marquette administration on behalf of the association to insist on due process in the case.[81]

The administration then initiated proceedings to revoke McAdams's tenure and fire him. Marquette's policies and procedures are largely consistent with AAUP standards. Under those policies a faculty hearing committee was convened to adjudicate the case. In a carefully crafted and admirably thorough 164-page report, that committee concluded that

> the interim suspension of Dr. McAdams pending the outcome of this proceeding, imposed by the University with no faculty review and in the absence of any viable threat posed by the continuation of his job duties, was an abuse of the University's discretion granted under the Faculty Statutes. The purpose of the suspension appears not to have been to prevent immediate harm to Dr. McAdams or members of the University community, but rather to impose a summary sanction on Dr. McAdams to satisfy the demands of external and internal audiences. This is an improper use of the interim suspension power that violated Dr. McAdams's right to due process under the Faculty Statutes.

However, the committee also concluded that

> the University has established sufficient discretionary cause under the Faculty Statutes to suspend Dr. McAdams without pay, but not sufficient cause to dismiss him. That conclusion has several parts to it. First, the Committee concludes that Dr. McAdams's conduct with respect to

his November 9, 2014 blog post violated his obligation to fellow members of the Marquette community by recklessly causing harm to Ms. Abbate, even though that harm was caused indirectly. The Committee concludes that the harm to Ms. Abbate was substantial, foreseeable, easily avoidable, and not justifiable. The Committee therefore concludes that the University has established by clear and convincing evidence that Dr. McAdams's conduct . . . clearly and substantially failed to meet the standard of personal and professional excellence that generally characterizes University faculties. Second, the Committee concludes that the University has demonstrated that Dr. McAdams's conduct was seriously irresponsible, and that his demonstrated failure to recognize his essential obligations to fellow members of the Marquette community, and to conform his behavior accordingly, will substantially impair his fitness to fulfill his responsibilities as a professor. . . .

However, the Committee also concludes that there are two mitigating circumstances in this case that preclude a finding that sufficient cause has been established to support a penalty of dismissal from the faculty. First, portions of Dr. McAdams's November 9 blog post did address a legitimate subject of intramural concern, namely the handling of his advisee's complaint that his advisee had been treated unfairly in terms of what views he could assert in Ms. Abbate's class. Second, despite multiple prior conflicts with professors, administrators, and students over his extramural and campus communications, Dr. McAdams has never been formally reprimanded, or even warned that his behavior was approaching a boundary that could lead to dismissal. The Committee therefore concludes that the University has established neither a sufficiently egregious failure to meet professional standards nor a sufficiently grave lack of fitness to justify the sanction of dismissal. Instead, the Committee concludes that only a lesser penalty than dismissal is warranted.

The Committee therefore recommends that Dr. McAdams be suspended, without pay but with benefits, for a period of no less than one but no more than two semesters.[82]

In the wake of the report, Marquette University president Michael Lovell suspended McAdams for two semesters but also imposed an additional penalty as a condition of his reinstatement, requiring McAdams to write a statement of apology and admission of wrong-doing. Predictably, McAdams refused (one suspects that such refusal was a goal of the condition). In January 2017, Marquette announced that, with the two-semester suspension completed, McAdams was no longer being punished for his criticism of the student instructor but would remain on indefinite suspension until he admitted he was wrong, acknowledged that "the blog post was reckless and incompatible with the mission and values of Marquette University," and apologized. McAdams filed suit.

The suit claimed that the faculty hearing committee suffered from serious procedural flaws, as Marquette withheld evidence from McAdams and allowed an allegedly biased professor to sit on it, but an AAUP observer, a professor from another university, concluded that the hearing process complied with AAUP due process standards. On May 4, 2017, a state circuit court trial judge granted summary judgment in favor of the university. On January 22, 2018, the Wisconsin Supreme Court agreed to hear McAdams's appeal of that judgment.

On February 27, 2018, the AAUP filed an amicus curiae brief in the case. The AAUP argued that the Faculty Hearing Committee (FHC) applied appropriate AAUP policies on extramural expression and urged the court to "adopt this standard in interpreting university academic freedom policies such as those provided in Marquette's Faculty Handbook and Faculty Statutes." The brief also argued that "Marquette violated Dr. McAdams's due process rights by unilaterally imposing a new penalty that required Dr. McAdams to write a statement of apology/admission as a condition of reinstatement. This severe sanction would compel Dr. McAdams to renounce his opinions, a fundamental violation of his academic freedom. It also amounted to a de facto termination that was imposed in contravention of the FHC's recommended lesser penalty."

The AAUP brief asserted,

The strong protection of academic freedom in extramural speech does not immunize faculty members from disciplinary charges. It does mean, however, that the administration carries a heavy burden of proving that extramural speech clearly demonstrates the faculty member's unfitness to serve, such as "fundamental violations of professional ethics or statements that suggest disciplinary incompetence."

The FHC report explicitly applies the AAUP's broad interpretation of academic freedom in extramural speech to Marquette's definition of academic freedom, modeled on the 1940 *Statement of Principles*. Further, the FHC accurately explains the relationship between the Committee A *Statement on Extramural Utterances*' "fitness to serve" standard and the "special obligations" described in the AAUP 1966 *Statement on Professional Ethics*: "Failure to abide by those special obligations . . . does not [alone] mean that the professor could be dismissed." The conduct in question must "clearly demonstrat[e] the faculty member's unfitness for his or her position. . . . A mere failure, for example, to be clear that one is not speaking for the university will not suffice unless it rises to that level."

Although the Circuit Court reiterated the FHC's use of the "fitness to serve" standard, unlike the FHC, the court did not identify the importance of examining "special obligations" only in the context of whether the administration has carried its burden of proving a faculty member's unfitness to serve. Instead, the court provides an imprecise summary of the scope of academic freedom that understates its protection: "In short, academic freedom gives a professor . . . the right to express his views in speeches, writings, and on the internet, so long as he does not infringe on the rights of others."

Such a formulation of limiting academic freedom to "views" that do "not infringe on the rights of others" vastly undermines academic freedom. The nature of offering opinions, particularly controversial ones, is that they may prompt vigorous responses, including assertions that the rights of others have been infringed. Views and opinions should be subject to debate, not to limitations based on claims that the expression of views infringes upon the rights of others. Adding such a component will only serve to limit the openness and breadth of the views expressed in academia, compromising essential rights of academic freedom.

In the McAdams case, the brief concluded, both due process protections and McAdams's academic freedom were violated. First, there is the matter of the additional penalty imposed by the university:

> President Lovell adopted the FHC's recommendation of a two-semester unpaid suspension, but increased the penalty by requiring that Dr. McAdams write a statement of apology/admission of wrongdoing as a condition of reinstatement. The Circuit Court incorrectly found that President Lovell's condition of reinstatement "was consistent with the recommendation of the FHC." Rather, this new penalty went well beyond the FHC's recommendation. . . . Additionally, the required written statement may put Dr. McAdams in legal jeopardy in a potential lawsuit by graduate student/instructor Cheryl Abbate. It was reasonable, and indeed predictable, that Dr. McAdams would refuse to write a statement with these required elements. Thus, making this written statement a condition of reinstatement was tantamount to removing tenure and dismissing Dr. McAdams. It also imposed the very penalty the FHC had explicitly rejected.

Lovell at minimum should have returned the case to the committee to consider the additional conditions he wished to impose: "it is fundamentally unfair for the administration to exercise unfettered power to assert that it accepts the FHC's recommendation, while simultaneously acting against that recommendation," the brief argued.

"The required written statement raises academic freedom concerns," the brief added:

> The required acknowledgement that "the blog post was reckless and incompatible with the mission and values of Marquette University" is not limited to the specific conduct that the FHC found to warrant discipline. The acknowledgment could reasonably be understood to extend to all the speech contained in the blog post. Yet, the vast majority of the speech in the blog post is on political and educational matters of

public concern, including "[t]he way classes are taught and the subjects that may be discussed . . ." The FHC found that this speech is clearly protected by the Faculty Handbook provisions for academic freedom in extramural speech, which are modeled on AAUP standards. In requiring Dr. McAdams to renounce his blog post as a condition of reinstatement, the administration used the threat of dismissal to force Dr. McAdams to choose between adhering to his protected political views and regaining his tenured position.[83]

On July 6, 2018, in a 4–2 decision, the Wisconsin Supreme Court ruled in favor of McAdams, ordering the circuit court to enter judgment for him on his claim that Marquette breached his contract by initially "suspending him without cause . . . , affirming the suspension . . . and then increasing the discipline."[84] The majority opinion, two concurrences, and the dissent in the case addressed multiple issues. These include the university's claim that its internal disciplinary procedures may substitute for McAdams's right to litigate (the court ruled that they do not) and McAdams's charge that the FHC was compromised by its inclusion of a faculty member who had previously signed a statement critical of the blog post at issue (the court ruled that it was), neither of which concern me here. But the court did address critical issues of academic freedom and shared governance in interesting, if at times confused, ways. Moreover, it is rare, if not unprecedented, for such a high judicial body to rely so extensively on AAUP policies as did the Wisconsin court. For these reasons the opinions merit consideration and analysis.

With respect to academic freedom, the majority opinion, written by Justice Daniel Kelly, fully embraced the AAUP's understanding of extramural expression:

> The analytical structure described by the AAUP, and adopted by the FHC, provides a stable framework within which to evaluate whether the doctrine of academic freedom protects a specific extramural comment. Although the doctrine may not be susceptible to precise definition, still it is sufficiently certain that it can inform faculty members

what is required of them. The AAUP properly limits the analysis to whether the actual extramural comment, on its face, clearly demonstrates that the professor is unfit to serve. This very narrow inquiry explains why the AAUP can confidently state that "[e]xtramural utterances rarely bear upon the faculty member's fitness for the position."[85]

In applying this strict standard, the majority found that McAdams's blog post had "nothing relevant to say about" his "fitness as a professor" and was therefore fully protected by academic freedom.[86]

Here the decision took issue with the FHC report, which found that portions of the blog post—and McAdams's actions subsequent to its initial posting—were indeed relevant to his fitness but did not rise to a level that would justify dismissal from his position. "Just because vile commentary followed the blog post doesn't mean the blog post instigated or invited the vileness," wrote Kelly.[87] But in dissent Justice Ann Walsh Bradley, joined by Justice Shirley S. Abrahamson, argued that such a conclusion can be reached only "by ignoring significant facts in the record." These facts include various actions by McAdams suggesting that he was aware in advance that his identification of Abbate would provoke the kind of abusive response it did and that he actively promoted the blog and distributed to the media copies of the surreptitiously obtained audio recording of Abbate's confrontation with the student. The dissent concluded "that McAdams indeed did 'instigate' or 'invite' the vileness that followed his blog post. He knew what would happen, and he actively ensured that it would happen."[88] I find both the FHC report and the dissent convincing about this, and that McAdams did engage in some conduct unprotected by academic freedom that might have merited the level of discipline proposed by the FHC. Others, however, might disagree. In any event, the majority's argument remains an important affirmation of the AAUP's understanding of academic freedom with respect to extramural expression.

One must wonder, of course, whether the conservative justices in the majority would have applied this strict standard in the same manner had McAdams been a leftist in a similar position. In his analysis of the decision, John K. Wilson thought that at best unlikely.[89] That he is probably correct is demonstrated by the concurring opinion authored by Justice Rebecca Grassl Bradley and joined by Justice Kelly, which histrionically embraced the prevailing rhetoric of a campus "free speech crisis." According to Bradley, "Academic freedom, and concomitantly, free speech, is increasingly imperiled in America and within the microcosm of the college campus. It is the expression of opinions divergent from what is currently politically correct that needs protection under the doctrine of academic freedom." In her view the question posed by the case was, would academic freedom "succumb to the dominant academic culture of microaggressions, trigger warnings and safe spaces that seeks to silence unpopular speech by deceptively recasting it as violence? In this battle, only one could prevail, for academic freedom cannot coexist with Orwellian speech police."[90]

Of course, microaggressions, trigger warnings, and safe spaces were totally irrelevant to this case, and claims of a leftist assault on free expression are, at minimum, grossly inflated (see chap. 8). Such rhetoric therefore suggests that at least two members of the court majority may have been motivated by politics as much as or more than by principle. In some respects, the decision offers a mirror opposite of the case a few years earlier of leftist Ward Churchill, dismissed from his tenured position by the University of Colorado. In that case, after a jury found in Churchill's favor, conservative majorities on the Colorado Court of Appeals and Supreme Court ruled that the university's internal procedures precluded Churchill's right to sue, as these procedures gave the university "quasi-judicial immunity."[91]

With respect to shared governance, Wilson is correct that "everybody on the court gets [it] wrong." Leaders of Marquette's academic senate expressed concern that the decision had "undermined the role—established by both tradition and contract—that faculty members play in determining what obligations they have to one another and to students."[92] In a separate concurrence Justice Kelly, joined by Justice Bradley, called into question the legitimacy of any internal review by a faculty committee. "The FHC cannot be considered impartial because, even though it was hearing the case, it was also one of the contending parties," he wrote. "The FHC is the University inasmuch as it is composed entirely of University employees."[93] By contrast, the dissent approvingly referenced the AAUP's requirement that "any proposed suspension or dismissal of a tenured faculty member come before an independent faculty committee for review prior to any adverse employment action."[94] Hence, the dissent accused the majority of "jettisoning the shared governance of colleges and universities."[95] However, the dissenters did so by arguing that the idea of academic freedom "embraces the academic freedom of the faculty as well as the academic freedom of the institution."[96] This reliance on the doctrine of institutional academic freedom is problematic, given that it may be and often has been employed to empower managerial prerogative to override both the collective and individual rights of faculty members. In this regard, the majority is more correct than not in arguing that a "university's academic freedom is a shield against governmental interference; the dissent, however, would reforge it as a sword with which to strike down contracts it no longer wishes to honor."[97]

The majority declined to base its ruling on the First Amendment, relying instead on contract law.[98] The distinction between institutional and individual academic freedom is, however, largely an artifact of First Amendment analysis. As Walter Metzger has argued, First Amendment jurisprudence protects institutional autonomy, while a professional interpretation of academic freedom depends on institutional neutrality. Academic freedom as the AAUP understands it protects both individual faculty members and the collective ability of the faculty as a whole to engage in shared governance because it is founded on the defense of professional norms. None of the opinions in this case, unfortunately, grasped this fundamental principle.[99]

While none of the justices seemed fully to understand shared governance and its connection to academic freedom, the majority opinion may prove less harmful to the faculty's role in governance than the Marquette senate leaders fear. Whatever reservations the court may have had about the FHC's composition or its conclusions, much of the majority opinion is based on the undeniable fact that, under Marquette's policies (like those of most American colleges and universities), the committee's report "resulted in mere advice, not in an authoritative decision."[100] While the university's discipline procedure provides guidance to the hearing committee, the majority noted, it "has nothing to say about how the actual decision-maker is to decide the case." Therefore, "it was President Lovell, not the FHC, who decided whether Dr. McAdams would be disciplined. It was President Lovell, not the FHC, who decided the nature of the discipline that should be imposed. It was President Lovell, not the FHC, who had the authority to impose the discipline. It was President Lovell who actually meted out the discipline when he sent Dr. McAdams the Discipline Letter. And it was President Lovell who created the conditions on reinstatement that have kept Dr. McAdams in suspension limbo."[101]

While the majority's implication might well be that it would be better for the university to rely on external arbitrators, there is a more favorable way to interpret this argument. According to Justice Kelly, "It is not our place to rewrite [Marquette's] management structure to give the faculty a more muscular role in the university's affairs than they currently have."[102] But such a role might be obtained by strengthening the policy. If shared governance is to be meaningful and, at least under the standard set by this decision, legally enforceable, the faculty role needs to be more than advisory. To be effective, shared governance must involve shared decision-making, not simply consultation and advice, and provide for appropriate deference to the professional judgment of duly constituted faculty bodies. Had President Lovell sought FHC approval of his imposition of a sanction that went beyond its recommendation, as the AAUP brief argued he should have, or had he deferred entirely to the FHC recommendation, this case might not have been decided differently, given the flaws the majority found in the composition and conclusions of the FHC and their indifferent attitude to shared governance. However, the decision's genuine potential for undermining shared governance would have been lessened substantially.

The 1966 *Statement on Government of Colleges and Universities*, jointly formulated by the AAUP, the American Council on Education, and the Association of Governing Boards of Universities and Colleges, declared that in matters in which the faculty has primary responsibility, including questions of faculty status, "the power of review or final decision lodged in the governing board or delegated by it to the president should be exercised adversely only in exceptional circumstances, and for reasons communicated to the faculty. It is desirable that the faculty should, following such communication, have opportunity for further consideration and further transmittal of its views to the president or board."[103] Marquette has announced that in response to the decision the university "will work with its faculty to re-examine its policies, with the goal of providing every assurance possible that this never happens again."[104] Hopefully such a reexamination will aim to strengthen, not weaken, the faculty's role in decision-making so as to avoid the pitfalls created by its relegation to an advisory capacity.

Organizing in the Age of Social Media

"If there's an organized outrage machine, we need an organized response." So declared one faculty member quoted in the *Chronicle of Higher Education*.[105] And surely if the experience of the AAUP teaches us anything, it is that academic freedom cannot be defended individually; an organizational response is essential.[106] But in the era of mass electronic communication organizing is itself being transformed. Digital tools offer new and exciting methods for mobilizing and "organizing" support. The rapid circulation of information afforded by social media—from simple email to Facebook, Twitter, or WhatsApp—greatly facilitates the gathering of signatures on a petition or the mobilizing of physical protests. As Zeynep Tufekci has pointed out in her book *Twitter and Tear Gas*, "The ability to organize without organizations, indeed, speeds things up and allows for great scale in rapid time frames. There is no need to spend six months putting together a single rally when a hashtag could be used to summon protesters into the streets; no need to deal with the complexities of logistics when crowdfunding and online spreadsheets can do just as well."[107] Tufekci calls the new style of organizing without organization "adhocracy," noting that "adhocracy allows for the organization, for example, of big protests or major online campaigns with minimal effort and advance-work, but this empowerment can come along with a seemingly paradoxical weakness. I find that many such movements lose out on network internalities or the gains in resilience and collective decision-making and acting capacity that emerge from the long-term work of negotiation and interaction required to maintain the networks as functioning and durable social and political structures."[108]

We need to ask, then, what does it mean to organize on behalf of academic freedom in today's wired world? And if academic freedom is under assault online, how can the faculty best respond? The good news is that while social media may greatly facilitate targeted harassment, their spread and growing use also provide opportunities for more effective and rapid sharing of information about threats to and violations of academic freedom.[109] But sharing information must be accompanied by improved organization. On the simplest level organizing involves education, enlightenment, and persuasion—in contemporary lingo, making people "woke." But organizing also involves getting people to take some action—sign a petition, attend a meeting, donate money, write or call a legislator, join a picket line, and so on. Yet organizing cannot be limited to specific actions, inevitably bound by time and place. To be both successful and sustained, organizing must involve getting people to join and then participate in some structure, some, well, *organization*. And that involves devoting resources, both money and time; developing leadership; hiring and supporting paid staff; and, perhaps most importantly, establishing formalized decision-making structures and procedures that are efficient but also representative and meaningfully democratic.

It's difficult to imagine forty faculty members agreeing on everything, much less more than forty thousand, which is the current membership of the AAUP. But that's what organizing and organization are about—working through differences to achieve larger shared goals over the long haul. As faculty members face the kind of online harassment and other challenges described in this chapter, as well as additional assaults on academic freedom, shared governance, and the common good sure to come in the Trump era, the necessity of such organization will only increase.

Chapter Five

Can Outside Donors Endanger
Academic Freedom?

In January 2015, the North Carolina–based John William Pope Center for Higher Education Policy, a right-wing think tank, issued a report purporting to demonstrate that conservative-leaning academic centers on college and university campuses founded by wealthy donors "are not just surviving but thriving," a development the report lauded. Most of the centers the report described were financed by a few private donors, among them the North Carolina–based BB&T Foundation, the Pennsylvania-based Jack Miller Center, the Manhattan Institute's Veritas Fund, and, of course, various philanthropies associated with the network of billionaire conservative activists David H. Koch and Charles G. Koch. These donors, the report triumphantly proclaimed, "have the leverage to negotiate the terms that can keep centers safe from faculty control at schools where the faculty is antagonistic to their missions." The prospect of opening an academic center financed entirely by outside donors "can melt the heart of university administrators" of any ideological leaning, the report declared, especially given that college presidents "are often judged primarily on their ability to raise funds."[1]

The Pope report was little more than a slick promotional piece filled with loaded language and unfounded and extreme political allegations, more a puff piece designed to promote, without even a shred of dispassion, privately funded conservative academic centers than an objective assessment of their value. It made two critical, if largely unsubstantiated, claims: first, that universities are dominated by leftist faculties, who hide behind the fig leaf of "academic freedom" to promote their own radical agendas, and second, that university governance "should primarily support the rights of a donor" over the " 'academic freedom' of the faculty."

In support of the tired charge that left-wing faculty dominate universities and impose their narrow political agenda on students and that as a consequence the academy is "being scrubbed of free market economics, traditional attitudes toward Western civilization, time-tested methods of scholarship, and the general philosophy of liberty," the sole piece of evidence the report managed to muster was a 2007 list of thirty-seven most-cited authors of books in the humanities and social sciences, most of whom were supposedly "leftist." The charge that universities are somehow dominated by "the Left" is now and has always been false and fantastical. Repeating it over and over again may comfort some ideological conservatives, but that doesn't make it true.[2] As one conservative scholar who studied the question noted, "The political gap on college campuses is less important than other sources of tension, which arise based on differences between faculty and administrators and differences in academic discipline, age, and gender."[3] No doubt more university faculty members vote Democratic than vote Republican. But so what? More business executives and generals surely do the opposite. The key point is that critics have consistently failed to prove that where such leanings exist this creates undue obstacles to conservative expression. In the great majority of cases, it manifestly does not.[4]

The report maintained that "the issue of academic freedom is not only about protection against administrative intrusion into the objective inquiry of faculty but also about the faculty evolving over time into a special interest group that limits the range of ideas expressed on campus." The first part of this is true; the second, not so much. As any faculty member will readily attest, the notion that "the faculty" is a uniform "special interest group" is at best an aspiration of some. Faculty members are divided by discipline, rank, and employment category (tenured, contingent, etc.), as well as by race, age, gender, and, of course, political leanings. If we are an interest group, we are a pretty fractured one.[5]

The report explicitly faulted the American Association of University Professors' position that academic institutions should not "relinquish autonomy and the primary authority of their faculty over the curriculum" when they accept outside donations. But this is not solely the AAUP's position, nor is it anything new. On the issue of outside interference in the university—whether from government or private interests—the AAUP's view is essentially that espoused in a concurring opinion in the 1957 case of *Sweezy v. New Hampshire* by US Supreme Court justice Felix Frankfurter. He identified "four essential freedoms of a university—to determine for itself on academic grounds who may teach, what may be taught, how it shall be taught, and who may be admitted to study."[6] Donors have every right to request that their donations be used for goals they support. It is the responsibility of the institution, however, to ensure that those goals do not violate these basic principles.[7]

The report did get one thing right, however: conservative academic centers, funded, often lavishly, by outside donors like the Koch brothers, have spread throughout higher education, engendering growing concern among many faculty members. These centers must also be understood within a broader context of conservative philanthropy that, as a 1997 report put it, amounts to "an impressively coherent and concerted effort to undermine—and ultimately redirect—what they and other conservatives have regarded as the institutional strongholds of modern American liberalism: academia, Congress, the judiciary, executive branch agencies, major media, and even philanthropy."[8] *New Yorker* writer Jane Mayer's best-selling 2016 exposé of the Koch network elevated these concerns, as has the work of the largely student-initiated UnKoch My Campus project.[9]

Lynn Pasquerella, president of the Association of American Colleges and Universities, told the *Boston Globe* that the higher education world has been watching the trend closely. "The Kochs have been an increasingly visible force on college campuses at a time when there is widespread criticism by conservative voices that higher education promotes progressive liberal causes," she said. But many are concerned that the Kochs and their ilk are trying to control curriculum and faculty hiring. "It is corrosive," opined Leon Botstein, president of Bard College. "Using money as an ideological club is a fact of life, but it's an unpleasant one. It's a nasty fact of life that you have to accept is nasty."[10]

The Koch Network and George Mason University

In 2012, foundations controlled by the Kochs combined to give more than $12.7 million to 163 colleges and universities. In 2016, the Kochs awarded $50 million in grants to 249 institutions. That represented a 49 percent increase from 2015, when the Charles Koch Foundation distributed $34 million to 222 institutions. According to Ralph Wilson of UnKoch My Campus, the purpose of the centers and programs funded by the Koch donor network is "political rather than educational. The network erodes institutional integrity to leverage donor control."[11]

George Mason University (GMU), a public institution in Virginia, has received $95.5 million from the Kochs since 2005—nearly $50 million between 2011 and 2014—making it by far the largest single beneficiary of Koch largesse. Much of this funding has gone to the university's Mercatus Center, which describes itself as the "world's premier university source for market-related ideas," and its Institute for Humane Studies, which researches "the practice and potentials of freedom." Charles Koch chairs the institute's board and serves on the board of the Mercatus Center. Koch Industries executive vice president Richard Fink, who founded Mercatus when he was a George Mason professor and has been described as "Koch's brain," also sits on both boards and served eight years on George Mason's Board of Visitors.[12]

The university's relationship with the Kochs drew increased attention when on March 31, 2016, the Board of Visitors approved renaming their law school the Antonin Scalia Law School after receipt of a combined gift of $10 million from the Charles Koch Foundation and $20 million from an anonymous donor. The university's faculty senate expressed "deep concern" about the renaming and, in particular, about terms of the donor agreements under which the university was obligated to create two new centers affiliated with the law school and to appoint twelve new faculty members, including several tenured full professors. A May 4, 2016, senate resolution called on the administration and Board of Visitors to "put the request for SCHEV [State Council of Higher Education for Virginia] approval and the enactment of the provisions of the grant proposals on temporary hold to allow for a more careful discussion of the many serious concerns expressed by faculty, students, staff, alumni, state legislators, and the general public." AAUP associate secretary Anita Levy wrote George Mason's president and the chair of SCHEV, noting that the association "shares these concerns."[13] The renaming and the grants were accepted nonetheless.

In 2014, George Mason students initiated a campaign to raise concerns about the school's close relationship to the Charles Koch Foundation and advocate for disclosure of the university's agreements with private donors. Students filed a Freedom of Information Act (FOIA) request that year, seeking grant and gift agreements between the university and the Koch Foundation. They were told that the documents were controlled by the GMU Foundation, which claimed to be exempt from freedom of information requests. In response, the students launched a grassroots effort asking for the university voluntarily to release the documents. For more than two years their requests were ignored despite broad support from alumni, students, faculty, and other concerned community members. On February 9, 2017, the student organization Transparent GMU filed a lawsuit against the university and the GMU Foundation seeking to make them comply with the Virginia Freedom of Information Act. At a hearing the following October, Fairfax County circuit judge John M. Tran said the case could become "historic."[14]

The suit was tried in just one day on April 24, 2018, with Tran holding his verdict under advisement.[15] But on April 27, faculty and staff received an email from GMU president Angel Cabrera. He wrote, "Last week I was made aware of a number of gift agreements that . . . raise questions concerning donor influence in academic

matters. . . . These agreements fall short of the standards of academic independence I expect any gift to meet." Given that before he
took office Cabrera was extensively briefed on all major donors
and prospects, the claim that he had just become aware of these
agreements—which coincidentally had been discovered in the files
of a campus dean—strained credulity, especially in light of the timing
of the message, just three days after the FOIA trial. Two hours later,
Samantha Parsons, a 2016 GMU graduate, cofounder of Transparent
GMU and activist with UnKoch My Campus, received copies of ten
gift agreements—three of which involved the Koch Foundation—
dating from 2003 to 2011 that she had requested under the FOIA, all
of which involved the Mercatus Center. Several days later, Cabrera
sent a second email promising "a thorough review of all active donor agreements supporting faculty positions throughout the university to ensure that they do not grant donors undue influence in
academic matters" and "a comprehensive review of our gift acceptance policies." Cabrera contended that all but one of the agreements
had expired and that the donor had agreed to void the remaining
2011 agreement and transfer leftover funds "to the university for general support."[16]

The disclosures were a bombshell, quickly gaining national attention. They revealed that as early as 1990 donors were given a seat on
a committee to pick candidates for a professorship. Similar arrangements continued through 2009. "In one 2003 agreement, the Mercatus Institute said it had received $900,000 from the Menlo F. Smith
Trust to fund a professorship in the economics department, and
would make the first payment 'conditional' upon the appointment
of Russell Roberts, an economist who advocates limited government. A person designated by Menlo Smith, a St. Louis businessman, was given a seat on the selection committee." A pair of 2009
agreements between the Koch Foundation and the Mercatus Center to fund professorships in economics included language defining the positions in highly political terms. "The objective of the Professorship is to advance the understanding, acceptance and practice
of those free market processes and principles which promote indi-

vidual freedom, opportunity and prosperity including the rule of law, constitutional government, private property and the laws, regulations, organizations, institutions and social norms upon which they rely," one agreement read. George Mason also allowed donors a role in evaluating faculty members' performance via advisory boards.[17]

"It's now abundantly clear that the administration of Mason, in partnership with the Mercatus Center and private donors, violated principles of academic freedom, academic control and ceded faculty governance to private donors," said Bethany Letiecq, associate professor of human development and president of GMU's AAUP chapter. She added, "These are all gross violations of academic freedom. Faculty hiring and faculty retention are not the business of donors, in any way, shape or form."[18]

But that was not all. On April 30, UnKoch My Campus released more than seven hundred pages of heavily redacted documents concerning the law school that were received in response to an FOIA request made by a 2004 graduate of that school, Allison Pienta. She had sought information on the source of the anonymous $20 million gift that was part of the decision to rename the school for Justice Scalia. The documents revealed that since April 2016 the conservative Federalist Society for Law and Public Policy had "been influencing faculty and student placement, recommending and establishing legal programs, redirecting large amounts of scholarship revenues to support the Law School's most-politicized centers for the 'Study of the Administrative State' and 'Liberty and Law,' and even reorienting the Law School's judicial law clerk programs to place 'conservative' law students associated with the Federalist Society as clerks to the nation's judges."[19]

George Mason administrators had previously claimed that "there are no conditions tied to this gift other than creating scholarship programs" with "no strings attached." At a faculty senate meeting in April 2016, Provost David Wu declared that "the entire $30 million is for scholarships for students and nothing else." The documents released to Pienta indicate otherwise. Even before the change in name of the school, there was already a close relationship between its dean, Henry Butler, and Leonard Leo, executive vice president of the Federalist Society, who would also direct President Donald J. Trump's search for a nominee to replace Justice Anthony Kennedy on the US Supreme Court. In October 2015, Leo emailed Butler recommending a potential faculty hire. A few minutes later, Butler replied, "We're on it." On March 31, 2016, grant agreements were finalized with the Koch Foundation and the anonymous donor, who had been referred by Leo. In addition to the renaming of the school, the agreements established the new centers on the "administrative state" and "liberty and law." They granted to an entity called the "BH Fund" the right to represent the anonymous donor. The BH Fund's president is Leonard Leo, and its secretary-treasurer is another Federalist Society officer.[20]

The emails released by the university confirmed that Leo and the Federalist Society have been closely involved in the development of programs at the law school. They have sent Dean Butler recommendations and opinions on faculty hires, as well as recommendations for prospective students. For example, Leo sent Butler a résumé of one "student prospect" whose "father is a senior executive at [redacted]" and is "very interested in Mason." Federalist Society members made several other student recommendations. Five days after one applicant was referred, Butler emailed the director of the Federalist Society's student division to say, "Just wanted to make sure that you are aware that we closed the deal with [redacted]." An email from one professor claimed, "We are hoping to place Scalia Law Alumni who are current members of our Fed Soc student chapter, alumni who were active in Fed Soc, and other Scalia Law conservative and libertarian alums in federal clerkships."[21]

On April 25, two days after the Transparent GMU FOIA trial hearing but before release of the agreements, members of George Mason's Institutional Conflict of Interest Committee, formed in the aftermath of the Scalia renaming, introduced motions to the faculty senate calling for changes in the university's gift acceptance policy that would mandate public review of all grant agreements by a gift acceptance committee, with faculty representation elected by the senate, within thirty days of their enactment. The proposals were approved overwhelmingly at a special senate meeting on May 4.[22]

On July 5, 2018, Judge Tran issued his decision. "As a matter of law, the foundation is not a public body under [the Virginia Freedom of Information Act] as it is presently situated," he declared. However, he added, "This decision does not absolve the university of the responsibility, as a public body, to maintain records of the use of funds and programs it decides to develop." The university, Judge Tran continued, does not have "unfettered right to keep secret its use of gifted funds to create programs in compliance with conditions and restrictions imposed upon those gifts." The decision noted that when conditions are attached to donations such gift agreements could become public records once they are accepted and used. George Mason has a gift-acceptance committee that is not exempt from the state's Freedom of Information Act, Tran said. Transparent GMU said it planned to appeal.[23]

The Centers at Work

Although, as at George Mason, many funding agreements remain shrouded in secrecy, in an extensive work in progress UnKoch My Campus has been documenting a long series of instances in which donors in the Koch network exerted "undue influence over academic and administrative decisions." These include influence over faculty hiring and program creation and faculty and student scholarship, including control over curriculum. Also documented are multiple incidents in which grant agreements violated existing institutional polices on academic freedom, faculty governance, donor policy, and search procedures. The study recounts reports by faculty members of "threats" and "intimidation" in response to questions raised about Koch funding and examines efforts by both donors and institutions to keep information about these grants secret.[24]

Probably the most well-documented example prior to the Mason disclosures is Florida State University (FSU), where the extent of donor influence on the university's economics department has included the ability to veto tenure hires, or any programming, with as little as fifteen days' notice and an annual donor review of curricular/extracurricular programs and non-tenure-track hires. According to a faculty investigation, the Koch gift violated principles of academic freedom and faculty governance. A "two-fold conflict of interest," it was executed through "administrative dictate," with the dean and department chair using "threats" to create an "atmosphere of intimidation."[25] An economics professor who sat on a department hiring committee for the two positions that the Koch Foundation eventually underwrote charged that the committee forwarded forty names of potential candidates to department leaders. Twenty-five were crossed off the list because, he was told, those candidates would not be acceptable to the Kochs. He also charged that, at an annual economic conference where the department interviewed candidates, the Koch Foundation conducted its own interviews with the candidates—without telling the hiring committee it was doing so.[26]

In 2015, under pressure from UnKoch My Campus and the university community, FSU administrators decided to secretly discontinue the controversial Koch agreement. However, nearly all of the programs and professorships affiliated with the agreement were reassembled under the L. Charles Hilton Jr. Center at FSU, which in 2016 received an additional $539,000 grant from the Charles Koch Foundation. Koch's 2016 donation to FSU also included $150,000 for the Project for Accountable Justice (PAJ), a criminal justice think tank with ties to private corrections contractors and a "Right on Crime" initiative led by the American Legislative Exchange Council (ALEC), the State Policy Network, and the Charles Koch Institute.[27]

At Auburn University, a Koch center was found to have been the result of a foregone hiring process that took place without faculty knowledge, largely outside of Auburn's hiring procedures.[28] At Troy University in Alabama, an economics professor called for using Koch funds to move ideological allies into positions of campus power.

The department chair crowed that the grant "has kind of let us get away with a lot, as far as hiring people very rapidly and ramming through some of this curricular kind of stuff."[29]

What kind of work has been done at these centers? Consider philosopher Matt Zwolinski, a product of the University of Arizona's Koch-funded Freedom Center, who has also received research funding from the Charles Koch Foundation. He has argued that because sweatshop laborers "choose to accept the conditions of their employment," there is a moral case against interfering in the working conditions of sweatshops. In another piece he argued that charging $12 for a bag of ice that normally costs $1.70 in order to exploit conditions of scarcity touched off by a natural disaster should be legal and may even be deemed virtuous. Zwolinski is now a full professor of philosophy at the University of San Diego and director of a new Koch-funded center on Christian ethics. As journalist David Johnson commented, "It is not a sin for a philosopher to be provocative, even outrageous. . . . On the contrary, such provocations can be quite salutary in philosophy, a field that ruthlessly questions all presuppositions. But these kind of intellectual provocations appear in a different light when incentivized by private money with the explicit aim of passing laws."[30]

A report from UnKoch My Campus charges that Koch Foundation funds have also supported white supremacist teaching. Florida Atlantic University political science professor Matthew DeRosa, who runs a Koch-funded prison education program, was from 2000 until at least 2009 a "faculty member" at the League of the South Institute, the "educational arm of the Southern independence movement" where "the South's finest unreconstructed scholars" teach. The institute acts as the charitable nonprofit of the League of the South, which the Southern Poverty Law Center considers a neo-Confederate hate group that supports a second Southern secession in order to form a nation ruled by "Anglo-Celtic" people.[31] DeRosa isn't the only former League of the South academic in the Koch network. The institute's founder, Donald Livingston, served on the Institute for Humane Studies Academic Review Committee, which grants Koch's "Humane

Studies Fellowships," from 1996 to 1999. In 2017, he lectured at an Institute for Humane Studies seminar at George Mason University.
Thomas DiLorenzo, an "affiliated scholar" of the League of the South
Institute as recently as 2008, was an economics professor at George
Mason and worked on policy for the Koch-funded Cato Institute.
"Through their support for these faculty, the Koch Foundation is
subsidizing and strengthening an already booming wave of violent, alt-
right anarcho-capitalists," said Ralph Wilson, who wrote the UnKoch
report.[32]

To be fair, however, it should be noted that the Charles Koch
Foundation has provided a $3.25 million grant to the Knight First
Amendment Institute at Columbia University to help fund a
litigation-focused initiative that has sued President Trump to prevent him from blocking Twitter followers and is trying to force the
Justice Department to disclose secret legal memorandums.[33] In addition, Koch Foundation grants to the Poynter Institute have supported independent student media projects, including efforts by
student journalists at Howard University to cover "the longest student occupation in the college's history, hold their own university
officials accountable and host bl(activism), a conference on black
activism." The Institute has also received funding from the Mac-
Arthur Foundation and from George Soros's Open Society Institute.
According to one Poynter official, under terms of the grants, "we
pick the schools. We set the curriculum. We hire the faculty. We occasionally update our contacts at the Koch Foundation about our
progress. I can personally attest that over the last year our contacts
at the Koch Foundation gave us complete independence to run the
program the way we saw fit."[34]

Faculty Resistance

According to Wilson, "the more that faculty know about Koch's
contracts and strategy, the more they are trying to resist its influence."[35] At a growing number of institutions grants from the Kochs
and other similar donors have attracted faculty scrutiny:

- At Western Carolina University the faculty senate issued a position statement on a proposed Center for the Study of Free Enterprise, to be funded by a $2 million Koch Foundation grant. The statement, approved by a vote of 24–2, raised concerns about the center's long-term financial cost, its necessity, constraints on academic freedom, "reputational costs," and absence of peer review. The senate voted 21–3, with four abstentions, to oppose the center.[36]

- A six-page letter to the University of Utah Academic Senate signed by eighty-five faculty members and doctoral candidates in political science, economics, and law warned that a $10 million grant from the Charles Koch Foundation and a like sum from the descendants of Marriner S. Eccles to establish an economics institute in Eccles's name "raises serious concerns" about academic freedom. The letter called on the university to incorporate meaningful "independent faculty governance in this new institute, especially as this relates to future faculty hiring and the distribution of student scholarships and fellowships."[37]

- A $10 million center for the study of free enterprise at the University of Kentucky—funded jointly by the Charles Koch Foundation and John Schnatter, founder of Papa John's Pizza, for whom the center would be named—won the support of the university senate for its academic mission, but not for the terms of the gifts, which will be distributed over five years, must be reviewed each year, and may be revoked on just thirty days' notice. Critics said such terms would leave the university liable to maintain funding on its own should the grant be revoked. More importantly, the risk of losing funding could chill the academic freedom of researchers.[38] Purdue University and Ball State University also have centers funded by Schnatter, who was also a trustee of the University of Louisville. He stepped down from that position, as well as from his Papa John's chairmanship, after revelations in July 2018 that he had used racial slurs.[39]

- At Chapman University in California a $5 million Koch gift funds a program in "Humanomics," defined as "reintegrating the study of the humanities and economics." The English department voted to reject two candidates for tenured professorships in the program. The two scholars were then hired by the business school, but only after the head of an economics hiring committee resigned in protest, citing a lack of objectivity. "No other donor would be allowed to pre-select professors based on their ideology," said Tom Zoellner, an English professor. "Appointments were hustled through without due process or necessary transparency."[40]

- In June 2016, Wake Forest University announced the creation of the Eudaimonia Institute, whose mission is to "study the nature of human flourishing." Two months later it was revealed that funding for the center would come from the Charles Koch Foundation to the tune of $3.69 million. The announcement prompted a petition from 189 concerned faculty members. The faculty senate looked into the matter and by a 17–9 vote called on the administration to "prohibit all Koch network funding for any of its centers or institutes." In an op-ed explaining the vote, the resolution's authors wrote, "We believe that there is an opportunity for Wake Forest University to make a powerful statement against such private/corporate efforts to use institutions of higher education and, most importantly, our students for such overtly political ends. Are there other foundations with political agendas? Of course. But we've encountered *nothing* comparable to this attempt to co-opt higher education—and all under the veil of secrecy. The donor agreement remains undisclosed. It was the conclusion of our committee that *any* association with this effort tarnishes the reputation and integrity of Wake Forest University."[41]

The Wake Forest project was an outgrowth of a "well-being initiative" begun by Charles Koch in 2014 in response to criticism of his efforts. Richard Fink, Charles Koch Foundation vice chairman, explained: "The Koch network needed to present its free-market ideology as an apolitical and altruistic reform movement to enhance the quality of life—as 'a movement of well-being.' The network should make the case that free markets forged a path to happiness, whereas big government led to tyranny, Fascism, and even Nazism." James Otteson, executive director of the BB&T Center for the Study of Capitalism (BB&T is a bank holding company), put it even more bluntly: "Who can be against well-being?" he rhetorically asked. "The framing is absolutely critical."[42]

Exploiting the Public Treasury

It's not difficult, of course, to understand why colleges and universities find such donations attractive. At public research universities the state share of funding has fallen from over 30 percent in 2001 to 17 percent in 2012.[43] And so schools turn to outside donors to make up the loss. Between 1970 and 2000 alone, the share of university research funding from private sources tripled. Donations are, however, decidedly top-heavy, with less than 1 percent of universities receiving nearly 30 percent of gifts. Private institutions don't get state funding, but intensified tuition competition has compelled them as well to embrace more aggressive fund-raising.[44] Of course, as Christopher Newfield has demonstrated, external private funding often disguises hidden institutional costs: "around 20 percent of the cost of *externally* funded research is supported *internally* by universities themselves." Newfield concludes, "Privatized research funding is not a way that public universities can cost-share with the private sector. It is a way for the private sector to extract value from the public."[45]

What value might donors like the Kochs extract? The experiences of Arizona State University and Texas Tech University may shed some light. Since the 2008 financial crisis, Arizona has slashed state funding and raised tuition more than any other state.[46] So it came as a surprise to many when Republican governor Doug Ducey's April 2016 budget included a new higher education line item of $5 million earmarked for "economic freedom schools." Arizona

State University boasted a Center for the Study of Economic Liberty, housed in the business school, which opened in 2014 after reportedly receiving a $3.5 million donation from the Charles Koch Foundation. The university had a second center funded in part by the Kochs as well, as did the University of Arizona, but the economic liberty center attracted attention because its executive director had just endorsed a controversial K–12 education funding plan proposed by Ducey. The proposal wasn't the first Ducey idea endorsed by the center. It's impossible to determine whether the $5 million in state funding came in exchange for such support, but it certainly appeared suspicious.[47]

Suspicions were heightened in 2017 when Arizona State launched a new School of Civic and Economic Thought and Leadership, which was funded by the state legislature but absorbed the two centers that had been supported by the Koch Foundation. Matthew Garcia, who directed Arizona State's School of Historical, Philosophical and Religious Studies from 2012 to 2017, left for Dartmouth College, "sickened" by the events that led to the establishment of the new school. The Koch-funded Center for Political Thought and Leadership had been housed in his school, where, as he related in the *Washington Post*,

> I trusted our agreement with the foundation because it guaranteed faculty control over the hiring process and required Center members to work within the school to create a curriculum that championed many perspectives. . . .
>
> This is why I was profoundly surprised and disappointed when President [Michael] Crow accepted the money from the state legislature to create an alternative school to our own, one that would absorb the original Koch-funded centers. Born in secrecy at the eleventh hour in the Arizona Assembly, a small group of conservative legislators inserted funding for the new school into the overall annual allocation for public universities. The maneuver forced Crow to make a choice—defend Arizona State University's curriculum or lay down to these political partisans.

He invited them in by hiring a group of conservative professors at private institutions to construct the foundations of the new school.

The report they produced reveals more about their intentions to use public moneys for ideological indoctrination than create intellectual diversity. The official justification for the School of Civic and Economic Thought and Leadership is full of assumptions that misrepresented our school as having a "conformity of opinion" that produced "an obvious lack of debate."

But neither the small group of legislators nor the architects of the new school showed any interest in debate. None of the external scholars charged with building the school ever talked to me or members of my faculty. If they had, they would have recognized our embrace of diverse political perspectives and the hiring of scholars that broadened our curriculum in ways that they claimed were lacking in higher education.

Michael Crow also exempted the new school from the usual budgets and hiring protocol. The recruitment of the first director, Paul Carrese, happened mostly outside the purview of his future colleagues in political science.

His hire was part of an overall commitment of ten costly new positions to populate the school's faculty, most of which have been filled through a "targeted" process normally reserved for exceptionally accomplished scholars or to address demographic under-representation on campus. So far, the faculty hired have not met these criteria. They appear to have been hired more for their right-wing commitments than academic stature.[48]

The Arizona legislature has so far approved $7 million for the new school. In addition to funding six new conservative professors, $430,000 was earmarked for rare manuscript acquisitions, including first editions of the *Federalist Papers* and Adam Smith's *Wealth of Nations*. An additional $75,000 pays for spring break trips to India for twelve students, who must take at least one of the school's classes as a condition of winning a spot on the trip—a carrot to increase the school's enrollment, which as of February 2018 stood at only about fifty students.[49] In total, since 2016 legislators have appropriated

$12 million to the two state universities for these ideologically driven centers established initially by Koch funding. As of spring 2018, the schools still had $9.8 million of that money on hand, but the legislature was poised to appropriate an additional $7.5 million. Neither university requested any of this funding.[50]

The Free Market Institute at Texas Tech University opened in 2013 with more than $11 million in funding from entities and individuals in the Koch network. But if the institute wasn't established with public funds, it soon secured an additional $1.4 million from the state budget through the Texas Research Incentive Program, created by the legislature to help boost research universities. And, of course, as in all such endeavors, the institute's faculty and staff offices, its internet access, and its maintenance expenses are still covered by the general university budget. Three departments rejected the institute and its proposed director before it landed in the business school, where it has thrived on a combination of private and public funding. Economics faculty said that the faculty recipient of the initial funding "didn't satisfy the minimum criteria for a tenure position," had a "weak vita," and had an "Austrian bent" that "wasn't consistent with the culture in our department." In March 2015, the institute held a three-day seminar promoted as a "weekend exploring liberty, freedom, entrepreneurship and innovation." As the *Texas Observer* reported,

> Attendees were treated to breakfast, lunch and dinner and put up at the swanky MCM Eleganté nearby. At the reception area, pamphlets from the Institute for Humane Studies, a Koch-funded group at George Mason University similar to the Free Market Institute, were neatly arranged. Sponsored by the Institute for Humane Studies and McLane Company, a supply chain service company headquartered in Carrollton, the event kicked off with a lecture from SMU's Robert Lawson titled "Why Do Leftists Hate Economic Freedom?"
>
> In his talk, Lawson pondered whether perhaps liberals just despise people in general. "I normally wouldn't say that in a lecture or conference because I wouldn't want to offend anyone, but I don't think that's going to be an issue here," Lawson said.[51]

Where legislators share the Kochs' sympathies, independent centers standing outside the normal disciplinary structures of the university can be established solely with public funds. In 2016, the North Carolina General Assembly established the North Carolina Policy Collaboratory—a title apparently chosen to avoid use of "center," given the legislature's continuing attacks on externally funded centers on poverty and civil rights. Its scientists are supposed to conduct research on environmental policy funded by a $4.5 million initial appropriation that had not been requested by the university. Apparently the brainchild of Republican state senate leader Phil Berger, the collaboratory was established to provide a conservative and no doubt climate change–denying alternative to the university's nationally recognized Institute for the Environment. One of Berger's staff members was quickly hired as the director of the new collaboratory.[52]

Funding Controversial Speakers

Efforts by the Kochs and similar foundations on behalf of independent centers promoting the study of free markets are paralleled by support provided by other conservative organizations for visiting campus speakers who promote right-wing ideas. Ann Coulter, for example, commands significant fees for her appearances, usually in the $20,000–$30,000 range per speech. Few student groups can afford that kind of money, but Coulter's appearances, while dependent on the willingness of a campus group (almost always the Young Republicans) to extend a formal invitation, are, like those of most prominent conservatives, actually sponsored and paid for by outside organizations. In the case of Coulter's controversial 2017 Berkeley invitation (see chap. 8), this was the Young America's Foundation (YAF).

Founded in the late 1960s as a nonprofit arm of the Young Americans for Freedom, YAF is a tax-exempt group that claimed more than $59 million in assets in 2014, with expenditures of $23 million. The organization boasts that campus groups can seek "logistical and financial assistance [from YAF] to host a big-name conservative speaker." About half its money goes to organizing and promoting campus speaking tours and paying generous honoraria to a roster of more than ninety conservative celebrities, including Dinesh D'Souza, David Horowitz, Ted Nugent, and Coulter. During the final three weeks in April, YAF sponsors roughly one event each day nationwide.[53]

Charles Murray's 2017 appearances at Columbia, Duke, Notre Dame, and Villanova—all without incident—as well as at Middlebury, where he was greeted with a demonstration that turned violent, were sponsored by the American Enterprise Institute, which gets most of its funding from prominent conservative donors, including members of the Koch, DeVos, and Bradley families. The smaller Intercollegiate Studies Institute, founded in the 1950s by William F. Buckley, also sponsors speakers, although it shies away from the kind of provocations in which YAF specializes, counting among its stable *New York Times* columnist Ross Douthat.[54] A newcomer to such activity is Turning Point USA (TPUSA), sponsor of the Professor Watchlist (see chap. 4). According to its founder, Charlie Kirk, "Most of the speakers we bring to campus are paid for by Turning Point USA but we do [have] several partnerships throughout the year with select organizations." The Foundation for Economic Education (FEE) provided its CEO Larry Reed to "speak on free markets and the purpose of limited government" at a TPUSA-sponsored event at the University of Colorado at Boulder. FEE is a recipient of donations from the Charles Koch Foundation and from TPUSA donor Dunn's Foundation for the Advancement of Right Thinking. Dennis Prager—CEO of digital media organization PragerU, a TPUSA sponsor—spoke at a TPUSA event at the University of Wyoming.[55]

There is nothing in principle wrong with this, of course. These groups have every right to support speakers with whom they agree, just as they are entitled to fund university programs with which they sympathize, provided that they conform to established norms of academic freedom and shared governance. But the growing and disproportionate influence of such outside right-wing money on the campus speech debate must be taken into account. It is completely wrong to demand that all political speech of one perspective be "balanced" by opposing speech. Nevertheless, the remarkable political imbalance in the funding of prominent speakers on campus should raise concern, especially insofar as it may be part of a broader and well-funded effort to reshape higher education in a specific ideological and political direction from outside both the academy and the democratic process.

Responding to Criticism

As criticism of the apparent Koch threat to academic freedom mounted, the Charles Koch Foundation released a set of "academic giving principles." The document proclaimed four tenets that "inform our university philanthropy and characterize our grants to universities." They were academic freedom, academic independence, donor intent, and public benefit. "We structure our gifts to support the vision of a faculty member or principal investigator and ensure her academic independence," the document proclaims. But these guidelines remained subordinate to the foundation's more central and long-standing "guiding principles," which continue to promote its ideological and political agenda.[56] In July 2018, the foundation announced that it would make public all future multiyear agreements with colleges and universities. With regard to past contracts, a Koch representative said that "many" already are public, "and we welcome that." Moving forward, "we'll share with schools the expectation that agreements will be published when news of the supported projects are announced." Ralph Wilson of UnKoch My Campus was critical, however, noting that "Koch is not providing clarity" unless the foundation releases all past agreements as well as future ones, in addition to other documents about academic programs. Anything less, he added, is "simply executing a strategic pivot to distract from the ways in which past and current donor agreements continue to violate academic principles and policies on potentially hundreds of campuses, and they are proposing that they be allowed to continue leveraging that influence for private gain."[57]

Charles Koch rejects charges that his donations compromise academic freedom. "The opposite is true," he told the *Washington Post*. "They're the ones campaigning to un-Koch our campuses and stuff. We're not saying, 'Un-Marxist our campuses.' Fine, bring it all on. Let a hundred flowers bloom. We love it. That's what we want."[58] John C. Hardin, director of university relations for the Charles Koch Foundation, said, "It's unfortunate that some folks have used political tactics to silence or attack scholars they don't agree with instead of dealing with the ideas themselves." Responding to the George Mason disclosures, Hardin said in a statement that the agreements have "evolved over time." He added, "To be clear we champion academic freedom and do not seek to influence the hiring practices of university departments nor have input on curricular or research decisions."[59]

Daniel Kovenock, who teaches economics at Chapman University, acknowledged that the Kochs had changed their approach. "Instead of explicit contractual provisions governing use of the funds, it's now a wink and a handshake," he said. Carrie Meyer, an associate professor of economics at George Mason, who describes herself as a political moderate, said she tries not to antagonize her conservative colleagues or the Kochs, although she has never received funding from Koch-connected sources. "I carefully chose my research so it wouldn't be objectionable to them," she said.[60]

Almost universally scholars funded by the Koch network or similar foundations claim that the funders have never interfered with their work. "I was doing this research, and I had this vision and mission" before the Koch Foundation offered money, said Rajshree Agarwal, who directs a Koch-funded center. "They don't micromanage, and I wouldn't be micromanaged."[61] Some Koch-funded scholars charge their critics with being the real enemies of academic freedom. They claim that UnKoch's efforts to expose terms of grant agreements and name those who receive them amount to a kind of left-wing blacklist. But while this sort of attention may make some grant recipients uncomfortable, it is hardly illegitimate, any more than publicizing how some scholars who denied the link between tobacco and cancer had received funding from tobacco companies. The issue is transparency. Colleges and universities—or, for that matter, individual faculty members—should not be able to hide or disguise their sources of funding.

Some of those opposed to the Koch efforts in higher education say that it is they who have been harassed. When Jane Mayer first began writing about the Kochs, she found herself trailed by a private investigator.[62] One Koch-funded scholar went on Twitter to charge UnKoch activists with being "Soviets" or even "Stalinist." He accused Ralph Wilson of being "quite the fanboy of genocidal Soviet types," offering as proof a tweet exposing how Wilson once participated in the carving of a Halloween pumpkin with the faces of Marx, Engels, and Lenin.[63]

Supporters of externally funded conservative centers were notably silent when, in 2015, the Board of Governors of the University of North Carolina voted to discontinue the UNC School of Law's Center on Poverty, Work, and Community, seen by its opponents as less a center for teaching law students and for scholarship than an advocacy program for the economic and social betterment and the civil rights of the poor, the disabled, and persons of color. There was never any real question about whether the center—wholly supported by outside funders—enjoyed support from the school's faculty or whether its governance was transparent and in accord with university policy. The decision was clearly political, in good measure motivated by hostility to its outspoken director, Gene Nichol.[64] In a statement to the board in advance of the vote the AAUP recalled previous cases and the North Carolina board's own history in defense of academic freedom. The AAUP statement quoted former UNC chancellor Molly Broad, the 2003 recipient of the association's Alexander Meiklejohn Award, who said, "We have a clear duty to uphold and passionately defend the right of faculty on every UNC campus to define the curriculum, to examine and to debate ideas, however popular or unpopular those choices might be, and however much the state's nonuniversity leaders may agree or disagree with a specific campus decision."[65]

This principle should also apply to scholars of conservative views and externally funded centers that promote those views, including those funded by Koch money. What is troubling about the efforts by the Kochs and other similar foundations, as well as those funding conservative speakers, however, is less the viewpoints they promote than that their donations are part of an ambitious and highly coordinated political strategy. As Koch Foundation administrator Kevin Gentry boasted to an audience of wealthy donors in 2014, "It's not just work at the universities with the students, but it's also building state-based capabilities and election capabilities, and integrating this talent pipeline. . . . No one else has this infrastructure." Faculty members at Wake Forest understood this to mean that the foundation funds academic projects not to promote scholarship—and, of course, no scholarship is entirely disinterested or "objective"—but "to 'leverage' higher education for ultimately political ends. Students are portrayed as cogs in a wheel of 'grass roots' political production."[66]

What about the "Left"?

Nevertheless, can it be said that the Kochs and similar right-wing funders are uniquely threatening? After all, concern over the impact of outside money on higher education is hardly new. As the late AAUP general secretary Mary Burgan pointed out in a 2009 essay,

> Centers, institutes, and schools are regularly proposed by well-meaning friends of the academy who want to sponsor some special program or by ideologues who aim to provide "balance" to redress the imagined biases of higher education. The programs that result tend to be narrowly defined and politically charged. Moreover, their sponsors are likely to assume the kind of ownership that demands a say in all of their operations—setting the curriculum, appointing faculty, granting scholarships, inviting visiting lecturers, and the like.
>
> The strategy of establishing centers to redress a purported blindness to neglected areas of study or a supposed resistance to oppositional

ideas is not a new development in higher education; indeed, it has been the basis for the creation of a number of respected academic centers. Since the late 1940s, many new programs, created through faculty approval and ongoing faculty governance, have enriched research and teaching by opening up neglected areas and new methodologies for study. . . .

Nevertheless, even such established programs may pose problems for faculty governance. For example, the locus of tenure for faculty is a besetting issue for almost every interdisciplinary center . . . traditional or newly established. And there is also the continuing problem of funding over the long term. Programs may be initiated with the promise of continuing resources, but all too often the funding priorities of foundations shift, private benefactions prove to be inadequate, or the promised money is never raised. The program then becomes anomalous, and the campus that hosts it is left holding the bag.[67]

To be sure, pressures to accede to the demands of outside funders have intensified. In 2005, Jennifer Washburn published *University Inc.*, which blisteringly surveyed overly cozy university-business relationships reaching back to the 1990s. Washburn exposed pro-Enron studies produced by Enron-funded faculty at the Harvard Business School, as well as the patenting by a private for-profit company of a human gene discovered at a public university, among many others.[68] These sorts of problematic relationships led the AAUP to initiate a comprehensive study of academy-industry relationships that in 2014 yielded a major book-length report.[69]

It would be foolish to assume that only money from the Right can be corrupting. "Shouldn't we be concerned about anyone who is funding any academic research centers on political and social subjects, no matter their ideological direction?" asked journalist David Johnson. Liberal centers may also advance their sponsors' economic or political interests. At Wake Forest the Pro Humanitate Institute, directed by political scientist and former MSNBC host Melissa Harris-Perry, received no scrutiny even as faculty mobilized opposition to the Koch donation. Yet her funders are unknown. At

Berkeley, Christina Romer, former chair of President Obama's Council of Economic Advisers, announced the opening of a new, privately funded Opportunity Lab. The lab immediately announced a search for a professional fund-raiser who can "develop new ideas for attracting prospective donors and private companies to research opportunities."[70] As the AAUP's report on academy-industry relationships noted, prior to the 2008 financial crisis a series of seemingly independent academic economists, including Berkeley's Laura Tyson, a prominent figure in Democratic circles, "strenuously defended high-risk investment vehicles like collateralized debt obligations and credit default swaps" while serving on hedge fund boards or as consultants to private funds. Tyson advised Credit Suisse.[71]

Take also the case of Ernest Moniz, one of President Obama's energy secretaries. Moniz was the founding director of the MIT Energy Initiative (MITEI), the university's self-described "hub for energy research, education, and outreach" on low-carbon and no-carbon energy options. Its founding donors were BP, ExxonMobil, Shell, Saudi Aramco, and Italian oil and gas company Eni. Its sustaining members included GE, Chevron, French oil and gas company Total, and Norwegian oil and gas company Statoil. Moniz personally served many of these companies in one capacity or another. As David Johnson reported,

> These investments were perhaps best recouped with MITEI's 2011 report "The Future of Natural Gas." Moniz was lead author. It argued that "natural gas truly is a bridge to a low-carbon future." As the Public Accountability Initiative detailed in its reporting on the fracking industry's influence on academic research, Moniz and his coauthors had numerous conflicts of interest over and above the limited number of energy-industry financial ties disclosed in the report. Moniz, for example, received compensation in excess of $300,000 as a board member of ICF International—a consulting firm to oil and gas companies that cited shale gas "as a key profit driver for its energy business," according to a report by the Public Accountability Initiative—before hiring Moniz to give his MITEI stamp of approval.[72]

"I worry that as an energy secretary he won't display the proper preference for independent research, which he didn't display at MIT," former AAUP president Cary Nelson, who coauthored the association's academy-industry report, told the *Boston Globe* during Moniz's confirmation process.[73]

As David Johnson caustically put it, "The pursuit of higher learning is returning to its pre-university roots: the patron-client model of the Renaissance. Privately funded research centers are the engine of this trend." This is an exaggeration, no doubt, but by no means outlandish. Certainly Johnson is correct in noting that for some academics, no matter their politics,

> brokering deals with moneyed interests is how they've advanced their careers. In the scientists' cases, in exchange for granting elite funders access to their universities' expertise, talent pool, and reputation, they have been freed from the very norms and governance structures that, for centuries, have allowed universities to build these resources in the first place. Such casually discarded conventions include departmental collaboration and voting, peer review, and—most important—independence from undue influence.
>
> It would be no exaggeration to say that the world of academic research centers and institutes, especially insofar as they deal with profitable industries such as energy, health care, pharmaceuticals, agriculture, and technology, is thoroughly awash in—indeed, wholly made possible by— corporate cash. The point is not only that this corporate money enables compromised research. . . . There is also the research that this money restricts, and even silences—the studies whose conclusions big-money funders may find disagreeable.[74]

Reflecting on the George Mason disclosures in the context of an increasingly competitive and restricted academic job market, one academic blogger complained, "These champions of libertarianism and the free market . . . couldn't earn a job in academe, they couldn't establish scholarly legitimacy through research and collaboration and free inquiry engaging with key debates and questions in their own field. . . . No. They had to have their appointments bought for them by the Kochs, and in return they surrendered whatever remnants of independent thought they may have once possessed."[75]

What Is to Be Done?

The problem lies less with individual faculty members than with a systematic failure to enforce clear guidelines. The AAUP's 2004 *Statement on Corporate Funding of Academic Research*, while mainly concerned with individual research contracts with private industry, enunciates a number of principles that apply as well to the kinds of activities funded by the Koch network and, indeed, by all outside funders:

1. Consistent with principles of sound academic governance, the faculty should have a major role not only in formulating the institution's policy with respect to research undertaken in collaboration with industry but also in developing the institution's plan for assessing the effectiveness of the policy. The policy and the plan should be distributed regularly to all faculty, who should inform students and staff members associated with them of their contents.

2. The faculty should work to ensure that the university's plan for monitoring the institution's conflict-of-interest policy is consistent with the principles of academic freedom. There should be emphasis on ensuring that the source and purpose of all corporate-funded research contracts can be publicly disclosed. Such contracts should explicitly provide for the open communication of research results, not subject to the sponsor's permission for publication.

3. The faculty should call for, and participate in, the periodic review of the impact of industrially sponsored research on the education of students, and on the recruitment and evaluation of researchers (whether or not they hold regular faculty appointments) and postdoctoral fellows.

4. The faculty should insist that regular procedures be in place to deal with alleged violations by an individual of the university's

conflict-of-interest policy. Should disciplinary action be contemplated, it is essential that safeguards of academic due process be respected.

5. Because research relationships with industry are not static, the faculty, in order to ensure that the assessment of conflict-of-interest policies is responsive to changing needs, should regularly review the policies themselves, as well as the instruments for conducting the assessment.[76]

The AAUP's 2014 *Recommended Principles to Guide Academy-Industry Relationships* expanded on these principles and is also relevant to nonindustrial external funding. It declared, "Academic freedom does not entitle faculty members to accept outside responsibilities that jeopardize or gravely compromise their primary university responsibilities. Academic freedom does not entitle faculty members to sign away their freedom to disseminate research results. Academic freedom does not entitle faculty members to ignore financial conflicts of interest that could dangerously compromise the informed consent process and the impartiality of research. It follows, therefore, that academic freedom does not guarantee faculty members the freedom to take money regardless of the conditions attached."[77] The report enunciated fifty-six principles—many specific to certain research endeavors, for example, medicine—but the first two general principles are universally applicable:

PRINCIPLE 1—Faculty Governance: The university must preserve the primacy of shared academic governance in establishing campuswide policies for planning, developing, implementing, monitoring, and assessing all donor agreements and collaborations, whether with private industry, government, or nonprofit groups. Faculty, not outside sponsors, should retain majority control over the campus management of such agreements and collaborations.

PRINCIPLE 2—Academic Freedom, Autonomy, and Control: The university must preserve its academic autonomy—including the academic freedom rights of faculty, students, postdoctoral fellows, and academic professionals—in all its relationships with industry and other funding sources by maintaining majority academic control over joint academy-industry committees and exclusive academic control over core academic functions (such as faculty research evaluations, faculty hiring and promotion decisions, classroom teaching, curriculum development, and course content).[78]

An analogy can also be drawn between the kind of funding provided by Koch interests and the China-sponsored Confucius Institutes, about whose practices the AAUP warned in a 2014 statement and that, ironically, have more recently been targeted by political conservatives who might otherwise turn a blind eye to similar practices by externally funded conservative centers. The association's objection to the Confucius Institutes was related not to the content they promoted but to their apparent lack of critical independence. "Allowing any third-party control of academic matters is inconsistent with principles of academic freedom, shared governance, and the institutional autonomy of colleges and universities," the association's Committee A declared. The statement continued,

> The AAUP joins CAUT [Canadian Association of University Teachers] in recommending that universities cease their involvement in Confucius Institutes unless the agreement between the university and Hanban [the Chinese state agency sponsoring the institutes] is renegotiated so that (1) the university has unilateral control, consistent with principles articulated in the AAUP's *Statement on Government of Colleges and Universities*, over all academic matters, including recruitment of teachers, determination of curriculum, and choice of texts; (2) the university affords Confucius Institute teachers the same academic freedom rights, as defined in the 1940 *Statement of Principles on Academic Freedom and Tenure*, that it affords all other faculty in the university; and (3) the university-Hanban agreement is made available to all members of the university community. More generally, these conditions should apply to any partnerships or collaborations with foreign governments or foreign government-related agencies.[79]

Taken together, these are the standards to which the Koch funders—and not only the Koch funders—should be held. Un-Koch My Campus, joined by many faculty members, may object to the political content of the work done by Koch-funded centers, which is their right, but insofar as academic freedom is concerned the viewpoints being advanced are mostly irrelevant. The real question is whether funding agreements conform to the criteria for institutional independence proposed by Justice Frankfurter. Moreover, given the financial straits faced by colleges and universities today, the fear that large amounts of politically directed funding could seriously distort an entire institution's basic mission is hardly unfounded. As AAUP president Rudy Fichtenbaum wrote in the aftermath of the George Mason disclosures, "The public defunding of higher education has already generated a host of terrible consequences. If politically motivated donors pick up the slack, things will only get worse. Higher education can't function properly when it is beholden to special interests. That bodes ill not just for colleges themselves. It bodes ill for our democracy."[80]

Chapter Six

Will Online Education Cure the
"Cost Disease"?

California governor Jerry Brown has long been notorious for his frugality, especially when it comes to higher education. During Brown's recent terms as governor, the doubling of tuition revenues in the state's two public university systems did not make up for massive state cuts followed by small annual increases. His budget proposal for 2018–19 was more of the same, but with a new twist. In 2017, Brown and California Community Colleges (CCC) chancellor Eloy Ortiz Oakley announced a fully online community college degree program called the Flex Learning Option for Workers. Brown's budget then proposed that this become a new and separate "online campus," building on the system's existing Online Education Initiative.[1]

Under the plan, approved by the legislature in June 2018, California will spend an initial $100 million to get the online community college going and then spend $20 million a year from a voter-approved pool of money in the general fund that already supports community colleges and K–12 education. Although anyone could enroll, the college is to focus on adults age 25 and older. "We're not targeting the traditional college student," Oakley said. "We're targeting people in apprenticeship programs, people who are trying to move from being a medical assistant to a supervisorial job. . . . They don't have the time to spend getting to know instructors and students on campus."[2] The online school will seek accreditation as the state's 115th community college.[3]

Speaking to the state's Community College Board of Governors after the proposal was approved, Brown gushed, "This is a no-brainer, it is obvious, it is inevitable, it is a juggernaut that cannot be stopped. California is a leader, it will lead in this. And I say, hallelujah." More soberly, Brown explained that the initiative "is targeted to several million people who can upgrade their skills by taking online courses and maintaining their employment, which they certainly need." That rationale failed to convince the state Legislative Analyst's Office, however. They complained that "the administration does not identify specific root causes responsible for low educational attainment among some groups. As a result, it is unclear if an online college would address these root issues." Jonathan Lightman, executive director of the Faculty Association of California Community Colleges, was more acerbic. The new college, he said, "has the appearance of a solution in search of a problem." Faculty unions also voiced opposition to the plan.[4]

Whatever the program's justification, Brown has long been a believer in the ability of online education to contain costs, and there can be little doubt that cost containment was also crucial to the proposal.[5] However, a much-ballyhooed partnership between online provider Udacity and San José State University, brokered by the governor earlier in his tenure, was abandoned after six months when a National Science Foundation study revealed that the online courses actually lowered remedial education outcomes.[6] Examining a similar partnership between Udacity and Georgia Tech, Christopher Newfield found no cost savings for the university and considerable profit for Udacity; that program continues only with massive subsidies from AT&T.[7]

Nevertheless, the assumption that technology "has moved the cost-quality curve, so online college is 'better faster cheaper, than face-to-face,'"[8] remains widespread among both politicians like Brown and a disturbing number of educational leaders. Take, for example, a small (161-page) book by former Princeton University president William Bowen, *Higher Education in the Digital Age*, published in 2013.[9] The book consists of edited and expanded versions of two lectures delivered by Bowen at Stanford University on the potential of online teaching to help control the rising cost of higher education. The lectures are accompanied by comments from Harvard professor Howard Gardner, then Stanford president John Hennessy, Columbia professor Andrew Delbanco, and Stanford professor Daphne Koller, who is also cofounder of the for-profit online provider Coursera.

The book offers a brief and readable introduction to some issues in online education, but it is most useful as a largely unintended demonstration of the unconscious myopia of leaders and some faculty members at elite institutions like Stanford. With the notable exception of Delbanco's remarks, the authors seem largely ignorant of how faculty teach and how students learn at the overwhelming majority of colleges and universities in the United States, which Bowen repeatedly and dismissively refers to as "less selective institutions." They draw examples largely from their own universities or from other research institutions and make little effort to address the problems faced by working and commuting students, by those with disabilities—two groups who might most benefit from online access—by students whose high schools were substandard, and by those who stand on the have-not side of the "digital divide." The entire book includes a mere three passing references to community colleges, by far the largest segment of American higher education, where issues of cost control and online learning are perhaps most critical.

Bowen's first lecture addressed what he and the late economist William Baumol previously named the "cost disease."[10] The term refers to the proposition that "in labor-intensive industries such as . . . education, there is less opportunity than in other sectors to increase productivity. . . . As a result, unit labor costs must be expected to rise faster in . . . education than in the economy overall."[11] With respect to higher education, Baumol put it this way: "The relatively constant productivity of college teaching . . . suggests that, as productivity in the remainder of the economy continues to increase, costs of running the educational organizations will mount correspondingly, so that whatever the magnitude of the funds they need today, we can be reasonably certain that they will require more tomorrow, and even more on the day after that."[12] In other words, according to Baumol and Bowen, a principal driver of cost inflation in higher education is the inevitably rising price of faculty time and the inability to replace faculty with less costly inputs.

This is not the place to examine this thesis in depth, but there is much to suggest that, whatever its theoretical appeal, it seems not to be borne out by reality. In a 2012 study, economists Robert Martin and Carter Hill found that "cost disease" accounted for just 16 percent of the total increase in spending at public research universities from 1987 to 2008.[13] The Delta Cost Project has labeled the idea that faculty compensation drives cost inflation a "myth." As researchers Dennis Jones and Jane Wellman demonstrated, "spending on faculty is a minority of total spending in most institutions, a proportion that has been declining in all sectors for the last two decades." According to Delta's figures, spending on instruction, mainly faculty salaries, in public master's-granting institutions, for example, amounted to just 34.3 percent of total spending in 2010. In private research institutions the figure was only 30.0 percent.[14]

The California State University (CSU) system, the country's largest four-year institution, enrolls almost five hundred thousand students. For the 2016–17 academic year, CSU reported $9.6 billion in expenses, of which only $3 billion, or 28.8 percent, went to instruction, including faculty compensation. In the CSU system, full-time equivalent enrollment increased by 51.6 percent from 1990 to 2017. But full-time-equivalent faculty numbers increased by only 23 percent during that period, and the number of tenure-track faculty actually declined by 4.7 percent. Yet from 1993 to 2016, the number of administrators and senior staff jumped by a whopping 88.5 percent.[15] And it's not just large public systems. At Pomona College, an elite private liberal arts school, John Seery reports that "the number of students . . . has increased 12 percent from 1990 to 2016; the number of faculty has increased 3 percent; tuition has increased 253 percent; the number of administrators has increased 384 percent. Pomona now employs far more administrators (271) than faculty (186) to fulfill its small college, nonprofit educational mission."[16]

While Bowen recognized that expenditures on faculty are but one factor driving costs up, Hennessy put the argument more baldly: "Faculty salaries have gone up faster than wages for most other workers," he declared, adding that for those in the academy, "financially, life is much more pleasant now than it was thirty years ago."[17] This may be true at the Princetons and Stanfords, but not elsewhere. According to the American Association of University Professors' *Annual Report on the Economic Status of the Profession*, salaries of full-time tenure-track faculty at all institutions, adjusted for inflation, actually declined by nearly 3 percent from 1971 to 2012.[18] More importantly, today less than one-third of all teaching faculty are on the tenure track. Among the remainder, the majority are either part-time and "temporary" or graduate student employees.

It is notoriously difficult to obtain accurate salary information for such non-tenure-track faculty, but based on limited data collected by the Coalition on the Academic Workforce and reported by the AAUP in its 2012–13 faculty compensation survey, even at private doctoral research institutions the median salary per course was just $3,800 in fall 2010. At public community colleges the median was only $2,250. From these figures it is difficult to sustain the notion that for such instructors—the great majority of the higher education instructional workforce—"life is much more pleasant" than it was for their largely full-time and tenured counterparts thirty years ago.[19]

Remarkably, both Bowen and Hennessy suggest that another driver of increased cost has been the proliferation of PhD-granting institutions and consequent overproduction of doctoral degrees, which are more expensive to generate than bachelor's or master's degrees. Yet neither acknowledges how the glut of doctoral candidates and degrees permits research institutions to cut costs by exploiting graduate students as instructors—and, for research in the sciences, as inexpensive postdocs—while "less selective institutions" may dip into a growing oversupply of underemployed PhDs for "temporary" instructors. Indeed, their outrage seems motivated less by genuine concern about cost containment or attention to basic fairness than by thinly disguised resentment that some "less selec-tive institutions" have the gall to compete with elite institutions in doctoral training.

In his second lecture, Bowen turned to "prospects for an online fix." In 2000 he posited that "sound online instruction is likely to cost more than traditional instruction," but by 2013 he concluded that conditions had changed. To be sure, his argument was hedged by numerous cautions, but Bowen became convinced that "greater access to the Internet, improvements in Internet speed, reductions in storage costs, the proliferation of increasingly sophisticated mobile devices, and other advances have combined with changing mind-sets to suggest that online learning, in many of its manifestations, can lead to at least comparable learning outcomes relative to face-to-face instruction at lower cost."[20]

Asking whether online formats are good or bad makes as little sense as asking whether, say, the lecture or the seminar format is good or bad. The answer depends on where, how, and for and by whom. Certainly online education has become a commonplace fea-ture on the educational landscape at all levels and has proven valuable to many students and faculty members. At the same time, however, "anyone who thinks teaching and learning are the same online as they are face-to-face is catastrophically wrong."[21] As Bowen acknowl-edged, we have little hard data to demonstrate whether—and, more importantly, in which subjects and for which students—online in-struction yields outcomes comparable to traditional methods.[22] A 2010 meta-analysis by the Department of Education found only seven rigorous studies of fully online, semester-length courses at four-year institutions. These studies showed little difference in learning outcomes, but the typicality of the courses was unclear, and the studies did not investigate completion rates, which are fre-quently much lower online.

Bowen placed considerable emphasis on one study of a hybrid statistics course offered by Carnegie Mellon University, which "found no statistically significant differences in standard measures of learn-ing outcomes" from those of students in traditional classes. But statistics may well be a subject especially suited to online formats. More importantly, the hybrid (or blended) format, in which online material is combined with face-to-face meetings, is probably the format least likely to cure Bowen's "cost disease." For instance, a hybrid engineering class at San José State University offered in cooperation with the online provider edX attracted considerable attention when it was reported that students in the class succeeded at remarkably higher rates than those in traditional sections. But these "online" students met face-to-face with instructors three hours each week, and their instructors acknowledged spending significantly more time preparing and evaluating student work than they did in traditional classes.[23]

Perhaps the most extensive studies of online outcomes were conducted by the Community College Research Center at Columbia University's Teachers College. Researchers there assessed the experience in fully online courses of multiple cohorts totaling more than fifty thousand students at twenty-three community colleges in Virginia and over one hundred thousand students at thirty-four community and technical colleges in Washington State. The findings were sobering. For one thing, withdrawal rates were consistently nearly double in online courses what they were in face-to-face classes. Moreover, regardless of academic subject, demographics, or academic background, investigators found that "the same student performs more poorly in a fully-online course than in a face-to-face course." Students with a stronger academic background showed a small dip in performance, while more poorly prepared students evidenced a larger decline. Finally, performance gaps between white and minority students tended to widen in online courses.[24]

Developments since Bowen's book was published tend to confirm the limits of online teaching's impact. There is an emerging consensus that "online instruction at community colleges isn't working." Researchers at the University of California, Davis, found that California community college students were 11 percent less likely to finish and pass a course if they opted to take the online version instead of the traditional face-to-face version.[25] In 2014, the Public Policy Institute of California examined community college students' online passing rates, as well as their grades in subsequent courses in related fields, and found that success rates in online courses were 10 to 14 percent lower than in traditional classes.[26] One 2017 study found that it took ten hours to plan an hour's lecture for online students compared with eight hours for a traditional lecture. It also took significantly longer to substantially review or update teaching materials for online courses, while student consultation and assessment moderation for online students were more time-consuming.[27] In 2016, George Washington University was sued by eleven graduates who claimed that their online education was inferior to what was offered on campus. The university's faculty senate, which had created a task force to investigate the quality of its degree programs, found that there were in some cases vast differences between those courses that were offered online and those that were offered on campus and that oversight of online education at the university was inconsistent.[28]

In a damning 2017 report, the Century Foundation found that "the vast majority of public colleges and universities that offer online education programs or courses are now relying upon external companies to do so." Analyzing over a hundred agreements between universities and so-called online program managers, Century found "a traditional outsourcing model with a dangerous twist" in which these management companies "may prioritize profit over the interests of online students, to whom they owe no loyalty, financial or otherwise." In search of profits, these firms may also provide private student information to marketers. The report found that "these programs are evading oversight from both sides, lacking the internal oversight that comes from a nonprofit or public structure and the governmental supervision that comes from operating a for-profit school." Its authors concluded that such "outsourcing of the core educational mission of public institutions of higher education, threaten[s] the consumer-minded focus that results from the public control of schools."[29]

In March 2018, the Boston Consulting Group (BCG) and Arizona State University (ASU) published a report, funded by the Bill and Melinda Gates Foundation, in which case studies of online programs at three research universities, including ASU, two community colleges, and a state-wide community college system, were said to reveal "the potential of digital learning to open the doors of higher education wider and to improve student outcomes, while operating more efficiently and at lower cost."[30] However, as one educational technology expert responded, "The problem with case studies is that the selection of cases to study may not be representative or appropriate to prove one's thesis." He accessed two online classes at one of the community colleges investigated—Rio Salado College in Tempe, Arizona, established in 1978 to be a "college without walls" that could enroll underserved student populations—and pointed out that those courses had "no student-to-student discussions, as the discussion board was unused for the course. There was one peer-review activity, but otherwise no interactions between students. . . . The primary feedback method in these two courses was faculty usage of the custom-developed Feedback Tool, which uses rubrics to grade assignments." A primary claim of the BCG-ASU study was that online education had improved Rio Salado's retention rates. This claim did not hold up to scrutiny. In fact, the college's retention rates for full-time and part-time students lie in "the bottom 10% of all community colleges at 33% and 27%, respectively. And the full-time rate is lower than it was prior to 2011."[31]

The BCG-ASU report's contention that online instruction reduces costs has also been subject to convincing critique. The section on cost savings "compared the overall costs of online courses with average costs at four of the institutions in the study" and "found that the savings for online courses ranged from 3% to 50%." In other words, the report found savings at just four of the six schools it handpicked to investigate. Those lower costs are possible, the report argued, in part because schools can save money on building costs for new students, which is true only if the institution is already at maximum on-campus capacity. Mostly, the report admitted, savings in online classes are found because these classes "have higher ratios of students to instructors." At ASU, the report boasted, "section sizes for online courses are significantly larger than those for on-campus courses: lower division online undergraduate courses are about twice the size of lower division face-to-face courses." Upper-division online classes at ASU are about 50 percent larger than on-campus ones.[32]

Moreover, the study added, "Some universities and community colleges among our case study institutions use more adjunct or part time faculty—who tend to be less costly to hire than tenure-track faculty—to teach online courses." At one unnamed "major university" studied, adjunct professors teach 85 percent of online courses compared with 70 percent of those on campus. For upper-division classes about 60 percent of campus classes were taught by adjuncts; online classes were taught by the "less costly" teachers 90 percent of the time. As one of the report's critics wryly noted, "Having more students per class learning from less costly, less experienced teachers is sure to be less expensive." Johann Neem, professor of history at Western Washington University, told *Inside Higher Ed*, "If, as the report concludes, much of the savings come by relying on contingent faculty to teach larger classes," then "these savings have nothing to do with technology."[33]

Responding to the BCG-ASU study, Shanna Smith Jaggars, director of student success research for the Office of Distance Education and E-Learning at Ohio State University and lead investigator in the Columbia community college studies, called it "limited in utility" for several reasons:

> First, it neglects an existing body of evidence showing that the impacts of online learning are very different for different populations. For example, a 30-year-old middle-income working mother will probably perform as well or better online, while a low-income 19-year-old will probably perform more poorly online than face-to-face. Second, the report's authors explicitly selected six institutions with very large and high-quality online programs, and at those institutions, they observed a

number of good outcomes. Yet it's entirely possible that many other institutions have experienced similarly good or better outcomes with small or nonexistent online programs, or have invested in large and expensive online programs without good outcomes. Third, the six institutions' online learning outcomes are reported only in a descriptive way, without controlling for factors such as gender, age or underrepresented minority status, which makes it impossible to draw conclusions about the effectiveness of the colleges' online courses or programs in comparison to their face-to-face programs.[34]

Defending the Brown-Oakley proposal for an independent online community college, Laura Hope, a CCC executive vice chancellor, told the *Los Angeles Times*, "Improved classes and tools for online orientation, counseling and tutoring have significantly narrowed the performance gap between online and traditional classes. Nearly two-thirds of online students completed their courses in 2015–16, compared with just over half a decade earlier. Over the same period, the percentage of students who completed traditional classes stayed roughly the same, at about 71%."[35] According to Oakley's office, the proportion of California community college students taking at least one online course per year (for credit or noncredit) rose from 19.5 percent in 2011–12 to around 33 percent five years later.[36]

But has this translated into equivalent quality and lower cost? Analyzing the same California data, Christopher Newfield and Cameron Sublett concluded that it hasn't, at least not for everyone, especially in introductory courses, which are at the heart of community college academic offerings. They wrote,

> Online continues to deliver a significant drop in success rates in basic skills courses. The convergence trend CCC claimed on aggregate is much weaker here. In addition, online makes the racial disparity of in-person courses somewhat worse. The success rates of underrepresented minority students, to use the standard classification, are poor. In addition, they are not improving, as CCC claims for the aggregated results.

One reasonable policy conclusion would be quite the opposite of Brown's and Oakley's—Black and Latinx basic skills students should never be placed in online courses—not until researchers are given the time (and data) to explore and overcome the mechanisms underlying the racial disparities. And even though white and Asian students outperform the state averages, a face-to-face/online gap also exists for these student groups. Consequently, it seems reasonable that even they should use them sparingly.[37]

A 2018 study published by Stanford University found that online courses may also exhibit disturbing levels of racial and gender bias in their discussion forums. The researchers posted comments in the forums of 124 different online courses. "Each comment was randomly assigned a student name connoting a specific race and gender." The study found that instructors were 94 percent more likely to respond to forum posts by white male students. "Our results show compelling experimental evidence that instructor discrimination exists in discussion forums of online classrooms," the paper concluded. "Because online courses are typically asynchronous, these forums provide a uniquely important venue for instructor-to-student and student-to-student engagement. Our field experiment produced evidence that the comparative anonymity granted by asynchronous, digitally mediated interactions in online discussion forums does not eliminate bias among instructors."[38]

Newfield and Sublett offer these general conclusions about the use of online instruction:

- Online education is valuable and important as a selective and supplemental approach to extending in-person higher ed. It helps students who cannot stop full-time work or family care. It is especially good at dealing with the repetition that is part of all learning. This is an area where it has a clear advantage over human teachers, as language labs (and books!) have been proving for generations.
- State leaders are wrong to continue to push online as a categorical good. This current push depends on aggregating data in a way that

conceals how online disadvantages African-American and Latinx students. Online education is currently an engine of racial inequality, and no good higher ed policy can be created by ignoring that fact.

- It is still unclear how learning in online environments compares to learning in traditional environments. The chancellor's office seeks to justify the growth of distance education by pointing to improvements in the success rates of students in these courses. But by reducing "success" to completion, the CCCCO [California Community Colleges Chancellor's Office] masks the differential impact of DE [distance education] course taking on traditional measures of successful education, including both cognitive (e.g., learning, retention) and noncognitive (e.g., interpersonal skills and attitudes) growth. It is doubtful that the prospective employers in the state will hold the same definition of success as the CCCCO. Consequently, we recommend a rigorous, longitudinal evaluation of the state's extant online courses prior to the new construction of an entirely online campus.

- Online should never be used to excuse state budgets that are too small to support the established features of educational quality. These features include the presence of fully-qualified teachers working with classes that are small enough to allow individual feedback. Online courses that approach the quality of face-to-face courses are actually "hybrid" courses that involve structured personal contact. We know of no hybrid courses that will save universities money. States should never budget by assuming the opposite.[39]

In short, whatever online teaching's virtues, it is by no means clear that comparable learning outcomes and completion rates can be sustained online for all students, especially students most "at risk," or in all subject areas. As information scientist and self-described "recovering technoholic" Kentaro Toyama concluded, "If history is a guide, new technologies will be absorbed by schools but will do little in the end to advance education."[40] And it is equally questionable whether online formats measurably reduce costs.

Of course, the online format with the greatest promise for cost reduction was the MOOC, or massive open online course. Bowen's lectures were delivered as "MOOC madness"—a bubble that burst as quickly as it inflated—was cresting, and his endorsement was appropriately tentative.[41] He argued, correctly, that MOOCs might save money only if they remain standardized and are not "customized" to a local student body or faculty preferences. This led Bowen to argue for "genuinely collaborative decision-making that includes faculty, of course, but that does not give full authority to determine teaching methods to particular professors or even to particular departments." In the past, he concluded, "it may have been sensible to leave almost all decisions concerning not just what to teach but how to teach in the hands of individual faculty members. It is by no means clear, however, that this model is the right one going forward."[42] Despite the obligatory nod to "collaboration," such remarks come close to a full-scale assault on fundamental principles of academic freedom and shared governance.

More important, however, is that what Bowen calls "customized" teaching formats are what most faculty members understand as the compelling need to address the reality that not all students learn in the same way. What may work—face-to-face or online—for students at Stanford may not be suitable for those at San José State or a community college nearby. If online courses amount to little more than canned video lectures combined with standardized online exercises and discussion boards, as far too many do, they will surely fail.

Koller, however, argued passionately that online teaching "is really a new educational paradigm." Teaching online, she claimed, compels instructors to "flip" the classroom—"not the kind of thing that we were trained to do," which was instead to "stand and orate."[43] Putting aside the fact that such "flipping" is possible only with hybrid and not fully online classes, the sheer parochialism of this comment is astonishing. In most teaching institutions, faculty have for several decades moved well beyond the lecture format to modes of instruction that involve greater active student participation, be it face-to-face or online. "Be a guide on the side, not a sage on the stage," we've been counseled repeatedly by administrators, faculty development officers, and many colleagues. Although interactive education may not be the norm at Stanford, it is quite common at institutions like CSU, in community colleges, and elsewhere, perhaps even more so in traditional than in online classrooms.

For Koller it was virtually a matter of faith that online formats will facilitate a transition from passive to active learning while simultaneously reducing the cost of college and potentially offering a Stanford education to all. Bowen was more cautious, but his enthusiasm for these new formats, like that of Governor Brown, was also largely faith based. As Jonathan Rees discovered in years of studying educational technologies, "there are actually a ton of really devoted people who are trying to develop and utilize various educational technologies to create useful and—at least in some cases—superior experiences to how colleges and classes operate now. These efforts are, as you might expect, hugely labor intensive."[44] Will they appeal to political leaders or university administrators seeking to cut costs while increasing "student success," much less tech companies seeking profit? One may hope so, but it would be advisable to remain at the least highly skeptical.

Chapter Seven

Do Students Have Academic Freedom?

In the fall of 2015, events at two major universities focused national attention on student protests and their implications for free expression and academic freedom to a degree not seen since the 1960s and early 1970s. At the University of Missouri in Columbia, a group of African American students, energized by events the preceding summer in Ferguson, Missouri, raised a series of demands in response to the university's failure to address racial problems on campus and in the community. As an investigation by the American Association of University Professors reported, "African American students, faculty members, and staff members spoke publicly of a long-standing pattern of abuse, with one professor writing that in eighteen years at the university she had been 'called the n-word too many times to count.'" Tension mounted as protesters blocked the university president's car during a homecoming parade and one student began a widely publicized hunger strike, gathering increasing support in the student body and among faculty and staff. After African American members of the football team threatened to strike, winning support from white teammates and their coaches, the system president and campus chancellor resigned.[1]

The Missouri events were preceded by an incident at Yale University involving, of all things, Halloween costumes. Things came to a head after Yale's Intercultural Affairs Committee, comprising many of the school's religious and cultural group leaders, sent an email to students urging them to be culturally sensitive in choosing costumes. Erika Christakis, a faculty member and residence adviser at Yale's Silliman College, responded with an email to students in her college questioning the need to exercise "implied control" over students' choice of dress. Hundreds of Yale students soon signed an open letter to Christakis taking issue with her argument. One group of angry students confronted Nicholas Christakis, Erika's husband and another residence adviser, and demanded a retraction, proclaiming that the residence should be a "safe space." Christakis defended his wife's message. The exchange grew heated and was captured on video by Foundation for Individual Rights in Education (FIRE) head Greg Lukianoff, who happened to be on campus. The video went viral, and soon accusations of "political correctness" and censorship spread like wildfire, with the issue becoming, in the eyes of many, one of free speech rather than cultural sensitivity.[2]

These events were followed by a series of highly publicized incidents involving student protests against provocative outside speakers (see chap. 8), which led to alarms about a "free speech crisis" on campus, with some charging that protesting students, in David Bromwich's words, have become "the leading actors in the pressure for campus censorship."[3] That charge seems exaggerated, to say the least. While the maintenance of restrictive speech codes, muddled harassment policies, and limitations on student due process rights no doubt have chilling effects on student expression, these derive more from administrative apprehension than student activism.[4] Can it really be said that academic freedom and free speech are more gravely threatened by student demands for "safe spaces" than by inappropriate political interference and massive public disinvestment or by other troubling aspects of the modern university's growing corporatization? Are student demands to remove monuments or rename buildings more dangerous to free expression than the increasing power that donors, granting agencies, and governments have in how colleges and universities make use of the resources they provide? Is concern over discussion of a racial slur in class more threatening to freedom than the ever-expanding censorship of student publications and other media by administrations obsessed above all with their institution's "image"?[5] Do a small number of highly publicized efforts to silence racist and misogynist speakers, no matter how misguided, pose a greater threat to free expression than well-funded blacklists of faculty members and orchestrated campaigns of racist and misogynist harassment?

One source of concern about student intolerance for provocative views came in a widely publicized survey released by the Brookings Institution, which reported that one-fifth of undergraduates say that it's acceptable to use physical force to silence a speaker who makes "offensive and hurtful statements."[6] The survey asked students whether it was more important for colleges to create an "open learning environment where students are exposed to all types of speech and viewpoints, even if it means allowing speech that is offensive or biased against certain groups of people," or "a positive learning environment for all students by prohibiting certain speech or expression of viewpoints that are offensive or biased against certain groups of people." It found that 53 percent of respondents said they supported the "positive learning environment" that required "prohibiting certain speech." However, the survey, funded by a grant from the Charles Koch Foundation, was not administered to a randomly selected group of students nationwide, what statisticians call a "probability sample." Instead, it was given to an opt-in online panel of people who self-identified as current college students. The study was conducted not by a reputable pollster or even a social scientist but an electrical engineer. Polling experts soon dismissed it as "malpractice" and "junk science."[7]

A more representative survey of student opinions on campus free speech conducted by Gallup and funded by the Knight Foundation and the Newseum Institute asked similar questions but found strikingly different results. That 2016 survey of more than three thousand college students, who had been selected in a carefully randomized process from a nationally representative group of colleges, found that 78 percent of students said that colleges should create an "open learning environment."[8] Large majorities of various subgroups—including 70 percent of black students—endorsed the primacy of such an open learning environment, hardly a ringing student endorsement of censorship. The survey also found that among nonstudent adults only 66 percent favor an open learning environment. The survey revealed that 73 percent of respondents viewed freedom of speech as secure or very secure, and 81 percent viewed freedom of the press as secure. Half of all respondents thought that free speech protections have grown stronger over the past two decades. As journalist Vann Newkirk concluded, "Students themselves seem to be less concerned about a wave of 'political correctness' overtaking free speech than some journalists."[9]

Nonetheless, media coverage obscured this finding, reporting that according to the survey, as the *Washington Post* phrased it, students "seek balance on free speech and hate speech."[10] Former Columbia University provost Jonathan Cole went so far as to cite the results as evidence that "core university values are being questioned again, but from a new source: the students who are being educated at them."[11] But this was not at all what the survey revealed. In fact, as journalist Matthew Yglesias and Canadian political scientist Jeffrey Adam Sachs have demonstrated, data from both the Gallup-Knight study and the annual General Social Survey suggest that since 1970 public support for free expression has actually been rising and that "in general, people with left-wing ideological commitments are overall more tolerant than people with right-wing ones." In addition, there is minimal differentiation by age on the right to speak. For instance, 56 percent of 18- to 34-year-olds support the right of a racist to give a speech, versus 60 percent of the overall population. And "there is a strong correlation between educational attainment and support for allowing free speech."[12]

A 2017 survey commissioned by FIRE and funded by the John Templeton Foundation found that overwhelming majorities of students "feel comfortable sharing ideas and opinions" both in classrooms (87%) and outside of class (86%). Almost all respondents (92%) said that "it is important to be part of a campus community where they are exposed to the ideas and opinions of other students." However, respondents said they were less likely to engage with comments they find offensive or hurtful than with those with which they simply disagree. Few very liberal students (17%) agreed they "should not have to walk past student protests," while a majority of very conservative students (64%) agreed. Lastly, only a handful of students said they might participate in actions that could shut down a speaking event. Just 5 percent said they might take down flyers publicizing the speech, 4 percent might try to prevent others from attending, 2 percent might make noise during the event, and a mere 1 percent said they might use violent means to disrupt a speaker.[13]

Do student protesters sometimes threaten free expression? Yes, they sometimes do. And too many students have bought into a culture that privileges security and comfort over liberty and challenge as, for example, in the movement to impose so-called trigger warnings, which the AAUP has rightly decried as "at once infantilizing and anti-intellectual."[14] As libertarian scholar Jacob Levy wittily put it, "It turns out that 18-year-olds seized of the conviction of their own righteousness are prone to immoderation and simplistic views. (Who knew?)"[15] But is the source of the problem activist students who make demands? Don't those students themselves have the right to express their views? As a group of faculty at the University of Chicago put it, "The right to speak up and to make demands is at the very heart of academic freedom and freedom of expression."[16]

This raises the question, Do students have academic freedom, and if so, of what sort? The concept of academic freedom for faculty has been more or less clearly defined over the years. Its three components—freedom in the classroom, freedom in research and publication, and freedom of expression as a citizen—are widely acknowledged. The AAUP's 1915 *Declaration on Academic Freedom and Academic Tenure* recognized that "academic freedom has traditionally had two applications: to the freedom of the teacher and to that of the student, *Lehrfreiheit* [to teach] and *Lernfreiheit* [to learn]." In 1929, an AAUP investigating team considered a case in which a student group was disciplined for "insubordination" after they invited a controversial speaker to campus. The investigation concluded that the association "cannot concern itself in a case of student discipline as such, even though such discipline may be unjust and excessive," adding that the university's discretion to punish "is not subject to review on the ground of academic freedom." However, the report continued, the faculty should be consulted in such matters. And "so long as a group of students speaks in its own name, we believe that it ought to be unmolested in its expression of opinion on public questions. Any other position implies an intolerable censorship of all student opinion by the administration."[17]

According to Ralph Fuchs, a former general secretary of the AAUP, "Student freedom is a traditional accompaniment to faculty freedom as an element of academic freedom in the larger sense."[18] But what, concretely, does student academic freedom entail? May students, like faculty, claim some version of academic freedom beyond their legal rights under the First Amendment? And if so, what kind of academic freedom is most appropriate for students? These questions were addressed more than fifty years ago in the wake of the civil rights movement in the South, the Free Speech Movement at the University of California, Berkeley, and the burgeoning national student movement against the Vietnam War. The AAUP and several other associations drafted the 1967 *Joint Statement on Rights and Freedoms of Students*. The proclaimed aim of that statement—a kind of Magna Carta for student rights—was "to enumerate the essential provisions for student freedom to learn."[19]

It's worth looking back at that seminal document in light of contemporary concerns about campus free speech.[20] The *Joint Statement* not only protects the free expression rights of students generally but also speaks specifically to student academic freedom in the classroom. It requires "the professor . . . [to] encourage free discussion, inquiry and expression, [and to evaluate students] solely on an academic basis, not on opinions or conduct in matters unrelated to academic standards."

The *Joint Statement* also addresses students' rights outside the classroom. "Students bring to the campus a variety of interests previously acquired and develop many new interests as members of the academic community," it declares. "They should be free to organize and join associations to promote their common interests." The *Joint Statement* adds, "Students and student organizations should be free to examine and discuss all questions of interest to them, and to express opinions publicly and privately. They should always be free to support causes by orderly means which do not disrupt the regular and essential operation of the institution." If only administrators at Fordham University had taken these words to heart when, in December 2016, they refused to permit students to create a chapter of Students for Justice in Palestine, alleging that the group's existence would lead to "polarization rather than dialogue." Fordham then sought to discipline a student trying to establish the group, who was charged with violating the school's "Demonstration Policy" for organizing a rally protesting the denial.[21]

The 1967 *Joint Statement* declared that "student publications and the student press are valuable aids in establishing and maintaining an atmosphere of free and responsible discussion and of intellectual exploration on the campus." It called for a student press "free of censorship and advance approval of copy," with student editors and managers "free to develop their own editorial policies and news coverage" and "protected from arbitrary suspension and removal because of student, faculty, administration, or public disapproval of editorial policy or content." Unfortunately, a 2016 joint report by the AAUP, the College Media Association, the Student Press Law Center, and the National Coalition Against Censorship found that today "many college and university authorities have exhibited an intimidating level of hostility toward student media, inhibiting the free exchange of ideas on campus."[22]

Of no small importance was the 1967 *Joint Statement*'s recognition of the right of students to participate in institutional governance: "As constituents of the academic community, students should be free, individually and collectively, to express their views on issues of institutional policy and on matters of general interest to the student body. The student body should have clearly defined means to participate in the formulation and application of institutional policy affecting academic and student affairs." The extent of such participation was left unclear, however. Nonetheless, in 1970 the AAUP's Committee on College and University Governance and its council did issue a *Draft Statement on Student Participation in College and University Governance.* Perhaps reflecting then-current student demands for black and ethnic studies, that statement proposed that "students should be consulted in decisions regarding the development of already-existing programs and the establishment of new programs." It added as well that "student opinion should also be consulted, where feasible, in the selection of presidents, chief academic and nonacademic administrative officers including the dean of students, and faculty."[23]

The 1967 *Joint Statement* considered students' freedom off campus, noting that "students are both citizens and members of the academic community" and as citizens "should enjoy the same freedom of speech, peaceful assembly and right of petition that other citizens enjoy." Moreover, the statement added this essential caution: "Faculty members and administrative officials should insure that institutional powers are not employed to inhibit such intellectual and personal development of students as is often promoted by their exercise of the rights of citizenship both on and off campus."

The detailed provisions of the 1967 *Joint Statement* suggest a more systematic and reasoned view of student unrest than the near-hysterical reactions—the *Wall Street Journal*, for instance, called Yale protesters "little Robespierres"—that seem to characterize some recent commentary.[24] It is certainly true that the rights defined by the *Joint Statement* would include the right of students to upset other students, perhaps by wearing offensive costumes on Halloween. But, in many ways, more important is the right of the offended students to express their distaste as forcefully as they can without undue disruption of the institution's mission.

In this light, despite all the hubbub and outside a few successful efforts to silence invited speakers (see chap. 8), it is difficult to identify more than a handful of instances where recent student protests have substantially violated the rights and freedoms of anyone, including faculty members and other students. It might also be noted that history suggests that the right to free speech itself has sometimes been won through means that may deny freedom of speech to others. In *Free Speech on Campus*, Erwin Chemerinsky and Howard Gillman rightly uphold Berkeley's 1964 Free Speech Movement as a watershed moment in opening campuses to "noncivilized and non-scholarly expression of ideas," noting that this was achieved only after students forcibly occupied the administration building, which led to 773 arrests. Yet, some pages later, they state without irony that "there is not a First Amendment right to occupy campus buildings" or "block access to them."[25]

The issue at Yale, Missouri, and other institutions has largely been one not of free expression but of communication, environment, and values. Bruce Shapiro, executive director of the Dart Center for Journalism and Trauma, put it well: "At a time of unprecedented economic inequality, students of color, immigrants and students from low-income backgrounds—at rich, elite universities and state schools alike—are painfully aware that the experiences they bring to campus are ill appreciated by many classmates, teachers and administrators, who come overwhelmingly from a culture of middle-class safety nets and an economy that rewards those who already have. That's the issue."[26] As University of Pennsylvania professor Sigal Ben-Porath has argued, "Often controversies surrounding free speech on campus involve negotiation and debate among multiple parties that generally seek the same goal: allowing or encouraging speech on matters of political and civic importance while maintaining a constructive atmosphere for learning and research." Hence, she urges "shifting the focus away from disputes about legality and harm and toward practical considerations linked to education and inclusion."[27]

This is why the sanctimonious claims of some college and university administrators and faculty are so tone-deaf, if not dangerous. The University of Chicago may stand as an example. Its administration likes to boast of its unwavering commitment to free expression, a claim too often taken on faith by others in and out of academia.[28] Consider the much-vaunted email sent by a University of Chicago dean to incoming freshmen in the fall of 2016. He wrote, "Our commitment to academic freedom means that we do not support so-called trigger warnings, we do not cancel invited speakers because their topics might prove controversial, and we do not condone the creation of intellectual 'safe spaces' where individuals can retreat from ideas and perspectives at odds with their own."[29] The letter was welcomed by some as an overdue rebuke to unruly student protesters. The conservative Heritage Foundation, for example, wrote on Facebook that "the letter will make you stand up and cheer."[30]

Others quickly pointed out, however, that a blanket ban on trigger warnings would itself violate faculty academic freedom and that "safe spaces" are essential to true freedom of expression. In fact, the University of Chicago has a few such spaces, including the official "University of Chicago LGBTQ Student Life Safe Space."[31] Jacob Levy has offered a particularly cogent defense of safe spaces, worth quoting at length. "Why do we need safe spaces?" he asked.

> We need safe spaces for a few different reasons. One of them is intellectual. Inquiry is hard. Research, teaching, and learning, require building blocks. And if you are never allowed to put one set of blocks down, you will never be able to move on to the next level. An intellectual world in which we are always doing nothing but challenging one another's basic assumptions gets very boring very quickly because no progress is possible. You can never build on what you've already learned because you're never allowed to take for granted that you've learned it. That requires communities and times and spaces that distinguish themselves from one another. . .
>
> Another reason is that that kind of thing is psychologically and emotionally draining. Adults commenting on university students from off-campus will often say "there is a real problem with students not understanding that their ideas should be up for challenge all of the time." But nobody who lives off of a university campus lives that way. We go home at the end of the day. . . . You can't do that all day every day, not if you take those challenges seriously or not if people get in your face beyond some minimal level. Because I'm a tenured professor I can actually just close my door if someone is getting on my nerves and that

serves to give me my own safe space in its own way. But if I'm actually going to be listening and to hear the arguments they make, I need it not to be all day every day. . . .

The arguments about freedom of speech that arose on American college and university campuses last fall, very many of them invoked the language of safe spaces. This is a language I've been using in a very unfamiliar or atypical way to describe classrooms, disciplines, and departments. I've been putting it in that context in order to make clear that communities of inquiry and debate depend on the ability of participants to sometimes go back, among the people who relatively agree with one another, and get some work done. Or, to get out of the circumstance of argument and debate entirely and take some time off.

Addressing the Halloween controversy at Yale, Levy continued,

When the student protestor was caught on video saying "I don't want a debate I want a safe space," I think it is almost certain that what she was saying was not "I want all of Yale to be an environment in which my feelings are protected." She was not saying "I don't want there to be debates at Yale." She was saying "this place, this residential college, this dorm that you are the faculty member associated with, this needs to be a place where I can go catch my breath." . . . And when the African American students say "we want a moment in our day, we want a space on the campus where we can step back," they aren't saying "we want to shut down debate on campus." They're saying something that is perfectly within everyone's range of reasonable emotional and psychological needs: "Stop boring me with this argument about whether I belong here or not, I have work to do."[32]

Berkeley economist Bradford DeLong has written that a university should be both "a safe space for ideas" and "a safe place for people—particularly young people."[33] Princeton political scientist Keith Whittington adds that "finding ways to accommodate the needs of students to sometimes be apart from the bustle of the campus at large will sometimes raise tensions and will often require compromise, but those difficulties are best negotiated if we are able to think about such demands as reflecting a universal desire rather than a special interest."[34]

But for some on the right the issue is more race than ideas. Fox News host Tucker Carlson complained that on campus "everybody gets a safe space except white men."[35] The claim is, of course, laughable. As a white man I've studied and taught at numerous colleges and universities in four different states. As an officer of the AAUP I have visited dozens of campuses, public and private, elite and open-access, across the country. But on all these campuses as a white male I have never failed to find a "safe space"—*the entire campus*! Safety is a justifiable concern on college and university campuses, but only someone who willfully ignores reality could believe that the specific safety of white males—by which, of course, Carlson really meant a small subset of obnoxiously conservative white males—is the main problem.[36]

Consider also the Chicago letter's declaration that "we do not cancel invited speakers because their topics might prove controversial." Of course, they shouldn't. But that's not the point. Why not instead encourage students to invite speakers they want to hear? Why not indicate that students who disagree with a speaker's viewpoint are free to protest that speaker's presence, so long as they do not deprive others of the right to hear that speaker? Without any such indications, the message is clear: accept the speakers we want you to hear; don't protest, don't organize opposition, don't speak out yourselves. (For extended discussion of outside speakers, see chap. 8.)

Responding to the email, a group of Chicago faculty members wrote their own letter to the entering class, which declared, "Those of us who have signed this letter have a variety of opinions about requests for trigger warnings and safe spaces. We may also disagree as to whether free speech is ever legitimately interrupted by concrete pressures of the political. That is as it should be. But let there be no mistake: such requests often touch on substantive, ongoing issues of bias, intolerance, and trauma that affect our intellectual exchanges. To start a conversation by declaring that such requests are not worth making is an affront to the basic principles of liberal education and participatory democracy."[37]

Chicago's fear of student protest is almost obsessive. Consider a report by the university's Committee on University Discipline for Disruptive Conduct, which has been thoroughly critiqued by John K. Wilson.[38] It mostly made proposals to "protect" free expression on campus by aiming to suppress protest, which seems to be the real goal of the university's Statute 21, which governs student expression. The committee recommended that disruptive protests be defined to include "blocking access to an event or to a University facility and shouting or otherwise interrupting an event or other University activity with noise in a way that prevents the event or activity from continuing in its normal course." As Wilson noted, "There is a fundamental difference between 'interrupting' an event and shutting it down. A protest can disrupt the 'normal course' of an event without preventing it from continuing altogether."

Statute 21 already included this questionable definition of disruption: "Disruptive conduct includes but is not limited to: (1) obstruction, impairment, or interference with University sponsored or authorized activities or facilities in a manner that is likely to or does deprive others of the benefit or enjoyment of the activity or facility." As Wilson comments, "The 'enjoyment' standard is absolutely unacceptable. 'Enjoyment' is a subjective standard, not an objective basis for punishment. A protest almost always affects the enjoyment people have at an event. It can annoy and inconvenience people. But being annoying shouldn't be punishable behavior." He concludes, "The University [of Chicago] Statutes are the foundational document for the structure of the University. Yet the Statutes have no mention of academic freedom and freedom of speech, or due process, or the right to dissent and protest. The Statutes do not mention a word about campus disciplinary processes or rules, with the sole exception of Statute 21, which presumably was adopted with the goal of suppressing campus protests."[39]

Writing in the *American Conservative*, where he was an editorial assistant, Chicago student Malloy Owen offered one of the most perceptive analyses of the Chicago administration's hypocrisy about free speech. "At one time," he concluded, "the University of Chicago might have been thought to be the one place above all others that was capable of preparing its students to acquit themselves well in difficult, valuable conversations about race, class, and violence. As my experience in seminars attests, though, Chicago is no longer fully committed to humanizing its students the old-fashioned way, through books and discussion. The left's attacks on free speech may endanger the academic project, but the greater threat to the free exchange of ideas comes from academic corporatization. As long as that process continues unchecked, the university's bold rhetorical defense of an art that it no longer teaches us how to practice will be nothing better than posturing."[40]

One of the Chicago committee's recommendations was that "the University create free-speech deans-on-call with special training to deal with disruptive conduct" and add educational programming to train students on "the rights and responsibilities of participation in the free speech commons."[41] Such proposals, responded Harvard Law School professor Jeannie Suk Gersen, "are bureaucratic responses that mirror what many universities have done in recent years to address bias and discrimination: appoint deans and administrative staff to run new offices for training and discipline related to diversity and inclusion." It is often the efforts of these offices that, critics charge, threaten the expression of those with dissenting views on tolerance. "Not much clairvoyance is needed to see what is coming," Suk Gersen concluded. "A clash is imminent—not just between ideas and students but also between the campus structures embodied in deans for diversity and inclusion and deans for free speech. The training and orientation programs run by these dedicated offices will have to negotiate a tense balance to avoid coming to blows."[42]

These Chicago proposals resemble provisions of legislation introduced in many states that allegedly aim to "restore and protect freedom of thought and expression" on college campuses. These bills are largely based on a model bill, entitled the Campus Free

Speech Act, prepared by the Goldwater Institute, a conservative think tank. The model bill would prevent public colleges and universities from disinviting controversial speakers, require institutions to abolish speech codes and "free speech zones," and require colleges to publish a formal statement affirming that its "primary function is the discovery, improvement, transmission, and dissemination of knowledge by means of research, teaching, discussion, and debate." In addition, the proposed bill would instruct institutions "to strive to remain neutral, as an institution, on the public policy controversies of the day." The model legislation also states that colleges should create disciplinary policies for students "who interfere with the free expression of others," with harsh mandatory punishments and organizational structures to ensure enforcement. As of March 2018, such legislation had been approved in Arizona, Colorado, Missouri, North Carolina, Tennessee, Utah, and Virginia. In Wisconsin the bill passed in the assembly but died in the state senate. However, the University of Wisconsin regents adopted almost all its provisions as system policy. In February 2018, Senator Orrin Hatch (R-UT) introduced the Free Right to Expression in Education Act, also based on the Goldwater Institute model, which would "amend the Higher Education Act of 1965 to ensure that public institutions of higher education protect expressive activities in the outdoor areas on campus."[43]

The Goldwater Institute model and state legislation derived from it have been critiqued extensively in reports by PEN America and the AAUP's Committee on Government Relations.[44] In a May 2017 statement, the AAUP declared, "Given the important role of colleges and universities in debate, dissent, and the free exchange of ideas, the AAUP strongly supports freedom of expression on campus and the rights of faculty and students to invite speakers of their choosing. We oppose, however, any legislation that interferes with the institutional autonomy of colleges and universities by undermining the role of faculty, administration, and governing board in institutional decision-making and the role of students in the formulation and application of institutional policies affecting student affairs."[45]

The PEN America report acknowledged that the bills were "intended to foster respect for civil rights and open expression, and contain certain elements that would advance these objectives." But the organization raised questions about several provisions that "pose serious risks for free speech." Among the group's concerns were proposals for "mandatory minimum" punishments—including yearlong suspension or expulsion—for conduct judged to interfere with vaguely defined "expressive rights" that could be used to deter and discipline peaceful protesters.

In Wisconsin an especially controversial provision in the proposal, drawn from the Goldwater Institute model, would compel university officials—and arguably faculty members—not to take political stances on controversial issues. One problem with such a provision was highlighted by this extraordinary exchange at a hearing on the bill, as reported in the *Madison Capital Times*:

> Rep. Terese Berceau, a Madison Democrat, was quizzing Rep. Jesse Kremer, her Republican colleague from Kewaskum, at a hearing for his proposed Campus Free Speech Act. . . .
>
> Berceau wondered what would happen under the bill—which requires University of Wisconsin System institutions to be neutral on "controversies of the day"—if a student in a geology class argued the Biblical theory that the earth is only 6,000 years old.
>
> "Is it okay for the professor to tell them they're wrong?" Berceau asked during the lengthy session on May 11.
>
> "The earth is 6,000 years old," Kremer offered. "That's a fact."
>
> But, he said, "this bill stays out of the classroom."
>
> Yet Kremer immediately speculated that students who felt intimidated from expressing their opinions in class could bring their complaints to the Council on Free Expression, an oversight board created in the bill. . . .
>
> "How are we to be taken seriously as an institution of higher learning and research if our professors can be called before a 'Council on Free Expression' to defend their teaching of geology?" University of Wisconsin at Madison professor Dave Vanness wondered.[46]

A similar bureaucratic structure is part of "free speech" legislation passed in North Carolina. Following the Goldwater Institute model, the legislation declared the "primary function" of the state's public colleges and universities to be "the discovery, improvement, transmission, and dissemination of knowledge by means of research, teaching, discussion and debate." It adds that to "fulfill this function [universities] must strive to ensure the fullest degree of intellectual freedom and free expression." So far, so good. But then the legislation continues,

> The University of North Carolina System Board of Governors shall establish the Committee on Free Expression and appoint 11 individuals from among its membership to the Committee. . . . Each . . . member shall serve . . . at the pleasure of the Board of Governors. . . . In the event of a vacancy on the Committee, the Board of Governors shall appoint a replacement from among its membership. . . . All employees of the [university system] shall cooperate with the Committee on Free Expression by providing information requested by the Committee. . . . [The Committee] shall, annually, provide assessments, criticisms, commendations or recommendations [on the handling of free speech issues on campuses].[47]

As UNC law professor Gene Nichol acidly commented, "There are, surely, no two institutions in the state of North Carolina, based on behavior, less appropriate to be trusted with the determination of free expression rights than the General Assembly and the University's Board of Governors. I would rather have Joe McCarthy and J. Edgar Hoover cast lots to decide my First Amendment liberties."[48]

A stunning example of elitist condescension to students came in the fall of 2017, when fifteen professors from Harvard, Yale, and Princeton Universities published their own message to the nation's entering first-year students. "Our advice," they wrote, "can be distilled to three words: Think for yourself." The message continued,

> In today's climate, it's all-too-easy to allow your views and outlook to be shaped by dominant opinion on your campus or in the broader

academic culture. The danger any student—or faculty member—faces today is falling into the vice of conformism, yielding to groupthink.

At many colleges and universities what John Stuart Mill called "the tyranny of public opinion" does more than merely discourage students from dissenting from prevailing views on moral, political, and other types of questions. It leads them to suppose that dominant views are so obviously correct that only a bigot or a crank could question them. . . .

Don't get trapped in an echo chamber. Whether you in the end reject or embrace a view, make sure you decide where you stand by critically assessing the arguments for the competing positions.[49]

As if no one had thought of this before! The message is both preachy and a bit pathetic. No one doubts that higher education should be about developing independence of mind, but to assume that this can be accomplished via simplistic exhortation is absurd. In over forty years of teaching I found that my students all thought for themselves. Well, at least they *believed* they did. And that's one reason why this simple call to "think for yourself" is so pointless. Even the most conformist often tout their intellectual independence.

Moreover, the statement, signed by a group of scholars whose views are largely on the conservative end of the political spectrum, is clearly disingenuous. With its repeated contrast between independent thought, on one side, and "fashionable opinion" and "campus orthodoxies" on the other, can anyone doubt that the conformism the message decries is only a certain brand of conformism? That this statement is directed at those who "conform" to "fashionable opinions" about racism and Black Lives Matter, about misogyny and abortion rights, about gay marriage and transgender bathroom rights, about microaggressions and safe spaces, or about Antifa? In short, that it's directed at those student protesters whom right-wing critics demean as thuggish illiberal "snowflakes"?

Higher education is about developing independent critical thinking, to be sure, but such thinking must always be informed by knowledge and expertise. And higher education is also about providing those. Truly independent minds are expert and knowledgeable enough to know what they don't know and when they need to rely on the knowledge and wisdom of better-informed others to make up their minds.

By challenging campus administrations through organized protest, the student demonstrators of today may well be doing more to advance the cause of free expression than their occasionally intolerant demands may now and then hinder it. It's necessary to credit their courage and determination in addressing the sometimes unconscious but nonetheless real and persistent racism and misogyny that infect our society and our campuses. In doing so, they have made and will again make mistakes. They will offend others even as they respond to deeper offenses against their own dignity. They may demonstrate indifference to the rights of others, as protesters everywhere always have. But, in doing so, they will learn. And that, it seems to me, is the essential point. Student academic freedom, in the final analysis, is about the freedom to learn. And learning is impossible without error.

"Those who see the recent rash of free speech–related incidents on U.S. campuses as a sign of the decline of higher education and of a generation of coddled students are misdiagnosing the problem," declared Scholars at Risk executive director Robert Quinn. "These incidents might just be an opportunity and a cry for more: More inclusivity. More nuance. More understanding. And yes, more speech."[50]

What is therefore most remarkable about today's student movements is not their alleged intolerance or immaturity. It is not their intemperance or supposed oversensitivity to insult and "offense."[51] It is that they have begun to grapple with issues that their elders have resisted tackling for far too long. Geoffrey Stone is right that "a university can legitimately educate students about the harms caused by the use of offensive, insulting, degrading and hurtful language and behavior and encourage them to express their views, however offensive or hurtful they might be, in ways that are not unnecessarily disrespectful or uncivil."[52] But the university, and especially its faculty, must also be willing to learn from students. Faculty members should welcome the challenges protesting students have posed. Student movements offer countless opportunities for students—as well as their teachers—to learn. To approach them in this way, in the spirit of the student academic freedom proclaimed and defined by the AAUP and its collaborators in 1967, is therefore simply to fulfill our responsibility as educators.

Chapter Eight

Are Invited Speakers Entitled to a Platform?

A university without student protests against visiting speakers would be like a forest without birds.

—Timothy Garton Ash

When minor moronic bigot Milo Yiannopoulos attempted to speak on the University of California, Berkeley, campus on February 1, 2017, protesters set fires, smashed windows, and attempted to assault police officers. The speech was canceled. Yiannopoulos had gained undeserved notoriety through a series of vile assaults on liberals, minorities, women, gays, and transgender people, initially via the Breitbart News website and Twitter and then in a self-described "dangerous faggot" campus lecture tour. In his talks he sometimes singled out individuals for mockery and harassment.

Repulsive as his ideas and actions are, Yiannopoulos has the right to speak publicly, including on college campuses. Under the First Amendment public colleges and universities are legally bound not to bar him or to create viewpoint-based obstacles (like inordinately high "security fees") to his appearances. Under the broader principles of free expression, all institutions, public or private, and all members of the higher education community should refrain from efforts to block his appearances, should an authorized campus group invite him, if for no other reason than that this is precisely the response he seeks to provoke. It is important, however, to emphasize that at Berkeley, while some student demonstrators claimed Milo's views so hateful that his ideas should be proscribed—a viewpoint they too have a right to express—the few who employed violence were not mainly students. Milo had the right to speak and his opponents had the right to protest, but the appearance was terminated by the actions of a relatively small group, most of whom had no connection whatsoever to the university. Nevertheless, within hours President Donald J. Trump, in office for less than two weeks, posted this tweet: "If U.C. Berkeley does not allow free speech and practices violence on innocent people with a different point of view—NO FEDERAL FUNDS?"[1]

While the violence at Berkeley gained perhaps the most extensive publicity, that incident was but one of several around the same period involving efforts to silence other right-wing firebrands like Ann Coulter and Richard Spencer, as well as the less obviously provocative conservatives Charles Murray and Heather MacDonald. Spencer, a self-professed white supremacist, spoke at Auburn University only after a court ordered the school to allow his appearance, even though he had not been invited by any campus group. Talks by Murray at Middlebury College and by MacDonald at Claremont-McKenna College were obstructed in ways that physically endangered the speakers, as well as those who wished to hear—or protest against—them.[2] In the wake of the abortive Yiannopoulos event a much-ballyhooed appearance by Coulter at Berkeley was canceled after the university claimed it could not find a safe venue for her talk on the date and time requested. The following autumn Berkeley spent a reported $4 million on security costs for an appearance by conservative blogger Ben Shapiro, who spoke without incident, and preparations for a much-hyped week-long series of events organized by Yiannopoulos, which never materialized.[3] In November 2016, Shapiro's appearance at the University of Wisconsin–Madison had been interrupted by hecklers, although he managed to complete his talk. Nonetheless, Wisconsin legislators used the disruption as a rationale for passage of a problematic campus free speech bill.[4]

Predictably, the affected speakers and their supporters used these incidents to argue that American colleges and universities have become bastions of intolerance and left-wing "political correctness." In a statement, Coulter called Berkeley a "thuggish institution" that had snuffed out the "cherished American right of free speech." In the *National Review*, Stanley Kurtz alleged that "campus free speech is more besieged nowadays than it's been in decades." Fox News host Tucker Carlson went so far as to claim that "millions of students and professors have made far left politics their only reason for being at school." Speaking before the conservative student group Turning Point USA in July 2018, Attorney General Jeff Sessions declared, "Rather than molding a generation of mature, well-informed adults, some schools are doing everything they can to create a generation of sanctimonious, sensitive, supercilious snowflakes." Concern for free speech on campus was not limited to right-wing voices. Donald Downs, Alexander Meiklejohn Professor of Political Science at the University of Wisconsin, said that on campus "free speech is more threatened than ever." Writing in the *Chronicle of Higher Education*, Jonathan Haidt, a social psychologist at New York University, claimed that "intimidation is the new normal on campus."[5]

Such sweeping claims are at minimum exaggerated. In reality, despite all their many flaws, colleges and universities are probably still the places in America where the diversity of views to be found is most extensive and least restricted, certainly when compared to the mass media, the corporate world, or religious institutions. And despite their reputation as both frightened "snowflakes" and bullying "thugs," student protesters have been far more willing to engage in constructive dialogue than sensationalist media reports would suggest.[6] On the other hand, as Corey Robin observed, the challenge at many, maybe even most, colleges and universities "has never really been how to keep speakers off campus; it has almost always been how to get them on campus."[7]

Still, it would be a mistake to minimize the danger to free expression posed by attacks on controversial speakers. As the American Association of University Professors declared in its 1994 statement *On Freedom of Expression and Campus Speech Codes*, "On a campus that is free and open, no idea can be banned or forbidden. No viewpoint or message may be deemed so hateful or disturbing that it may not be expressed. . . . An institution of higher learning fails to fulfill its mission if it asserts the power to proscribe ideas—and racial or ethnic slurs, sexist epithets, or homophobic insults almost always express ideas, however repugnant. Indeed, by proscribing any ideas, a university sets an example that profoundly disserves its academic mission."[8]

But the discussion cannot end there. For as legitimate as concern for the rights of controversial speakers surely is, the rights of those who object to and protest their ideas must also be a concern, as must the safety of all on campus. As one commentator argued, at least for some, "what is under severe attack, in the name of an absolute notion of free speech, are the rights, both legal and cultural, of minorities to participate in public discourse."[9]

Oxford scholar Alan Ryan has written, "Fascism is not a creed looking for an interesting debate with its rivals."[10] While neither Yiannopoulos nor Anne Coulter can usefully be labeled fascist (Spencer is another matter, however), the lack of interest in genuine debate fits their approach as well. Neither Yiannopoulos nor Coulter was invited to Berkeley to discuss ideas; they came instead merely to provoke, some might argue to brawl. "Coulter is like a distorted Tinker Bell," commented *Washington Post* blogger Alyssa Rosenberg. "It's not applause that saves her from falling out of existence, it's shock and jeers."[11]

Moreover, these controversies raise difficult questions about the relationship between free speech, a liberal democratic value, and academic freedom, which is largely a meritocratic value. Academic freedom aims to protect scholars from retaliation based on their teaching, research, or work as public intellectuals. Academic freedom is therefore not founded on the "free marketplace of ideas," but on professional expertise. Hence, from the perspective of the professoriate, threats to academic freedom from politicians, trustees, and corporatizing administrators appear much more ominous than efforts by impassioned sophomores to silence outside provocateurs like Coulter. As David Faris of Roosevelt University put it, "At Berkeley, Ann Coulter actually has more free speech rights than a tenured professor," whose teaching and research must conform to disciplinary standards irrelevant to someone like Coulter.[12] I don't generally agree with Stanley Fish's cramped definition of academic freedom (see chap. 2), but I must admit he has a point when he argues that "free speech is not an academic value."[13]

This chapter explores these issues and comments on some of the responses to these events in a series of mini-essays covering the history of the AAUP's position on invited speakers, the "heckler's veto," the academic Left's alleged intolerance, the extent and nature of the student threat to free expression, the legitimacy of free speech claims, academic freedom's relation to freedom of speech, and the principle of tolerance.

The Position of the AAUP

In July 2007, the AAUP's Committee A published a statement entitled *Academic Freedom and Outside Speakers*, which declared,

> Because academic freedom requires the liberty to learn as well as to teach, colleges and universities should respect the prerogatives of campus organizations to select outside speakers whom they wish to hear. . . .
>
> This principle has come under growing pressure. Citing an inability to guarantee the safety of outside speakers, or the lack of balance represented by the invitation of a college or university group, or the danger that a group's invitation might violate Section 501(c)(3) of the Internal Revenue Code, college and university administrators have displayed an increasing tendency to cancel or to withdraw funding for otherwise legitimate invitations to non-campus speakers. Committee A notes with concern that these reasons for canceling outside speakers are subject to serious abuse, and that their proper application should be limited to very narrow circumstances that only rarely obtain. Applied promiscuously, these reasons undermine the right of campus groups to hear outside speakers and thus contradict the basic educational mission of colleges and universities.
>
> It is of course the responsibility of a college or university to guarantee the safety of invited speakers, and administrators ought to make

every effort to ensure conditions of security in which outside speakers have an opportunity to express their views. The university is no place for a heckler's veto. . . . We have always been clear that colleges and universities bear the obligation to ensure conditions of peaceful discussion, which at times can be quite onerous. Only in the most extraordinary circumstances can strong evidence of imminent danger justify rescinding an invitation to an outside speaker. . . .

As part of their educational mission, colleges and universities provide a forum for a wide variety of speakers. There can be no more appropriate site for the discussion of controversial ideas and issues than a college or university campus. . . . Invitations made to outside speakers by students or faculty do not imply approval or endorsement by the institution of the views expressed by the speaker. . . . Institutions may also clearly affirm that sponsorship of a speaker or a forum does not constitute endorsement of the views expressed.[14]

This statement reinforced long-standing positions taken by the association in the past. In 2007, the late Jordan Kurland, who worked for more than half a century in the AAUP's Department of Academic Freedom, Tenure, and Governance, reviewed the association's historic opposition to efforts to ban outside speakers. "Since its founding," he wrote, "the AAUP has been concerned with infringements of academic freedom when colleges interfere with invited speakers."[15] In 1957, the association's annual meeting adopted a resolution in response to the issuance of a list of "radical and/or revolutionary speakers" by the House Un-American Activities Committee, which led many institutions to cancel appearances by individuals on the list. The resolution declared that "it is educationally desirable that students be confronted with diverse opinions of all kinds" and that "any person who is presented by a recognized student or faculty organization should be allowed to speak on a college or university campus."

In 1963, the North Carolina legislature considered a bill sponsored by the American Legion that would prohibit the use of state facilities, including universities, for speeches by any person known to be a member of the Communist Party or to advocate the overthrow of the federal or state constitutions, or to have pleaded the Fifth Amendment when asked about allegedly subversive associations. After civil rights demonstrators staged sit-ins, the bill was fast-tracked and enacted into law. Efforts to repeal the ban led the AAUP to respond with "Restraints on Visiting Speakers" resolutions at its 1966 and 1967 annual meetings. These referred to the "freedom to hear" as "an inseparable part of academic freedom."

In the 1970s, Nobel Prize–winning physicist William Shockley began to argue abrasively (and ignorantly) that differences in intelligence had a racial basis, a position also advocated by educational psychologist Arthur Jensen, although not by any but a minuscule number of qualified experts. The two began well-publicized lecture tours that led to disruptions of their talks and to college and university administrations withdrawing invitations. In response, AAUP's Committee A in 1974 approved a statement entitled *On Issues of Academic Freedom in Studies Linking Intelligence and Race*. The committee, the statement said, "categorically rejects any proposal to curtail the freedom to report research studies or the interpretive conclusions based on them, however unpalatable either may be. Mindful that the quality of research endeavors and the conclusions drawn from them may reflect varying degrees of scientific rigor, we assert nonetheless the paramount virtue of the open forum for the dissemination of ideas through publication, exposition, and debate. No less importantly, we commend open channels of expression as the basic source of counterpositions and correctives, where critics of distasteful views can express themselves without restraint."

One result of the turmoil surrounding the two men was that they became famous, while the overwhelming majority of cognitive scientists who forcefully rejected their ideas remained all but anonymous. This was hardly the fault of the academy. It was the mass media—and, ironically, to some degree the protesters who sought to silence them—that built a platform for Shockley and Jensen to spread their views despite the near-total rejection of their work by qualified peers.

Of course, both Shockley and Jensen were themselves scholars and faculty members, however far out of the mainstream. Hence, the protections the AAUP sought to extend to their research were those of academic freedom, not the freedom of speech the association advocates for nonscholarly invited speakers. Such a speaker, however, was US ambassador to the United Nations Jeane Kirkpatrick, who in 1983 was prevented from speaking at several campuses by disruptions from students and others who objected to the foreign policy of the Reagan administration. In a few cases violence was threatened, and one institution withdrew an invitation to speak because, it was claimed, Kirkpatrick's safety could not be guaranteed. Much like today, the incidents were highly publicized and led Committee A to issue a statement entitled *On Issues of Academic Freedom in Interference with Invited Speakers* in April 1983. The statement read,

> In recent weeks there have been widely reported accounts of several instances in which the United States ambassador to the United Nations, invited to address a university audience, was prevented from completing her remarks because of disruptions by persons in attendance, presumably because they disagreed with her views or those of the administration which she represents. On one occasion, an invitation to her to serve as commencement speaker was withdrawn by college officials because they could not assure her security while visiting the campus.
>
> The Association's Committee A on Academic Freedom and Tenure, responding to these incidents as it has to similar incidents on previous occasions, emphasizes that the freedom to hear is an essential condition of a free university and an inseparable part of academic freedom. Committee A deplores interference with the right of members of an academic community to hear on campus those whom they have invited to speak. The right to access to speakers on campus does not in its exercise imply either advance agreement or disagreement with what may be said, or approval or disapproval of the speaker as an individual. There can be no more appropriate forum for the discussion of controversial ideas and issues than the college and university campus.

Committee A reaffirms its expectation that all members of the academic community will respect the right of others to listen to those who have been invited to speak on campus and will indicate disagreement not by disruptive action designed to silence the speaker but by reasoned debate and discussion as befits academic freedom in a community of higher learning.

This was followed by a joint statement issued by the AAUP, the American Council on Education, the National Coalition of Independent College and University Students, the National Organization of Black University and College Students, and the United States Student Association, which called "upon our fellow students, teachers, and administrators to reaffirm our traditional commitments to the freedom to speak and to listen . . . so that the hecklers' veto does not drown out free speech and debate."

Kurland concluded his account of the AAUP's engagement with this issue by noting several instances of attempts to cancel the appearance of an invited speaker owing to alleged threats to national security after September 11, 2001:

Pressures to cancel a scheduled speech were unsuccessful in the cases of a leading Palestinian spokesperson at Colorado College and at the University of Colorado and of an Irish poet at Harvard University. Pressures on the sponsors did, however, bring about the cancellation of a speech by a British cleric at the College of the Holy Cross in Massachusetts, and at Rockford College in Illinois a commencement speech by a Pulitzer Prize reporter who opposed the war in Iraq was drowned out by audience members who continually chanted "God Bless America."

Several professors in Middle East studies programs at major American colleges and universities have been under steady attack by various pressure groups for being too sympathetic in their teaching and writing to Islamic interests. Those professors have by and large had their academic freedom supported by the administrations of their own institutions, but opposition to their scheduled speaking on other campuses has brought threats of cancellation.

Thoughts on the "Heckler's Veto"

In the strict legal sense, a heckler's veto occurs when a speaker's right is curtailed or restricted by the government in order to prevent the possibility of a violent reaction by hecklers or other protesters. In common parlance, the term is used to describe situations where hecklers or demonstrators themselves silence a speaker without legal intervention.

The courts have in the past upheld the right of authorities to shut down speech out of concern for safety. In *Feiner v. New York*, the Supreme Court in 1951 held that police officers acted within their power in arresting a speaker if the arrest was "motivated solely by a proper concern for the preservation of order and protection of the general welfare."[16] But in *Hill v. Colorado*, the Supreme Court in 2000 found that the government cannot grant power to a private actor, the heckler, to unilaterally silence a speaker because of a concern for the violent reaction by the heckler.[17]

Outside of the legal arena the term has come to mean that the heckler creates the veto and suppresses the speech by creating the violent reaction or the threat of violent reaction. The end result may be that the individual who is potentially being heckled will self-censor for fear of negative reaction. Alternately, the heckling will be so effective as to prevent any meaningful communication from the speaker to the audience. The late Nat Hentoff wrote that "First Amendment law is clear that everyone has the right to picket a speaker, and to go inside the hall and heckle him or her—but not to drown out the speaker, let alone rush the stage and stop the speech before it starts. That's called the 'heckler's veto.'"[18] The great First Amendment scholar Thomas Emerson wrote, "Up to a point heckling or other interruption of the speaker may be part of the dialogue. But conduct that obstructs or seriously impedes the utterance of another, even though verbal in form, cannot be classified as expression. Rather it is the equivalent of sheer noise. It has the same effect, in preventing or disrupting communication, as acts of physical force."[19]

Permitting speakers to be shouted down, allowing demonstrators to block access to speeches, or failing to provide sufficient security to ensure that a speech will be delivered—all forms of the heckler's veto—amount to impermissible violations of the principles of free expression and, in public institutions, of the protections guaranteed by the First Amendment. But, one might ask, what about the expressive rights of those who heckle?

In a discussion of free speech on campus, Greg Lukianoff, executive director of the Foundation for Individual Rights in Education, said, "Universities should be a chaotic paradise. It should be an exciting, challenging, sometimes difficult place but never all that quiet." Historian of student movements Angus Johnston went further: "I think it's crucial that free speech not just be an idea, and it not just be something that is safe and civil. There has to be space for speech that is not only rowdy, and disruptive, and aggressive, and obnoxious, but also speech that is attempting to change things."[20] In some ways both sides in the recent incidents have embodied aspects of this rough-and-tumble vision of free speech. Coulter and Yiannopoulos are nothing if not obnoxious, but it is equally true that their campus critics can be rowdy and disruptive, even when they eschew overt efforts to silence opponents. And if hecklers must be deprived of their veto, should they not still retain their right to heckle? Surely, for example, a woman who laughed out loud at Attorney General Jeff Sessions's confirmation hearing could be considered a heckler of sorts. But did her outburst warrant the jail sentence she initially received?[21]

When do impassioned disruption and uncivil dialogue cross the line into silencing behavior? Are a few boos or jeers sufficient to constitute a heckler's veto? And does it matter whether the speaker being heckled is a powerful figure with a near-guaranteed platform or someone less well known, struggling to promote novel or unpopular ideas? Of course, academics should promote reasoned discourse and polite consideration of the rights of others. But protest that fails to disrupt is hardly protest at all. Is there a point at which denying the heckler's veto simply creates what David Pozen calls "the provocateur's privilege?"[22] And the extraordinary amounts spent by the Berkeley administration to ensure Shapiro's safety and the success of the abortive Milo free speech week raise the question whether "the parameters of free speech are set not just by the limits of public tolerance but also by the practical budgetary concerns of ensuring a safe forum."[23] In May 2018, for instance, the University of California, Los Angeles announced that it would cover only $100,000 in total security costs each academic year for speakers who are not invited by a student group.[24]

One celebrated case involving a heckler's veto was that of the so-called Irvine 11. On February 8, 2010, Israeli ambassador to the United States Michael Oren spoke at the University of California, Irvine. Protesters began to disrupt the event by having a series of students yell so that the ambassador could not be heard. After the first disruptions, the audience was admonished that such behavior was not acceptable and that those who engaged in such conduct would be arrested and face student disciplinary proceedings. Still, eleven individuals rose and shouted so that the ambassador could not be heard. At one point he left the stage, but he was persuaded to return and deliver his address. All eleven were arrested and ultimately convicted of criminal conduct.

First Amendment scholar Erwin Chemerinsky, then UC Irvine law dean and current dean of the law school at UC Berkeley, wrote this about the incident:

> A person who comes into my classroom and shouts so that I cannot teach surely can be punished without offending the First Amendment. Likewise, those who yelled to keep the ambassador from being heard were not engaged in constitutionally protected behavior.
>
> Freedom of speech, on campuses and elsewhere, is rendered meaningless if speakers can be shouted down by those who disagree. The law is well established that the government can act to prevent a heckler's veto—to prevent the reaction of the audience from silencing the

speaker. There is simply no First Amendment right to go into an audi-
torium and prevent a speaker from being heard, no matter who the
speaker is or how strongly one disagrees with his or her message.

The remedy for those who disagreed with the ambassador was to
engage in speech of their own, but in a way that was not disruptive.
They could have handed out leaflets, stood with picket signs, spoken
during the question-and-answer session, held a demonstration elsewhere on campus or invited their own speakers.[25]

But Chemerinsky also spoke out against prosecuting the students:

> The students violated California law, which makes it a misdemeanor
> offense to disrupt a public meeting.... But the fact that conduct vio-
> lates a law does not mean that it should be prosecuted. Prosecutors,
> state and federal, constantly make choices about which crimes to
> prosecute....
>
> Although campus demonstrations are common, rarely have they led
> to criminal charges or convictions. Unless there is harm to persons or
> property—or a serious threat of this—district attorneys are almost
> always content to leave discipline to school authorities.... No one was
> hurt, and no property was damaged. After the disruptive students were
> escorted away, Ambassador Oren finished his speech. The students
> acted wrongly, and they were punished by the campus; there was no
> need for anything more.[26]

During the Vietnam War in the 1960s, UN ambassador Arthur
Goldberg came to Berkeley to debate the war at a mass meeting of
over ten thousand. Chairing the meeting was the late Reginald Zelnik, my mentor and an early faculty supporter of the Free Speech
Movement. To put it mildly, Goldberg's defense of the war was not
popular with Berkeley students, and his remarks were repeatedly
interrupted by catcalls and jeers. Zelnik—whose prestige among
campus radicals was high—repeatedly silenced the crowd, allowing
the discussion to proceed to its conclusion, after which a straw vote
was held and those attending overwhelmingly, and even more

powerfully because they had heard him out, rejected Goldberg's position.

I thought a lot about this story when on two different occasions I was thrust into a position not unlike that of my late mentor. In 2009, Mark Rudd, my college classmate, leader of the 1968 student rebellion at Columbia University and participant in the notorious Weather Underground, published a memoir, *Underground*, in which he advocated nonviolence and was self-critical of his past actions. As a Columbia student Rudd had disrupted a talk by the director of the New York City selective service office by shoving a cream pie in his face. The speech went on, but the point was made. Heckler's veto? Learning that Rudd would be in San Francisco to promote his book, I invited him to speak at my university nearby. A local public television station agreed to film the talk. But when we arrived, among those who packed the room to overflow were several retired police officers convinced that Rudd was responsible for the death of a fellow officer during the 1970s (Rudd denies it, and no one was ever charged in the case), as well as one Larry Grathwohl, the only law enforcement agent to successfully infiltrate the Weather Underground.

I was chairing the event and soon had my work cut out for me. The shouted curses and insults from the officers' group commenced even before Rudd began his talk. I repeatedly pleaded for calm, urging the protesters to allow Rudd to speak and promising they could ask questions or make brief statements later. One of the ex-officers used a handheld camcorder to record not only Rudd's remarks but also reactions from the largely student audience, which several of those attending later told me intimidated them from speaking during the question period. However, because we had agreed to allow filming of the event, I could not, I believed, ask the cameraman to stop without also terminating the TV station's efforts.

There was quite a ruckus, and soon campus police officers arrived. Although they later confessed to me their own sympathies for the hecklers, they offered to remove and if necessary arrest the disrupters. It would have been within our rights under the law governing the heckler's veto to do that, but I was certain such action would mark a defeat for free speech, so I declined the offer. The officers stood by as tensions waxed and waned and the program proceeded. Those in attendance saw history come to life, as the passions of the past were reenacted. In the end, Rudd did something masterful. He had begun with a reading of excerpts from his memoir and proceeded to respond to questions, both friendly and hostile. Then, after reading a passage from his book describing Grathwohl's treachery, Rudd invited Grathwohl himself to the stage to offer a response. Grathwohl too had his say, the audience heard him out, and the event concluded successfully.

Some time later I had occasion to direct our university's short-lived program in Jewish studies. Although the program was to be largely secular and represent multiple views of Judaism and the Jewish community, it was clear that we could hardly turn down an offer to speak on campus from the Israeli consul general in San Francisco. This was around the time of the Irvine events, and I was concerned about possible disruption, even violence. So I met with leaders of the Muslim Student Association (MSA) and invited them to attend the talk with assurance that there would be a question period during which they could freely speak.

The results were positive. The MSA members ended up composing almost half the audience. They were respectful and listened attentively, offering only the mildest of potentially disruptive comments. Encouraged, the consul general extended his question period and engaged in a fascinating dialogue with the students that went on for nearly an hour. Was anyone's mind changed? I doubt it, but this was precisely the kind of reasoned discussion of a heated issue that universities—and perhaps only universities—can best facilitate. A few weeks later the consul general spoke at nearby San José State University, where unfortunately no one had worked in advance to ensure a successful and safe event. He was compelled to leave the stage midspeech. "I wish you'd been at San José to help," he later told me.

These incidents from my own career may illustrate some of the complexities associated with the current debate over outside speakers and the heckler's veto. In the first case, it was not left-wing students who sought to silence a right-wing speaker; it was the opposite. And in the second example, it is clear that not all protesting students are disrespectful. Both incidents demonstrate that dialogue is indeed possible, that speakers and protesters can both be accommodated, although sometimes it can be difficult.

Is the Academy Intolerant?

To hear some critics tell it, American college and university campuses have become centers of illiberal intolerance, where a supposedly "leftist" orthodoxy championed by protesting students and their faculty allies seeks to effectively silence all dissent, especially that from the right side of the political spectrum. Stanley Kurtz decried the "chronic, pervasive, and steadily growing vice-grip of campus orthodoxy, punctuated and enforced by occasional shout-downs and meeting takeovers" that has produced a "tattered campus climate of free speech." Efforts to silence outside speakers, he declared, are "no longer occasional embarrassing episodes but the fruit of a deliberate strategy devised by influential sectors of the campus left."[27]

Charles Cooke, *National Review*'s editor, went so far as to declare that arguments claiming that speech may cause "harm" will result in nothing less than "the death of the West," an idea echoed by *New York Times* columnist David Brooks, who suggested that "fragile thugs who call themselves students" are partly responsible for an existential "crisis of Western Civ[ilization]." The editors of *USA Today* feared that "respect for free speech is withering on campus," while claiming in a headline that "campus mobs muzzle free speech." Between May 2016 and January 2018, the *New York Times* published twenty-one columns or articles decrying the alleged silencing of conservatives on campus, devoting only three to efforts to silence those on the left, including the epidemic of targeted harassment of left-leaning and minority faculty members.[28]

Jonathan Chait described student protests as a "war on the liberal mind" and the "manifestation of a serious ideological challenge to liberalism." Fareed Zakaria went perhaps the furthest. Speaking on his CNN show, Zakaria declared that "conservative voices and views are being silenced entirely" on campuses. "American universities these days seem to be committed to every kind of diversity—except intellectual diversity," he charged, adding that "an attitude of self-righteousness" is leading to "the ideas we find offensive" being drowned out. As evidence Zakaria cited the walkout of some graduates at Notre Dame to protest the appearance of Vice President Mike Pence and a protest by graduates at Bethune-Cookman University of a commencement talk by Secretary of Education Betsy DeVos.[29] Pence's speech was not even interrupted by the walkout, however, and in no sense was he silenced. And while some Bethune-Cookman graduates did boo DeVos, their principal mode of protest was to turn their backs silently on her. She too was able to speak with minimal interruption.[30] Indeed, that these two were invited to speak at all suggests that conservative politics are far from entirely unwelcome. But when has a cable news pundit allowed stubborn facts to interfere with a good rant?

Such arguments are—at minimum—overwrought exaggerations. To be sure, efforts to silence outside speakers and impose some sort of orthodoxy are both wrong and ill-advised, whether these originate on the left, right, or center of the political landscape. But to conclude that such efforts are broadly characteristic of American higher education today or that they pose a major threat to liberal democracy more generally—or that they are the main threat to free expression on campus—is, to be blunt, totally wrongheaded, even absurd.

For one thing, if one seeks sources of intolerance in American society today—or even in American colleges and universities—there are culprits far more frightening and obvious than protesting college students and their allegedly complicit left-leaning teachers.

As Colby College professor Aaron Hanlon commented, "The greater threat to free speech is not people on campuses judging the value of each other's speech, but powerful people calling on the state to criminalize speech, and the state obliging."[31] While student protests are decried as assaults on free speech by critics right and left, notes Adam Serwer, "Republican legislators have proposed 'Blue Lives Matter' bills that essentially criminalize peaceful protest; bills that all but outlaw protest itself; and bills that offer some protections to drivers who strike protestors with automobiles [particularly chilling after the events of August 2017 at the University of Virginia in Charlottesville]. GOP lawmakers have used the state to restrict speech, such as barring doctors from raising abortion or guns with patients, opposition to the construction of Muslim religious buildings, and attempts to stifle anti-Israel activism."[32]

Moreover, the most provocative outside speakers may bring their own violence. In Seattle, just days before the Berkeley protests, an anti-Milo demonstrator was shot in the abdomen by two Milo supporters.[33] When Spencer spoke in October 2017 at the University of Florida, the protests were peaceful. Yet there was violence in Gainesville nonetheless, although thankfully no one was hurt. A few hours after Spencer concluded his event, police arrested three of his supporters, charging them with attempted murder after one of them, egged on by his friends, fired a gun at protesters "with the intent to kill."[34] At Colorado State University peaceful, nondisruptive protesters at a speech by Turning Point USA founder Charlie Kirk were assaulted by a group chanting a Nazi slogan and wielding riot shields, large flashlights, and face masks emblazoned with skulls.[35]

And the Left hardly has a monopoly on disruption. On October 5, 2017, at Whittier College in Los Angeles, California, attorney general Xavier Becerra, who filed a lawsuit against the Trump administration over its attempts to end the Deferred Action for Childhood Arrivals (DACA) program, was confronted by pro-Trump hecklers, who "continuously shouted slogans and insults at Becerra and [Ian] Calderon," majority leader of the California Assembly. According to an eyewitness account, "Becerra and Calderon were to have an hour-long question-and-answer session using audience questions randomly selected from a basket. As soon as they began the discussion, however, hecklers decked in 'Make America Great Again' hats began a continuous and persistent chorus of boos, slogans, and insults." The event ended abruptly after just thirty-four minutes.[36]

Then there is the growing threat to freedom of the press, a threat that extends to student media. President Trump has famously referred to the press as "enemies of the people." One lawyer and former newsman fears that "the First Amendment will soon be tested in ways we haven't seen before." Evoking the experience of the late eighteenth-century Alien and Sedition Acts, historian Bernard Weissberger warned that with respect to a free press "genuine trouble is at our doorstep."[37] Incidents of student media censorship occur far more frequently than the more attention-grabbing—and usually less successful—protests against controversial speakers. In 2016, the AAUP, the College Media Association, the National Coalition Against Censorship, and the Student Press Law Center issued a report, entitled *Threats to the Independence of Student Media*, which documented how many "college and university authorities have exhibited an intimidating level of hostility toward student media, inhibiting the free exchange of ideas on campus." Sadly, commentators who eagerly echo charges that student protesters create a "tattered climate" for free speech overwhelmingly ignored this important report.[38]

The fact is that at almost every American college and university each day there occur meaningful exchanges of ideas far more extensive and unfettered than just about anywhere else in our society. As Eddie Glaude Jr., chair of the Department of African American Studies at Princeton, eloquently put it,

> Thousands of lectures across the ideological spectrum happen on campuses. Students go to classes, participate in various organizations and attend lectures without incident. Imagine how many times Murray or [Condoleeza] Rice or Ben Shapiro have actually spoken on campuses without it becoming a national spectacle. The protests we have witnessed

recently are not the norm, but conservatives and even some liberal columnists would have us believe otherwise.

In many ways, the university setting is the most vibrant space for the free exchange of ideas in this country. That doesn't mean that universities and colleges are free from the passions of political debate. Just as those passions inflame partisanship in national and local politics, they show up on campuses, especially in the hearts and minds of young people who fight it out, sometimes with abandon.

Not all conservative speech is hateful speech, and we ought to be able to distinguish the difference. Most conservatives aren't like Yiannopoulos, Spencer and Coulter. Such conservatives should, and do, speak on campuses every day. But if they hold controversial views, like any speaker of whatever ideological bent, they should expect a passionate response that may take the form of protests. And in those cases, students have every right to exercise their freedom of speech.[39]

Moreover, those institutions that stand as exceptions to such extensive free expression are, by and large, colleges—often religiously based—that openly bar ideas and expression most usually associated not with the Right but with the Left. Take, for instance, Jerry Falwell Jr.'s flagrantly misnamed Liberty University. After Shane Claiborne, a Christian pacifist, invited Falwell to participate in a prayer breakfast with him, Claiborne was threatened with arrest if he even set foot on campus.[40] *Politico* reported, "A member of the Board of Trustees who criticized Trump and questioned Falwell's endorsement of him was pushed into resigning. In the student newspaper, the *Liberty Champion*, a student-penned column criticizing Trump's grotesque 'Access Hollywood' comments about women was preemptively censored at Falwell's request (that writer has since resigned). And Liberty's faculty—all of whom work without the possibility of tenure—are reluctant to speak out, with many fearing retribution and the loss of their positions." Then there is Liberty's faculty handbook, which declares, "All employees of the University are expected to conduct themselves in matters of language and morality in a manner compatible with the Mission of the University and The Liberty Way. Unsuitable conduct may be grounds for disciplinary action, up to and including termination."[41]

Indeed, incidents in which both students and faculty have had their free expression rights violated at conservative Christian colleges may be far more frequent—if less frequently reported—than the highly publicized incidents of censorship by an allegedly intolerant Left. As journalist Sarah Jones concludes, "Jerry Falwell, Jr. isn't some random evangelical but a prominent figure with the ear of the president of the United States. Christian colleges train the next generation of the religious right, and enrich the current generation with speaking gigs and lucrative positions. Their policies have serious political implications, and they reveal how far the right-wing will go to preserve its doctrinal purity. The left isn't the real threat to free speech, not on campus, and not anywhere else."[42]

In a remarkable Twitter thread University of Wisconsin–Milwaukee professor Joel Berkowitz vividly described the sorts of exchanges that take place regularly in college classrooms: "The countless fruitful discussions that happen all the time in college classrooms don't grab headlines," he wrote. "They're the 'dog bites postman' of higher ed news, minus the biting. I couldn't tell you how many animated, but entirely civil disputes I've facilitated in my classes in over 25 years of teaching."

After recounting a particularly poignant interaction between a black female graduate student and a white police officer in a discussion of policing and race informed by readings of African American literature, Berkowitz continued, "'Students With Diametrically Opposed Views Smile & Nod at One Another' is not a headline. But maybe it should be. Neither is 'Student Raises Voice in Heated Class Discussion, but No Harm Done, and People Learned Stuff.' The truly worrying class sessions, btw, aren't when voices get raised. When managed well, those are the best ones. The worst are when it's like pulling teeth to get anyone to participate at all. Maybe someone could endow a center to combat that sort of thing. Seriously, though, we already have that: it's called a university." Returning to his example, Berkowitz asked,

> If they hadn't enrolled in my class, would Ron & Lisa ever have met? Maybe. Would they have debated central themes in *Invisible Man*? In that class, they & a couple of dozen classmates from diverse backgrounds & w/ diverse views did so, for several months. MILLIONS of students do that all the time, guided by skilled, dedicated instructors who facilitate civil debates & steer discussions—not toward the "moral of the story," but to something less obvious, & unlikely to be wrapped up in a pretty bow. But discussions in which numerous points of view are encouraged b/c you know what? Otherwise, TEACHING & LEARNING WOULD BE REALLY BORING! So spare us the sanctimony about conservatives needing platforms, please. Spare us the cherry-picked moments of a Coulter deciding she can't or won't take the heat. How about directing resources to where they're really needed? . . . The insistence on giving any particularly political agenda a "platform" on campus either misunderstands or distorts the civil, constructive debates & disagreements that happen in higher ed classrooms every single day.[43]

To be sure, the widespread complaint from the Right that faculty in the humanities and social sciences are overwhelmingly liberal, while highly exaggerated, is not entirely without basis. And it would be foolish to deny that this preponderance may sometimes inappropriately narrow the scope of discourse in these disciplines. But even here, as conservative scholars themselves attest, diversity of views and freedom of debate are more extensive on campus than critics would have it.[44] Does attending college turn students into intolerant liberals, as some on the right seem to think? One group of scholars tried to find out. They started following a nationally representative sample of over seven thousand undergraduates at more than 120 colleges when they entered college in 2015, tracking, among other things, how their attitudes toward liberals and conservatives changed from their first to second years: "We measured how students viewed each political group separately along four dimensions. Specifically, we asked respondents the extent to which they thought liberals and conservatives were ethical, made positive contributions to society, and were people the student had something in common with. We also asked students if they had a positive attitude toward each group. The same questions were asked at the beginning of each student's freshman and sophomore years." Interestingly, 48 percent of those surveyed viewed liberals more favorably in their second year of college than when they arrived on campus. However, among the same students, 50 percent also viewed conservatives more favorably. And 31 percent developed more negative attitudes toward conservatives, while just about the same number, 30 percent, developed more negative attitudes toward liberals. "In other words," the study concluded, "college attendance is associated, on average, with gains in appreciating political viewpoints across the spectrum, not just favoring liberals."[45]

Another survey, this time of University of Wisconsin–Madison students, found that politically conservative students, far from feeling intimidated, are actually more likely to report feeling safe, respected, and like they belong than students holding other political views. The 2016 Campus Climate Survey garnered 8,652 responses, representing some 21 percent of the student body. The online survey also found that conservative students were more likely than liberal students to say they feel comfortable approaching faculty members with their concerns. They were also less likely than liberal or moderate students to be expected to represent their point of view in class, but they felt more positive about doing so than the others.[46]

As Adam Serwer concluded, the story of left-wing campus intolerance "survives in disproportion to its importance because it involves the children of financial and scholarly elites who drive press coverage; because it allows elders to sneer at a younger generation; and because of conservative media outlets which see these stories as politically useful and amplify such stories for their audience."[47] One must wonder whether all this hand-wringing is even about free speech.

The Main Threats to Free Speech on Campus

How extensive are challenges to outside speakers? Do incidents like those involving Yiannopoulos at Berkeley, Murray at Middlebury, or MacDonald at Claremont McKenna represent the tip of a larger iceberg? And, if so, does the iceberg menace all of higher education or only a relatively small number of mainly elite institutions?

Writing in response to the Middlebury incident, Yale Law School professor and novelist Stephen L. Carter opined that what he found most frightening about that confrontation was how "it felt like an everyday event." Carter explained,

> According to the Foundation for Individual Rights in Education [FIRE], 2016 saw a record number of efforts to keep controversial speakers from being heard on campus—and that's just in the U.S. To be sure, not all of the attempts succeeded, and the number catalogued, 42, is but a small fraction of the many outsiders who give addresses at colleges and universities each year. The real number of rejected speakers is certainly much higher, once we add in all the people not invited in the first place because some member of this or that committee objects to their views, or because campus authorities fear trouble. But even one would be too many.[48]

I admire much of the excellent work FIRE has done in defense of campus free expression, but their "disinvitation" database, to which Carter referred, is not one of their more commendable efforts. Indeed, it actually makes the case that the problem it seeks to track—assaults on the rights of outside speakers—is in reality much less severe than the organization claims. That was the contention of Paul Campos, a professor at the University of Colorado Law School, who pointed out that "the total number of talks on potentially politically sensitive topics at American colleges and universities in any one year must reach seven figures (There are four thousand such institutions in the US, so if you assume an average of one such talk per day per institution—surely a gross underestimate—that's 1,460,000 opportunities for civil discourse-destroying protest). So tens of thousands—at least—politically controversial talks take place at American institutions of higher learning for every one that leads to any (overt) attempt to keep that talk from taking place."[49]

The point was further developed by *Los Angeles Times* columnist Michael Hiltzik, who called attention to

> the chief problem with the FIRE database: It treats every protest against a speaker as a blow against free speech, whether it resulted in a genuine disinvitation or not, whether the event was a commencement address or campus talk or panel discussion, and whether the protest came from on campus or off. . . .
>
> Then there's the question about what qualifies as a "disinvitation." The details of protests or expressions of disapproval of speakers show that many of these are not genuine attempts "to prevent those with whom they disagreed from speaking on campus," as FIRE describes them.
>
> Consider a dual appearance of Vice President Joe Biden and former House Speaker John Boehner at Notre Dame's commencement last year. FIRE lists these as the targets of disinvitations, but its only evidence is a letter from 89 students saying they were "disappointed and discouraged" by the invitations chiefly because of Biden's tolerance for abortion. But the students didn't call for the invitations to be rescinded or for Biden and Boehner to be prevented from speaking.
>
> Then there's the disinvitation of the physician Emily Wong as commencement speaker at Hampshire College in Massachusetts. FIRE asserts that this happened because Wong "could not 'directly address student concerns' such as transphobia, racial issues, and sexual violence," which makes the episode sound like the height of loony leftism. But that's a gross misrepresentation of what happened.
>
> The truth is that the college president, Jonathan Lash, had selected Wong on his own because the students' choices, including writer Ta-Nehisi Coates and Bernie Sanders, weren't available. After students and faculty protested Lash's high-handedness, he relented. The students, faculty and administration then settled on Reina Gossett, an activist writer and filmmaker whose "life and work," according to Hampshire's press release, "engage the issues that have been raised by students around anti-blackness, transphobia, and sexual violence."

FIRE took a phrase that applied to Gossett and turned it, inaccurately, into a critique of Wong.

Hiltzik observed that "only 24 'disinvitations' in 2016 resulted in a true withdrawn invitation; in FIRE's full database of 331 incidents going back to 2000, only 145 were true disinvitations. Is a protest that fails to result in a withdrawn invitation a blow against free speech?" he asked. "Hardly. In many if not most cases, it's an expression of free speech."[50]

And then there is the problem of conflating protests against commencement speakers with other protests. Commencements account for about 40 percent of the incidents in FIRE's database of 331 "disinvitations" dating back to 2000, and 7 of the 43 cases in 2016. It is surely true that in some instances student objections to controversial commencement speakers may inappropriately chill discussion. But a closer look at the phenomenon reveals that students are often more concerned about whether speakers were chosen with meaningful participation by student representatives than they are with the content of the speeches or the pedigree of the speakers. Protesting students often point out that a commencement speaker is not an ordinary campus speaker. Those invited are generally given some honor, usually a symbolic degree, and hence their words are provided a sort of official "stamp of approval" that would not necessarily be the case for those invited during the school year by an academic program or a student group. So, for example, in 2016 President Barack Obama castigated Rutgers graduates for their "misguided" protest against a commencement address by Condoleezza Rice two years earlier. But the protesters did not dispute Rice's right to speak. They complained that the university would also be giving her an honorary degree and that administrators had usurped the power of a student-faculty committee that in the past had selected commencement speakers.[51] In addition, students say, commencement is not a classroom or a traditional forum for debate; it is a celebration of the graduates and their achievements, and speaker choices should recognize that. On ordinary occasions when an objection-able speaker comes to campus, students who disagree can boycott the speech or peacefully protest outside. But is it fair to ask them to boycott or demonstrate at their own commencement?

Responding to Hiltzik's column, FIRE's Ari Cohn identified two problems with his argument. First, Cohn wrote, "While there may be 4,000 colleges and universities, the universe of schools to which controversial, big-name speakers are invited is likely significantly smaller." Second, he contended, Hiltzik's "criticism belies a misunderstanding of the purpose of not only the database but also our disinvitation work more generally. FIRE is concerned with disinvitations not only because of the severity of each individual incident's impact on free speech, but also because it exemplifies a trend."[52]

With respect to the first point, Hiltzik responded that while it may be the case that only a subset of the nation's four thousand colleges and universities are impacted by this sort of controversy, nevertheless "FIRE's universe is fairly inclusive. Its database includes big campuses like Berkeley and the University of Michigan, but also places like Earlham College of Indiana (enrollment 1,019) and Anna Maria College of Massachusetts (1,462). So what's the real size of the 'universe'? Cohn doesn't say. Nor are all the targets appearing on his list 'big name speakers': They include state legislators, authors of self-published political screeds, and local activists unknown outside their homes and surrounding counties."[53]

Moreover, elsewhere FIRE has argued against the notion that the problem is limited to a smaller subset of institutions. In January 2017, University of Wisconsin–Madison professor Donald Moynihan published an op-ed in the *New York Times*, in which he argued that outside a relatively small circle of selective private institutions "like Oberlin or Yale," conservative state legislators pose a far greater threat to academic freedom than do student protesters.[54] In response, FIRE's Samantha Harris wrote that "as someone who has been tracking threats to free speech on campus for more than 11 years, I can say this is not the case."[55] But it is impossible to have it both ways; FIRE cannot convincingly argue in one context that the universe of institutions impacted by "disinvitations" is limited, as does Cohn, and elsewhere, as in Harris's piece, that it is not.

With respect to Cohn's second argument against Hiltzik, it is illogical to contend that the aim of the FIRE database is to collect incidents that "exemplify a trend" when the limitations of the list itself actually suggest that the trend, insofar as it can be documented, is not all that impressive. It would seem that FIRE has actually assumed a priori that a trend exists and now seeks anecdotes to confirm that assumption rather than compiling evidence sufficient to test it. As Hiltzik concludes, "Anecdotes can be useful, but not when they deflate at the slightest poking."[56]

The point is not to dismiss the significance of those incidents in which speakers have been truly "disinvited" or even silenced, in a few instances violently. The issue, however, is not the legitimacy of the problem but how extensive it is—whether these incidents are, as Carter put it, "everyday events"—and, in addition, where the problem ranks among the full panoply of threats to free expression and academic freedom on college and university campuses.

Moynihan clearly spoke for thousands of faculty members at public colleges and universities when he wrote that "my colleagues and I have been given much more reason to worry about the ideological agendas of elected officials and politically appointed governing boards" than the actions of censorious student protesters. "Students can protest on the campus mall, demanding that policies be changed; elected officials can pass laws or cut resources to reflect their beliefs about how a campus should operate. One group has much more power than the other."

"Policy makers who accuse students of weakening campus speech should lead by example," Moynihan concluded. "Free speech on campus has survived and will survive challenges from students and other members of civil society. Its fate is much less certain when the government decides to censor discomforting views."[57]

In an April 2017 Twitter thread Angus Johnston listed a number of threats to academic freedom discussed in a workshop on the topic at a national meeting of unionized faculty, in which "Ann Coulter's name didn't come up":

- "Administrators interfering with faculty members' attempts to share information with campus boards of trustees."
- "The challenges in protecting student and faculty free speech rights in the classroom."
- "Attempts to roll back or compromise faculty control over curriculum."
- "Threats to professors' freedom to criticize their own institutions."
- "Faculty misunderstanding of the scope and limits of academic freedom."
- "Administrators' and legislators' use of budgeting power to constrain professors' freedom of speech and inquiry."

He concluded, "Some of these reflect profs' concerns about restrictions on their own freedoms, others [are] worries about violation of students' rights. And none of them is likely to gain any serious attention from the nation's self-appointed media champions of campus free speech. . . . There's a lot happening right now around academic freedom and campus free speech that the media is missing."[58]

In this context it is difficult to accept the notion that attempts by protesting students to silence controversial speakers—however inappropriate or foolish—are even near the top of the list of threats to academic freedom and free expression on campus.

Moreover, it is by no means clear that attacks on outside speakers are even directed overwhelmingly at avowed conservatives. In September 2017, the Theological College of Catholic University disinvited the Rev. James Martin, a popular priest who published a book encouraging a bridge between the LGBTQ community and the Catholic Church, from giving an address.[59] Princeton University professor Keeanga-Yamahtta Taylor was forced to cancel a speaking tour after she received violent threats from the right wing. The threats began after Fox News covered her commencement speech at Hampshire College, in which she called Donald Trump "a racist, sexist megalomaniac."

"Since last Friday, I have received more than fifty hate-filled and threatening emails," she said. "Some of these emails have contained specific threats of violence, including murder. I have been threatened with lynching and having the bullet from a .44 Magnum put in my head."[60] Taylor's situation garnered considerably less attention than did the efforts to deny platforms to Murray, Coulter, and Yiannopoulos. "There are no columns in *The New York Times* or *The Atlantic or New York* magazine," wrote Sarah Jones in the *New Republic*. "There are no fevered tweets, no hand-wringing on her behalf. Instead, we have yet another *Times* column about the excesses of college liberals." Concluded Jones, "Coverage of free speech fights in the U.S. casts the left as illiberal antagonists and lets the right off the hook for its own, much more serious history of censorship. By defending Charles Murray, and not Taylor, the media has shown some revealing inconsistencies in its concerns about free speech."[61] Fred Smith Jr., a constitutional scholar and assistant professor at the University of California's Berkeley School of Law, told the *New York Times*, "There are a few people who have been very effective in branding the left at shutting down free speech, but the moment they are confronted with leftist speech they don't like, they are equally outraged and poised to suppress that speech."[62]

While attacks on the right of controversial figures to speak on campus pose a problem that needs to be addressed, the problem cannot be said to be limited to attacks by leftists against those with more conservative views. Nor can such attacks be said to merit greater attention than quite a few other challenges to free expression and academic freedom that have, as yet, attracted much less public notice, several of which pose considerably more ominous dangers. To suggest that leftist threats to outside speakers constitute the main menace to free expression and academic freedom on campus today is to exaggerate and mislead, or worse.

Are Some Free Speech Claims Illegitimate?

In an April 2017 op-ed in the *New York Times*, New York University vice provost Ulrich Baer argued that campus speaker protests

> should be understood as an attempt to ensure the conditions of free speech for a greater group of people, rather than censorship. Liberal free-speech advocates rush to point out that the views of these individuals must be heard first to be rejected. But this is not the case. Universities invite speakers not chiefly to present otherwise unavailable discoveries, but to present to the public views they have presented elsewhere. When those views invalidate the humanity of some people, they restrict speech as a public good.
>
> In such cases there is no inherent value to be gained from debating them in public. . . .
>
> The idea of freedom of speech does not mean a blanket permission to say anything anybody thinks. It means balancing the inherent value of a given view with the obligation to ensure that other members of a given community can participate in discourse as fully recognized members of that community. Free-speech protections—not only but especially in universities, which aim to educate students in how to belong to various communities—should not mean that someone's humanity, or their right to participate in political speech as political agents, can be freely attacked, demeaned or questioned.[63]

At first glance this argument merits sympathy. After all, if the university has an obligation to protect free speech, it must also be obliged to protect members of the scholarly community, including the community's minority members, from attack, including via verbal assaults. However, as Conor Friedersdorf responded, implicit in Baer's argument "are lazy stereotypes common to many who share his views on speech."[64] Friedersdorf stressed what

> any observer of American life ought to know: that the opinions of African Americans, Hispanics, Asian Americans, gays, lesbians, trans people, undocumented immigrants, foreign students, people from

minority religious groups, and those of members of every other identity group on campus are hugely diverse. . . . Baer seems not to realize
that there are millions of black and Hispanic Americans whose views
on, say, illegal immigration or transgender rights run afoul of his standards for what is even mentionable. How much speech by historically
marginalized groups will be stifled in Baer's effort "to ensure the conditions of free speech for a greater group of people"?[65]

For Friedersdorf, Baer's contention that freedom of speech
"means balancing the inherent value of a given view with the obligation to ensure that other members of a given community can
participate in discourse as fully recognized members of that community" is "so pernicious that it is vital to reject it. . . . It is inaccu-
rate and disempowering to tell undergraduates that any bigot can
render them unable to participate in public discourse merely by
speaking on campus; or can render them less than fully recognized
in their community merely by addressing it," he argued. "In fact, minorities are not only free to participate in discourse on college campuses, they are doing so vigorously."[66]

A similar argument to Baer's was offered by Traci Yoder, director
of research and education for the National Lawyers Guild. "When
the views of speakers are actually dangerous to other people," she
asserted, "universities should consider the implications and balance
the need for a diversity of viewpoints with the consequences of in-
validating the humanity or rights of entire groups of already disadvantaged people."[67] Yoder makes two arguments in opposition to
what she calls "the commonsense liberal approach" advocated, for
instance, by the American Civil Liberties Union (ACLU). That approach, she claims, "assume[s] that allowing all speech under any circumstances will ensure that the best ideas win out and that it is ideal
to have even potentially dangerous ideas out in the open where they
can be challenged." (This is a simplistic caricature of that argument,
but it can pass here.)

First, she writes, "Far right conservative and fascist ideology is
not simply based on logical and reasonable arguments; rather, these

movements depend on the irrational mobilization of hate, fear, and anger against some of the most marginalized and vulnerable populations. Offering them an open forum and vigorously defending their right to promote harmful speech confers legitimacy on their positions as being equally as acceptable as any other."[68] Second, according to Yoder,

> The liberal free speech model . . . does not take into account the asymmetry of different positions and the reality of unequal power relations. Arguments about free speech rarely address the significant imbalances in power that exist between, for example, a wealthy white speaker with the backing of a multi-million dollar organization and members of the populations affected by their words (i.e. immigrants, people of color, queer and trans people, low-wage workers, etc.). What are lost in the abstract notion of free speech are the rights of those who do not have the connections or wealth to equally participate in public discourse. The "marketplace of ideas" is like any other marketplace; those with the most resources dominate.[69]

It is true, of course, that speakers like Coulter, Spencer, and Yiannopoulos appeal to irrational emotion and disdain reason, although the same might be said about some on the far left. But so what? That is hardly cause not to confront and demolish their appeals with bold and aggressive reasoned argument. Indeed, it is higher education's very mission to confront irrationality with reason. Silencing irrational arguments may only allow them to fester. As legal scholar Frederick M. Lawrence has written, "The required response to hateful speech is to describe it as such and to criticize it directly. Supreme Court Justice Louis D. Brandeis wrote in *Whitney v. California* that, except in those rare cases in which the harm from speech is real and imminent, the answer to harmful or hateful speech is not 'enforced silence' but, rather, 'more speech.' "[70]

And while Yoder fears that combating hateful speech with "more speech" will legitimize the hate-mongers, in practice combating rather than disallowing hate speech is precisely her own recommended response: "Challenges to reactionary speakers have included putting up flyers with information about the speakers and their back-ground, circulating petitions to have the event cancelled, organizing counter-events and speakers, writing op-ed pieces for campus and lo-cal publications, sending students to the event with a list of critical questions, and protesting outside or within the event by walking out or holding signs."[71] All of this amounts, more or less, to the "more speech" approach that Yoder ostensibly dismisses. That even includes petitioning to have an event canceled. I don't support cancellation of speaking events, but the right to raise that demand is itself protected. It is up to the institution hosting the event to reject such calls and to ensure that the event can proceed safely and with minimal disrup-tion. All of Yoder's other suggestions are entirely legitimate, fully rea-sonable, and consistent with Brandeis's proposed remedy.

"We bind ourselves to an impoverished choice set if we believe that we can either punish speech or validate it," writes Lawrence. "There is a middle position, expressed in Brandeis's dictum of 'more speech,' that allows us to respond without punishing. In the face of hate speech, the call for more speech is not merely an option; it is a professional or even moral obligation."[72]

Yoder's second argument about the asymmetry of power rela-tions is more interesting and compelling. One thinks immediately of the famous quote from Anatole France: "In its majestic equality, the law forbids rich and poor alike to sleep under bridges, beg in the streets and steal loaves of bread." One thinks too of the infamous US Supreme Court ruling in *Citizens United v. FEC*, which granted First Amendment speech protections to corporations as if they were people. As Jim Sleeper points out, "The First Amendment is abused when it's interpreted not only to protect dissenters' right to rant but also to empower corporations, which already dominate individuals' options as employees and customers, to use expensive megaphones in public debate, leaving dissenters with laryngitis from straining to be heard."[73]

There can be little doubt about the disparity in resources be-tween the powerful and the still to be empowered and about the potent impact this has on speech and discourse. Speakers like Coulter,

Yiannopoulos, and Murray enjoy extensive financial support (see chap. 5). Even when their events are canceled, no reasonable person can doubt that their message is still being delivered and may even be more accessible than the counterarguments of their critics. Moreover, it is not just that power relations are unequal. Freedom of speech is by definition a right conferred on individuals (and associations of individuals). But racism, misogyny, and other forms of oppression are collective and structural.

In a controversial essay Georgetown University law professor Louis Michael Seidman asks, "Can Free Speech Be Progressive?" Specifically, he argues that "the constitutional right to free speech is actually at war with free thought. . . . It provides an excuse for not speaking, for not listening, and for not thinking."[74] Seidman's piece builds on an argument by University of Chicago law professor Laura Weinrib, who has complained that while "the early ACLU viewed free speech as a tool of social justice, suited to particular purposes under particular conditions," it has since embraced a more legalist and abstract vision of the First Amendment. As a consequence, "in recent years, nearly half of First Amendment victories have gone to corporations and trade groups challenging government regulation. Free speech has served to secure the political influence of wealthy donors."[75]

How can we then ensure that all viewpoints may be fully aired, considered, discussed, and either accepted or rejected fairly, when some viewpoints are structurally disadvantaged compared to those with far greater access to power? I will try to address this knotty problem, which calls into question the limits of tolerance in a diverse democracy, shortly. For now, however, let us recognize that it is not a problem easily resolved, if it can be resolved at all, either in the context of actually existing society or in the abstract. That said, it should also be recognized that nearly all solutions offered to this conundrum have proven as problematic as or worse than the imbalance they seek to remedy.

Moreover, it is important not to turn every political conflict into a free speech battle. Writing in the *Atlantic*, Walt Hunter pointed out that "representing campus protests under the heading of free speech helps to obscure the actual struggles occurring over the allocation of resources and the revision of curricula—struggles being led by students. In the context of campus rape, structural racism, gender-based wage discrimination, and skyrocketing expenses over student housing, battles over 'free speech' might as well be waged on a different planet."[76]

In important respects student protesters today have revived the '60s-era radical critique of the university as an integral part of the "Establishment." There was, of course—and still is—considerable truth to that assessment. One of the most trenchant critics of the contemporary university, philosopher Robert Paul Wolff, acknowledged as much in his still-relevant 1969 book *The Ideal of the University.* "So long as the lion's share of the money for universities comes from industry, foundations, and state and federal governments," he wrote, "society at large [and not faculty and students] can effectively dictate the form and content of the education within the academy."[77]

Nevertheless, Wolff rejected the radical critique of the university, even as he found much of it "true and important." Instead, he also found it "wrong on several counts":

> To begin with, despite the pressures and constraints of contemporary higher education, it seems to me clearly the case that university life is liberating for most students, and that the liberation occurs because of what the university is rather than in spite of what it is. . . . A great many colleges and universities are much freer, much more conducive to serious questioning and open debate, much more committed to human values, than any other major institution in the United States. . . . American universities today, despite their defense contracts and ROTC programs, their businessman trustees and Establishment presidents, are the only major viable institutional centers of opposition to the dominant values and politics of the society. . . . There, if anywhere, new and deeper attacks on the evils of American society will be mounted. Here again, the opposition role of the university flows from its very nature as a center of free inquiry.[78]

Nearly a half century later, these words remain pertinent. For while we cannot separate the university from the larger society—nor should we wish to do so; the "ivory tower" is neither Wolff's model nor mine—it is also our job to defend the university as a center of inquiry, reason, and, growing inevitably out of these, critique and change. "I have no illusion that universities somehow evade the logic of the marketplace," writes University of Tennessee professor Lisi Schoenbach. "But no other institution is designed so intentionally to provide structures in which free intellectual inquiry can take place. It is no accident that most scholars work under the protection of these spaces. . . . Universities are not perfect, but they are the only protection we have."[79]

Properly conceived and functioning well, colleges and universities should not fear repugnant viewpoints and odious language. Our institutions should be strong enough to meet the challenges these present. But if the university stops being a center of free inquiry, it will have no purpose at all. It will then indeed be just another part of the "Establishment." And if that happens, the important struggles for justice that protesting students have initiated will suffer most.

Academic Freedom and Freedom of Speech

Among the many responses to recent controversies over campus free speech, Stanley Fish's "Free Speech Is Not an Academic Value" may have been the most provocative.[80] Fish began by taking to task a statement by a faculty committee at the University of Minnesota, which proclaimed the university's "larger normative commitment to the free exchange of ideas." Fish disagreed: "The university's normative commitment is to freedom of inquiry, which is quite a different thing." He continued,

> The phrase "free exchange of ideas" suggests something like a Hyde Park corner or a town-hall meeting where people take turns offering their opinions on pressing social matters. The right to speak is held by all. . . .

The course of free inquiry in universities is not like that at all. Before one can speak, in a classroom or in the research seminar or in a journal publication, one will have been subjected to any number of vetting procedures. . . . To put it another way, the free exchange of ideas between persons who want in on the conversation is a democratic ideal; but the university is not a democracy; it is (or is supposed to be) a meritocracy, one in which those who get to put their ideas forward are far outnumbered by those who don't.

"Freedom of speech," Fish therefore concluded, "is not an academic value. Accuracy of speech is an academic value; completeness of speech is an academic value; relevance of speech is an academic value. Each of these values is directly related to the goal of academic inquiry: getting a matter of fact right."[81]

I have been critical of Fish's unduly cramped interpretation of academic freedom, what he has called the "It's just a job" school (see chap. 2). But in this essay he makes a valid point: academic freedom and freedom of speech are founded on differing justifications and should not be confused. Libertarian scholar Jacob Levy confirms that "academic freedom is not just the same thing as 'free expression of ideas.'" While it "has some overlap of form and purpose with liberal freedom of speech," academic freedom "is genuinely not the same thing. . . . It is the professional ethic of a purposive community."[82] As Joan W. Scott has pointed out, "Free speech makes no distinction about quality; academic freedom does."[83]

Robert Post, Sterling Professor of Law at Yale University and former AAUP general counsel, writes, "The scope of academic freedom is not determined by First Amendment principles of freedom of speech, but by the metrics of professional competence." He adds, "The freedom of inquiry characteristic of a disciplinary community is quite different from the classic First Amendment tradition."[84]

Post criticizes the position articulated by FIRE that "a university exists to educate students and advance the frontiers of human knowledge, *and does so by acting as a 'marketplace of ideas'*" (emphasis added). But speech within college and university classrooms and in scholarly exchange bears little resemblance to a free market and doesn't serve the purposes of the First Amendment. Astrology, creationism, and Holocaust denial, for example, are protected in the open market but not in the classroom. Indeed, even within public universities, Post argues, "FIRE and overblown public rhetoric notwithstanding, it makes little sense to apply core First Amendment principles of freedom of speech."

Academia itself has too often confused the relationship between academic freedom in the service of teaching and research and a broader liberal commitment to free expression. Take, for example, the famous Yale University Woodward Report of 1974.[85] It opens with the clear declaration that "the primary function of a university is to discover and disseminate knowledge by means of research and teaching." Almost immediately, however, the report goes on to claim that "the paramount obligation of the university is to protect the right to free expression." As Post points out, the report's commitment to research and teaching and its "overriding" commitment to free speech "cannot be reconciled except through a theory of education that, at its extreme, runs contrary to the experience of virtually all university teachers and administrators. It is no wonder, therefore, that the Report is almost always read to subordinate the goal of teaching and to elevate 'free speech' over every other university goal or purpose."

The reality at Yale, one might add, has differed from the ideals the institution so piously claimed to embrace. The report's dissenting statement noted several "interferences with the free market of ideas at Yale," including an "article by Dr. Spock which the Alumni Magazine refused to print; the termination of the employment of such radical faculty members as Staughton Lynd (History), Mills and McBride (Philosophy), and Resnick, Hymer, Weisskopf (Economics); censorship by the Administration of the Yale Band; punishment of streakers." More recently, one might point to Yale's unusual relationship with the National University of Singapore, about which the AAUP raised significant questions with respect to academic freedom and free expression; its administration's 2006 rejection of Juan Cole for a tenured position despite overwhelming faculty support after an intensive media campaign against Cole's appointment by pro-Israel and right-wing groups; or the adoption of Standards of Faculty Conduct that, according to one prominent professor, paid lip service to free expression in the preamble but "gave little if any thought to the importance of safeguards: for academic freedom, for freedom of expression, for dissent and for diversity."[86]

The classic elements of academic freedom encompass freedom in teaching, in research, and in the professor's right to speak as a citizen. But what about when these are not directly applicable, as in the regulation of outside speakers? Is there some common ground that must be shared by academic freedom, strictly defined, and by free speech, as articulated in what Post labels "the classic First Amendment tradition?"

Fish, not surprisingly, takes a rather extreme view: "Neither free speech—speech uttered by anyone who has something to say—nor political speech—speech intended to nudge students in one direction or the other—is a legitimate part of the academic scene," he contends. Such speech is strictly "extracurricular," a "sideshow." To be sure, "the university lets this stuff go on, but . . . it neither affirms nor repudiates any of the positions that vie for attention in the circus it allows on its grounds; it doesn't take those positions seriously, and it shouldn't."[87]

As far as Fish is concerned, there really is no free speech controversy on campus; there is, instead, what he deems a crisis of management. Fish is untroubled that protesting students can be "obnoxious, self-righteous, self-preening, shallow, short-sighted, intolerant, and generally impossible." In short, "they are students, doing what students do." It is, therefore, he argues, not the job of students (or, by implication, of their teachers) either to guarantee or to police free expression; that "is what administrations are supposed to do and what they are paid to do: Set up procedures for establishing, maintaining, and managing the various enterprises, academic and nonacademic, that fall within their purview." In short, he concludes, if nonacademic expression is to be permitted on campus, administrators must become more responsible "managers of crowd control."[88]

There are several problems with this approach. First, of course, is Fish's constricted view of academic governance, in which faculty have little to no responsibility for institutional affairs outside their closely defined roles in the classroom, the lab, and the library. As far as he is concerned, or so it would appear, faculty members need not concern themselves with the "sideshow" of outside speakers, but should leave that to the administration. The problem, of course, is that the line between the curricular and the extracurricular, the scholarly and the political, is hardly a bright one. For faculty to abdicate a role in the definition of this border, leaving it to managers, would be an obvious disaster. Just as advocates of free speech repeatedly point out how yielding to government the right to determine who may speak and what may be said will end up disproportionately limiting the rights of minorities and dissidents, advocates for academic freedom should recognize that empowering administrations to regulate the freedoms of outside speakers will ultimately empower administrative regulation of the faculty's own professional liberty.

Aaron Hanlon has argued that speaker invitations should always be products of discussion. He writes, "We should think about campus speakers less in terms of the so-called marketplace and more in the terms that guide other kinds of educational programming on campus. Inviting quality speakers to share expertise and experience is an important part of the educational mission. Just as scholars routinely disagree about which material belongs on the syllabus, administrators, faculty, and students can understandably and productively disagree over what makes a quality speaker. The process of reconciling that disagreement is bound to involve vocal opposition to some invited speakers, arguments made with varying degrees of merit and coherence."[89]

Under Fish's approach such discussion would for all intents and purposes be shunned. Since outside speakers are "extracurricular" and largely irrelevant to the university's mission, each group would be free to invite whomever it may please—or perhaps not be free to invite anyone at all—with minimal faculty participation but with the administration obliged to guarantee security. This is both impractical and wrong.

More to the point, another issue with Fish's argument is that he fails to address the problem of defining not only how speech is to be managed but also which speech is to be permitted. Since for him free speech is not even "a legitimate part of the academic scene," he'd clearly be content if there were never outside speakers, excluding perhaps a few visiting scholars invited by the faculty. But once such speakers are permitted—and there is hardly a college or university, public or private, that does not do so—how to establish which among them should be deemed acceptable remains undetermined. In short, Fish's view seems to be this: if you want to have speakers, fine, but it's not an academic concern, so just deal with it. Not much help.

Post, on the other hand, takes this bull by the horns. He concludes that while "the conceptual framework of academic freedom has not been elaborated to include outside speakers, the scope and bounds of the proper regulation of the speech of outside speakers must nevertheless be justified by reference to their contributions to the twin missions of the modern university," teaching and research.[90]

Do outside speakers contribute to one or the other of those missions, and if so, how? The assumption is that speakers invited by the institution or its faculty will have things to say relevant to teaching or research. If not, it is hard to justify their appearance. But what about when students, who "are accountable neither for the research mission of the university nor for its educational responsibilities," invite a speaker? Students may invite speakers for entertainment purposes, someone like, say, Chris Rock. Or speakers may be brought to campus for political purposes that have little to do with institutional mission. (Arguably, Milo Yiannopoulos fits both categories.) Even when students seek to invite speakers with greater academic credibility, their choices may be poor. Nevertheless, there are multiple reasons why the faculty of a university might yet encourage students to invite speakers of their choosing. Insofar as these reasons are left unstated or unquestioned, however, it will be difficult for the institution to decide how speaking events might be regulated. Colleges and universities, Post therefore suggests, must "determine how policies of authorizing student-invited speakers serve institutional purposes of education and the expansion of knowledge." On that basis they may be able to limit the terms under which speakers who do not advance those purposes may speak.

Starting from the assumption that "a college or university campus is an associational space, deliberately shaped in all sorts of ways to promote the university's purposes," Levy arrives at a rationale similar to Post's. Although "freedom of association vests primarily in the university itself," a campus may authorize the existence of closed student clubs under the rationale that "the quality of intellectual exchange is enhanced by allowing ideas to be developed, explored, and refined among those who share them. . . . Like academic freedom, clubs' associational freedom is justified and also shaped by the purposes of university life." From this Levy concludes, "While normally a secular university should not have viewpoint-based restrictions on, e.g., the sponsored speakers that student clubs bring to campus, its rules and its reasons here will differ from those of the liberal state" and may be "more restrictive."[91]

Some college and university administrations have sought to limit the access of provocative outside speakers on the grounds that their talks will result in violence. Universities are surely entitled to bar or severely restrict speakers whose declared or transparent goal is the initiation of violence, especially where a speaker's retinue may be armed (a situation rendered more difficult in "campus carry" states). Often, however, such justifications are little more than thinly veiled capitulations to the heckler's veto. Therefore, Post's approach may provide a firmer basis on which those who seek to limit the speech of provocateurs and bigots like Yiannopoulos or Coulter may found their arguments. Indeed, in many respects his idea that outside speakers must serve institutional missions provides the soundest basis for restricting speakers on the basis of what they have to say.

Nonetheless, in the end I don't find Post's remedy entirely persuasive. For one thing, Post's argument is in important respects a continuation of his long-standing effort to clarify the incoherence that surrounds academic freedom jurisprudence, driven by his growing concern about judicial efforts to apply First Amendment protections to "speech as such" rather than to public discourse.[92] Post contends that "the predictable over-extension of First Amendment rights will in the long run prove unsustainable." I agree; we can see negative impacts of this already in other spheres, most famously in campaign finance (*Citizens United*) and public employment (*Janus*) law. But it is hardly clear that Post's position, irrespective of its merit, has as yet been embraced by influential segments of the judiciary. As a consequence, it is questionable whether a public institution seeking to bar a student-invited speaker on the Postian grounds that the speaker's words are not relevant to the university's educational mission would prevail in court. Moreover, even the wisest efforts to limit controversial speech on the basis advocated by Post are likely only to fuel the impact of those whose ostensibly liberal advocacy of "free speech" thinly veils illiberal political aims.

In a footnote Post explains that he does "not consider situations where speakers come to campus based exclusively on private resources and without explicit university sanction, because in such circumstances the connection between speakers and universities becomes particularly difficult to define." However, some of the most controversial outside speakers (e.g., Coulter and Murray) are often privately funded and promoted, sometimes quite generously, with the institution providing only the venue and a student organization formal sponsorship.

More substantively, Post's approach demands a prior discussion of not only when but why colleges and universities should permit or even encourage nonacademic speech. Unlike Fish, who simply suggests that there is no academic justification at all for such speech, Post argues that justifications must derive from the university's central missions. "Unless they are wasting their resources on a frolic and detour," he says, universities "can authorize students to invite speakers only because it serves university purposes to do so. The problem is that universities typically undertheorize these purposes." *That, however, is quite a significant problem.* What purposes are served by permitting student-invited speakers? As much as conversations about this would be salutary, it is not at all clear that they could reach a common answer to this question, perhaps even at a single institution.

One response that many will no doubt advocate is that insofar as a purpose of higher education is training for better citizenship, the institutional purpose served will be to allow students to practice civic engagement in the relatively sheltered environment of the campus. But for this a First Amendment regime, so to speak, will be essential, much as editorial freedom is essential to the training of student journalists working in campus media. In addition, if colleges and universities remain by and large places where the diversity of views to be found is most extensive and least restricted, such diversity may not be a function entirely of the institutions' academic mission and may in good measure stem from permissive attitudes to the ideas and speech of nonacademic outsiders.

As Scott has suggested, societal benefit was a central concern of the AAUP's founders. "It was in defense of the university's role as the crucible of critique that the doctrine of academic freedom was formulated," she says.[93] The AAUP's 1915 *Declaration of Principles on Academic Freedom and Academic Tenure* emphasized the university's role as "an intellectual experiment station" serving the common good. It quoted (as does Scott) one university president: "It is better for students to think about heresies than not to think at all; better for them to climb new trails, and stumble over error if need be, than to ride forever in upholstered ease in the overcrowded highway." However, in the next sentence that president continued, "It is a primary

duty of a teacher to make a student take an honest account of his
stock of ideas, throw out the dead matter, place revised price marks
on what is left, and try to fill his empty shelves with new goods."[94] It
is difficult to see how that primary duty can be fully achievable without
allowing first for the expression of heresies, and not only academic
ones. And it is also difficult to imagine how the faculty themselves
can model "heresy" sufficiently enough to facilitate learning without employing examples from outside the realm of scholarship and
expertise.

In short, as Scott concludes, "We can respect the right of free
speech without having to respect the ideas being uttered." It is the
responsibility of the faculty to engage critically with ideas that enter higher education not only from the realm of scholarship but
also, perhaps in some areas even more, from the external "free
marketplace of ideas." But such engagement requires that heretical ideas, however repugnant or wacky, may be expressed in the
first place.

On Tolerance

In a previously cited essay published in response to the Middlebury events, Stephen L. Carter wrote, "Students who try to shut
down debate are not junior Nazis or proto-Stalins. If they were, I
would be content to say that their antics will wind up on the prover-
bial ash heap of history. Alas, the downshouters represent something more insidious. They are, I am sorry to say, Marcusians. A
half-century-old contagion has returned."[95]

Carter refers here to Herbert Marcuse, the late Frankfurt School
Marxist philosopher who in the 1960s gained notoriety as a supposed "theorist" of the New Left. Marcuse has long been scape-
goated by conservatives for his supposedly dangerous influence on
college youth. Liberals too have been highly critical of some of his
work. The problem lies with one of Marcuse's more notorious writings, his 1965 essay "Repressive Tolerance," one of three pieces in
the small but influential volume *A Critique of Pure Tolerance*.[96]
Here, according to Carter, Marcuse "sets out the argument that the

downshouters are putting into practice." This is how Carter describes that argument:

> For Marcuse, the fact that liberal democracies made tolerance an absolute virtue posed a problem. If society includes two groups, one powerful and one weak, then tolerating the ideas of both will mean that the voice and influence of the strong will always be greater. To treat the arguments of both sides with equal respect "mainly serves the protection and preservation of a repressive society." That is why, for Marcuse, tolerance is antithetical to genuine democracy and thus "repressive."
>
> He proposes that we practice what he calls a "liberating" or "discriminating" tolerance. He is quite clear about what he means: "tolerance against movements from the Right, and tolerance of movements from the Left." Otherwise the majority, even if deluded by false consciousness, will always beat back efforts at necessary change. The only way to build a "subversive majority," he writes, is to refuse to give ear to those on the wrong side. The wrong is specified only in part, but Marcuse has in mind particularly capitalism and inequality.

In the end, Carter concludes, "Marcuse lives. The downshouters will go on behaving deplorably, and reminding the rest of us that the true harbinger of an authoritarian future lives not in the White House but in the groves of academe."[97] (Yes, he wrote this during the Trump administration!)

I have always thought that Marcuse's influence and the influence in particular of this essay have been exaggerated. I encountered Marcuse's tolerance essay in college soon after it came out, but I'm pretty sure I was unusual among my fellow student radicals, some of whom may have heard of it but few of whom actually read it. And I doubt that any more than a tiny handful of today's protesters are even aware of Marcuse, much less dedicated to the promotion of his ideas. I will also acknowledge, on the other hand, that "Repressive Tolerance" is not one of Marcuse's more profound or persuasive writings and that important elements of its argument are questionable. That said, however, Carter's overwrought alarmism is both simplistic and misleading and merits rebuttal.

To begin, the question of tolerance or toleration may encompass but is hardly identical to the question of free speech. As the concept's leading intellectual historian, Rainer Forst, has demonstrated exhaustively, discussions of tolerance go back to the ancient Greeks and Romans. In those discussions "the demand for toleration is not situated above or beyond social disputes but emerges within them, so that its concrete shape is always tied to a particular social and historical context." Tolerance may be understood as "vertical," a form of state policy, or "horizontal," exercised mutually by members of a community in their behavior toward each other.[98] Historically, tolerance arose as a mode of managing religious conflict and not within the search for truth in the scholarly sense. Today, as another scholar of the concept, Wendy Brown, points out, tolerance has expanded its object from faith to identity.[99]

Tolerance is plagued by paradox. Most obvious is that in order to safeguard tolerance it may be necessary to be intolerant toward those who are themselves intolerant. But tolerance is also both authoritarian and majoritarian, since it is those in authority or in the majority who must agree to tolerate difference and dissent. Hence, tolerance will tend to favor the persistence of existing distinctions and inequalities. This was in fact Marcuse's main argument: "Generally, the function and value of tolerance depend on the equality prevalent in the society in which tolerance is practiced. . . . In other words, tolerance is an end in itself only when it is truly universal, practiced by the rulers as well as by the ruled." But in divided societies "the conditions of tolerance are 'loaded': they are determined and defined by the institutionalized inequality . . . i.e., by the class structure of society."[100]

"The liberating force of democracy was the chance it gave to effective dissent," Marcuse acknowledged. "But with the concentration of economic and political power and the integration of opposites in a society which uses technology as an instrument of domination, effective dissent is blocked where it could freely emerge."[101] Hence, Marcuse was raising a critical question I posed earlier: how can we ensure that all viewpoints may be fully aired, considered, discussed, and either accepted or rejected fairly, when some viewpoints are so structurally disadvantaged compared to those with far greater access to power?

"The telos of tolerance is truth," Marcuse states.[102] By this he refers to the classically liberal argument, articulated most famously in John Stuart Mill's *On Liberty*. According to that argument, we tolerate speech not because, as may be the case with religious faith, there is no objective truth to be found, or because truth must be a compromise among faiths, but precisely because there *is* objective truth that can be discovered, but only in the contest of ideas. However, Marcuse contends, such a contest cannot be rightly decided politically, much less democratically, given the power inequities of society and their extension into intellectual life—hence his controversial conclusion that "the realization of the objective of tolerance would call for intolerance toward prevailing policies, attitudes, opinions and the extension of tolerance to policies, attitudes, and opinions which are outlawed or suppressed."[103]

The question of toleration's relationship to scholarly inquiry was explored, more persuasively than by Marcuse in my view, by Barrington Moore Jr. in his essay "Tolerance and the Scientific Outlook," the second contribution to the 1965 *Critique*. Moore's argument may be encapsulated in this quote:

> According to the scientific outlook, every idea, including the most dangerous and apparently absurd ones, deserves to have its credentials examined. Still, examining credentials means exactly that. It does not mean accepting the idea. Toleration implies the existence of a distinctive procedure for testing ideas, resembling due process in the realm of law. No one holds that under due process every accused person must be acquitted. A growing and changing procedure for the testing of ideas lies at the heart of any conception of tolerance tied to the scientific outlook. That is genuine tolerance. It has nothing to do with a cacophony of screaming fakers marketing political nostrums in the public square. Nor does the real article exist where various nuances of orthodoxy pass for academic freedom.[104]

As I understand them, both Moore and Marcuse distinguish tolerance of ideas from tolerance of difference more generally. Both would suggest that ideas must be tolerated only prior to their decisive refutation. At least that would be the case in a college or university. In this sense their attitude to tolerance resembles Post's distinction between free speech in the societal marketplace of ideas and the more restrictive limits of academic freedom.

In his contribution to the *Critique*, "Beyond Tolerance," Robert Paul Wolff identified tolerance as the "virtue" of democratic pluralism. However, he wrote, "the application of the theory of pluralism always favors the groups in existence against those in process of formation. . . . Pluralism is a philosophy of equality and justice whose concrete application supports inequality by ignoring the existence of certain legitimate social groups."[105] As a consequence, "the unwillingness of the government to impose its own standards or rules results not in a free play of competing groups, but in the enforcement of the preferences of the existing predominant interests." Such may well be the case in the university as well. "The theory says justice will emerge from the free interplay of opposed groups; the practice tends to destroy that interplay."[106]

Taken together, the critique of tolerance offered by Wolff, Moore, and Marcuse is a powerful one and more sophisticated than the similar arguments offered by Ulrich Baer and Tracey Yoder discussed earlier. But only Marcuse offered the radical remedy that so terrifies Carter. In a postscript published in 1968, Marcuse concluded, "The tolerance which is the life element, the token of a free society, will never be the gift of the powers that be; it can, under the prevailing conditions of tyranny by the majority, only be won in the sustained effort of radical minorities, willing to break this tyranny and to work for the emergence of a free and sovereign majority—minorities intolerant, militantly intolerant and disobedient to the rules of behavior which tolerate destruction and suppression."[107]

But do those "conditions of tyranny" prevail in the contemporary American university? Just a few years after the *Critique* and in the wake of the 1968 student rebellion at Columbia, where he was a member of the faculty, Wolff stepped away from such an assumption. He concluded—as I would today—that "a great many colleges and universities are much freer, much more conducive to serious questioning and open debate, much more committed to human values than any other major institution in the United States. . . . There, if anywhere, new and deeper attacks on the evils of American society will be mounted. *Here again, the opposition role of the university flows from its very nature as a center of free inquiry.*"[108]

What then are we to make of the relationship between tolerance and free expression? I am not entirely certain, torn as I am between the critique of tolerance and the concomitant meritocratic definition of academic freedom, on the one hand, and my sense of the university as an ideal locus for the sort of unfettered "testing of ideas," even rotten ones, that Mill celebrated and Moore sought to identify with the scientific outlook, on the other. As Wendy Brown puts it, "To remove the scales from our eyes about the innocence of tolerance in relation to power is not thereby to reject tolerance as useless or worse." However, she continues,

> When the ideal or practice of tolerance is substituted for justice or equality, when sensitivity to or even respect for the other is substituted for justice for the other, when historically induced suffering is reduced to "difference" or to a medium of "offense," when suffering as such is reduced to a problem of personal feeling, then the field of political battle and political transformation is replaced with an agenda of behavioral, attitudinal, and emotional practices. While such practices often have their value, substituting a tolerant attitude or ethos for political redress of inequality or violent exclusions not only reifies politically produced differences but reduces political action and justice projects to sensitivity training, or what Richard Rorty has called an "improvement in manners." A justice project is replaced with a therapeutic or behavioral one.[109]

In other words, current controversies over free speech on campus, outside speakers, microaggressions, safe spaces, harassment, and dehumanization are not about civility, behavior, respect, or, as Fish might have it, the regulation and management of student life. They are at root about justice and, ultimately, power, and they can only be addressed intellectually through genuinely open and critical debate leading to concrete action. As Wolff concluded from his experience at Columbia, "There is not a single 'extracurricular' campus activity which can beat the appeal of a free and honest interplay of ideas."[110]

Chapter Nine

Can Unions Defend Academic Freedom?

Almost from its inception, the American Association of University Professors has been frequently referred to as a union.[1] The *New York Times*, for example, titled a scathingly hostile editorial greeting the association's formation "The Professors' Union." Although the association's first president, John Dewey, was a proud member of the American Federation of Teachers (AFT), the AAUP's founders went to great lengths to reject the union label. At the third annual meeting in 1917, President Frank Thilly argued that the AAUP's growth could be attributed to convincing faculty members that the group would refrain from union tactics. One member's letter, published in the AAUP *Bulletin*, seemed to validate that view, declaring it "unfortunate that we should have become identified in the public mind with a movement whose immediate concern is with the fortunes of the professors. It goes all right in a jocular way to be spoken of as a labor union, but an impression of this kind could do great damage to us if it becomes more than a joke. I fear that it has already reached that stage."[2] As Walter Metzger has written, "There was a deep aversion among academic men to entering into an organization whose purpose smacked of trade unionism." Writing in the early 1920s, Upton Sinclair was more brutal: "The first aim of the Association has apparently been to distinguish itself from labor unions," he wrote, "whereas the fact is that it is nothing but a labor union, an organization of intellectual proletarians, who have nothing but their brain-power to sell." If it was such a union, however, it was not, as Metzger noted, "'one big union for all,' but a union of the aristocrats of academic labor."[3]

The AAUP's early leaders saw their organization less as a defender of its members or even of the interests of the professoriate as a whole and more as a custodian of "higher education's contribution to the common good," a goal that remains an important element of the association's mission to this day.[4] However, as Hans-Joerg Tiede has demonstrated, the AAUP's initial focus on the defense of academic freedom was "set by events rather than by design and not without dissent." The "broader goal was to further the professionalization of the professoriate."[5]

Actually, in pursuit of professional ends the AAUP was from the start not wholly reluctant to address the "bread and butter" issues of salary, pensions, and working conditions that regularly concern trade unions. The 1915 *Declaration of Principles on Academic Freedom and Academic Tenure* acknowledged that one of the "ends to be accomplished" by means of tenure was "to render the profession more attractive to men of high ability and strong personality by insuring the dignity, the independence, and the *reasonable security* of tenure."[6] More practically, one of the association's earliest efforts involved negotiations with the Carnegie Foundation over the fate of the foundation's pension fund for teachers at select colleges and universities, which led eventually to the formation of what became the Teachers Insurance and Annuity Association.[7]

In such efforts, as in its defense of academic freedom, what distinguished the AAUP's approach from that of most unions was its aversion to agreements with individual institutions and its preference for establishing professional standards and persuading other national organizations and individual institutions to adhere to them. While the association considered faculty "the appointees, but not in any proper sense the employees," of university trustees, it also recognized that, unlike doctors and lawyers, faculty are not independent professionals and were indeed employees, albeit of a special kind.[8]

During the association's first few decades, this approach was not without foundation, especially when contrasted with the failures of union organizing. The AFT, founded just one year after the AAUP, began organizing university faculty with the establishment of the Howard University Teachers Union in 1918. But that local disbanded in 1920. In 1919, the AFT established a local at the University of Illinois, but it too soon collapsed. Similar stories can be told of early AFT and independent union efforts in New York and at a series of normal schools in the Midwest, Montana, and the Dakotas.[9]

According to Timothy Reese Cain, "AAUP leaders did not take the AFT lightly." In 1919, President Arthur Lovejoy, a longtime opponent of unionization, devoted a major portion of his presidential address to arguing against union membership. He was, however, challenged by members of the AAUP who also belonged to the Missouri University Teachers' Union, a short-lived AFT affiliate. Lovejoy argued that were AAUP members to join unions this would divide the professoriate and lessen its influence. The Missouri members responded that labor affiliation could achieve the opposite. The discussion continued later that year when Lovejoy and others participated in a symposium on faculty unionization in the pages of *Educational Review*.[10] This suggests that even at this early date the AAUP was not of one mind about the benefits of unionization in higher education.

Sentiment for collective bargaining could be found even among faculty members at the sorts of elite institutions most associated with the AAUP in those years. For instance, a faculty member at the University of Chicago declared, "The average milk driver is paid more than any assistant professor in the University of Chicago. A janitor gets more than a school principal. Plumbers get more than teachers. That is because milk drivers and plumbers and janitors have unions."[11] But many union locals, in both the AFT and the National Education Association (NEA), were unsuccessful or exceptionally small, with only a handful gaining majority support. Indeed, the initial flurry of organizing at both the K–12 and college levels in the immediate aftermath of World War I quickly subsided, as AFT membership declined from over ten thousand in 1919 to just three thousand two years later. By the end of the 1920s, only one AFT higher education local remained active.[12]

It may well be argued that the AAUP's approach had been vindi-cated. But this hardly meant that the organization did not remain concerned about the material situation of the profession. In 1937, the AAUP issued its first major report on the economic status of the professoriate, *Depression, Recovery, and Higher Education*, which would evolve into the association's much-vaunted annual reports on faculty compensation. Moderate in its tone, the report nonethe-less documented the sweeping impact of the Great Depression on faculty status, salaries, and benefits. "The depression raises the question of whether or not adequate consideration has been given to the men and women of lowest rank," the report concluded. "There is much to suggest that it has not."[13]

The report gave rise to renewed discussion of unionization. In a paper first read at a 1937 regional AAUP conference and reprinted in the *AAUP Bulletin*, Earl Cummins and Eric Larrabee, using a noto-rious phrase echoed by California governor Jerry Brown in the 1970s, argued,

> That any college professor who is worth his salt receives more in so-called "psychic income" than in his monthly pay-check is obvious. We know that during the depression literally thousands of teachers suf-fered actual want without quitting their posts, often increasing instead of diminishing their teaching loads, and we honor their magnificent devotion. But there are limits to which the substitution of emotional satisfaction for bread-and-butter can go; and most teachers live on such a narrow margin that they are swiftly reached. The pleasantness of our labors can not replace entirely the tangible rewards for very long, with most of us, at least.[14]

"Our colleges are no longer in the hands of their faculties," Cummins and Larrabee continued. "The final authority lies elsewhere; and the faculty members have the choice of dealing with it individually or collectively." Their preference was unequivocally for the latter, but they also firmly rejected "demands for the transformation of our pro-fessional association into a labor union, entailing the adoption of some, at least, of the common union methods of reaching its goals."[15]

Even this middle-ground approach attracted the ire of Lovejoy, who opined in a 1938 speech, reprinted in the *Bulletin*, "Any plan for 'unionizing' academic teachers is essentially inimical to the union of academic teachers in the discharge of what is at once their common and their special and peculiar responsibility—the defense of the standards and the integrity of their calling against dangers which threaten them from without, the energizing and improvement from within, through investigation and wide and free discussion, of the institutions and the processes devoted to the higher education of youth and the increase of man's knowledge and understanding." Yet Lovejoy also acknowledged that the association "*is* analogous to a trade union because the economic status of teachers is legally the same as that of most industrial workers. We are employees of corporations, private or public, not, like most doctors and lawyers, independent entrepreneurs."[16]

Lovejoy's comments prompted a response from one George Coe, who wrote,

> Almost immediately after reading your address there fell into my hands a statement of the objectives of the Northwestern University branch of the American Federation of Teachers. The main difference that I discern between this declaration pro and your declaration anti is that this professors' union, after going the whole way with you in your definition of professional standards, assumes that still other aims and standards are obligatory upon our profession. Further, it places the problem of academic freedom within the concrete social context that provides the dynamics and the contemporary meaning of higher education. It explains the attitude of some professors to the labor movement. They see in this movement an expression of basic meanings in American history; they regard the emancipation of labor as necessary to the maintenance and development of democracy; they are convinced that if democracy goes down, science will go down with it; hence, even as upholders of the freedom of science, they find themselves participating in the struggles of labor.[17]

Ultimately this discussion reached no conclusion.

In the aftermath of World War II, the left-leaning United Public Workers of America–CIO (UPWA), now largely forgotten, began efforts to organize college and university faculty and staff, winning some successes in New York and at historically black colleges and universities, including Howard University. At its second national convention in 1948, the UPWA adopted the *Statement on Academic Freedom*, which incorporated professors' right to unionize, "the right to join and be active in any political party or organization of their choice," and "the right as citizens to speak their minds and to act on public issues without fear of reprisal from their superiors." The *Statement* also declared "the right and obligation" of teachers "to develop an atmosphere of free inquiry in the classroom; to encourage students to discuss all sides of controversial issues." It failed, however, to include any reference to freedom in research and publication. The UPWA's efforts were short-lived, as the organization soon fell victim to the anti-Communist hysteria of the time.[18]

With the extraordinary expansion and democratization of higher education in the 1950s and 1960s and the ebbing of the anti-Communist panic of the 1950s—which, as Ellen Schrecker has shown, all but paralyzed the AAUP—discussions of collective bargaining in the association resumed, albeit slowly and hesitantly. At the 1957 annual meeting the membership amended the organization's constitution to add the word "welfare" to the phrase "to advance the standards and ideals of the profession," rejecting, however, an initial proposal to add the phrase "economic welfare." The meeting also asked the association "to establish as immediate objectives the discovery of tactical ways and means of securing proper salary levels throughout the country."[19]

Spurred by the rapid growth of higher education in the postwar decades, AAUP membership increased from 20,671 in 1946 to 68,900 in 1965.[20] With chapters emerging at former "normal schools" and in community colleges, and with the requirement that new members be nominated by current ones long abandoned, the association was no longer an organization of academic aristocrats.

In 1965, a special Self-Survey Committee reported, "The coming era in higher education is already showing features markedly different from those of the college and university world in which the older members of the Association grew up. If the Association expects to play an effective role in this new era, it should not allow itself to be taken by surprise; nor can it assume that the future into which we are moving is already determined without benefit of our effort and counsel."[21] By 1962, Melvin Lurie, an economics professor at the University of Rhode Island, was arguing in the *Bulletin* that "university professors are currently in an economic position that could, under effective unionism, result in a large increase in income over the next two decades. We could disguise our real goals by asking for and imposing higher standards on those desiring to enter the teaching profession."[22]

During the 1960s, the principal advocate for collective bargaining within the AAUP was Israel Kugler, then at the New York State Institute of Applied Arts and Sciences (currently New York City College of Technology). An AFT chapter vice president, Kugler responded to Lurie by calling on the AAUP to "recognize the true nature of the power structure in American education." He urged the association to transform "itself into a union" and "shed the illusion that college teachers are not professional employees but professionals on appointment."[23]

Lurie and Kugler were reacting to increased activity by the AFT and the NEA in higher education. The early 1960s saw the AFT's first major successes in organizing university faculty, especially in Wisconsin and New York, where enabling legislation opened opportunities in both two-year and four-year public institutions. The NEA, which had previously abjured collective bargaining, committed itself to the concept in 1962 and quickly entered the field of higher education organizing. As Philo Hutcheson noted, "With 1962 membership at 812,497, 1962 dues income at nearly $7,358,000, and sixty-nine national staff members plus many state staff members, the NEA's resources were far greater than those of the AFT or the AAUP."[24]

Hence, by the mid-1960s the AAUP was compelled to respond both to intensified discontent among faculty with their economic status and to the increasingly vigorous efforts of union rivals. The response, however, was slow and deliberate. In October 1964, the AAUP Council decided to plan and finance a national conference on collective bargaining. Although there was "a real sense of urgency because the profession was growing so fast" and "faculty members were feeling more and more remote from the administrators," former AAUP general secretary Bertram Davis later recalled that it was also "very, very difficult to see just what collective bargaining would mean for higher education and for the AAUP, whose approach was totally different."[25]

The December 1964 conference took only cautious steps in the direction of collective bargaining. While the meeting did suggest similarities between AAUP's activities and collective bargaining, there was as yet little enthusiasm for unionism among the association's leaders. As President David Fellman put it, "I think our position is that we would not suggest to a chapter becoming a union but would suggest to a chapter acting as a union. . . . We bring pressure on the administration and I suppose this in a sense is collective bargaining."[26]

The association's ambivalence was soon challenged by events at St. John's University in New York. The AAUP first learned of "strained relations between the faculty and the administration" at St. John's in 1963. A group of faculty members at the university organized an AAUP chapter, but the administration only agreed to negotiate with the AAUP after the AFT began to organize a union local. The association devoted much effort to settling disagreements at St. John's, but initial progress was reversed when, in December 1965, the university informed the AAUP that termination notices had been sent to thirty-one faculty members, including twenty-one who were "summarily separated from their classroom duties" because, the administration alleged, they had engaged in "organized opposition amounting to a rebellion."[27]

The AAUP responded in its usual manner, conducting a formal investigation that led to the administration's censure in 1966. But the St. John's AFT local responded by calling for a faculty strike, and when classes opened on January 4, 1966, about two hundred faculty pickets were at the university's gates. Two days later the AAUP responded with an ambiguous statement. The association declared that it "has never looked upon the strike as an appropriate mechanism for resolving academic controversies or violations of academic principles and standards. . . . Accordingly, the Association does not endorse a strike against an academic institution." At the same time, however, the statement argued that "a refusal by individual faculty members to cross picket lines maintained by colleagues, when their refusal is based upon personal dictates of conscience and their intimate familiarity with the facts, should not be considered a violation of professional ethics."[28]

While the strike was defeated (St. John's faculty would win union recognition, with AAUP representation, a few years later), the conflict highlighted the limits of AAUP's traditional approach to violations of academic freedom. As Hutcheson concluded,

> The AAUP had expended tremendous resources in its attempts to negotiate with the administration and the Board of Trustees at St. John's University, but the administration and the board refused to negotiate about the summary dismissals, which the AAUP deemed to be blatant violations of principles of academic freedom and tenure. Given that the board had announced support for the 1940 *Statement* not only before the dismissals but also in the spring of 1966, St. John's University in this period presents a remarkable example of administrative and governing board intransigence. They would accept the principles of academic freedom and tenure as and when they cared to do so; they clearly saw themselves as managers of the university, and the professors as employees to be dismissed at will.[29]

In 1966, in the wake of the St. John's events and expanding activities by the AFT and the NEA, the Special Committee on the Representation of Economic Interests, appointed after the December 1964 conference, presented its report, recommending AAUP adoption of the *Statement of Policy on the Role of Association Chapters as Exclusive*

Bargaining Representatives. The statement, ultimately approved by the council, continued the association's guarded ambivalence on the question of collective bargaining, declaring, "If these conditions [of effective faculty voice and adequate protection and promotion of faculty economic interests] are not met, and a faculty feels compelled to seek representation through an outside organization, the Association believes itself, by virtue of its principles, programs, experience and broad membership to be best qualified to act as representative of the faculty in institutions of higher education." Presenting the statement, Clyde Summers, chair of the special committee, explained its reasoning in these terms:

> The question confronting the Association is not whether it shall become a "union," or whether it shall engage in "collective bargaining," for to cast the issue in those terms is to submit to the tyranny of labels. The Proposed Statement makes as plain as words permit that the Association shall continue, and with all means at hand, to assert and implement its historic role as a professional organization which views the university as a community of scholars in which all faculty shall participate through democratic structures of university government. It is true that a chapter may become an "exclusive representative" similar to a union, but only when state laws or administrative policies of the institution leave the chapter with no viable alternative. And in acting as exclusive representative, the chapter must reject methods and devices commonly associated with unions. The chapter must not assert exclusive right to present grievances but must provide a procedure open to any individual or group. The chapter must disown the use of the strike or work stoppage. And the chapter cannot require any member of the faculty to join or pay dues to the chapter. The underlying premise of the Proposed Statement is that the Association, in confronting the practical problem, shall seek to evolve through experience procedures and structures for faculty representation which are not those of unions, but which are especially designed for the special status of faculty members within an academic community.[30]

Not long after, in February 1967, the faculty at Belleville College in Illinois (now Southwest Illinois College) voted to designate the AAUP chapter as its exclusive bargaining representative, replacing an AFT local that had negotiated on its behalf alongside local K–12 teachers. Although the 1966 statement of policy required individual chapters to obtain permission from the national office before initiating representation, the Belleville faculty failed to do so. Thus, wrote AAUP president Clark Byse, "did collective bargaining come to the AAUP—in Belleville, Illinois, without the knowledge, encouragement, or consent of the General Secretary or the officers or Council of the AAUP."[31]

Nonetheless, the association did not disavow the Belleville move. From that point on, growing pressure from below pushed leaders into ever more active support of collective bargaining by the AAUP. In 1970, Rutgers University, St. John's, and Oakland University in Michigan became the first three AAUP collective bargaining agents at four-year universities.

In 1968, after another strike over academic freedom—this one successful—at Catholic University the previous year,[32] the council issued a new statement on strike participation, declaring that "situations may arise affecting a college or university which so flagrantly violate academic freedom of students as well as of faculty or the principles of academic government, and which are so resistant to rational methods of discussion, persuasion, and conciliation, that faculty members may feel impelled to express their condemnation by withholding their services, either individually or in concert with others."[33] In 1969, the association inched further toward endorsement of collective bargaining when in a revised version of the 1966 statement it recognized "the significant role which collective bargaining may play in bringing agreement between faculty and administration on economic and academic issues. Through the negotiation of a collective agreement, it may in some institutions be possible to create a proper environment for faculty and administration to carry out their respective functions and to provide for the eventual establishment of necessary instruments of shared authority."[34]

Then, after a 1971 "Summer Study" by a committee led by law professor Robert Gorman, the AAUP's executive committee submitted a confidential report to the council that endorsed collective bargaining. The Gorman report presented two alternative approaches. The first would incorporate collective bargaining as an essential activity of the association. The second approach would divide the AAUP, with one component functioning in the traditional manner and the other as a union. The Gorman report also included dissenting statements from the association's vice president and chair of Committee A, William Van Alstyne, supported by all but one member of that body. They argued that entry into collective bargaining would limit the association's impact on campuses where other unions represented the faculty, lessen support for AAUP principles among administrations, and lead to a loss of membership. Nevertheless, on October 31, 1971, the council voted to "pursue collective bargaining as a major additional way of realizing the Association's goals," effectively accepting the Gorman report's first approach. The decision was endorsed at the June 1972 annual meeting, and the next year the association adopted the *Statement on Collective Bargaining*, which both accepted such activity as an "effective instrument for achieving" the AAUP's traditional goals and trumpeted the association's unique qualifications to shape bargaining consistent with professional standards of academic freedom and shared governance.[35]

The AAUP's endorsement of collective bargaining led to a rapid expansion of its union activities, fueled in part by a dues increase adopted by the membership meeting to fund union organizing. In 1972, the AAUP won certification as bargaining agent for faculty at eight additional four-year institutions, four private and four public. By the end of 1975, the association represented faculty at thirty-five colleges and universities, about half the present number. However, while collective bargaining membership grew, overall membership declined, as opponents of unionization had predicted, going from

78,000 in 1969 to about 60,000 in 1976. It is unclear, however, whether these losses might not have been equaled or even exceeded had the association declined to enter the bargaining arena, because losses among those opposed to bargaining might easily have been matched by losses at institutions where pro-bargaining members could desert the association for other unions.[36]

The transition to bargaining was facilitated by the election in 1974 of law professor Van Alstyne, initially an opponent of unionization, as AAUP president. Although two pro–collective bargaining candidates divided a majority of voters, Van Alstyne won with support from major collective bargaining leaders, who hoped his election would unify the organization. Van Alstyne made good on this hope, successfully defeating efforts to limit funding for collective bargaining organizing. In his 1976 presidential address Van Alstyne proclaimed the association "more effective in more ways than at any time in its history." He identified two concerns for the AAUP: that the association develop its own distinct approach to bargaining and that it not be reticent about involvement in such activity. On the latter point, he declared, "We have not been half-hearted, and we have in fact made it a resounding success." In sharp contrast to his previous opposition to collective bargaining, the former Committee A chair now boasted, "The presence of the Association in collective bargaining has also brought with it the flattery of widespread imitation: not only do our own agreements reflect the enforceable contractualizing of the 1940 *Statement* and related AAUP standards, but the other associations and unions have now reached the point where negotiation for recognition of AAUP standards is commonplace throughout collective bargaining in higher education."[37]

Nevertheless, tensions remained. In 1980, the US Supreme Court, in the case of *National Labor Relations Board v. Yeshiva University*, ruled that tenured and tenure-track faculty members at private universities are managers and hence exempt from the protections of the National Labor Relations Act.[38] As Ernst Benjamin has argued, *Yeshiva* "was inimical to not only faculty bargaining but also the core principles of the Association." Further, "the decision disproportionately impaired the development of AAUP bargaining because the AAUP was more competitive at private than at public universities. . . . The consequent need to focus on public-sector organizing reinforced the argument in favor of joint ventures [with the AFT or NEA] with their attendant difficulties."[39] In short, by overlaying a public-private divide on the distinction between collective bargaining and non–collective bargaining chapters, *Yeshiva* could tend to exacerbate divisions.

A second Supreme Court case proved more traumatic, albeit mainly in the short term. Shortly after ruling in *Yeshiva*, the court granted certiorari in the case of *Minnesota Board for Community Colleges v. Knight*, decided in 1984. In that case the Minnesota NEA argued that its exclusive right to bargain on behalf of community college faculty outweighed the rights of individual professors, including twenty individual faculty members who filed suit, to participate in shared governance. The association prepared an amicus brief in support of the appellants and shared governance, but the leadership of the AAUP Collective Bargaining Congress (CBC), which had emerged as the national representative of the unionized chapters, rejected its claims. The court ultimately ruled in favor of the NEA that governance arrangements of the sort it had cited in finding the Yeshiva faculty to be managers were not constitutionally protected under state laws affording the faculty collective bargaining rights.

In a sharply worded report delivered shortly after the decision, and reflecting some of the bitterness the *Knight* controversy had engendered, Committee A chair Matthew Finkin argued that for the association the question in *Knight* had been clear: "This arrangement was plainly violative of the joint *Statement on Government of Colleges and Universities*."[40] According to Finkin, the leaders of the CBC offered four arguments against the AAUP brief: "(1) The AAUP should not appear on the same side as the Right to Work Foundation, which had supported the suit; (2) the AAUP should not attack the principle of exclusive representation; (3) the AAUP should not attack the contract of a sister union; and (4) the AAUP should not advance a position that the CBC does not support." In Finkin's view, the first argument "could not be taken seriously," since, like the American Civil Liberties Union, the association had more than a few times in the past found itself defending academic freedom in the company of groups it otherwise found distasteful. The second argument he found "even more disturbing, for it would place a new, much higher emphasis upon exclusive representation," which the association had previously seen "as a desirable way of achieving recognition of AAUP principles" but not "as an end in itself." The third and fourth arguments, Finkin concluded, were essentially political and not principled, but he feared that "the CBC leadership sees every issue as political."

Finkin had been an advocate of the association's entry into collective bargaining, and he hastened to assure members that his remarks were "not an attack on the validity of collective bargaining for the professoriate." Nonetheless, citing precipitous declines in AAUP membership at major research universities and selective private colleges and the growing dominance of the membership by a relatively small number of collective bargaining chapters, several of whom were only affiliates, he expressed fear of "the demise of the Association's mission as the paramount professorial voice in defense of academic freedom and tenure." He worried that "when the profession comes to see Committee A as speaking, in essence, for a couple of dozen collective bargaining organizations, the usefulness of Committee A in its traditional mission will be at an end. We will be perceived, and rightly, as just another faction, parochial and self-serving."[41]

Fears that a commitment to collective bargaining might undermine the AAUP's traditional commitment to academic freedom and tenure were somewhat assuaged by events at Temple University in 1985. Here the association investigated and censured the university administration for laying off faculty in violation of AAUP principles, even though the layoffs were legal under a "retrenchment" provision of Temple's collective bargaining agreement with the university's AAUP chapter, a provision approved by a vote of the chapter membership even after imposition of censure. This censure decision made clear that the association would not weaken, much less abandon, its historic commitment to academic freedom and tenure even at institutions where its own collective bargaining agreements authorized administrations to take actions inconsistent with that commitment.[42]

In addition, as Ernst Benjamin has recalled, his selection as the first general secretary from a collective bargaining unit also facilitated the association's stability. He concluded,

> I believe that the Association and to a remarkable extent the profession have successfully integrated collective bargaining with the commitment to academic freedom, tenure, shared governance, and professional standards. . . . Where the Association and faculty generally have adopted it collective bargaining has tended to strengthen AAUP-supported standards and procedures. Moreover, the collective bargaining faculty who now provide the greater share of Association resources and make the AAUP's continued support of national standards possible are plainly subsidizing those many faculty members who do not contribute to the organization's work. In view of the ever-increasing managerialism that confronts us throughout academe, and the consequent erosion of the shared values between faculty and academic administrators that have helped sustain the AAUP's core principles, I do not see an alternative to pursuing collective bargaining and advocacy organizing.[43]

Collective bargaining agreements, it might be argued, share much with noncontractual arrangements like shared governance policies and faculty handbooks. If some contracts are weak and ineffective, so too are many academic senates. But by and large, as one recent empirical study has demonstrated, "faculty unions have a positive effect on the level of faculty influence at public institutions." Predictably, the study found, faculty at unionized institutions have more say in determination of their salaries, but "they also have more influence in many other areas, such as appointments of faculty and department chairs, tenure and promotion, teaching loads and the curriculum, and governance."[44]

Nevertheless, the tensions highlighted by Finkin have not disappeared. As I have argued, however, they've existed from the origins of the association. Indeed, these tensions may be inherent in the very position that faculty occupy in society. Sociologist Erik Olin Wright has pointed out, as the AAUP itself has always implicitly recognized, that college and university faculty occupy an "objectively contradictory class location." Professors are similar to independent professionals in many ways, but they are actually employees of large private and state bureaucracies. Faculty members are also increasingly similar to salaried workers with respect to employer-employee relations, but they are not such workers. Thus, as Clyde Barrow has concluded, "faculty ambivalence toward competing forms of organization is anchored in their objective structural location in capitalist society."[45]

In his useful and detailed, but conceptually somewhat muddled, study of the AAUP's gradual embrace of collective bargaining, Philo Hutcheson argued that the shift to collective bargaining arose as a consequence of the increasing tension between the bureaucratization of the university and the professionalism of its faculty. But the proper distinction is not between professionalism and bureaucracy. As Benjamin perceptively put it in a review of Hutcheson's book,

> AAUP policies recognize that faculty as professionals are employed in bureaucratic organizations . . . and seek to protect professional autonomy through the construction of bureaucratic rules and procedures defining appointments, tenure, and academic governance. Moreover, the distinguishing characteristic of managerialism is in fact the search for entrepreneurial 'flexibility' through a systematic deconstruction of established institutional rules, including AAUP-recommended standards. Bargaining to reinforce orderly personnel procedures and long-standing AAUP policies was not, as Hutcheson suggests, a triumph of bureaucracy over professionalism, but an extension of AAUP's efforts to safeguard professional autonomy and academic governance against entrepreneurial managerialism within an established bureaucratic framework.[46]

Similarly, it is equally incorrect to oppose professionalism to unionism, as the early AAUP leaders did and too many faculty members still do today. The concept of a union of professionals that not only seeks improvements in salaries, benefits, and working conditions but also strives to enforce broader professional standards and principles is not unique to the AAUP or even to academia. For example, attorneys in the public sector, including district attorneys and public defenders, are frequently represented by unions, but this hardly constrains their engagement with and conformity to the standards of the professional bar. The same can certainly be said of K–12 teachers, whose unions help defend and define professional standards. Moreover, as a historian of Tsarist Russia, I cannot help but mention the emergence during the first Russian Revolution of 1905—a decade before the founding of the AAUP—of unions of railwaymen (defined to include not only engine drivers and switchmen but also, even mainly, midlevel managers and professional engineers), teachers, agronomists, and pharmacists. These professional groups came together to form a Union of Unions, which the more "proletarian" socialists in the factories considered petty bourgeois.[47]

In 2005, the AAUP's CBC endorsed a lengthy statement defining the association's approach to academic unionism, which both underpins current AAUP collective bargaining efforts and helps explain the appropriate relationship between unionism and professionalism:

> Academic unions are the most recent in a long line of collegial struc tures forged to protect the rights and professional roles of academics. Increasingly, tenure-track and contingent faculty, academic professionals, and graduate assistants have formed unions to ensure their professional standing and protect themselves from the threats and challenges presented by the corporatization of American colleges and universities. . . .
>
> Academics generally regard their primary obligations to be to their professional communities, their students, and the larger public rather than to political edicts or ideologically biased mandates from above. . . .

An AAUP union is not an off-campus organization. It is the profession, in an organized form. It is an amplified voice of the faculty and other academic professionals—a voice they use to achieve their needs. . . .

A union of professionals committed to retaining power and autonomy in their work must be organized differently from other institutions in modern America. . . . Faculty and academic professionals join unions not just to get higher wages, but also to maintain authority and a primary role in the university. . . .

The nation's campuses have carved out vital public spheres in American society. They have been the training ground for its future citizens. By ensuring an open and challenging education for college students, conducted by trained and committed academics, a renewed academic union movement can be crucial in continuing the American experiment of making a high-quality liberal education available to all U.S. citizens.[48]

These principles are consistent with those first enunciated by the AAUP's founders a century ago and with principles of shared governance. As Mary Burgan pointed out, "In the AAUP model of unionism, the faculty senate is not replaced by a collective bargaining unit but rather supported and informed by it." Moreover, it should also be stressed that the AAUP's distinctive combination of union organization and professional association may provide the most effective method of defending professional principles today. "One often-ignored reason for the faculty's choice of collective bargaining," argued Burgan, "is that the culture and expertise of unions can improve faculty effectiveness and efficiency. The definiteness in the procedures and rules set up in union contracts offers more clarity than less formal modes of institutional agreements can do."[49]

Unfortunately, many faculty members at US institutions of higher learning are by law currently unable to engage in collective bargaining. There is, of course, the *Yeshiva* decision. Moreover, in many states, the lack of appropriate enabling legislation leaves employees at public colleges and universities, including faculty, without the right to bargain collectively. Even where this right exists, faculty unions, including those affiliated with the AAUP, have been weakened by the Supreme Court's 2018 decision in the *Janus* case, which barred the collection of fair representation fees from nonmember public employees. And in an increasing number of states—recent events in Wisconsin, Michigan, and Iowa come to mind—expanded restrictions on union activity, including so-called right-to-work laws, hamstring organizing efforts (see chap. 10). Such restrictions limit not only academic unionism but also the union movement as a whole, which now represents a much-diminished portion of the US labor force.

In this environment the AAUP's continuing commitment to represent not only its own unionized membership but also its thousands of nonunionized "advocacy" members and, indeed, the profession as a whole; to organize and recruit for both union and nonunion chapters; and to continue developing and defending meaningful professional standards in support of "the common good" has become more essential—and arguably more practical—than ever. If unions are to remain viable defenders of those who work, be their labor physical or mental, they will need to organize and act in new ways. They will need to organize and act across workplaces and across industries, locally and regionally, both in traditional union structures and in new forms—some akin to associations like the AAUP—employing new strategies and tactics capable of mobilizing public support and exerting political pressure and moral suasion beyond the workplace. If this be true, the AAUP's creative blending of professionalism and unionism, developed slowly and fitfully over the past century, may provide a model not only for other professions but also for the union movement as a whole in the century to come.

Chapter Ten

What Is the Future of Academic Freedom under the Trump Regime?

On November 9, 2016, faculty members across the country awoke to the realization that Donald J. Trump would be the next president of the United States. Many wondered what this would mean for our country in general and academia in particular. We are now well into the Trump regime, and it is clear that President Trump is doing exactly what candidate Trump promised: trying to enact an extremist version of the recent Republican program, assaulting the rights of Muslims and immigrants, and promoting an agenda that many of its own proponents proudly call "white nationalism."

Within hours of Trump's victory, the American Association of University Professors issued a statement to its members. While acknowledging that the association does not engage in partisan politics and has never endorsed a candidate for national office, the statement also recognized the widespread fear that Trump's election "threatened some of the core institutions of our democracy and may be the greatest threat to academic freedom since the McCarthy period."[1] The statement noted in particular that Trump's campaign remarks about minorities, immigrants, and women on some campuses already had a chilling effect on the rights of students and faculty members. It pointed out how Trump's call for an "ideological screening test" for admission to the United States could make it difficult for colleges and universities to attract students and scholars from abroad and engage in the international exchange of ideas vital to academic freedom and the pursuit of knowledge. Lastly, it expressed alarm that the Republican denial of climate change, and often of the validity of science itself, represents a dangerous threat to the essential core of higher education's mission.

In response, the AAUP pledged to

1. oppose the privatization of our public higher education system and fight for higher education as a common good, accessible and affordable to all;

2. oppose discrimination on the basis of race, gender, sexual orientation, disability, religion, or national origin and fight for an equitable and welcoming educational environment in which all can freely and safely learn, discuss, differ, debate, and grow;

3. oppose attacks on unions and the economic security of college and university faculty and staff and fight for expanding and strengthening the rights of all those engaged in teaching and research in higher education—tenured and tenure-track faculty members, faculty members in contingent positions, and graduate student employees—to organize and bargain collectively; and

4. oppose violations of academic freedom and of the broader rights to free expression in the academic community and fight for strengthened protections for and renewed commitment to the 1940 *Statement of Principles on Academic Freedom and Tenure* and the 1966 *Statement on Government of Colleges and Universities.*

The statement also emphasized that "the problems facing higher education today and the growing assault on the professionalism and freedoms of faculty members over the past several decades can hardly be attributed to the results of a single election. Many of these problems stem from ill-conceived policies developed and implemented on a bipartisan basis." Nevertheless, it must be acknowledged that, in light of Trump's subsequent appointments and executive orders, as well as his proposed federal budgets, under his presidency these assaults are intensifying.

This concluding chapter looks at each of these pledges in turn, shedding some light on what has already occurred, what may yet occur, and what the AAUP has been trying to do in response.

Privatization

Well before Donald Trump emerged as a national political figure, the AAUP was concerned about the decades-long movement to privatize America's public colleges and universities in the spirit of "academic capitalism."[2] In *The Great Mistake: How We Wrecked Public Universities and How We Can Fix Them*, University of California professor Christopher Newfield wrote, "Submitting public universities to private sector standards hasn't increased their overall wealth and made their education more efficient. It has increased their costs and shifted resources from the educational core. . . . Private sector 'reforms' are not the cure for the college cost disease—they are the college cost disease."[3] Some forty years of privatization and academic capitalism have yielded declining quality, decreased access, and burgeoning student debt. Underlying these developments has been a steady abandonment of the core principle that the AAUP has stressed since its founding in 1915: higher education, both public and private, is a common good, not a private commodity.[4] Today, however, higher education is treated increasingly as a benefit available only to those able to pay for it, or those willing to amass crushing debt to gain its benefits.

Temple University professor Sara Goldrick-Rab has noted that colleges and universities promote the idea that they can regularly increase tuition so long as they also increase financial aid. But, she concludes, "we've failed to actually implement that model. We told ourselves a story over and over where our students are actually all right, or they must be, or we wouldn't be able to sleep at night, quite frankly." But our students are *not* all right. As Goldrick-Rab has exhaustively documented, shocking numbers of college students go hungry, and many are homeless.[5] Now, as previously underserved populations—ethnic minorities, the poor, immigrants—have entered higher education, the resources provided to serve them have steadily diminished.

In every state except Wyoming, the share of revenue that public colleges receive from tuition—students and families—has grown since 2001. "Tuition is far too high, grant aid is far too insufficient," says Mark Huelsman, a senior policy analyst at Demos who has studied the issue. "If you add on top of that minimum wages that haven't increased in a lot of states, the affordability crisis becomes a pretty massive issue." More specifically, Huelsman added, the challenges of paying for college have become "both a racial justice issue, and also an economic justice issue." On average, the cost of a public, four-year degree—*after* scholarships and grant aid are accounted for—is equivalent to about one-third of the median income of black families and one-quarter of the median income of Latino families. For white families, that so-called net price amounts to about one-fifth of the median income.[6]

Although President Trump has not articulated a clear program for higher education, it is not too daring to say that his administration is embracing and even accelerating the privatization agenda, with its ominous implications for educational quality and the survival of academic freedom and shared governance. Secretary of Education Betsy DeVos initially appeared woefully ignorant about higher education (among other things), but her demonstrated devotion to extreme privatization of K–12 education in Michigan hardly boded well. Deep cuts to public higher education under Republican governors such as Scott Walker in Wisconsin, Bruce Rauner in Illinois, John Kasich in Ohio, and Mike Pence in Indiana, and under Republican legislatures in Iowa and North Carolina, suggest the likelihood of similar cuts in federal aid, including student aid, under Trump. Hence, it was hardly a surprise when, in February 2018, Trump and DeVos proposed a fiscal 2019 federal budget that would slash nearly $4 billion in annual funding for student aid programs. Over time the cuts could amount to as much as $200 billion, according to Senator Patty Murray (D-WA), ranking Democrat on the Senate Committee on Health, Education, Labor and Pensions.[7]

And it appears that Trump and DeVos have begun to seriously weaken, if not entirely eliminate, efforts begun under President Obama to rein in abuses characteristic of many for-profit institutions.[8] In June 2017, the Department of Education blocked two rules, set to take effect the next month, that would have clarified how student borrowers can have their loans forgiven if they were defrauded or misled by their college. In July 2018, DeVos proposed curtailing Obama administration loan forgiveness rules for students defrauded by for-profit colleges, requiring that to be eligible for the forgiveness program borrowers must demonstrate how they have fallen into hopeless financial straits or prove that their colleges knowingly deceived them. The next day it was revealed that the department has been planning to eliminate the rule requiring for-profit and vocational programs to prove that they are preparing graduates for gainful employment.[9] "Unlike the last Republican administration, this one seems to lack any proactive agenda to make higher education more affordable and improve student outcomes," opined two former Department of Education officials. "Instead, DeVos's only agenda so far is to undo critical policies through an ongoing assault on meaningful reforms. . . . This deregulatory agenda constitutes no less than an attack on the very heart of higher education."[10]

As this book was in its final stage of editing, the Department of Education announced an ambitious round of negotiated rulemaking, a public comment and deliberation process, on over a dozen higher education topics, most notably accreditation. Also up for review are "rules about how the government measures learning for the purpose of awarding federal aid; whether and how distance learning must be authorized in the states; and allowing a wider range of noninstitutional providers and religious schools access to federal student aid," the *Chronicle of Higher Education* reported.[11] According to *Inside Higher Ed*, "The changes the department is mulling give the clearest sign so far of an affirmative higher education agenda from the Trump administration."[12]

Under Secretary of Education Diane Auer Jones said that the administration wants to allow accreditors to "tolerate some risk." For example, she said, the department wants to encourage colleges to offer degrees through new online models at more affordable prices. Earlier in the year DeVos reinstated the Accrediting Council for Independent Colleges and Schools, which had certified both Corinthian

Colleges and ITT Tech, two enormous for-profit colleges that collapsed in scandal. The department now proposes "simplifying the Department's process for recognition and review of accrediting agencies."[13]

Among the most significant long-term changes proposed by the administration may be elimination of the standard credit-hour definition and overhaul of the so-called regular and substantive requirements for faculty member interactions with students. Under current rules, distance education courses must have a certain amount of student-instructor contact to be more than simply correspondence courses. In an audit last year of Western Governors University, a non-profit, online entity, the department's inspector general found violations of this standard and called for penalties. The audit found that the institution's "mentors" were not faculty but more like advisers and that most lecture-like content is delivered through videos, not in real time. The audit was simply advisory, however, and the department is free to ignore its recommendations, which so far it has. A department spokesperson said, "It is important to note that the innovative student-first model used by this school and others like it has garnered bipartisan support over the last decade."[14]

The rulemaking process was set to begin in 2019 and would allow "experts and stakeholder groups" to consider how best to encourage "innovative" delivery models. But experts warned that the administration is taking on too many issues in too little time for negotiators to engage in meaningful discussion, much less reach consensus. "They've made it clear they are interested in lowering regulatory burden and don't seem to be invested in finding out how to do that responsibly," said Clare McCann, deputy director for federal higher education policy at New America, a nonpartisan think tank.[15]

Discrimination

In recent years student demands for so-called safe spaces have come under criticism, with a few voices charging—quite inaccurately— that such demands have become the principal threat to academic freedom and free expression on campus (see chap. 7). Far more dangerous, however, have been those who would deny that increasingly it is the physical safety of scholars—both students and faculty—that is endangered, often by racially motivated violence.

As the Southern Poverty Law Center (SPLC) reported in 2017, "In the immediate aftermath of Election Day, a wave of hate crimes and lesser hate incidents swept the country—1,094 bias incidents in the first 34 days." While hate crimes typically spike during election years, FBI statistics analyzed by the *Washington Post* revealed that "there were more reported hate crimes on November 9 than any other day in 2016, and the daily number of such incidents exceeded the level on Election Day for the next ten days." Moreover, the SPLC reported, the number of hate groups in the country rose from 892 in 2015 to 917 in 2016 and 954 in 2017, not much fewer than the 1,018 tallied in 2011, which was the all-time high in some thirty years of SPLC counts.[16] According to a February 2018 SPLC report, over one hundred people were killed or injured in 2017 by alleged perpetrators influenced by the so-called alt-right. The Anti-Defamation League reported that white supremacists and other far-right extremists were responsible for 59 percent of all extremist-related fatalities in the United States in 2017, up from 20 percent in 2016. Another study found that white supremacist Twitter accounts have increased by more than 600 percent since 2012 and outperform ISIS accounts by every possible metric.[17]

Such developments have profound implications for colleges and universities. In early 2017, National Public Radio reported "an unprecedented spike in white supremacist activity on campuses across the U.S." They noted that "hate watch groups have tracked 150 incidents of white supremacist propaganda on campuses since" the presidential election. The Anti-Defamation League reported that incidents of white supremacist propaganda on US campuses more than tripled in 2017. These reports were bolstered in early 2018 when the US Department of Education revealed that the number of campus hate crimes reported under the Clery Act increased by

25 percent from 2015 to 2016. In 2016, the department found, colleges and universities reported a total of 1,250 hate crimes, defined as offenses motivated by biases of race, national origin, ethnicity, religion, sexual orientation, gender, or disability. Over the previous four years, colleges reported an average of 970 hate crimes annually, with little variation from year to year. Additional college-specific data, collected by the FBI, suggested that the election itself played a role in the surge of reported cases. From 2012 to 2015, police departments at select public colleges, universities, and medical schools reported an average of twenty hate crimes to the FBI in the month of November. In November 2016, however, the same group of departments reported forty-eight hate crimes. Before that, the most hate-related incidents the group of colleges had reported in one month was forty, in February 2014.[18]

In the weeks after the election, a black woman studying at Villanova University was attacked on campus by a group of white men chanting "Trump! Trump! Trump!" In Oregon, two bathrooms at Reed College's library were defaced with racist, homophobic, anti-semitic, and pro-Trump graffiti. In Massachusetts, at Wellesley College, Hillary Clinton's alma mater, students awoke after the election to find a large truck driving slowly through campus with a Trump flag flying off its back. Two men in the truck went to the house for students of African descent, rode around campus yelling at students, and spit toward a student when asked to leave. Other incidents included the alleged robbery of a Muslim student at San Diego State University by two men who "made comments about President-elect Donald Trump and the Muslim community," before stealing her purse, rucksack, and car. At San José State University, a sophomore said someone grabbed her hijab from behind and yanked it backward, choking her. White students at Southern Illinois University reportedly decided to put on blackface and pose in front of a Confederate Flag to celebrate Trump. A student from Baylor University said she was walking home from class when a man shoved her off the pavement. "He said 'no n*****s allowed on the sidewalk.'" At Texas State University in San Marcos fliers posted in bathrooms throughout the campus declared, "Now that our man Trump is elected. Time to organize tar-and-feather vigilante squads and go arrest and torture those deviant university leaders spouting off that diversity garbage."[19]

The AAUP Council, at its November 2016 meeting, passed a resolution condemning such attacks and calling on college and university administrators, faculty, staff, and students to unite against them. "Violence, threats of violence, and harassment have no place on campus," the council declared.[20]

Nevertheless, fall 2017 witnessed another wave of racist incidents. These included the physical assault of a student at Cornell University; the hanging of Confederate flags festooned with balls of cotton at American University; a swastika carved into a campus elevator and the n-word written on a whiteboard belonging to a black student at Drake University; the n-word scrawled on door name tags of black students at the University of Michigan; and fliers encouraging students to join openly "white nationalist" groups at the University of Louisville, Stockton University, and Purdue University.

Unfortunately, in this environment and despite increased congressional appropriations to the Department of Education's Office of Civil Rights (OCR), Education Secretary DeVos decided—without a public comment period—to allow that office to ignore a large number of complaints of discrimination, explaining that the high number of complaints imposes "an unreasonable burden." Under new rules, OCR will streamline reviews of institutional practices when complaints about discrimination are filed. A new case-processing manual also included changes mandating that complaints be dismissed under a range of circumstances, including a failure to state a violation of a law or regulation enforced by the OCR; an allegation that lacks sufficient detail; or a failure to file a complaint in a timely manner. Within a little more than a month after the new policies were adopted, OCR reportedly dismissed hundreds of civil rights complaints, including five hundred disability rights violations. In May 2018, the NAACP, the National Federation of the Blind, and the Council of Parent Attorneys and Advocates filed suit against the department for abandoning civil rights policies without public notice and a comment period, in violation of the federal Administrative Procedures Act.[21]

The AAUP Council resolution noted the special vulnerability of "those among our students who are undocumented, many of whom have been in this country since early childhood," and declared the AAUP's support for sanctuary campuses. "While colleges and universities must obey the law," the resolution declared, "administrations must make all efforts to guarantee the privacy of immigrant students and pledge not to grant access to information that might reveal their immigration status unless so ordered by a court of law. Nor should colleges and universities gather information about the citizenship or immigration status of people who have interactions with the administration, including with campus police. College and university police should not themselves participate in any efforts to enforce immigration laws, which are under federal jurisdiction. Faculty members should join efforts to resist all attempts to intimidate or inappropriately investigate undocumented students or to deny them their full rights to due process and a fair hearing."[22]

The Trump administration soon announced its intention to terminate the rights of the "dreamers," those who entered the country without documentation as children with their families, by ending the Obama administration's Deferred Action for Childhood Arrivals (DACA) program. As of this writing, that program's fate remains undetermined. Because so many of the "dreamers" are college students, faculty members have a special obligation to persist in opposing attacks on their status and pressuring Congress to act. The AAUP joined eighty-one other higher education associations in a September 2017 letter to congressional leaders urging passage of "bipartisan legislation as soon as possible that will include all the protections currently provided under DACA and allow these young people to continue contributing to our society and economy by working, serving in the military or attending college."[23] A week earlier AAUP president Rudy Fichtenbaum issued a statement denouncing the administration's decision "in the strongest possible terms."[24]

Then there are the president's notorious series of executive orders banning immigration from a number of Muslim countries. As the AAUP has stated, "Those being excluded from the US will doubtless include faculty and students who seek to travel here to speak, participate in conferences, or conduct other academic work. Their exclusion is at odds with fundamental AAUP principles and with our nation's historic commitment to the free exchange of ideas."[25]

In September 2017, the AAUP joined with the American Council on Education and twenty-eight other higher education groups in an amicus brief to the US Supreme Court opposing the first travel ban. The brief noted that foreign scholars have been deterred from accepting faculty positions in the United States or have pulled out of academic conferences here, either because they were directly affected by the ban or because they feared its potential impact. It explained how the ban "jeopardizes the vital contributions made by foreign students, scholars, and faculty by telling the world in the starkest terms that American colleges and universities are no longer receptive to them." The executive order, the brief continued, "sends a clarion message of exclusion to millions around the globe that America's doors are no longer open to foreign students, scholars, lecturers, and researchers" and "severely undermines the ability of American colleges and universities to fulfill their commitment to serving their students, their communities, the United States, and the world through innovative teaching and research."[26]

On March 28, 2018, the AAUP again joined with the American Council on Education and thirty-two other higher education groups in submitting another amicus brief to the Supreme Court opposing the third iteration of the travel ban. The new ban "jeopardizes the many contributions that foreign students, scholars, and researchers make to American colleges and universities, as well as our nation's economy and general well-being," the brief said. The brief argued that "foreign students, faculty and researchers come to this country because our institutions are rightly perceived as the destinations of choice compared to all others around the globe." The most recent ban, together with the first two travel ban executive orders, "altered those positive perceptions with the stroke of a pen."[27] In conjunction with the Knight First Amendment Institute, the AAUP has also looked into legal issues related to a regulation authorizing border patrol officers to search a traveler's electronic devices without any basis for suspicion.[28]

On June 26, 2018, in a 5–4 decision the high court ruled in favor of the ban. Writing for the majority, Chief Justice John Roberts was silent about the ban's potential impact on academia. Nor was this a major concern in the two concurring and two dissenting opinions, although Justice Sonia Sotomayor, writing in dissent, noted that among "a multitude of harms" likely to come from the ban were "constraints to recruiting and retaining students and faculty members to foster diversity and quality within the University community."[29]

Trump's actions on immigration are likely just a start. Faculty members and administrators must be prepared for further assaults on the rights of a broad array of minority groups on our campuses. We will need to stand firmly in defense of the rights of those so assaulted. We must also be prepared for efforts by individuals and groups that support the "white nationalist" agenda to intimidate and silence opposition on campus. To be sure, efforts to deny such individuals, including even noxious provocateurs like Milo Yiannopoulos, their own right to speak are misguided, if perhaps understandable (see chap. 8). But we cannot let legally protected, if invidious, speech develop into genuine harassment and intimidation. The rights of all members of our campus communities not only to speak freely but also to develop, test, and debate their views in safety must be protected.

Attacks on Unions

Ever since the US Supreme Court's 1980 decision in the *Yeshiva* case, most tenure-track faculty in American private institutions are considered to be "managers" under the National Labor Relations

Act and hence ineligible for federal protection of efforts to organize unions and bargain collectively.[30] And in a majority of states faculty in public institutions also lack such rights. Still, as the use—and widespread abuse—of faculty on short-term, often part-time, contingent contracts has expanded exponentially, efforts to organize faculty members into unions have intensified. In the first three quarters of 2016, twenty new faculty unions were certified. Almost two-thirds represent both full- and part-time contingent faculty members. According to the National Center for the Study of Collective Bargaining in Higher Education and the Professions, in 2016 over 20 percent of postsecondary teachers were unionized. For the growing numbers excluded from the tenure system—which for more than a century the AAUP has seen as the best and most important protection for academic freedom—unionization is perhaps the only way such freedom can be defended.[31]

Before the election, the legal environment for organizing, at least at the federal level, seemed to be improving. In key decisions the National Labor Relations Board (NLRB) made it easier for instructors at private institutions, including graduate student employees, to organize.[32] Now, however, the situation is different. During the campaign, Trump pledged to nominate Supreme Court justices in the mold of Antonin Scalia, whose death deprived antiunion forces of a majority in *Friedrichs v. California Teachers Association*, a case that could have denied public employee unions, including faculty unions, the right to collect fair share fees from nonmembers. With Trump appointee Neil Gorsuch having replaced Scalia, the court agreed to hear the case of *Janus v. AFSCME Council 31*, which reopened that issue. It thus quickly became likely that the justices would overturn precedent and bar such fees in the public sector, which would pose a profound threat to public employee unions, including the AAUP. In response, the AAUP began working with its unionized chapters to increase membership and strengthen ties with the faculty members they represent. The AAUP also joined an amicus brief in the case, as it had in the *Friedrichs* case.[33]

On June 27, 2018, to no one's surprise, the court by a 5–4 vote in *Janus* overturned a unanimous 1977 decision, declaring agency fee payments by nonunion members in the public sector violations of the First Amendment. The decision made little logical or legal sense, running counter to the justices' own recent case law governing public employee speech. If proof were still needed that the court majority is more concerned with the raw exercise of political power than with legal principle, *Janus* alone should be adequate. As Justice Elena Kagan put it in her blistering dissent, the decision "weaponized the First Amendment" against working people.[34]

Justice Samuel Alito's flawed argument for the majority was demolished in advance in an amicus brief filed by the unlikely pairing of Charles Fried, professor of law at Harvard University and a former Republican solicitor general of the United States, and Robert Post, professor of constitutional law and former dean at Yale University Law School, a former general counsel to the AAUP, and current member of AAUP's Committee A.[35] They argued that according to petitioner Mark Janus (and now the court majority as well),

> all union speech directed to the government is "political speech indistinguishable from lobbying the government." That is manifestly incorrect. When a union discharges statutory duties, it engages in speech that "owes its existence" to the State's chosen system for managing its workforce; funding such speech—which is directed to the government as an employer, not to the government as a sovereign—does not implicate "any liberties the employee might have enjoyed as a private citizen." (Garcetti, 547 U.S. at 422.) Concluding otherwise would set in motion drastic changes in First Amendment doctrine that essentially threaten to constitutionalize every workplace dispute and, further, to unsettle other constitutional doctrines that distinguish between the government as employer (or proprietor) and as sovereign.

Most striking here is the brief's reliance on the court's 2006 decision in *Garcetti v. Ceballos*, a decision that raised considerable concern among faculty and in the AAUP over its potential to restrict academic freedom.[36] But it turns out that *Garcetti* is a two-edged sword. "Public-sector bargaining regimes involve the same state managerial prerogatives to which the Court has expressed deference in the *Garcetti* line of cases," Fried and Post argued. "This Court has interpreted the First Amendment, consistent with *Garcetti*, to give ample room to state employers to structure public workplaces as they believed most effective, without undue First Amendment restrictions." The brief continued,

> The essential insight of the *Garcetti* line of cases is that if public employees are accorded categorical First Amendment rights, public employers will be denied the broad discretion they need to manage their workplaces. . . . It is inconsistent with *Garcetti*'s carefully drawn distinction between speaking as an employee and speaking as a citizen to hold that the compulsory payment of agency fees is categorically protected under the First Amendment. Any such holding would therefore threaten to transform every workplace dispute into a constitutional controversy. . . . Indeed, public employees are routinely compelled to speak pursuant to their official duties, and courts have rejected First Amendment challenges to such compulsion under *Garcetti*. If the employee speech at issue here can be restricted or compelled without First Amendment challenge, so too can the funding of such speech.

The brief went on to argue that a "categorical rule holding agency fees unconstitutional would also blur the limits the Court has been careful to place on what constitutes a 'matter of public concern' for constitutional purposes." The record shows that the kinds of activities funded by agency fees "cover the very types of routine workplace matters that the Court has carefully refrained from constitutionalizing with First Amendment protections. . . . A ruling categorically prohibiting agency fees would necessarily elevate these types of pedestrian workplace matters into matters of public concern. . . . If the Court in this case holds that employee grievances are a matter of public concern, it will have to accept the same result in countless other scenarios."

While *Janus* creates obstacles to union effectiveness, it also imperils the ability of the AAUP and other academic labor organizations to devote resources to the defense of academic freedom. As John Wilson has noted, "What few people realize is that union members (and fair share fees) subsidize academic freedom for all faculty members in America." Wilson also warned that the decision may endanger the speech and associational rights of college and university students. In the 2000 case of *Board of Regents of University of Wisconsin System v. Southworth*, the Supreme Court declared that public colleges and universities may charge student fees to support the activities of student organizations, including organizations whose outlook is abhorrent to other students, provided that there is no viewpoint discrimination. The decision, written by Justice Anthony Kennedy, who also authored the majority opinion in *Garcetti* and joined Justice Alito's ruling in *Janus*, relied explicitly on the *Abood* case, the 1977 decision that the *Janus* court overturned. But if *Abood* is no longer valid, students who do not want to pay fees for extracurricular activities in which they do not participate or to which they object may now challenge such fees on grounds that they entail the same sort of "compelled speech" invalidated by *Janus*. "If *Southworth* is overturned in the wake of the *Janus* ruling ... it would mean the end of student fees supporting student organizations or any controversial speech at public colleges," Wilson cautioned.[37]

The Senate has now confirmed a Trump appointee to the NLRB, creating an antiunion majority and increasing the likelihood that important Obama-era decisions will be reversed. Indeed, that is what trustees and administrators at elite private research institutions such as Columbia University, the University of Chicago—where graduate employees voted overwhelmingly in October 2017 to be represented by Graduate Students United, a joint affiliate of the AAUP and the American Federation of Teachers—and Yale University were counting on in their efforts to derail unionization of their graduate student employees. In 2016, the NLRB reversed a Bush-era decision, ruling that such students are employees and entitled to union representation.[38] Now these universities—despite their often-lofty language in opposition to Trumpism and in support of free expression—are counting on a Republican-dominated

NLRB to overturn that decision. In response, in February 2018 the graduate student employee unions on these campuses reluctantly withdrew their requests for representation, seeking to avoid yet another reversal by the NLRB and hoping to win voluntary recognition, as had happened previously at New York University. In April 2018, graduate student employees at Columbia staged a one-week walkout in an effort to compel the university administration to come voluntarily to the bargaining table.[39] They were not successful, but two months later the union for graduate employees at Brown University signed an agreement with the university for a union election outside the scope of the NLRB. It came after graduate employees at Georgetown University signed a similar agreement with their administration.[40]

Efforts are also underway to undermine other labor-friendly NLRB decisions, including the 2014 decision in *Pacific Lutheran University*, which expanded the organizing rights of non-tenure-track private-sector faculty. On December 28, 2017, the AAUP submitted an amicus brief to the US Court of Appeals for the District of Columbia Circuit urging the court to uphold the NLRB's determination that such faculty at the University of Southern California (USC) are not managers and therefore eligible to unionize. The case arose when the Service Employees International Union petitioned to represent non-tenure-track full-time and part-time faculty in two colleges within USC. The university objected, arguing that the faculty were managers under *Yeshiva*. The board applied the test established in *Pacific Lutheran*, finding that the faculty members were not managerial. After the union won the election in one college, USC refused to bargain, citing its objection, and the board ordered USC to do so. USC appealed to the court. The AAUP brief challenged the "paper authority" universities attribute to faculty they deem managerial without granting them actual authority in university policy making.[41]

Of course, assaults on unions and collective bargaining in states where Republicans dominate legislatures and governorships predate the Trump victory. Wisconsin is clearly the model. There, Governor Scott Walker successfully pushed through legislation that almost entirely destroyed public employee unions, including unions of public university faculty. And this attack was followed by an assault on the tenure system and massive cuts to funding. University of Wisconsin–Green Bay professor Chuck Rybak cautioned that Wisconsin was "a laboratory for the nation's direction" and "a national warning."[42] Goldrick-Rab, one of many prominent faculty members who left the state in the aftermath of the Walker assault, agreed. Now, she says, "We're all living in Wisconsin."

In Iowa legislation was enacted in 2017 under which most public-sector union contract negotiations are limited to base wages. Iowa unions are now barred from negotiating over issues such as health insurance, evaluation procedures, staff reduction, and leaves of absence. They are barred as well from having dues deducted from paychecks, and unions now need to be recertified prior to every contract negotiation.

Such efforts, however, can be resisted. In Wisconsin, devastation of the unions was followed by a remarkable growth of interest in the AAUP, with new non–collective bargaining chapters emerging and membership growing at several University of Wisconsin campuses. And the effort of Governor Kasich in Ohio a few years ago to destroy public employee unions was reversed by an overwhelming two-thirds majority in a public referendum, in which the Ohio AAUP played a critical part.[43] Still, the AAUP and other faculty unions must be prepared to absorb the blows to their finances and ability to organize that Trump's appointments and emboldened antiunion legislators are likely to bring.

The Threat to Learning

Violations of academic freedom and free expression on campus are becoming part of a broader assault on learning itself. The Trump administration's initial budget proposal issued in March 2017 contained deep cuts that would have severely damaged scientific research, the arts and humanities, and access to higher education. Congress did not go along with these draconian proposals, but the administration's priorities became clear.

Nowhere is this administration's disdain for learning more apparent than in the sphere of climate science. In the summer of 2017, the Union of Concerned Scientists released an exhaustive report, *Sidelining Science since Day One*, which described in detail the administration's assault on science, especially climate science. It concluded, "A clear pattern has emerged over the first six months of the Trump presidency: multiple actions by his administration are eroding the ability of science, facts, and evidence to inform policy decisions, leaving us more vulnerable to threats to public health and the environment. The Trump administration is attempting to delegitimize science, it is giving industries more ability to influence how and what science is used in policymaking, and it is creating a hostile environment for federal agency scientists who serve the public."[44]

In December 2017, the AAUP issued its own report, entitled *National Security, the Assault on Science, and Academic Freedom*. That report documented how even before Trump took office the academic freedom of foreign-born scientists, especially those of Chinese background, has been unduly endangered by inflated concerns about security. In Senate testimony in early 2018, Trump's FBI director Christopher Wray claimed that Chinese "professors, scientists, students [in] basically every discipline" working in the United States may be covertly gathering intelligence for the Chinese government. Speaking to a House of Representatives panel, former national counterintelligence executive Michelle Van Cleave called the United States "a spy's paradise," declaring that US R&D is "systematically targeted by foreign collectors to fuel their business and industry and military programs at our expense." In May 2018, it was revealed that the Trump administration was considering new provisions that would limit access of Chinese citizens to the United States, including by greatly expanding rules pertaining to Chinese researchers who work on projects with military or intelligence value at American universities. The proposals were widely criticized by higher education organizations.[45]

The AAUP report acknowledged that anti-scientific policies were characteristic of the Bush administration, but it concluded that under the Trump regime politically motivated threats to scientific research "threaten not only the academic freedom of scientists but also the ability of American science to maintain its international stature and continue to contribute to the improvement of American lives." The report demonstrated too how "well-funded and powerful interest groups have also sought to intimidate those conducting scientific research with which they disagree, especially through freedom of information fishing expeditions."[46]

The AAUP can celebrate one important victory in this area. In September 2017, the Arizona Court of Appeals rejected attempts by a "free market" legal foundation to use public records requests to compel faculty members to release emails related to their climate research.[47] In an amicus brief supporting the scientists, the AAUP argued that Arizona statute creates an exemption to public release of academic research records and that a general statutory exemption protecting records when in the best interests of the state, in particular the state's interest in academic freedom, should have been considered. The appeals court agreed.[48]

That case surely won't end such efforts to intimidate academic researchers, however, and it demonstrates that threats to academic freedom come not only from the government directly but also from well-funded think tanks and other organizations. Indeed, we should expect the various forces that have always threatened the faculty's rights and responsibilities—politicians, donors, and media, among others—to grow emboldened by the administration's rhetoric and its policy decisions.

Tenure and the Assault on Liberal Education

In recent years the AAUP has argued that the single greatest threat to academic freedom has been the erosion of the tenure system, resulting from overreliance on part-time and other contingent faculty, a product of academic capitalism and privatization (see chap. 1). But now we are experiencing once again a frontal assault on both tenure and shared governance that may intensify under the Trump regime, even if the president is not directly implicated.

Direct assaults on tenure have been launched in Iowa and Missouri, where proposed legislation would have barred any public college or university from providing tenured status to any faculty member. In a public statement, the AAUP called these bills "a concerted attack on academic freedom." Also in Iowa a bill was introduced that would prohibit the hiring of a professor or instructor at a public university or college if his or her most recent party affiliation would "cause the percentage of the faculty belonging to one political party to exceed by ten percent" the percentage of the faculty belonging to the other dominant party. In North Carolina, legislation was introduced that would require tenure-track and tenured faculty members to "reflect the ideological balance of the citizens of the state," so that no campus "shall have a faculty ideological balance of greater or less than 2 percent of the ideological balance" of North Carolinians. By requiring all faculty to disclose their personal political affiliations and views, such proposals revive the very essence of what made McCarthyism so dangerous.[49]

The good news is that these and similarly odious proposals have not as yet succeeded. Still, there is reason for concern that such efforts may be opening salvos in an all-out attack on a tenure system already dangerously weakened by "adjunctification"—and hence an attack on academic freedom itself.

In Wisconsin, until recently tenure for public college and university faculty members was enshrined in statute. Governor Walker removed this provision from the state's laws, leaving it to the University of Wisconsin system's governing board to ensure tenure through policy. But the policy the board adopted now provides for the dismissal of faculty members after post-tenure review without the protections of academic due process and on the sole initiative of an administrator and makes it markedly easier to use program elimination to lay off instructors.[50] These rules may be employed in the aftermath of major proposed program changes at two campuses.

In October 2017, administrators at the University of Wisconsin–Superior shocked faculty members and students by suspending twenty-five academic programs, including nine majors, fifteen minors, and one graduate program. This came on top of fifteen programs dropped since 2014. Some of the majors suspended were sociology, theater, journalism, and political science. In addition, another fifteen programs were placed "on warning," with departments required to make changes to their curriculum, meet "regional needs," and be more "attractive for students." Administrators claimed that the cuts were aimed at improving student success, not trimming a $2.5 million budget deficit, contending without basis that first-generation students are confused by too many academic options. In response, the university's faculty voted overwhelmingly in favor of a "no confidence" resolution. Students held sit-ins in front of the chancellor's office and gathered over five thousand signatures on a petition to reverse the suspensions.[51]

"Three people behind closed doors made a decision without consulting anyone," said Brent Notbohm, a film studies professor and former faculty senate chair. "There's been a lot of talk about whether they have the right to do this, and according to the rules of the UW System, they needed to consult faculty shared governance first. We never had a conversation about the programs being cut, so I think they're being disingenuous." Meanwhile, the administration contracted with a private company to increase enrollment in online graduate programs. While initially limited to the online master of education program, the contract gave right of first refusal to the company for any similar contracts and required at least "three high-demand designated programs," which must be in a format that takes eight weeks or less to complete.[52]

At the University of Wisconsin–Stevens Point, in Wausau, administrators proposed dropping thirteen majors in the humanities and social sciences—including English, philosophy, history, sociology, and Spanish—while adding or expanding sixteen programs "with high-demand career paths." If implemented, the proposal would ostensibly address a $4.5 million deficit over two years. The added or expanded programs, the administration claimed, "have demonstrated value and demand in the region" and include marketing, management, graphic design, fire science, and computer information systems.[53]

The proposal prompted massive opposition, with the campus Save Our Majors coalition mounting the school's biggest protest since the Vietnam War. In a public statement opposing the proposal, twenty-three national scholarly associations in the humanities and social sciences declared, "There is convincing evidence that college graduates can be expected to change careers—not just jobs, but careers—several times in their working lives. By focusing on preparation only for narrowly defined jobs, Stevens Point administrators risk leaving students with considerably poorer preparation for the full range of careers most Americans will experience in a working lifetime." Moreover, the statement added, "access to humanities studies is essential for all students, no matter their career paths, as is the opportunity to major in these disciplines."[54]

As Christopher Newfield concluded in a lengthy and perceptive analysis of the Stevens Point proposal, "The plan relegates the students of central Wisconsin to second class citizenship."[55] Its disparate impact was also highlighted by an anonymous blogger, who wrote,

> The next closest four-year college to Wausau is 90 minutes west or 90 minutes east (Eau Claire or Green Bay). Such a distance would be an impossible commute for many of the students who are placebound or who want to live at home to cut costs. These changes mean that a student could still start and complete their first two years of general education at UW Stevens Point . . . but they would no longer be able to complete a liberal arts four-year degree in any of those degree programs that students are most likely to require as a foundation for some of the most influential professional fields. . . .
>
>   For central Wisconsin parents, that means that you will have no choice but to send your students away to college somewhere else if you, or they, have professional ambitions beyond the bachelor's degree, or who hope to be prepared by their liberal arts education for success in their career beyond their "first job out."[56]

"Here's the takeaway," concluded Paula Krebs, executive director of the Modern Language Association: "If you are a working-class student, a first-generation college student, someone without the means to get you to a private college or to a public research university, then you should be channeled into job training."[57]

"Questioning forms the basis of thought and education, and whether you're a plumber or a professor, it is an essential part of human experience and progress," wrote a contributor to *Forbes*. "Stripping higher education, especially public higher education, of anything but pragmatic, technical or transactional courses completely undermines the mission of a college or university." As University of Wisconsin–Milwaukee faculty member Christine Evans wrote, "The humanities train critical thinkers and citizens. That may be inconvenient for politicians who see their constituents as merely a 'work force,' but it is definitely good for our democracy, as well as our economy."[58]

To be sure, "pursuing the liberal-arts track isn't a quick path to riches," business journalist George Anders acknowledged. "First-job salaries tend to be lower than what's available with vocational degrees in fields such as nursing, accounting, or computer science. That's especially true for first-generation students, who aren't as likely to enjoy family-aided access to top employers. . . . Yet over time, liberal-arts graduates' earnings often surge, especially for students pursuing advanced degrees."[59]

A study released in February 2018 by the American Academy of Arts and Sciences—based on data from the US Census and other government sources, plus Gallup polling of workers nationwide—revealed that the median salary for those with a terminal bachelor's degree in the humanities was $52,000 in 2015, less than the median for all graduates ($60,000) and much less than those in engineering ($82,000). However, the report noted that pay gaps narrow over time. Only 4.3 percent of those with terminal bachelor's degrees were unemployed in 2015, and the figure was under 3 percent for those with a bachelor's in a humanities field and an advanced degree in any field.[60]

As Newfield argued, if higher education's purpose is to serve the public good, then "study should not be rationed according to ability to pay" and "the full range of human interests and capabilities need to be brought to bear on public problems." He continued, "For every possible combination, 21st century learning requires depth through immersion and integration across fields, not surface familiarity through a handful of electives. . . . We have to undo the stratification that afflicts the current system, and that has lowered overall U.S. university outcomes to its current level of international mediocrity. UWSP's [University of Wisconsin–Stevens Point's] administration proposes to perpetuate and intensify stratification by ignoring the results of educational research, to the obvious disservice of its students and its region."[61]

Nonetheless, Newfield pointed out, in its own way the Stevens Point plan offers "a rational response to . . . the default budget logic of bipartisan austerity politics." Resisting that logic involves recognizing its political context, in particular the decades-long push to subordinate higher education to "workforce needs and business norms." But it also demands careful analysis of any proposed changes. In the case of Stevens Point, Newfield concluded, such analysis reveals "that the plan is grounded in flawed assumptions. . . . I've found no public evidence that UWSP's new curriculum may put its budget back in the black. On the contrary, there is indirect evidence that the change will make the budget deficit worse—new program costs, stagnant enrollments, alienated liberal arts and liberal-practical double majors, general disruption and lowered morale, and the continued influence of the dominant incumbents, all so far left undiscussed."[62]

Efforts to eliminate access to liberal arts majors, as at Stevens Point, were criticized in a May 31, 2018, joint statement by the AAUP and the Association of American Colleges and Universities. The groups declared "that institutions of higher education, if they are truly to serve as institutions of higher education, should provide more than narrow vocational training and should seek to enhance students' capacities for lifelong learning. This is as true of open-access institutions as it is of highly selective elite colleges and universities."

Linking defense of the liberal arts to academic freedom, the statement concluded, "Almost eighty years ago, in their joint 1940 *Statement of Principles on Academic Freedom and Tenure*, the AAUP and AAC&U [Association of American Colleges and Universities] emphasized that 'institutions of higher education are conducted for the common good' and that 'the common good depends upon the free search for truth and its free exposition.' The free search for truth and its free exposition in the liberal arts are essential components of a functioning democracy. Higher education's contributions to the common good and to the functioning of our democracy are severely compromised when universities eliminate and diminish the liberal arts."[63]

Shared Governance Imperiled

"Taking a cue from UW System president Ray Cross's open contempt for shared governance," one Wisconsin faculty member wrote, "administration at both UW-Superior and UW-Stevens Point crafted these radical policy changes without any apparent input from faculty, relying instead on shared governance groups to do the heavy lifting of implementation—shared governance ex post facto."[64]

A system of shared governance, as described in the AAUP's 1966 *Statement on Government of Colleges and Universities*, formulated jointly with the American Council on Education and the Association of Governing Boards of Universities and Colleges, is almost as central to the defense of academic freedom as tenure.[65] As the AAUP put it in the 1994 statement *On the Relationship of Faculty Governance to Academic Freedom*, "A sound system of institutional governance is a necessary condition for the protection of faculty rights and thereby for the most productive exercise of essential faculty freedoms. Correspondingly, the protection of the academic freedom of faculty members in addressing issues of institutional governance is a prerequisite for the practice of governance unhampered by fear of retribution."[66]

Unfortunately, however, at both private and public institutions shared governance has come increasingly under siege. The poisonous notion that colleges and universities should be run more like business enterprises has empowered authoritarian administrators and out-of-touch governing boards at the expense of faculty. Yet the perpetrators of these changes are almost never held to account for their failures.[67]

In 2011, the Idaho State Board of Education voted to suspend the operation and bylaws of the faculty senate at Idaho State University and to direct the university president to "implement an interim faculty advisory structure." The board acted on the recommendation of the president, one week after the faculty voted no confidence in his leadership. When faculty members elected to lead the new structure the same individuals they had elected previously, the body was summarily dissolved and its chair, a professor of physics, was deprived of the ability to send emails to the faculty.[68]

In 2014, the administration of Union County College in New Jersey, with the concurrence of the trustees and the governor, ended, or severely restricted, the faculty's role in choosing its own representatives to committees; eliminated most faculty committees, including the key Faculty Executive Committee; and replaced departments headed by faculty-chosen chairs with new academic divisions headed by deans selected with little or no faculty involvement.[69]

The summer of 2017 saw a crisis in shared governance in the California State University (CSU) system, the nation's largest public university system, with nearly five hundred thousand students. The promulgation of two executive orders, which capped general education credits and eliminated placement tests and remedial English classes, prompted widespread opposition among the faculty. The uncertain merits of the orders aside, these decisions were made without participation by the statewide and campus academic senates and without appropriate consultation with the California Faculty Association, the AAUP-affiliated union representing all 28,000 faculty members in the system.[70]

The CSU administration claimed that it "consulted" with faculty. But the 1966 *Statement on Government* does not call for mere "consultation." It calls for "joint effort." With regard to the faculty's role, it states, "The faculty has primary responsibility for such fundamental areas as curriculum, subject matter and methods of instruction, research, faculty status, and those aspects of student life which relate to the educational process. On these matters the power of review or final decision lodged in the governing board or delegated by it to the president should be exercised adversely only in exceptional circumstances, and for reasons communicated to the faculty." Specifically, the statement adds, "The faculty sets the requirements for the degrees offered in course, determines when the requirements have been met, and authorizes the president and board to grant the degrees thus achieved."[71] These executive orders were created not by faculty members, and certainly not by representative faculty bodies, but by the CSU Chancellor's Office. As such, they should be considered illegitimate, at least from the perspective of good governance practice.

In a letter to CSU chancellor Timothy White, AAUP associate secretary Hans-Joerg Tiede wrote,

> Disagreements about the adequacy of the faculty's involvement in a "consultation process" frequently hinge upon disparate understandings of the term consultation. The Association's Committee on College and University Governance has defined the term as follows: "Consultation means that there is a formal procedure or established practice which provides a means for the faculty (as a whole or through authorized representatives) to present its judgment in the form of a recommendation, vote, or other expression sufficiently explicit to record the position or positions taken by the faculty. This explicit expression of faculty judgment must take place in time to affect the decision to be made."

Tiede urged White "to hold the executive orders in abeyance, as requested" by CSU faculty representatives, and "to allow the faculty to exercise primary responsibility in the curricular decisions implicated by the executive orders."[72]

In Wyoming faculty resistance led the University of Wyoming's Board of Trustees in May 2018 to postpone a vote on changes to institutional regulations that would make it easier to end academic programs and terminate tenured faculty members. The proposed revision declared that university regulations may be "adopted, changed or amended at any regular or special meeting of the trustees without prior formal notice." Another regulation stressed that "final authority" for eliminating programs and tenured faculty jobs as a result of such education-related factors as low enrollment or loss of accreditation lies with the board. The proposed revision would empower the trustees "to reorganize, consolidate, reduce and/or discontinue an academic program for educational, strategic, realignment, resource allocation, budget constraints or combinations of educational, strategic and/or financial reasons." Dave Vanness, a faculty leader who in May 2018 announced that he was leaving the University of Wisconsin for Pennsylvania State University, said that Wyoming's trustees "appear determined to outrace" the Wisconsin system "to the bottom."[73]

In the Maricopa Community College District in Arizona the governing board in 2018 unilaterally terminated a "meet-and-confer" provision of the faculty policy manual and ordered the creation of a new manual that would limit participation of the faculty in institutional governance. Of particular concern was the board's directive that the new manual, to be prepared solely by the administration, may not allow faculty members to participate in matters related to "compensation, benefits, accountability, and organizational operations." Following adoption of the board's resolution, Provost Karla Fisher wrote college presidents to inform them that "Senate Presidents and Representatives must be dutiful in avoiding any [Faculty Executive Council] or Faculty Association–related work or conversations during business hours," thereby interfering with the academic freedom of the identified faculty members to express their views on matters of institutional concern.[74]

One especially troubling development in university governance has been the growing tendency of governing boards to conduct searches for college and university presidents, chancellors, and provosts entirely in secret, with no public vetting of finalists. In November 2015, the AAUP issued a statement on presidential searches, which read in part,

At a number of colleges and universities across the country controversy has emerged over decisions by governing boards to conduct searches for new presidents or chancellors in secret, abandoning the previously standard practice of inviting a select group of finalists to visit the campus and meet publicly with faculty and other members of the campus community. The rationale for such secrecy is that open meetings discourage applications from highly qualified candidates, although no evidence has ever been offered to suggest that this is in fact the case.

AAUP policy statements make clear that such decisions to forgo public campus visits and public forums by finalists violate longstanding principles of shared governance.[75]

However, even ostensibly open searches may be subject to abuse. Take, for instance, the search for a new president of the University of Iowa in 2015. Although four finalists were invited to campus and met publicly with faculty members and other stakeholders, an AAUP investigation determined that—in contrast to prior practice, which had been to involve faculty fully in presidential searches— the board designed this search process specifically to prevent any meaningful faculty role in the selection. A legal challenge to the appointment revealed that board members held secret meetings, in an effort to circumvent if not openly flaunt open meetings laws.[76] As the AAUP's investigation concluded, "The board acted throughout in bad faith, and not toward the faculty alone." Indeed, its behavior was a "serious disservice to the people of the state as well as the institutions to which it owes the highest standard of care."[77]

That investigation also warned that "there may well be an emerging crisis in American public higher education. The crisis is occasioned by headstrong, thoughtless action by politically appointed regents who lack any respect for the faculties of the institutions over which they preside." Such crude interventions are almost always accompanied by the appointment of university administrators whose first loyalty is not to the faculty that such officers had in the past represented and emerged from, much less to the broader public good, but to the values and practices of the academic capitalism increasingly embraced by governing boards and legislatures. According to John Seery,

> The real reason tuitions are skyrocketing and educational integrity has been compromised is because administrators, not educators, now run the show, all across America. They call the shots. They build the fancy buildings. They call for and approve the costly amenities. They fund what they want to fund. They hire the people they want to hire and pay them top dollar. They make the decisions about branding campaigns, and they set the agenda for student affairs staffs. They fund the kind of curriculum they want. They control the purse strings. They hold the power.
>
>   That pyramidal model in which intellectual labor is transferred from the faculty to the president and his administrators and their strategic plans systematically siphons money and attention and purpose away from what matters most, the classroom. . . . It doesn't have to be this way.[78]

Don't Mourn; Organize!

This account has not been optimistic about the current condition and imminent future of higher education and academic freedom. But if there is a silver lining, it is that more faculty members have grown more alert to the dangers they face, and many are organizing to respond. "Nothing will serve but organization," wrote the Marxist literary scholar Granville Hicks following his 1935 dismissal from the faculty at Rensselaer Polytechnic Institute, which was investigated by the AAUP. "Conditions in education, if left to themselves," he wrote, "are not going to become better but worse. If teachers do not want to be reduced to a nauseating, boot-licking slavery, they had better start organizing now."[79]

That warning remains timely, but there are signs that faculty members are once again taking such sentiments to heart. The remarkable women's marches, which involved between three and four million people nationwide, resonated especially on college and university campuses, as did the April 2017 March for Science and the

March 2018 March for Our Lives for gun control. And the extraordinarily rapid responses of so many, including many administrators as well as faculty members, to the proposed immigration ban and attacks on "dreamers" are another reason for optimism. Still, if assaults on academic freedom, shared governance, and what the AAUP's founders called "the common good" are to be resisted successfully, the faculty must step forward not only as individuals but also as a collective body, uniting wherever possible with sympathetic administrators, students, and concerned citizens. "All the fights that we thought belong to the future are owned by the present," Chuck Rybak cautions. "Without that fight, without our contributions to it, and without new coalitions, the unthinkable will arrive: there will be no public education to serve as a pathway to a brighter future."[80]

In remarks delivered to the annual conference of the AAUP in 2010, Patricia McGuire, president of Trinity Washington University and one of higher education's most fearless and bold champions, concisely and eloquently summed up why academic freedom is so imperative. Her words are more significant than ever:

> Higher education is one of the great counterbalances to government in a free society, but that balance only works through the free and frequent exercise of the muscle of our mission. We are the stewards of democracy's brain, the guarantors of informed citizen voices, the producers of much of the knowledge that fuels innovation stimulating social and economic progress. Lilliputian bureaucracies will certainly always try to tie down our free sails as we venture into uncharted waters—whether condemning a speaker or forbidding a play or investigating a scholar. Our stewardship— as presidents, as faculty, as trustees, all stewards of the freedom of higher education to do its work uninhibited and unintimidated—our stewardship requires us to swing mighty axes against the restraints that compromise our ability to conduct research freely, publish whatever we choose, teach as we must, and speak openly without fear.

McGuire acknowledged that "the biggest threat to our academic freedom and health of our enterprise is our own tendency to self-censorship." We can, she added, "either cower under our desks to escape the noise, hoping no one calls us out, resolving to remain silent. . . . Or, we can do our jobs, with responsibility, with integrity and with audacity. . . . Academic freedom rarely dies in one egregious event; academic freedom erodes in a thousand small concessions. . . . But we lose everything when we refuse the engagement, when we sit back and hope that this wave will just pass over us, naively thinking that our freedom will remain intact even as the ebb tide washes it away."[81]

Surely the time for engagement is now.

Notes

Preface

Epigraph: Hank Reichman, "Einstein on Academic Freedom and Political Inquisitions," *Academe* (blog), June 11, 2017, https://academeblog.org/2017/06/11/einstein-on-academic-freedom-and-political-inquisitions/.

1. For an illuminating symposium on the relationship between advocacy, activism, and scholarship, see Laura W. Perna, ed., *Taking It to the Streets: The Role of Scholarship in Advocacy and Advocacy in Scholarship* (Baltimore: Johns Hopkins University Press, 2018).

2. Louis Menand, *The Marketplace of Ideas: Reform and Resistance in the American University* (New York: W. W. Norton, 2010), 131.

3. "1915 Declaration of Principles on Academic Freedom and Academic Tenure" and "1940 Statement of Principles on Academic Freedom and Tenure with 1970 Interpretive Comments," in American Association of University Professors, *Policy Documents and Reports*, 11th ed. (Baltimore: Johns Hopkins University Press, 2015), 3–19; Sheila Slaughter, "Academic Freedom, Professional Autonomy, and the State," in *The American Academic Profession: Transformation in Contemporary Higher Education*, ed. Joseph C. Hermanowicz (Baltimore: Johns Hopkins University Press, 2011), 243.

4. "1940 Statement," 14.

5. Judith Butler, "The Criminalization of Knowledge: Why the Struggle for Academic Freedom Is the Struggle for Democracy," *Chronicle of Higher Education*, May 27, 2018, www.chronicle.com/article/The-Criminalization-of/243501.

6. Slaughter, "Academic Freedom," 244. For a thorough explication of these principles based on AAUP "case law," see Matthew W. Finkin and Robert C. Post, *For the Common Good: Principles of American Academic Freedom* (New Haven, CT: Yale University Press, 2009). The AAUP's "Recommended Institutional Regulations on Academic Freedom and Tenure" derive from the 1940 Statement and serve as both standards of "sound academic practice" and rules that the AAUP seeks to enforce through its investigations. See AAUP, *Policy Documents and Reports*, 79–90.

7. Neil Gross, "American Academe and the Knowledge-Politics Problem," in Hermanowicz, *American Academic Profession*, 134.

8. Jack H. Schuster, "The Professoriate's Perilous Path," in Hermanowicz, *American Academic Profession*, 4. Teresa A. Sullivan, "Professional Control in the Complex University: Maintaining the Faculty Role," in Hermanowicz, *American Academic Profession*, 315.

9. Chuck Rybak, *UW Struggle: When a State Attacks Its University* (Minneapolis: University of Minnesota Press, 2017), 36.

10. Schuster, "Professoriate's Perilous Path," 15. But consider this: "Universities have proven adaptable to social and economic challenges in the past, but there is no guarantee that they will continue to serve the same important functions in American life into the future." Keith E. Whittington, *Speak Freely: Why Universities Must Defend Free Speech* (Princeton, NJ: Princeton University Press, 2018), 12.

11. Chapter 1 expands on an essay of the same title published in recognition of the AAUP's centennial in *Academe* 101 (Nov.–Dec. 2015) and incorporates material from talks delivered at the University of Pittsburgh in March 2016 (Hank Reichman, "Academic Freedom: Challenges and Opportunities," *Academe* [blog], Apr. 5, 2016, https://academeblog.org/2016/04/05/academic-freedom-challenges-and-opportunities/) and a conference organized by the Faculty Advisory Committee to the Connecticut State Colleges and Universities Board of Regents for Higher Education in April 2015 (Hank Reichman, "Current Hurdles to Academic Freedom and Shared Governance," *Academe* [blog], Apr. 13, 2015, https://academeblog.org/2015/04/13/current-hurdles-to-academic-freedom-and-shared-governance/).

12. Reprinted with additions from "Academic Freedom and the Common Good: A Review Essay," *Journal of Academic Freedom* 7 (2016).

13. Chapter 3 expands on a December 28, 2016, post to the AAUP's *Academe* blog (Hank Reichman, "On Extramural Expression: A Response to Jonathan Helwink," *Academe* [blog], Dec. 28, 2016, https://academeblog.org/2016/12/28/on-extramural-expression-a-response-to-jonathan-helwink/). Chapter 4 expands significantly on a talk delivered at Wright State University on March 30, 2015, and posted to the *Academe* blog (Hank Reichman, "Can I Tweet That? Academic Freedom and the New Social Media," *Academe* [blog], Apr. 1, 2015, https://academeblog.org/2015/04/01/can-i-tweet-that-academic-freedom-and-the-new-social-media/).

14. Chapter 6 is an expanded version of a review, "Online Education and the 'Cost Disease,'" published in *Academe* 99 (Nov.–Dec. 2013).

15. Chapter 7 incorporates material from Henry Reichman, "On Student Academic Freedom," *Inside Higher Ed*, Dec. 4, 2015, www.insidehighered.com/views/2015/12/04/what-does-student-academic-freedom-entail-essay. Chapter 8 includes material from a four-part series, "On Outside Speakers and Academic Freedom," originally posted on the *Academe* blog on May 9 (https://academeblog.org/2017/05/09/on-outside-speakers-and-academic-freedom-part-i/), June 11 (https://academeblog.org/2017/06/11/on-outside-speakers-and-academic-freedom-part-ii/), June 13 (https://academeblog.org

/2017/06/13/on-outside-speakers-and-academic-freedom-part-iii/), and
September 8, 2017 (https://academeblog.org/2017/09/08/on-outside
-speakers-and-academic-freedom-part-iv/).

16. Reprinted with additions from "Professionalism and Unionism:
Academic Freedom, Collective Bargaining, and the American Association of
University Professors," *Journal of Academic Freedom* 6 (2015).

17. Chapter 10 expands on "Facing the Reality of the Trump Regime,"
Academe 104 (Jan.–Feb. 2018) and includes material from talks delivered at
Whitman College and to the California and Georgia State Conferences of the
AAUP in 2017.

Chapter 1. Does Academic Freedom Have a Future?

1. "Academic Freedom and Tenure: Community College of Aurora
(Colorado)," *AAUP Bulletin* 103 (2017): 2–11, www.aaup.org/sites/default/files
/JA17_CC_Aurora_CO.pdf.

2. "Academic Freedom and Tenure: College of Saint Rose (New York),"
AAUP Bulletin 102 (2016): 8–24, www.aaup.org/sites/default/files
/CollegeSaintRose.pdf.

3. The AAUP's letter to Trinity may be found at www.aaup.org/sites
/default/files/files/Trinity-Williams-6-27-17.pdf. For additional coverage, go
to https://academeblog.org/?s=Trinity.

4. In his history of (mainly elite) American universities, James Axtell
writes, "One of the defining features of American higher education is its firm
belief in academic freedom for faculty and students alike. . . . The much-
misunderstood institution of tenure, with its familiar trial periods but also its
virtually ignored annual or short-term evaluations thereafter, has long been the
bulwark of the faculty's freedom to teach and research as their disciplinary
guilds advise and allow." *Wisdom's Workshop: The Rise of the Modern University*
(Princeton, NJ: Princeton University Press, 2016), 368.

5. "1915 Declaration of Principles on Academic Freedom and Academic
Tenure" and "1940 Statement of Principles on Academic Freedom and Tenure
with 1970 Interpretive Comments," in American Association of University
Professors, *Policy Documents and Reports*, 11th ed. (Baltimore: Johns Hopkins
University Press, 2015), 3–19.

6. The prime example is David Horowitz's campaign on behalf of a
so-called Academic Bill of Rights. See the 2003 AAUP Committee A
statement, "Academic Bill of Rights," www.aaup.org/report/academic-bill
-rights. For a retrospective on the Horowitz campaign, see Adria Battaglia,
"Opportunities of Our Own Making: The Struggle for 'Academic Freedom,' "
Journal of Academic Freedom 5 (2014), www.aaup.org/JAF5/opportunities-our
-own-making-struggle-academic-freedom#.Wz5Hh7bMygQ.

7. "Trends in the Academic Labor Force, 1975–2015," www.aaup.org/sites /default/files/Academic_Labor_Force_Trends_1975-2015_0.pdf. See also Adrianna Kezar and Daniel Maxey, "The Changing Academic Workforce," *Trusteeship*, May/June 2013, www.agb.org/trusteeship/2013/5/changing -academic-workforce.

8. "The Annual Report on the Economic Status of the Profession, 2016–17," *Academe* 103, no. 2 (Mar.–Apr. 2017): 7, www.aaup.org/system/files /members/MarchApril2017_with_appendices.pdf.

9. Jack H. Schuster, "The Professoriate's Perilous Path," in *The American Academic Profession: Transformation in Contemporary Higher Education*, ed. Joseph C. Hermanowicz (Baltimore: Johns Hopkins University Press, 2011), 11. For an exhaustive study of the changing composition and roles of the faculty, see Jack H. Schuster and Martin J. Finkelstein, *The American Faculty: The Restructuring of Academic Work and Careers* (Baltimore: Johns Hopkins University Press, 2008).

10. Joseph E. Stiglitz, *The Price of Inequality: How Today's Divided Society Endangers Our Future* (New York: W. W. Norton, 2013); James Kwak, *Economism: Bad Economics and the Rise of Inequality* (New York: Pantheon, 2017).

11. Sheila Slaughter and Gary Rhoades, *Academic Capitalism and the New Economy: Markets, State, and Higher Education* (Baltimore: Johns Hopkins University Press, 2004), 305. According to Slaughter and Rhoades, academic capitalism is "characterized by the development of new networks of actors who develop organizations that span and blur the boundaries between public and private sectors." In this context "colleges and universities (and academic managers, professors, and other professionals within them)" are seen "as actors initiating academic capitalism, not just as players being 'corporatized.'" In a May 2018 talk at the University of Wisconsin–Milwaukee the Indian writer Arundhati Roy opined that "America has taken the lead in confusing universities with business enterprises." For a global perspective, see Brendan Cantwell and Ilkka Kauppinen, eds., *Academic Capitalism in the Age of Globalization* (Baltimore: Johns Hopkins University Press, 2014). For a somewhat different but not incompatible approach, see Michael Burawoy, "Redefining the Public University: Developing an Analytical Framework," *Transformations of the Public Sphere*, Aug. 5, 2011, publicsphere.ssrc.org /burawoy-redefining-the-public-university/.

12. "The education of citizens has taken a dramatic turn in recent decades, away from John Dewey's conception of education as the means of realizing individual potential towards a vision of a nation of students performing according to national 'standardized tests.' At the same time, the great 'research universities' have become interlocked with corporate interests and with the propaganda machines represented by well-funded think tanks and conserva-

tive foundations. As a result the critical independent intellectual seems an endangered species." Sheldon Wolin, *Politics and Vision: Continuity and Innovation in Western Political Thought*, expanded ed. (Princeton, NJ: Princeton University Press, 2004), 594.

13. Gordon Lafer, "The Corporate Assault on Higher Education," *Chronicle of Higher Education*, Apr. 30, 2017, www.chronicle.com/article/The-Corporate -Assault-on/239902; Gaye Tuchman, *Wannabe U: Inside the Corporate University* (Chicago: University of Chicago Press, 2009).

14. Gary Rhoades, "Extending Academic Capitalism by Foregrounding Academic Labor," in Cantwell and Kauppinen, *Academic Capitalism*, 122.

15. Roger L. Geiger, "Optimizing Research and Teaching: The Bifurcation of Faculty Roles at Research Universities," in Hermanowicz, *American Academic Profession*, 21–43; Gary Rhoades, "Whose Educational Space? Negotiating Professional Jurisdiction in the High-Tech Academy," in Hermanowicz, *American Academic Profession*, 92–110.

16. David Graeber, "Are You in a BS Job? In Academe, You're Hardly Alone," *Chronicle of Higher Education*, May 6, 2018, www.chronicle.com/article /Are-You-in-a-BS-Job-In/243318. For an insightful and biting, albeit dark, satire on the excesses of "assessment," see B. K. Stevens, "Living Underwater," in *Jewish Noir*, ed. Kenneth Wishnia (Oakland, CA: PM, 2015), 52–71. For a discussion of bullshit, see Harry G. Frankfort, *On Bullshit* (Princeton, NJ: Princeton University Press, 2005).

17. Schuster and Finkelstein, *American Faculty*, 363. See also Mary Burgan, *What Ever Happened to the Faculty? Drift and Decision in Higher Education* (Baltimore: Johns Hopkins University Press, 2006); and Benjamin Ginsberg, *The Fall of the Faculty: The Rise of the All-Administrative University and Why It Matters* (New York: Oxford University Press, 2011).

18. On tenure and its relation to academic freedom, see Ralph S. Brown and Jordan E. Kurland, "Academic Tenure and Academic Freedom," *Law and Contemporary Problems* 53, no. 3 (Summer 1990): 325–55. On financial exigency, see "The Role of the Faculty in Conditions of Financial Exigency," *AAUP Bulletin* 99 (2013): 118–47. An abbreviated version may be found in AAUP, *Policy Documents and Reports*, 292–308.

19. Hans-Joerg Tiede, "The Front Rank: On Tenure and the Role of the Faculty in the Defense of Academic Freedom," *History of Education Quarterly* 58, no. 3 (Aug. 2018): 441–47.

20. For one sobering report on the conditions faced by many "adjunct" faculty members, see Caprice Lawless, "Summer Series: Summertime, and the Living's Not Easy (for Adjunct Faculty)," *Academe* (blog), June 10, 2018, https://academeblog.org/2018/06/10/summertime-and-the-livings-not-easy -for-adjunct-faculty/.

21. "On Full-Time Non-tenure-track Appointments," in AAUP, *Policy Documents and Reports*, 190–96.

22. Ronald G. Ehrenberg and Liang Zhang, "Do Tenured and Tenure-Track Faculty Matter?," *Journal of Human Resources* 40, no. 3 (2005): 647–59. "Other factors held constant, a 10 percentage point increase in the percentage of part-time faculty at a public masters' level institution is associated with about a 3 percentage point reduction in the graduation rate at the institution and a 10 percentage point increase in the percentage of full-time faculty that are not on tenure-track lines is associated with about a 4.4 percentage point reduction in the graduation rate at the institution" (657).

23. Steven Hurlburt and Michael McGarrah, *The Shifting Academic Workforce: Where Are the Contingent Faculty?* (Delta Cost Project, 2016). For a useful bibliography of research on the impact of adjunct teaching suggesting a more complex picture, see Jane Hikel and Kevin Kean, "Annotated Bibliography to Accompany Changing the Narrative: What the Research Really Says about Adjunct Teaching," prepared for the 2017 AAUP Annual Conference and available from the authors.

24. Chuck Rybak, *UW Struggle: When a State Attacks Its University* (Minneapolis: University of Minnesota Press, 2017), 54.

25. Rybak, *UW Struggle*, 39.

26. A. J. Carlson, "So This Is the University?," *AAUP Bulletin* 24, no. 1 (Jan. 1938): 15.

27. For a critique of one such suggestion, see Hank Reichman, "Is It Time to Abandon Tenure?," *Academe* (blog), July 7, 2016, https://academeblog.org/2016/07/07/is-it-time-to-abandon-tenure/.

28. "Tenure and Teaching-Intensive Appointments," in AAUP, *Policy Documents and Reports*, 186–89.

29. Michael Bérubé and Jennifer Ruth, *The Humanities, Higher Education, and Academic Freedom: Three Necessary Arguments* (New York: Palgrave Macmillan, 2015).

30. For a compelling argument on behalf of "tenure now," see Burgan, *What Ever Happened to the Faculty?*, chap. 8.

31. Geoffrey Stone, "A Brief History of Academic Freedom," in *Who's Afraid of Academic Freedom?*, ed. Akeel Bilgrami and Jonathan Cole (New York: Columbia University Press, 2015).

32. "Academic Freedom and National Security in a Time of Crisis," Oct. 2003, www.aaup.org/report/academic-freedom-and-national-security-time-crisis.

33. Peter Augustine Lawler, "Higher Education vs. Competency and Diversity," *Modern Age* 59, no. 3 (2017), https://home.isi.org/higher-education-vs-competency-and-diversity-afterword.

34. "The limiting, distorting, and corrupting power of money is the biggest single cause for concern around free speech." Timothy Garton-Ash, *Free Speech: Ten Principles for a Connected World* (New Haven, CT: Yale University Press, 2016), 369.

35. The most influential early statement on the conflict between scholarship and business was Thorstein Veblen, *The Higher Learning in America* (Baltimore: Johns Hopkins University Press, 2015), originally published in 1918 but written during the preceding decade. See also Upton Sinclair, *The Goose Step: A Study of American Education* (Pasadena, CA: self-pub., 1923). In a 1929 case involving dismissal of a prolabor graduate student instructor at the University of Pittsburgh, a dean reportedly asserted that "the Chancellor depends on wealth for financing . . . and running the University and he cannot permit anything to happen which might antagonize these wealthy interests or individuals." "Academic Freedom at the University of Pittsburgh," *AAUP Bulletin* 15, no. 8 (Dec. 1929): 583.

36. Matthew Dolan and David Jesse, "How a Down-and-Out Broker Got University of Michigan to Invest $95M," *Detroit Free Press*, June 22, 2018, www.freep.com/story/news/local/michigan/2018/06/22/university-michigan-donor-endowment-broker/656708002/; Dolan and Jesse, "University of Michigan Pours Billions into Funds Run by Contributors' Firms," *Detroit Free Press*, Feb. 1, 2018, www.freep.com/story/news/local/michigan/2018/02/01/university-michigan-endowment-donor-funds/1066143001/; Dolan and Jesse, "How Stephen M. Ross' Gift to the University of Michigan Ended Up in Tax Court," *Detroit Free Press*, Aug. 27, 2017, www.freep.com/story/news/local/michigan/2017/08/27/stephen-ross-tax-break-gift-michigan/563170001/.

37. Brendan Cantwell, "The New Prudent Man: Financial-Academic Capitalism and Inequality in Higher Education," in *Higher Education, Stratification, and Workforce Development*, ed. Sheila Slaughter and Barrett Jay Taylor (New York: Springer, 2016), 173–92; Matthew Dolan and David Jesse, "U-M Socks Away Millions in Endowment as Families Face Rising Tuition," *Detroit Free Press*, Feb. 2, 2018, www.freep.com/story/news/local/michigan/2018/02/02/u-m-socks-away-millions-endowment-families-face-rising-tuition/875225001/.

38. Walter P. Metzger, *Academic Freedom in the Age of the University* (New York: Columbia University Press, 1955), 228–29.

39. Sweezy v. New Hampshire, 354 U.S. 234 (1957).

40. The agreement did not in the end produce the intellectual property expected and was not renewed after Novartis was acquired by Syngenta, a Swiss firm. See Sheila Slaughter, "Academic Freedom, Professional Autonomy, and the State," in Hermanowicz, *American Academic Profession*, 246–55. Slaughter concludes, "The issues that the Novartis case raises for academic

freedom are (1) creation of new circuits of knowledge that link the academy to the economy; (2) development of an administrative preference for science and technology able to generate external revenues, which undermines academic autonomy and credibility and threatens institutional potential for critique; and (3) weakening of faculty self-governance, which underpins academic freedom" (250). She cautions that "as segments of the professoriate align themselves with the market and make great personal gains from the synergy between their university work and their corporate endeavors, their claims about the need for buffers from external pressures ring less true, undermining their historic stance as disinterested scientists and experts, which is the foundation on which the claim of academic freedom rests" (251). See also AAUP, *Recommended Principles to Guide Academy-Industry Relationships* (Urbana-Champaign, IL: AAUP, 2014), 78–80.

41. Jacob H. Rooksby, *The Branding of the American Mind: How Universities Capture, Manage, and Monetize Intellectual Property and Why It Matters* (Baltimore: Johns Hopkins University Press, 2016), 7, 9. Bayh-Dole, however, "does not require universities to retain ownership over their faculty's inventions" (144). See also AAUP, *Recommended Principles*, 47–62.

42. Stanford University v. Roche Molecular Systems, Inc., 563 U.S. 776 (2011).

43. "Defending the Freedom to Innovate: Faculty Intellectual Property Rights after *Stanford v. Roche*," Nov. 2013, www.aaup.org/report/defending -freedom-innovate-faculty-intellectual-property-rights-after-stanford-v-roche -0; Jacob Rooksby and Brian Pusser, "Learning to Litigate: University Patents in the Knowledge Economy," in Cantwell and Kauppinen, *Academic Capitalism*, 88, 87.

44. It is, however, unclear whether this trend will continue. Beginning in 2026, it is predicted, the number of college-aged students will drop almost 15% in just five years. See Nathan D. Grawe, *Demographics and the Demand for Higher Education* (Baltimore: Johns Hopkins University Press, 2018)

45. Donna M. Desrochers and Steven Hurlburt, *Trends in College Spending: 2003–2013* (Washington, DC: American Institutes for Research, 2016); James B. Steele and Lance Williams, "Who Got Rich off the Student Debt Crisis," Center for Investigative Reporting, June 28, 2016, www.revealnews.org /article/who-got-rich-off-the-student-debt-crisis/.

46. SHEEO, *State Higher Education Finance: FY 2017* (State Higher Education Executive Officers, 2018), www.sheeo.org/sites/default/files /SHEF_FY2017.pdf.

47. Michael Mitchell, Michael Leachman, and Kathleen Madison, "Funding Down, Tuition Up: State Cuts to Higher Education Threaten Quality and Affordability at Public Colleges," Center on Budget and Policy

Priorities, Aug. 15, 2016, www.cbpp.org/research/state-budget-and-tax /funding-down-tuition-up; Government Accountability Office, *Higher Education: State Funding Trends and Policies on Affordability*, Dec. 2014, www .gao.gov/assets/670/667557.pdf.

48. Michael Mitchell, Michael Leachman, and Kathleen Masterson, "A Lost Decade in Higher Education Funding," Center on Budget and Policy Priorities, Aug. 23, 2017, www.cbpp.org/research/state-budget-and-tax/a-lost -decade-in-higher-education-funding; "Public Universities Struggle as Ohio, Other States Put Brakes on Funding," *Columbus Dispatch*, Jan. 29, 2018.

49. Ronald Brownstein, "American Higher Education Hits a Dangerous Milestone," *Atlantic*, May 3, 2018, www.theatlantic.com/politics/archive/2018 /05/american-higher-education-hits-a-dangerous-milestone/559457/.

50. California Faculty Association, *Equity Interrupted: How California Is Cheating Its Future*, Jan. 2017, www.calfac.org/sites/main/files/file -attachments/equity_interrupted_1.12.2017.pdf.

51. On student finances, see Sara Goldrick-Rab, *Paying the Price: College Costs, Financial Aid, and the Betrayal of the American Dream* (Chicago: University of Chicago Press, 2016); and Mark Huelsman, *The Unaffordable Era: A 50-State Look at Rising College Prices* (New York: Demos, 2018), www .demos.org/publication/unaffordable-era-50-state-look-rising-college-prices -and-new-american-student.

52. "Academic Freedom and Tenure: University of Southern Maine," *AAUP Bulletin* 101 (2015): 62–77, www.aaup.org/report/USM; "Academic Freedom and Tenure: Felician College," *AAUP Bulletin* 101 (2015): 48–61, www.aaup.org/report/Felician; "Academic Freedom and Tenure: National Louis University," *AAUP Bulletin* 99 (2013): 17–29, www.aaup.org/report /academic-freedom-and-tenure-national-louis-university.

53. "Tenure Weakened in Wisconsin," Mar. 10, 2016, www.aaup.org/news /tenure-weakened-wisconsin. For a passionate and perceptive account of these Wisconsin events, see Rybak, *UW Struggle*. See also Jon Marcus, "The Decline of the Midwest's Public Universities Threatens to Wreck Its Most Vibrant Economies," *Atlantic*, Oct. 15, 2017, www.theatlantic.com/business /archive/2017/10/midwestern-public-research-universities-funding/542889/; Christine Evans, "Save the Wisconsin Idea," *New York Times*, Feb. 16, 2015, www.nytimes.com/2015/02/16/opinion/save-the-wisconsin-idea.html.

54. N. D. Drezner, O. Pizmony-Levy, and A. Pallas, *Americans Views of Higher Education as a Public and Private Good* (New York: Teachers College, Columbia University, 2018), www.tc.columbia.edu/thepublicmind/reports /PublicMind_ResearchBrief_HigherEd.pdf.

55. "Statement on Government of Colleges and Universities," in AAUP, *Policy Documents and Reports*, 117–22. For additional AAUP resources on

shared governance, see "Resources on Governance," www.aaup.org/our
-programs/shared-governance/resources-governance.

56. It is encouraging that in 2017 the Association of Governing Boards
issued a white paper and Statement on Shared Governance that declared the
1966 Statement "the bedrock on which shared governance in most of
America's colleges and universities is based" and recommended specific
reference to the statement in institutional governing documents as "an
important foundation" for shared commitment among faculty, administration,
and board members. "Shared Governance: Changing with the Times," AGB
White Paper, Mar. 2017, www.agb.org/reports/2017/shared-governance
-changing-with-the-times; "AGB Board of Directors' Statement on Shared
Governance," Oct. 10, 2017, www.agb.org/statements/2017-1010/agb-board-of
-directors-statement-on-shared-governance.

57. "College and University Governance: The University of Iowa
Governing Board's Selection of a President," *AAUP Bulletin* 102 (2016): 52–68,
www.aaup.org/sites/default/files/UIowa_0.pdf.

58. Elahe Izadi, "The Incidents That Led to the University of Missouri
President's Resignation," *Washington Post*, Nov. 9, 2015, www.washingtonpost
.com/news/grade-point/wp/2015/11/09/the-incidents-that-led-to-the
-university-of-missouri-presidents-resignation/.

59. "Academic Freedom and Tenure: University of Nebraska–Lincoln,"
AAUP Bulletin 104 (July–Aug. 2018): 2–12; Steve Kolowich, "State of
Conflict," *Chronicle of Higher Education*, Apr. 27, 2018, www.chronicle.com
/interactives/state-of-conflict.

60. Gene Nichol, "Lessons on Political Speech, Academic Freedom, and
University Governance from the New North Carolina," *First Amendment Law
Review* 16 (2018): 39–72.

61. Nichol, "Lessons on Political Speech," 52.

62. Jane Stancill, "Board Bans Legal Actions at Civil Rights Center,"
Raleigh News and Observer, Sept. 8, 2017, www.newsobserver.com/news/local
/education/article171979707.html, quoted in Nichol, "Lessons on Political
Speech," 64.

63. Leah Moore, "Former UNC Faculty, Staff Explain Reasoning for
Taking Offers at Duke," *Daily Tar Heel*, Mar. 9, 2017, www.dailytarheel.com
/article/2017/03/unc-has-a-net-faculty-gain-despite-offers-faculty-cannot
-refuse, quoted in Nichol, "Lessons on Political Speech," 57.

64. Nichol, "Lessons on Political Speech," 71.

65. Dan Bauman et al., "Executive Compensation at Private and Public
Colleges," *Chronicle of Higher Education*, Dec. 10, 2017, www.chronicle.com
/interactives/executive-compensation#id=table_private_2015. See also Peter
Schmidt, "High Pay for Presidents Is Not Shown to Yield Any Fund-Raising

Payoff," *Chronicle of Higher Education*, Nov. 7, 2015, www.chronicle.com/article /High-Pay-for-Presidents-Is-Not/234079.

66. William G. Tierney, "As Max Nikias Pushed USC to Prominence, Checks and Balances Were Missing," *Los Angeles Times*, May 28, 2018, www .latimes.com/opinion/op-ed/la-oe-tierney-usc-tyndall-nikias-future -20180528-story.html.

67. Hank Reichman, "200 Faculty Members Call on USC President to Step Down," *Academe* (blog), May 22, 2018, https://academeblog.org/2018/05/22 /200-faculty-members-call-on-usc-president-to-step-down/; "Statement on Presidential Searches," Nov. 3, 2015, www.aaup.org/sites/default/files/AAUP _Statement_on_Presidential_Searches_0.pdf.

68. John Seery, "Somewhere between a Jeremiad and a Eulogy," *Modern Age* 59, no. 3 (2017), https://home.isi.org/somewhere-between-jeremiad-and -eulogy.

69. Ron Srigley, "Whose University Is It Anyway?," *Los Angeles Review of Books*, Feb. 22, 2018, https://lareviewofbooks.org/article/whose-university-is -it-anyway/.

70. Christopher Newfield, *The Great Mistake: How We Wrecked Public Universities and How We Can Fix Them* (Baltimore: Johns Hopkins University Press, 2016), 283. Adds Newfield, "Under plutonomic drift, public universities are succeeding at something big, which is to use limited learning to knock lots of college-educated people out of the middle class. While a lucky minority gets full-service college, the majority gets the fast-food version" (299). See also Christopher Newfield, *Unmaking the Public University: The Forty-Year Assault on the Middle Class* (Cambridge, MA: Harvard University Press, 2008).

71. "Joint Statement Opposing Campus Carry Laws," Nov. 12, 2015, www .aaup.org/sites/default/files/CampusCarry.pdf.

72. "Campus Carry Violates Academic Freedom," Nov. 20, 2017, www.aaup .org/news/campus-carry-violates-academic-freedom#.WntkXHxG1Ah.

73. "Glass v. Paxton," No. 17-50641, Aug. 16, 2018, www.ca5.uscourts.gov /opinions/pub/17/17-50641-CV0.pdf; Scott Jaschik, "Federal Appeals Court Rejects Challenge to Campus Carry Law," *Inside Higher Ed*, Aug. 20, 2018, www.insidehighered.com/news/2018/08/20/federal-appeals-court-rejects -challenge-texas-campus-carry-law.

74. Timothy Reese Cain, " 'Friendly Public Sentiment' and the Threats to Academic Freedom," *History of Education Quarterly* 58, no. 3 (Aug. 2018): 430.

75. Hank Reichman, "Is 'Incivility' the New Communism?," *Academe* (blog), Sept. 8, 2014, https://academeblog.org/2014/09/08/is-incivility-the -new-communism/; Michael Meranze, "The Order of Civility," *Remaking the University* (blog), Sept. 7, 2014, https://utotherescue.blogspot.com/2014/09

/the-order-of-civility.html; Greg Lukianoff, "Free Speech at Berkeley—So Long As It's 'Civil,' " *Wall Street Journal*, Sept. 8, 2014, www.wsj.com/articles /greg-lukianoff-free-speech-at-berkeleyso-long-as-its-civil-1410218613; Hank Reichman, "FSMers Respond to 'Civility' Appeal," *Academe* (blog), Sept. 13, 2014, https://academeblog.org/2014/09/13/fsmers-respond-to-civility -appeal/. See also Henry Reichman, "Civility and Free Speech," *Inside Higher Ed*, Oct. 14, 2014, www.insidehighered.com/views/2014/10/14/essay-argues -recent-statements-college-leaders-about-civility-are-threat-academic. On the Free Speech Movement, see Robert Cohen and Reginald E. Zelnik, eds., *The Free Speech Movement: Reflections on Berkeley in the 1960s* (Berkeley: University of California Press, 2002). In the wake of the charged rhetoric of both the Trump administration's supporters and opponents, calls for "civility" have spread beyond academia. For a persuasive, if passionate, treatment, see Marc Cooper, "In Praise of Incivility: The Appropriate Posture in a State of Emergency," *Los Angeles Review of Books*, July 10, 2018, https://lareviewof books.org/article/in-praise-of-incivility-the-appropriate-posture-in-a-state -of-emergency/.

76. "Academic Freedom and Tenure: The University of Illinois at Urbana-Champaign," *AAUP Bulletin* 101 (2015): 27–47, www.aaup.org/report /UIUC.

77. The case, *Cohen v. California*, 403 U.S. 15 (1971), involved a man who was arrested for wearing a jacket bearing the words "Fuck the Draft."

78. "Academic Freedom and Electronic Communications," in AAUP, *Policy Documents and Reports*, 42–57.

79. "Academic Freedom and Tenure: The University of California at Los Angeles," *AAUP Bulletin* 57 (1971): 382–420.

80. For a discussion of legal problems associated with prosecuting threats on social media, see Enrique A. Monagas and Carlos E. Monagas, "Prosecuting Threats in the Age of Social Media," *Northern Illinois University Law Review* 36, no. 3 (2016).

81. Scott Jaschik, "The Pressure on Provosts," *Inside Higher Ed*, Jan. 24, 2018, insidehighered.com/news/survey/2018-inside-higher-ed-survey-chief -academic-officers.

82. "Taking a Stand against Harassment, Part of the Broader Threat to Higher Education," Sept. 7, 2017, www.aaup.org/taking-stand-against -harassment-part-broader-threat-higher-education.

83. Metzger, *Academic Freedom*, 129.

84. "On Freedom of Expression and Campus Speech Codes," in AAUP, *Policy Documents and Reports*, 361. On "hate speech" and free expression, see Henry Louis Gates Jr. et al., *Speaking of Race, Speaking of Sex: Hate Speech, Civil Rights, and Civil Liberties* (New York: NYU Press, 1994).

85. "On Trigger Warnings," Aug. 2014, www.aaup.org/report/trigger
-warnings. One recent study suggests that some trigger warnings may actually
increase perceived emotional vulnerability to trauma, increase belief that
trauma survivors are vulnerable, and increase anxiety to written material
perceived as harmful. Benjamin W. Bellet, Payton J. Jones, and Richard J.
McNally, "Trigger Warning: Empirical Evidence Ahead," *Journal of Behavior
Therapy and Experimental Psychiatry*, July 27, 2018, www.sciencedirect.com
/science/article/pii/S0005791618301137. For a useful discussion of trigger
warnings, see Keith E. Whittington, *Speak Freely: Why Universities Must
Defend Free Speech* (Princeton, NJ: Princeton University Press, 2018),
57–66.

86. Geoffrey R. Stone, "Understanding the Free Speech Issues at Missouri
and Yale," *Huffington Post*, Nov. 11, 2015, www.huffingtonpost.com/geoffrey-r
-stone/understanding-the-free-sp_b_8535304.html.

87. This argument has been made in Sigal R. Ben-Porath, *Free Speech on
Campus* (Philadelphia: University of Pennsylvania Press, 2017).

88. Slaughter, "Academic Freedom, Professional Autonomy, and the State,"
in Hermanowicz, *American Academic Profession*, 266.

89. Burgan, *What Ever Happened to the Faculty?*, 207.

Chapter 2. How Can Academic Freedom Be Justified?

1. Books discussed in this chapter include Michael Bérubé and Jennifer
Ruth, *The Humanities, Higher Education, and Academic Freedom: Three
Necessary Arguments* (New York: Palgrave Macmillan, 2015); Akeel Bilgrami
and Jonathan Cole, eds., *Who's Afraid of Academic Freedom?* (New York:
Columbia University Press, 2015); Stefan Collini, *What Are Universities For?*
(New York: Penguin, 2012); Alice Dreger, *Galileo's Middle Finger: Heretics,
Activists, and the Search for Justice in Science* (New York: Penguin, 2015);
Stanley Fish, *Versions of Academic Freedom: From Professionalism to Revolution*
(Chicago: University of Chicago Press, 2014); Greg Lukianoff, *Unlearning
Liberty: Campus Censorship and the End of American Debate* (New York:
Encounter, 2012); Robert Post, *Democracy, Expertise, and Academic Freedom: A
First Amendment Jurisprudence for the Modern State* (New Haven, CT: Yale
University Press, 2012); and Hans-Joerg Tiede, *University Reform: The
Founding of the American Association of University Professors* (Baltimore: Johns
Hopkins University Press, 2015).

2. David Bromwich, "Academic Freedom and Its Opponents," in *Who's
Afraid of Academic Freedom?*, ed. Akeel Bilgrami and Jonathan Cole (New
York: Columbia University Press, 2015), 27. This view is echoed by Keith
Whittington, who writes, "Academic freedom is a specialized application of
general free speech principles." *Speak Freely: Why Universities Must Defend Free*

Speech (Princeton, NJ: Princeton University Press, 2018), 141. However, his argument is not founded on this position.

3. If there is a starting point for "academic freedom studies," it is likely Richard Hofstadter and Walter P. Metzger, *The Development of Academic Freedom in the United States* (New York: John Wiley, 1955). A selection of other important books would include, in addition to those reviewed here, William Van Alstyne, ed., *Freedom and Tenure in the Academy* (Durham, NC: Duke University Press, 1993); Louis Menand, ed., *The Future of Academic Freedom* (Chicago: University of Chicago Press, 1996); Beshara Doumani, ed., *Academic Freedom after September 11* (New York: Zone, 2006); John K. Wilson, *Patriotic Correctness: Academic Freedom and Its Enemies* (New York: Paradigm, 2008); Robert M. O'Neil, *Academic Freedom in the Wired World* (Cambridge, MA: Harvard University Press, 2008); Matthew W. Finkin and Robert C. Post, *For the Common Good: Principles of American Academic Freedom* (New Haven, CT: Yale University Press, 2009); Cary Nelson, *No University Is an Island: Saving Academic Freedom* (New York: NYU Press, 2010); Ellen Schrecker, *The Lost Soul of Higher Education: Corporatization, the Assault on Academic Freedom, and the End of the American University* (New York: New Press, 2010); and James L. Turk, ed., *Academic Freedom in Conflict: The Struggle over Free Speech Rights in the University* (Toronto: James Lorimer, 2014). Journal articles are too numerous to mention, as a quick search in Google Scholar will demonstrate. Moreover, there is a vast literature among legal scholars on the law governing academic freedom, as demonstrated by the many examples cited by Michael LeRoy in his 2016 article "How Courts View Academic Freedom," *Journal of College and University Law* 42, no. 1 (2016): 3n8.

4. For a different view of *Urofsky v. Gilmore*, see Sheila Slaughter, "Academic Freedom, Professional Autonomy, and the State," in *The American Academic Profession: Transformation in Contemporary Higher Education*, ed. Joseph C. Hermanowicz (Baltimore: Johns Hopkins University Press, 2011), 255–59.

5. Finkin and Post, *For the Common Good*.

6. Robert Post, "Why Bother with Academic Freedom?," *FIU Law Review* 9 (2013): 9, http://ecollections.law.fiu.edu/lawreview/vol9/iss1/4. In "Academic Freedom and the Constitution," his contribution to the Bilgrami/ Cole collection, Post distinguishes academic freedom from a broader intellectual freedom: "All persons are entitled to intellectual freedom, but only academics are entitled to academic freedom. Intellectual freedom does not presume the responsibility of competence, but academic freedom does. Intellectual freedom is not bound to any specific institution, like a university, but academic freedom is."

7. Post, "Why Bother with Academic Freedom?," 9–10.

8. Fish has advanced these arguments before, as in his *Save the World on Your Own Time* (New York: Oxford University Press, 2008). For a balanced and persuasive assessment of that book, see Joan W. Scott, "Back to Basics," *History and Theory* 49, no. 1 (Feb. 2010): 147–52.

9. William W. Van Alstyne, "Academic Freedom and the First Amendment in the Supreme Court of the United States: An Unhurried Historical Review," *Law and Contemporary Problems* 53, no. 3 (1990): 87.

10. John K. Wilson, "Stanley Fish and the Politics of Academic Freedom," *FIU Law Review* 79 (2013): 79, http://ecollections.law.fiu.edu/lawreview/vol9/iss1/28.

11. Post, "Why Bother with Academic Freedom?," 19.

12. John Dewey, "Academic Freedom," in *John Dewey: The Middle Works, 1899–1942*, ed. Jo Ann Boydston (Carbondale: Southern Illinois University Press, 1976), 57.

13. Post, "Why Bother with Academic Freedom?," 20.

14. Collini's book reprints several occasional pieces published in response to various British government initiatives. Are these works of scholarship? Collini seems to think so, and I agree. But I suspect that to Fish such crassly political interventions, incapable of being judged by strictly disciplinary norms, lie beyond the scholarly pale and would hence by his logic not be protected by academic freedom.

15. James Duderstadt, "Governing the Twenty-First-Century University: A View from the Bridge," in *Competing Conceptions of Academic Governance: Negotiating the Perfect Storm*, ed. William G. Tierney (Baltimore: Johns Hopkins University Press, 2004), 145, as quoted by Fish. Consider also Louis Menand's comment that "faculty members are by nature contentious and inefficient self-governors, but faculties must govern themselves." *The Marketplace of Ideas: Reform and Resistance in the American University* (New York: W. W. Norton, 2010), 131.

16. On the connection between shared governance and academic freedom, see Larry Gerber, " 'Inextricably Linked': Shared Governance and Academic Freedom," *Academe* 87, no. 3 (May–June 2001): 22–24; and Larry Gerber, *The Rise and Decline of Faculty Governance: Professionalization and the Modern American University* (Baltimore: Johns Hopkins University Press, 2014).

17. See also Whittington, *Speak Freely*, 144: "Academic freedom secures for faculty members a carefully constrained freedom of speech. They have earned the 'platform' of the post of professor at a university not by gaining some notoriety in the public sphere but by demonstrating the qualifications of expertise and by making careful, measured contributions to their field of study."

18. This point is also made for a rather different purpose by Judith Butler in "Exercising Rights: Academic Freedom and Boycott Politics," her own contribution to the Bilgrami/Cole collection: "Academic freedom is not just the name for the freedom we exercise when we teach and write, but also the name for this entire conundrum: we are dependent on a funded infrastructure to exercise academic freedom at the same time that academic freedom requires protection against the incursions by those very funding sources into the domain of teaching, writing, and scholarship." See also Louis Menand's discussion of interdisciplinarity, which engages these issues from a different angle, in *Marketplace of Ideas*, 95–125.

19. The AAUP's mission today is still not restricted to defense of academic freedom, which the organization continues to conceive as one facet, albeit a critical one, of a broader professional defense. Hence, the complaint by Matthew Goldstein and Frederick Schaffer in "Academic Freedom: Some Considerations," their essay in the Bilgrami/Cole collection, that "there is hardly any aspect of university life on which the AAUP has not expressed an opinion and which, according to the AAUP, is not an aspect of academic freedom" is misguided. AAUP policies and statements address multiple aspects of academic life, and not only academic freedom, as is wholly appropriate for a professional association of college and university faculty.

20. Whittington, *Speak Freely*, 164.

21. Judith Butler, "Academic Norms, Contemporary Challenges: A Reply to Robert Post on Academic Freedom," in *Academic Freedom after September 11*, ed. Beshara Doumani (New York: Zone, 2006).

22. For a thorough discussion from both sides, see *Journal of Academic Freedom* 4 (2013), http://aaup.org/reports-publications/journal-academic -freedom/volume-4. For arguments critical of the boycott movement, some of which address issues of academic freedom, see Cary Nelson and Gabriel Noah Brahm, eds., *The Case against Academic Boycotts of Israel* (Detroit: Wayne State University Press, 2014).

23. More recently Butler has offered a more nuanced and complete, but still not entirely convincing, view, arguing that "academic freedom relies on democratic public institutions. . . . Thus the struggle for academic freedom belongs to the struggle for democracy." Judith Butler, "The Criminalization of Knowledge: Why the Struggle for Academic Freedom Is the Struggle for Democracy," *Chronicle of Higher Education*, May 27, 2018, www.chronicle.com /article/The-Criminalization-of/243501.

24. Walter Metzger, "Profession and Constitution: Two Definitions of Academic Freedom in America," *Texas Law Review* 66 (June 1988): 1265.

25. Michael H. LeRoy, "How Courts View Academic Freedom," *Journal of College and University Law* 42, no. 1 (2016). As Sigal Ben-Porath notes, "The legal

framework alone cannot do all the work required to protect free speech on campus or to respond to challenges and violations of this principle." *Free Speech on Campus* (Philadelphia: University of Pennsylvania Press, 2017), 19.

26. Philip Lee, "A Contract Theory of Academic Freedom," *Saint Louis University Law Journal* 59 (2015). Ralph K. M. Haurwitz, "UT: Professors Have Academic Freedom, Despite What We Say in Court," *Austin American-Statesman*, July 18, 2018, www.mystatesman.com/news/local/professors-have -academic-freedom-despite-what-say-court/5oW6MvVHYKAahEsBKQoJvL /; Lindsay Ellis, "What Is Academic Freedom? Statement That Alarmed Professors at U. of Texas Sets Off Debate," *Chronicle of Higher Education*, July 24, 2018, www.chronicle.com/article/What-Is-Academic-Freedom- /244004. On institutional academic freedom, see David M. Rabban, "Professors Beware: The Evolving Threat of 'Institutional' Academic Freedom," in Turk, *Academic Freedom in Conflict*, 23–48.

27. Lee, "Contract Theory of Academic Freedom." Lee develops his ideas more fully in *Academic Freedom at American Universities: Constitutional Rights, Professional Norms, and Contractual Duties* (Lanham, MD: Lexington, 2014).

28. In one of the most important recent court cases involving academic freedom, *McAdams v. Marquette* (discussed in chap. 4), the court ruled in favor of a tenured professor's academic freedom rights solely on the basis of contract law, without reference to the First Amendment, noting explicitly that "the court . . . does not rely upon the United States Constitution for any part of its decision." John McAdams v. Marquette University, 2018 WI 88, July 6, 2018, 63n35, www.wicourts.gov/sc/opinion/DisplayDocument.pdf?content =pdf&seqNo=215236.

29. Fredrik deBoer, "Watch What You Say: How Fear Is Stifling Academic Freedom," *Chronicle of Higher Education*, Jan. 22, 2016.

30. Eric L. Dey et al., *Engaging Diverse Viewpoints: What Is the Campus Climate for Perspective-Taking?* (Washington, DC: Association of American Colleges and Universities, 2010), www.aacu.org/sites/default/files/files/core _commitments/engaging_diverse_viewpoints.pdf.

31. The argument that speech codes are products of the "pragmatic, almost utilitarian, considerations of college administrators" was previously made by Jon B. Gould, *Speak No Evil: The Triumph of Hate Speech Regulation* (Chicago: University of Chicago Press, 2005).

32. John Seery, "Somewhere between a Jeremiad and a Eulogy," *Modern Age* 59, no. 3 (2017), https://home.isi.org/somewhere-between-jeremiad-and -eulogy.

33. In 1967, the AAUP and several other organizations sought to define more precisely "student academic freedom" in a "Joint Statement on the Rights and Freedoms of Students," in American Association of University

Professors, *Policy Documents and Reports*, 11th ed. (Baltimore: Johns Hopkins University Press, 2015), 381–85. Student academic freedom is discussed in chapter 7.

Chapter 3. Can Faculty Speak Freely as Citizens?

1. Walter Metzger, *Academic Freedom in the Age of the University* (New York: Columbia University Press, 1955), 153–54.

2. Hans-Joerg Tiede, *University Reform: The Founding of the American Association of University Professors* (Baltimore: Johns Hopkins University Press, 2015), 35.

3. Metzger, *Academic Freedom*, 163–66. See also Tiede, *University Reform*, 35–37; and James C. Mohr, "Academic Turmoil and Public Opinion: The Ross Case at Stanford," *Pacific Historical Review* 39 (1970): 39–61.

4. Another early case of note involving a faculty member's political expression as a citizen was the 1915 non-reappointment of assistant professor Scott Nearing at the University of Pennsylvania in response to "a long continued effort on the part of a number of alumni of conservative views to use pressure, of various sorts, to prevent the expression . . . of teachings which those alumni regarded as unduly radical." In Nearing's case this involved his advocacy of laws restricting use of child labor. The AAUP's investigation established two key principles: first, "if a continuance in office which he might otherwise expect to enjoy is refused a teacher because of objections to his opinions, or his public expression of opinion, it makes little practical difference, so far as the injury to academic freedom is concerned, whether the result is called 'non-reappointment,' or 'removal,' or 'dismissal' "; and second, that "recommendation from the responsible and accredited representatives of the educational staff of a university . . . should be disregarded by governing boards of laymen only on grave occasions, and after definite charges have been brought against the teachers concerned, and opportunity for judicial hearings has been afforded, and that the grounds for removal should be clearly stated, and communicated to the faculties concerned." "Report of the Committee of Inquiry on the Case of Professor Scott Nearing of the University of Pennsylvania," *AAUP Bulletin* 2, no. 3 (May 1916): 19, 11, 13. See also Scott Nearing, "Thou Shall Not Speak," in *It Did Happen Here: Recollections of Political Repression in America*, ed. Bud Schultz and Ruth Schultz (Berkeley: University of California, 1989), 5–12; and Tiede, *University Reform*, 104–10.

5. Matthew W. Finkin and Robert C. Post, *For the Common Good: Principles of American Academic Freedom* (New Haven, CT: Yale University Press, 2009), 127. *Extramural* means, literally, "outside the walls," but as William Van Alstyne observed, "The phrase 'extramural' is used figuratively in reference to statements made outside of the employment relationship and not

merely to statements made outside the walls of the campus." William Van Alstyne, "The Constitutional Rights of Teachers and Professors," *Duke Law Journal*, no. 5 (Oct. 1970): 846.

6. "1915 Declaration of Principles on Academic Freedom and Academic Tenure," in American Association of University Professors, *Policy Documents and Reports*, 11th ed. (Baltimore: Johns Hopkins University Press, 2015), 10–11.

7. "1940 Statement of Principles on Academic Freedom and Tenure with 1970 Interpretive Comments," in AAUP, *Policy Documents and Reports*, 14.

8. "1915 Declaration," 9.

9. Oliver Bok, "Karega Fired after Split Faculty Recommendations," *Oberlin Review*, Nov. 18, 2016, https://oberlinreview.org/11914/news/karega -fired-after-split-faculty-recommendations/.

10. Jonathan Helwink, "Oberlin College Did the Right Thing by Firing Joy Karega for Anti-Semitism," *Federalist*, Dec. 23, 2016, http://thefederalist.com /2016/12/23/oberlin-college-right-thing-firing-joy-karega-anti-semitism/.

11. I am indebted here and throughout this chapter to an unpublished May 17, 2018, memorandum to Committee A on extramural utterances written by AAUP associate secretary Hans-Joerg Tiede.

12. "1940 Statement," 14n6.

13. The Koch case has been chronicled in John K. Wilson, "Academic Freedom and Extramural Utterances: The Leo Koch and Steven Salaita Cases at the University of Illinois," *Journal of Academic Freedom* 6 (2015).

14. Wilson, "Academic Freedom and Extramural Utterances."

15. "Academic Freedom and Tenure: The University of Illinois," *AAUP Bulletin* 49 (1963): 25–43.

16. Tiede, May 17, 2018, memorandum.

17. "Committee A Statement on Extramural Utterances," in AAUP, *Policy Documents and Reports*, 31.

18. For a judicial endorsement of the AAUP's fitness doctrine, see John McAdams v. Marquette University, Supreme Court of Wisconsin, 2018 WI 88, July 6, 2018, www.wicourts.gov/sc/opinion/DisplayDocument.pdf?content =pdf&seqNo=215236, which states, "The analytical structure described by the AAUP . . . provides a stable framework within which to evaluate whether the doctrine of academic freedom protects a specific extramural comment. . . . The AAUP properly limits the analysis to whether the actual extramural comment, on its face, clearly demonstrates that the professor is unfit to serve. This very narrow inquiry explains why the AAUP can confidently state that '[e]xtramural utterances rarely bear upon the faculty member's fitness for the position.'" The McAdams case is discussed in chapter 4.

19. The extent to which the 1964 *Statement on Extramural Utterances* vindicated Emerson's approach has been disputed. Finkin and Post, *For the*

Common Good, 144–48, suggest that it did, as does Wilson, "Academic Freedom and Extramural Utterances."

20. "Academic Freedom and Tenure: The University of California at Los Angeles," *AAUP Bulletin* 57 (1971): 382–420. The Davis investigation was conducted by philosophy professor Richard Brandt of the University of Michigan and law professor Hans Linde of the University of Oregon, who would later serve with distinction on the Oregon Supreme Court.

21. "Academic Freedom and Tenure: The University of Illinois at Urbana-Champaign," *AAUP Bulletin* 101 (2015): 27–47. For more on the Salaita case, see chapters 1 and 4.

22. It is sometimes noted that the fitness standard creates an awkward anomaly. Since, for example, Holocaust denial could well be grounds for the discipline or dismissal of a historian of Europe, the standard creates a situation in which the greater the qualifications of a faculty member to opine on a topic, the less freedom is afforded. So, for example, law professor Phillip Johnson could freely argue for "intelligent design," but the fitness of a biology professor might legitimately be questioned were that professor to do the same. See Eugenie C. Scott, "Darwin Prosecuted: Review of Johnson's *Darwin on Trial*," *Creation Evolution Journal* 13, no. 2 (1993): 36–47; and Brian Spitzer, "The Truth, the Whole Truth, and Nothing but the Truth?," *Talk Reason*, Aug. 4, 2002.

23. Steven Lubet, "The Mess at Oberlin," *Faculty Lounge*, Aug. 4, 2016, www.thefacultylounge.org/2016/08/the-mess-at-oberlin.html.

24. Jonathan Marks, "Is Anti-Semitism a Firing Offense?," *Commentary*, Nov. 27, 2016, www.commentarymagazine.com/anti-semitism/is-anti-semitism-a-firing-offense/.

25. Helwink, "Oberlin College Did the Right Thing."

26. Marks, "Is Anti-Semitism a Firing Offense?"

27. Colorado Conference of the AAUP, "Report on the Termination of Ward Churchill," *Journal of Academic Freedom* 3 (2012).

28. Judith Butler, "The Criminalization of Knowledge: Why the Struggle for Academic Freedom Is the Struggle for Democracy," *Chronicle of Higher Education*, May 27, 2018, www.chronicle.com/article/The-Criminalization-of /243501.

29. Finkin and Post, *For the Common Good*, 133.

30. "1915 Declaration," 11.

31. "Academic Freedom: Professor Lovejoy's Criticism of Professor Wigmore's Proposals and the Latter's Reply," *Nation* 103 (1916): 561–62. Tiede, *University Reform*, 119.

32. Finkin and Post, *For the Common Good*, 140.

33. Keith Whittington, *Speak Freely: Why Universities Must Defend Free Speech* (Princeton, NJ: Princeton University Press, 2018), 153–54.

Chapter 4. Can I Tweet That?

1. Scott Jaschik, "Fireable Tweets," *Inside Higher Ed*, Dec. 19, 2013, www.insidehighered.com/news/2013/12/19/kansas-regents-adopt-policy-when-social-media-use-can-get-faculty-fired.

2. Kansas Board of Regents, *Policy Manual*, 97–98, www.kansasregents.org/resources/PDF/About/BoardPolicyManual.pdf.

3. The survey was conducted by the Babson Survey Research Group on behalf of Pearson Learning Solutions. See Jeff Seaman and Hester Tinti-Kane, *Social Media for Teaching and Learning* (Boston: Pearson Learning Solutions, 2013), www.pearsonlearningsolutions.com/higher-education/social-media-survey.php.

4. "Academic Freedom and Electronic Communications," in American Association of University Professors, *Policy Documents and Reports*, 11th ed. (Baltimore: Johns Hopkins University Press, 2015), 50. Parts of this chapter summarize or paraphrase portions of this report, of which I was the lead author.

5. Natasha Singer, "What You Don't Know about How Facebook Uses Your Data," *New York Times*, Apr. 11, 2018, www.nytimes.com/2018/04/11/technology/facebook-privacy-hearings.html. See also Thomas Fox-Brewster, "Facebook Is Playing Games with Your Privacy and There's Nothing You Can Do about It," *Forbes*, June 29, 2016, www.forbes.com/sites/thomasbrewster/2016/06/29/facebook-location-tracking-friend-games/#21bdaf5b35f9. For detailed background and additional resources, see Electronic Privacy Information Center, "Facebook Privacy," www.epic.org/privacy/facebook/; and Siva Vaidhyanathan, *Anti-social Media: How Facebook Disconnects Us and Undermines Democracy* (New York: Oxford University Press, 2018).

6. Peter Bruce, "The Facebook Controversy: Privacy Is Not the Issue," *Scientific American*, Apr. 18, 2018, https://blogs.scientificamerican.com/observations/the-facebook-controversy-privacy-is-not-the-issue/.

7. Zeynep Tufekci, "It's the (Democracy-Poisoning) Golden Age of Free Speech," *Wired*, Feb. 2018, www.wired.com/story/free-speech-issue-tech-turmoil-new-censorship/.

8. Jack Balkin, "The Political Economy of Freedom of Speech in the Second Gilded Age," *Law and Political Economy* (blog), July 4, 2018, https://lpeblog.org/2018/07/04/the-political-economy-of-freedom-of-speech-in-the-second-gilded-age/.

9. Kate Klonick, "The New Governors: The People, Rules, and Processes Governing Online Speech," *Harvard Law Review* 131 (2018): 1598–670. According to Timothy Garton Ash, "there are at least three ways in which some combination of private and public power produces what are arguably illegitimate restrictions" on the exchange of ideas and information on the

internet that "we will find hard to identify because they result from hidden, untransparent, nonaccountable interventions." *Free Speech: Ten Principles for a Connected World* (New Haven, CT: Yale University Press, 2016), 360.

10. "Academic Freedom and Electronic Communications," 42.

11. For the sake of conceptual convenience, this definition adds to the usual tripartite definition a separate freedom to speak on institutional matters, usually treated as implicit in the definition of faculty members as "officers" of their institutions with the right to speak as citizens.

12. Robert M. O'Neil, *Academic Freedom in the Wired World* (Cambridge, MA: Harvard University Press, 2008), 181.

13. "Academic Freedom and Electronic Communications," 45–46. See also Steve Kolowich, "The Academic Twitterazzi," *Inside Higher Ed*, Oct. 2, 2012, www.insidehighered.com/news/2012/10/02/scholars-debate-etiquette-live -tweeting-academic-conferences; and Noah Berlatsky, "The Dangers of Tweeting at Conferences," *Chronicle of Higher Education*, Nov. 15, 2017, www .chronicle.com/article/The-Dangers-of-Tweeting-at/241767.

14. "1940 Statement of Principles on Academic Freedom and Tenure with 1970 Interpretive Comments," in AAUP, *Policy Documents and Reports*, 14.

15. Quoted in Jonathan Rees, "More than MOOCs: What Are the Risks for Academic Freedom?," *Academe* 100, no. 3 (May–June 2014), www.aaup.org /article/more-moocs#.WniYrnxG1Ag.

16. Rees, "More than MOOCs."

17. "Academic Freedom and Electronic Communications," 47.

18. Quoted in Beckie Supiano, "What Happens in the Classroom No Longer Stays in the Classroom. What Does That Mean for Teaching?," *Chronicle of Higher Education*, July 19, 2018, www.chronicle.com/article/What -Happens-in-the-Classroom/243974.

19. Colleen Flaherty, "Didn't Mean to Offend," *Inside Higher Ed*, Sept. 6, 2013, www.insidehighered.com/news/2013/09/06/michigan-state-suspends -professor-teaching-following-anti-republican-remarks.

20. Colleen Flaherty, "Not-So-Great Expectations," *Inside Higher Ed*, Oct. 18, 2013, www.insidehighered.com/news/2013/10/18/professors-afforded -few-guarantees-privacy-internet-age.

21. Colleen Flaherty, "Don't Smile (You're on Camera)," *Inside Higher Ed*, Dec. 12, 2016, www.insidehighered.com/news/2016/12/12/student-secretly -records-professors-anti-trump-comments.

22. California Code, Education Code - EDC § 78907, http://codes.findlaw .com/ca/education-code/edc-sect-78907.html.

23. "OCC Rescinds Suspension of Student Who Recorded Teacher's Anti-Trump Comments," *Orange County Register*, Feb. 24, 2017, www

.ocregister.com/2017/02/24/occ-rescinds-suspension-of-student-who
-recorded-teachers-anti-trump-comments/.

24. "Targeted Online Harassment of Faculty," Jan. 31, 2017, www.aaup.org
/file/2017-Harassment_Faculty_0.pdf.

25. John K. Wilson, "Why the AAUP Is Wrong about Secret Recordings,"
Academe (blog), June 2, 2017, https://academeblog.org/2017/06/02/why-the
-aaup-is-wrong-about-secret-recordings/.

26. L. D. Burnett, "Rehearsal Space," *U.S. Intellectual History* (blog),
Aug. 13, 2016, https://s-usih.org/2016/08/rehearsal-space/; Supiano, "What
Happens in the Classroom."

27. Gary Rhoades, "Compromising Academic Freedom and Creating a
Hostile Classroom Environment," Apr. 28, 2011, www.aaup.org/AAUP
/newsroom/prarchives/2011/Ancel.htm#.Wnd98HxG1Ah.

28. "1915 Declaration of Principles on Academic Freedom and Academic
Tenure," in AAUP, *Policy Documents and Reports*, 10. The 1940 Statement asks
instructors not to introduce "controversial matter which has no relation to the
subject." A 1948 AAUP investigation at Evansville College in Indiana
emphasized that "this admonition is a guiding principle, and not a formula.
Aside from uncertainties as to what is 'controversial' and what is 'related,' all
experienced teachers realize that it is neither possible nor desirable to exclude
rigidly all controversial subjects, or all topics upon which the teacher is not an
expert." Moreover, the report added, "judgments concerning the handling of
controversial material will frequently depend not so much on the *what* as the
how. . . . The total effect of what a teacher says on controversial subjects in the
classroom depends a great deal upon the manner, the spirit in which he says it,
and the emphasis he places upon it. It depends also upon the previous
existence of a relationship of confidence and understanding between the
teacher and his students." "Academic Freedom and Tenure: Evansville
College," *AAUP Bulletin* 35, no. 1 (Spring 1949): 91–92.

29. Quoted in "Academic Freedom and Electronic Communications,"
56n19.

30. On *Garcetti*, see "Protecting an Independent Faculty Voice: Academic
Freedom after *Garcetti v. Ceballos*," Nov.–Dec. 2009, www.aaup.org/file
/Protecting-Independent-Voice.pdf.

31. Tim McGettigan, "The Children of Ludlow: Fighting for Free Speech
on Campus," *Academe* (blog), Sept. 29, 2017, https://academeblog.org/2017
/09/29/the-children-of-ludlow-fighting-for-free-speech-on-campus/; Scott
Jaschik, "Is Citing History a Threat?," *Inside Higher Ed*, Jan. 20, 2014, www
.insidehighered.com/news/2014/01/20/colorado-state-removes-email
-account-professor-who-criticized-cuts.

32. "Academic Freedom and Tenure: The University of Illinois at Urbana-Champaign," *AAUP Bulletin* 101 (2015): 27–47.

33. Claire Potter, "Natalie Zemon Davis 'Gets' Twitter, Supports Steven Salaita," *Chronicle of Higher Education*, Aug. 29, 2014, www.chronicle.com /blognetwork/tenuredradical/2014/08/natalie-zemon-davis-gets-twitter -supports-steven-salaita/.

34. The relevant case is Elonis v. U.S., 135 S. CT. 2001 (2015). See Enrique A. Monagas and Carlos E. Monagas, "Prosecuting Threats in the Age of Social Media," *Northern Illinois University Law Review* 36, no. 3 (2016): 69. In a rare case of a criminal charge brought against someone who threatened a faculty member for protected expression, in May 2018 a Boston man was charged with threatening to commit assault after he allegedly left a voicemail declaring "I'm coming for you" for a Bridgewater State University professor who had criticized President Trump on social media. Colleen Flaherty, "Man Charged with Threatening Professor," *Inside Higher Ed*, June 1, 2018, www .insidehighered.com/quicktakes/2018/06/01/man-charged-threatening -professor. In 2013, a student was expelled and criminally charged after threatening on Twitter to slit his professor's throat in front of the class. In 2017, a New Jersey man was arrested on charges of calling in telephone threats to Evergreen State College in Washington State after a series of student protests there drew national attention. William Westhoven, "Man Arrested for Phone Threat to College in Washington State," *Morris County Daily Record*, July 5, 2017, www.usatoday.com/story/news/nation-now/2017/07/05/new-jersey -man-arrested-threat-washington-college/450850001/.

35. Tim Wu, *Is the First Amendment Obsolete?* (New York: Knight First Amendment Institute, 2017), 7, 11, https://knightcolumbia.org/content/tim -wu-first-amendment-obsolete.

36. Tufekci, "It's the (Democracy-Poisoning) Golden Age."

37. "Taking a Stand against Harassment, Part of the Broader Threat to Higher Education," Sept. 7, 2017, www.aaup.org/taking-stand-against -harassment-part-broader-threat-higher-education.

38. Michael Mann, "I'm a Scientist Who Has Gotten Death Threats. I Fear What May Happen under Trump," *Washington Post*, Dec. 16, 2016, www .washingtonpost.com/opinions/this-is-what-the-coming-attack-on-climate -science-could-look-like/2016/12/16/e015cc24-bd8c-11e6-94ac-3d324840106c _story.html.

39. "Academic Freedom and Tenure: University of Missouri (Columbia)," *AAUP Bulletin* 102 (2016): 25–43.

40. Joshua A. Cuevas, "A New Reality? The Far Right's Use of Cyberharassment against Academics: A Firsthand Account by a Targeted Faculty Member," *Academe* 104 (Jan.–Feb. 2018).

41. Dan Lieberman, "Death Threats Are Forcing Professors off Campus," CNN.com, Dec. 28, 2017, http://edition.cnn.com/2017/12/21/us/university-professors-free-speech-online-hate-threats/index.html. See also the AAUP's October 12, 2017, letter to Drexel provost M. Brian Blake, https://1cohn81j5mw92tftq84ejugf-wpengine.netdna-ssl.com/wp-content/uploads/2018/01/Drexel-Ciccariello-Maher-10-12-17-2.pdf. Ciccariello-Maher came to his own defense in an op-ed piece; see "Conservatives Are the Real Campus Thought Police Squashing Academic Freedom," *Washington Post*, Oct. 10, 2017, www.washingtonpost.com/news/posteverything/wp/2017/10/10/conservatives-are-the-real-campus-thought-police-squashing-academic-freedom/.

42. Chris Quintana, "Lecturer Who Tweeted 'Trump Must Hang' Apologizes and Deletes Account," *Chronicle of Higher Education*, Apr. 12, 2017, www.chronicle.com/blogs/ticker/lecturer-who-tweeted-trump-must-hang-apologizes-and-deletes-account/117759.

43. Cleve R. Wootson and Susan Svrluga, "Fresno State Says It Can't Discipline the Professor Who Called Barbara Bush an 'Amazing Racist,' " *Washington Post*, Apr. 25, 2018, www.washingtonpost.com/news/grade-point/wp/2018/04/25/fresno-state-says-it-cant-discipline-the-professor-who-called-barbara-bush-an-amazing-racist/.

44. "University of Tampa Should Immediately Reinstate Lecturer Fired over Tweet," *Academe* (blog), Aug. 31, 2017, https://academeblog.org/2017/08/31/university-of-tampa-should-immediately-reinstate-lecturer-fired-over-tweet/.

45. Colleen Flaherty, "Furor over Philosopher's Comments on Violence against White People," *Inside Higher Ed*, May 11, 2017. See also Steve Kolowich, "Tough Talk," *Chronicle of Higher Education*, July 26, 2017, www.chronicle.com/article/Who-s-Left-to-Defend-Tommy/240757.

46. Colleen Flaherty, "Threats for What She Didn't Say," *Inside Higher Ed*, June 19, 2017, www.insidehighered.com/news/2017/06/19/classicist-finds-herself-target-online-threats-after-article-ancient-statues.

47. Colleen Flaherty, "Concession to Violent Intimidation," *Inside Higher Ed*, June 1, 2017, www.insidehighered.com/news/2017/06/01/princeton-professor-who-criticized-trump-cancels-events-saying-shes-received-death.

48. Hank Reichman, "Online Harassment of Faculty Continues; Administrators Capitulate," *Academe* (blog), Aug. 29, 2017, https://academeblog.org/2017/08/29/online-harassment-of-faculty-continues-administrators-capitulate/.

49. Hans-Joerg Tiede, "Action on Behalf of Dr. Laurie Rubel at Brooklyn College," *Academe* (blog), Jan. 17, 2018, https://academeblog.org/2018/01/17/stand-with-dr-laurie-rubel-at-brooklyn-college/.

50. "Academic Freedom and Tenure: The University of Nebraska–Lincoln," *AAUP Bulletin* 104 (July–Aug. 2018): 2–12.

51. Rick Shenkman, "Manisha Sinha Got Death Threats after Writing an Article Comparing Donald Trump to Andrew Johnson," *History News Network*, July 30, 2018, https://historynewsnetwork.org/article/169667.

52. Anita Levy, "State of the Profession: Targeted Harassment—Faculty Report Back," *Academe* 104 (Jan.–Feb. 2018).

53. Levy, "State of the Profession."

54. Michael Harriot, "Neo-Nazi Leader Orders White Supremacists to Harass American University's 1st Black Female Student Body President," *Root*, May 10, 2017, www.theroot.com/neo-nazi-leader-orders-white-supremacists -to-harass-ame-1795094288; "Student Sues Neo-Nazi Website Publisher after 'Troll Storm' of Harassment," *Guardian*, May 1, 2018, www.theguardian.com /us-news/2018/may/01/student-sues-daily-stormer-troll-storm-neo-nazi -harassment.

55. Arvind Dilawar, "How Universities Facilitate Far-Right Groups' Harassment of Students and Faculty," *Pacific Standard*, July 2, 2018, https:// psmag.com/social-justice/how-far-right-campaigns-are-pressuring -universities-to-censor-speech.

56. Quoted in Noëlle Liley, "Are Social Media Normalizing Campus Racism?," *Nation*, May 21, 2018, www.thenation.com/article/is-social-media -normalizing-campus-racism/.

57. Tressie McMillan Cottom, "The Real Threat to Campuses Isn't 'PC Culture.' It's Racism," *Huffington Post*, Feb. 19, 2018, www.huffingtonpost.com /entry/opinion-cottom-campus-racism_us_5a8afb80e4b00bc49f471b41.

58. "Academic Freedom and National Security in a Time of Crisis," Oct. 2003, www.aaup.org/report/academic-freedom-and-national-security -time-crisis.

59. Roger Cohen, "Israel Banishes a Columbia Law Professor for Thinking Differently," *New York Times*, May 4, 2018, www.nytimes.com/2018/05/04 /opinion/israel-columbia-katherine-franke.html; Dina Kraft, "Two Lead-ing U.S. Human Rights Activists Refused Entry to Israel, One for BDS Ties," *Haaretz*, May 3, 2018, www.haaretz.com/israel-news/.premium-two-leading-u -s-human-rights-activists-deported-from-israel-1.6052515.

60. Alex Kane, "The FBI Is Using Unvetted, Right-Wing Blacklists to Question Activists about Their Support for Palestine," *Intercept*, June 24, 2018, https://theintercept.com/2018/06/24/students-for-justice-in-palestine-fbi -sjp/.

61. Rebecca Schuman, "Oh Good, a 'Professor Watch List,'" *Slate*, Nov. 23, 2016, www.slate.com/articles/news_and_politics/education/2016/11 /professor_watchlist_is_a_grotesque_catalog_of_left_leaning_academics

.html; Matthew Boedy, "Responding to the 'Professor Watch List,'" *Academe* (blog), Feb. 8, 2017, https://academeblog.org/2017/02/08/responding-to-the-professor-watch-list/.

62. "Targeted Online Harassment of Faculty."

63. Kelly Hand, "Add Your Name to the Professor Watchlist!," *Academe* (blog), Dec. 14, 2016, https://academeblog.org/2016/12/14/add-your-name-to-the-professor-watchlist/.

64. Michael Vasquez, "Inside a Stealth Plan for Political Influence," *Chronicle of Higher Education*, May 7, 2017, www.chronicle.com/article/Inside-a-Stealth-Plan-for/240008. See also David Perry, "The Right-Wing Plot to Take Over Student Governments," *Pacific Standard*, Apr. 20, 2018, https://psmag.com/.amp/education/the-right-wing-plot-to-take-over-student-governments.

65. Quoted in Steve Kolowich, "State of Conflict," *Chronicle of Higher Education*, Apr. 27, 2018, www.chronicle.com/interactives/state-of-conflict.

66. Lachlan Markay, "Exclusive: Pro-Trump Group, Turning Point USA, Has Finances Revealed," *Daily Beast*, June 28, 2018, www.thedailybeast.com/exclusive-pro-trump-group-turning-point-usa-has-finances-revealed; Alex Kotch, "Who Funds Conservative Campus Group Turning Point USA? Donors Revealed," *International Business Times*, Nov. 28, 2017, www.ibtimes.com/political-capital/who-funds-conservative-campus-group-turning-point-usa-donors-revealed-2620325.

67. Young America's Foundation, "Advising Our Students about TPUSA," May 25, 2018, www.yaf.org/news/yaf-memo-advising-our-students-about-tpusa/; James Hohmann, "The Daily 202: Koch Network Warns of 'McCarthyism 2.0' in Conservative Efforts to Harass Professors," *Washington Post*, Aug. 1, 2018, www.washingtonpost.com/news/powerpost/paloma/daily-202/2018/08/01/daily-202-koch-network-warns-of-mccarthyism-2-0-in-conservative-efforts-to-harass-professors/5b611a871b326b0207955e90/.

68. Hank Reichman, "George Ciccariello-Maher Resigns: 'We Are All a Single Outrage Campaign Away from Having No Rights at All,'" *Academe* (blog), Dec. 28, 2017, https://academeblog.org/2017/12/28/george-ciccariello-maher-resigns-we-are-all-a-single-outrage-campaign-away-from-having-no-rights-at-all/.

69. "Targeted Online Harassment of Faculty."

70. "Syracuse University Chancellor Defends Prof after Tweet Sets off Right-Wing Backlash," syracuse.com, June 26, 2017, www.syracuse.com/su-news/index.ssf/2017/06/syracuse_university_chancellor_defends_prof_after_tweet_sets_off_right-wing_back.html.

71. Jonathan Rees, "The Wrong Kind of Famous," *Chronicle of Higher Education*, Nov. 8, 2017, www.chronicle.com/article/The-Wrong-Kind-of-Famous/241701.

72. "Academic Freedom: Dr. Jonathan Higgins," July 26, 2017, www
.thismess.net/2017/07/academic-freedom-dr-jonathan-higgins.html.

73. "Taking a Stand against Harassment."

74. University of Iowa Office of the Executive Vice-President & Provost,
"Faculty Support & Safety Guidance," https://provost.uiowa.edu/sites
/provost.uiowa.edu/files/Faculty_Support_Safety_Guidance.pdf.

75. Adalberto Toledo, "UI Debuting Protocols for Handling 'Trolling'
Attacks on Faculty in Fall," *News-Gazette*, May 16, 2018, www.news-gazette
.com/news/local/2018-05-16/ui-debuting-protocols-handling-trolling-attacks
-faculty-fall.html.

76. Dana Cloud, "Responding to Right-Wing Attacks," *Inside Higher Ed*,
Nov. 7, 2017, www.insidehighered.com/advice/2017/11/07/tips-help
-academics-respond-right-wing-attacks-essay.

77. John K. Wilson, "Marquette to Fire John McAdams for His Blog,"
Academe (blog), Feb. 4, 2015, https://academeblog.org/2015/02/04
/marquette-to-fire-john-mcadams-for-his-blog/.

78. Peter N. Kirstein, "Beware of the Pedagogy Police: Cheryl Abbate v.
John McAdams at Marquette," *Academe* (blog), Feb. 9, 2015, https://
academeblog.org/2015/02/09/beware-of-the-pedagogy-police-cheryl-abbate
-v-john-mcadams-at-marquette-graphic-e-mail-in-appendix/.

79. Ira Allen, "Marquette to Fire McAdams for Dereliction of Duty,"
Academe (blog), Feb. 7, 2015, https://academeblog.org/2015/02/07
/marquette-to-fire-mcadams-for-dereliction-of-duty/.

80. Nicolette Perry, "Theology Professor Defends John McAdams on
Grounds of 'Due Process,'" *Marquette Wire*, Jan. 27, 2015, https://
marquettewire.org/3907918/tribune/tribune-news/theology-professor
-defends-john-mcadams-on-grounds-of-due-process/.

81. John K. Wilson, "AAUP Letter to Marquette on John McAdams,"
Academe (blog), Jan. 26, 2015, https://academeblog.org/2015/01/26/aaup
-letter-to-marquette-on-john-mcadams/.

82. Marquette University, University Academic Senate Faculty Hearing
Committee, "In the Matter of the Contested Dismissal of Dr. John C. McAdams:
Final Report," Jan. 18, 2016, www.marquette.edu/leadership/documents/20160118
-MUFHC-Final-Report-Contested-Dismissal-Dr-John-C-McAdams.pdf.

83. "Amicus Curiae Brief of the American Association of University
Professors in Support of Plaintiff-Appellant John McAdams' Petition to
Bypass," Feb. 27, 2018, www.aaup.org/sites/default/files/McAdams
_Marquette_Feb2018.pdf.

84. John McAdams v. Marquette University, 2018 WI 88, July 6, 2018, www
.wicourts.gov/sc/opinion/DisplayDocument.pdf?content=pdf&seqNo
=215236, Majority Opinion, 63.

85. *McAdams*, Majority Opinion, 48.

86. *McAdams*, Majority Opinion, 50.

87. *McAdams*, Majority Opinion, 52.

88. *McAdams*, Dissent, 17–20.

89. John K. Wilson, "Why *McAdams v. Marquette* Is a Victory for Academic Freedom and Shared Governance," *Academe* (blog), July 9, 2018, https:// academeblog.org/2018/07/09/why-mcadams-v-marquette-is-a-victory-for -academic-freedom-and-shared-governance/.

90. *McAdams*, Bradley Concurrence, 1–3.

91. I am indebted to Don Eron for calling my attention to this comparison. On the Churchill case, see Colorado Conference of the AAUP, "Report on the Termination of Ward Churchill," *Journal of Academic Freedom* 3 (2012).

92. Michelle Mynlieff, Sumana Chattopadhyay, and Bruce Boyden, "A Dangerous Precedent: Court's Ruling at Marquette," *Chronicle of Higher Education*, July 12, 2018, www.chronicle.com/article/A-Dangerous-Precedent- /243909. The senate leaders suggested that the result might have differed had the court simply sent the case back for a jury trial rather than deciding "for itself whether or not McAdams's actions exceeded the boundaries of academic freedom."

93. *McAdams*, Kelly Concurrence, 1.

94. *McAdams*, Dissent, 10.

95. *McAdams*, Dissent, 8.

96. *McAdams*, Dissent, 1.

97. *McAdams*, Majority Opinion, 58.

98. "The court . . . does not rely upon the United States Constitution for any part of its decision." *McAdams*, Majority Opinion, 63n35.

99. Walter Metzger, "Profession and Constitution: Two Definitions of Academic Freedom in America," *Texas Law Review* 66 (June 1988): 1265. I am indebted to Robert Post and Risa Lieberwitz for alerting me to this critical distinction.

100. *McAdams*, Majority Opinion, 30.

101. *McAdams*, Majority Opinion, 31.

102. *McAdams*, Majority Opinion, 39–40.

103. "Statement on Government of Colleges and Universities," in AAUP, *Policy Documents and Reports*, 120.

104. "Marquette University Statement on Wisconsin Supreme Court Decision," July 6, 2018, https://news.marquette.edu/news-releases/marquette -university-statement-on-wisconsin-supreme-court-decision/.

105. The remark is from Tressie McMillan Cottom of Virginia Commonwealth University, quoted in Chris Quintana, "If There's an Organized

Outrage Machine, We Need an Organized Response," *Chronicle of Higher Education*, July 18, 2017, www.chronicle.com/article/If-There-s-an-Organized /240683.

106. Hank Reichman, "Organizing, Organization, and the AAUP," *Academe* (blog), July 19, 2017, https://academeblog.org/2017/07/19/organizing -organization-and-the-aaup/.

107. Zeynep Tufekci, *Twitter and Tear Gas: The Power and Fragility of Networked Protest* (New Haven, CT: Yale University Press, 2017), preface.

108. Tufekci, *Twitter and Tear Gas*, 269.

109. This point has been made in Timothy Reese Cain, " 'Friendly Public Sentiment' and the Threats to Academic Freedom," *History of Education Quarterly* 103, no. 58 (Aug. 2018): 431.

Chapter 5. Can Outside Donors Endanger Academic Freedom?

1. Jay Schalin, *Renewal in the University: How Academic Centers Restore the Spirit of Inquiry* (Raleigh, NC: John William Pope Center for Higher Education and Policy, 2015), www.jamesgmartin.center/acrobat/pope _articles/centers_report-lores-final-rev.pdf.

2. The most exhaustive study of the political views of the American professoriate surveyed more than 1,400 full-time faculty members to find that only about half considered themselves "liberal," with just 9.4% "extremely liberal" and only 3% "Marxist." Neil Gross and Solon Simmons, "The Social and Political Views of American Professors," Working Paper, Sept. 24, 2007, www.conservativecriminology.com/uploads/5/6/1/7/56173731/lounsbery_9 -25.pdf. See also Neil Gross and Solon Simmons, "The Social and Political Views of American College and University Professors," in *Professors and Their Politics*, ed. Neil Gross and Solon Simmons (Baltimore: Johns Hopkins University Press, 2014), 19–52; and Jason Blakely, "Deconstructing the 'Liberal Campus' Cliche," *Atlantic*, Feb. 13, 2017, www.theatlantic.com/education /archive/2017/02/deconstructing-the-liberal-campus-cliche/516336/. Claims that college makes its graduates more liberal and less religious have also been debunked. See chapter 7, as well as Neil Gross, "The Indoctrination Myth," *New York Times*, Mar. 3, 2012, www.nytimes.com/2012/03/04/opinion /sunday/college-doesnt-make-you-liberal.html; and Christopher Newfield, "On Sympathy and Professionalism," *Remaking the University* (blog), Oct. 14, 2014, http://utotherescue.blogspot.com/2014/10/on-sympathy-and -professionalism.html.

3. Matthew Woessner, "Rethinking the Plight of Conservatives in Higher Education," *Academe* 98 (Jan.–Feb. 2012). Another conservative scholar, Keith Whittington, points out that "it marks a fundamental misunderstanding of academic life to conflate scholarly disagreements and political disagreements."

Speak Freely: Why Universities Must Defend Free Speech (Princeton, NJ: Princeton University Press, 2018), 165. A recent study based on 153 interviews with conservative faculty members found that "conservatives can survive and sometimes thrive in one of America's most progressive professions." Jon A. Shields and Joshua Dunn Sr., *Passing on the Right: Conservative Professors in the Progressive University* (New York: Oxford University Press, 2016).

4. See also Hank Reichman, "A Conservative Defense of Academia," *Academe* (blog), Mar. 15, 2016, https://academeblog.org/2016/03/15/a -conservative-defense-of-academia/; Hank Reichman, "Assault on Higher Education: A Conservative Critique," *Academe* (blog), Aug. 15, 2017, https:// academeblog.org/2017/08/15/assault-on-higher-education-a-conservative -critique/; and Hank Reichman, "Are Campus Conservatives Besieged? Not in Wisconsin," *Academe* (blog), Nov. 6, 2017, https://academeblog.org/2017/11 /06/are-campus-conservatives-besieged-not-in-wisconsin/.

5. Of course, hidebound and overly cautious thinking of any stripe may endanger the academic freedom of more iconoclastic scholars (see chap. 2), but there is little evidence that this is characteristic of the academy as a whole, or that it is limited to the imposition of some sort of "leftist" orthodoxy.

6. Sweezy v. New Hampshire, 354 U.S. 234 (1957). Frankfurter's opinion is a cornerstone of what Walter Metzger termed the "constitutional" view of academic freedom, which, unlike that of the AAUP, privileges the autonomy of the institution over the protection of professional norms by the faculty. Walter Metzger, "Profession and Constitution: Two Definitions of Academic Freedom in America," *Texas Law Review* 66 (June 1988): 1265. See also Marjorie Heins, *Priests of Our Democracy: The Supreme Court, Academic Freedom, and the Anti-Communist Purge* (New York: NYU Press, 2013).

7. For an elaboration of this conservative version of academic freedom, see Jay Schalin, *Academic Freedom in the Age of Political Correctness* (Raleigh, NC: John William Pope Center for Higher Education Policy, 2016).

8. Sally Covington, *Moving a Public Policy Agenda: The Strategic Philan- thropy of Conservative Foundations* (Washington, DC: National Committee for Responsive Philanthropy, 1997), www.ncrp.org/wp-content/uploads/2016/11 /Moving-a-Public-Policy-Agenda.pdf.

9. Jane Mayer, *Dark Money: The Hidden History of the Billionaires behind the Rise of the Radical Right* (New York: Doubleday, 2016). The book expanded on Mayer's essay "Covert Operations," *New Yorker*, Aug. 30, 2010, www.newyorker .com/magazine/2010/08/30/covert-operations. For more on the history of the Koch network, see Nancy MacLean, *Democracy in Chains: The Deep History of the Radical Right's Stealth Plan for America* (New York: Penguin, 2017). For information on UnKoch My Campus, see their website at www .unkochmycampus.org/.

10. Quoted in Annie Linskey, "With Patience, and a Lot of Money, Kochs Sow Conservatism on Campuses," *Boston Globe*, Feb. 2, 2018, www .bostonglobe.com/news/politics/2018/02/02/with-patience-and-lot-money -kochs-sow-conservatism-campuses/P6lrj1eIMNr4jPUZm8mbLO/story .html.

11. Ralph Wilson, "Conflicting Visions, Part I: Should Universities Accept Outside Funding for Free Market Centers?," James G. Martin Center for Academic Renewal, Nov. 2, 2016, www.jamesgmartin.center/2016/11 /conflicting-visions-part-universities-accept-outside-funding-free-market -centers/; Nell Gluckman, "Undeterred by Criticism, Koch Foundation Increases Spending in Higher Education," *Chronicle of Higher Education*, May 29, 2018, www.chronicle.com/article/Undeterred-by-Criticism-Koch /243528.

12. Jack Stripling, "How George Mason Became Koch's Academic Darling," *Chronicle of Higher Education*, May 13, 2016, www.chronicle.com/article/How -George-Mason-Became/236471.

13. "AAUP Expresses Strong Concern over Renaming GMU Law School and Issues of Shared Governance," May 10, 2016, www.aaup.org/news/aaup -expresses-strong-concern-over-renaming-gmu-law-school-and-issues-shared -governance#.WonuTnxG1Ah.

14. Angela Woolsey, "Students Suing GMU over Conservative Donations Could Become Historic Case," *Fairfax County Times*, Nov. 3, 2017; "George Mason University: Koch's Ground Zero," UnKoch My Campus, www .unkochmycampus.org/george-mason-university-1-2/.

15. Angela Woolsey, "GMU Student Lawsuit Challenges Privacy, Influence of Public University Donors," *Fairfax County Times*, Apr. 27, 2018, www.fairfaxtimes .com/articles/gmu-student-lawsuit-challenges-privacy-influence-of-public -university-donors/article_8da92c8a-4a60-11e8-8c17-635deab723b2.html.

16. The texts of Cabrera's emails may be found at https://ia601504.us .archive.org/19/items/CabreraEmails1and2/CabreraEmails1and2.pdf

17. Erica L. Green and Stephanie Saul, "What Charles Koch and Other Donors to George Mason University Got for Their Money," *New York Times*, May 5, 2018, https://mobile.nytimes.com/2018/05/05/us/koch-donors -george-mason.html; Nell Gluckman, "Why George Mason's Agreements with the Koch Foundation Raised Red Flags," *Chronicle of Higher Education*, May 2, 2018, www.chronicle.com/article/Why-George-Mason-s/243314; Colleen Flaherty, "Uncovering Koch Role in Faculty Hires," *Inside Higher Ed*, May 1, 2018, www.insidehighered.com/news/2018/05/01/koch-agreements -george-mason-gave-foundation-role-faculty-hiring-and-oversight.

18. Quoted in Sarah Larimer, "George Mason President: Some Donations 'Fall Short' of Academic Standards," *Washington Post*, Apr. 28, 2018, www

.washingtonpost.com/amphtml/local/education/george-mason-president
-some-donations-fall-short-of-academic-standards/2018/04/28/bb927576
-4af0-11e8-8b5a-3b1697adcc2a_story.html.

19. Allison Pienta, "The Federalist Society's Takeover of George Mason
University's Public Law School," UnKoch My Campus, www.unkochmycampus
.org/charles-koch-foundation-george-mason-mercatus-donor-influence
-exposed/.

20. Pienta, "Federalist Society's Takeover."

21. Pienta, "Federalist Society's Takeover"; Alex Kotch, "Right-Wing
Federalist Society Shaped Hiring and Admissions at George Mason
University, Emails Show," *Truthout*, May 2, 2018, www.truth-out.org/news
/item/44347-right-wing-federalist-society-shaped-hiring-and-admissions-at
-george-mason-university-emails-show.

22. George Mason University Faculty Senate, "Motions from Institutional
Conflict of Interest Committee," www.gmu.edu/resources/facstaff/senate
/Insitutional%20Conflict%20of%20Interest%20Committee%20Motions.pdf.

23. Sarah Larimer, "George Mason University Foundation Is Not Subject
to Public Records Laws, Judge Rules," *Washington Post*, July 6, 2018, www
.washingtonpost.com/amphtml/news/grade-point/wp/2018/07/06/george
-mason-university-foundation-is-not-a-public-body-judge-rules-in-records
-case/; Marc Parry, "George Mason's Foundation Does Not Need to Release
Records of Koch Foundation Agreements, Judge Finds," *Chronicle of Higher
Education*, July 6, 2018, www.chronicle.com/article/George-Mason-s
-Foundation/243868.

24. UnKoch My Campus, "Oversteps of Academic Freedom, Faculty
Governance, and Academic Integrity," www.unkochmycampus.org
/introduction/; and "Quid Pro Koch: Koch's Secret Higher Ed Agenda,"
Mar. 29, 2016, www.unkochmycampus.org/koch-campus-funding-whitepaper/.

25. FSU Progress Coalition and UnKoch My Campus, *A Case Study in
Academic Crime: The Charles Koch Foundation at Florida State University*,
Spring 2017, https://ia801907.us.archive.org/11/items
/FSUUnKochCaseStudy2017/FSU%20UnKoch%20Case%20Study%202017
.pdf. See also Alex Kotch, "Investigation Reveals the Extent the Koch Empire
Is Willing to Go to Take Over a University," *Alternet*, Feb. 3, 2017, www.alternet
.org/education/koch-brothers-fsu.

26. Jim Tankersley, "Inside Charles Koch's $200 Million Quest for a
'Republic of Science,'" *Washington Post*, June 3, 2016, www.washingtonpost
.com/news/wonk/wp/2016/06/03/inside-charles-kochs-200-million-quest
-for-a-republic-of-science/.

27. UnKoch My Campus, "*A Case Study in Academic Crime: Koch at Florida
State University*," press release, Jan. 12, 2017, www.unkochmycampus.org

/progress-coalition-2017/; Byron Dobson, "Charles Koch Foundation Provides More Than $800,000 in Research Grants to FSU," *Tallahassee Democrat*, June 15, 2016, www.tallahassee.com/story/news/2016/06/15 /charles-koch-foundation-provides-more-than-800000-research-grants-fsu /85931902/.

28. Jack Kochak, "Questions Raised about New AU Business Center," *Auburn Villager*, Sept. 18, 2008, www.auburnvillager.com/news/questions -raised-about-new-au-business-center/article_05141c93-cf21-5ab9-8ed5 -e0eae892744d.html.

29. Jeremy Gray, "Why Did the Koch Brothers Give Troy University $298,500?," al.com, Dec. 17, 2015, www.al.com/news/montgomery/index.ssf /2015/12/why_did_the_koch_brothers_give.html.

30. David V. Johnson, "Academe on the Auction Block," *Baffler* 36 (Fall 2017), https://thebaffler.com/salvos/academe-on-the-auction-block-johnson.

31. Southern Poverty Law Center, "League of the South," www.splcenter .org/fighting-hate/extremist-files/group/league-south.

32. "Advancing White Supremacy through Academic Strategy," UnKoch My Campus, www.unkochmycampus.org/los-preface; Alex Kotch, "How Charles Koch Is Helping Neo-Confederates Teach College Students," *Nation*, Mar. 21, 2018, www.thenation.com/article/how-charles-koch-is-helping-neo -confederates-teach-college-students/.

33. James Hohmann, "The Daily 202: Koch Network Warns of 'McCarthy-ism 2.0' in Conservative Efforts to Harass Professors," *Washington Post*, Aug. 1, 2018, www.washingtonpost.com/news/powerpost/paloma/daily-202/2018 /08/01/daily-202-koch-network-warns-of-mccarthyism-2-0-in-conservative -efforts-to-harass-professors/5b611a871b326b0207955e90/.

34. Tina Dyakon, "Poynter, Koch Foundation Expand Impact in Year Two of Program for College Journalists," Aug. 2, 2018, www.poynter.org/news /poynter-koch-foundation-expand-impact-year-two-program-college -journalists; Kelly McBride, "What We Do with Money from the Koch Foundation," Aug. 2, 2018, www.poynter.org/news/what-we-do-money-koch -foundation. In an email to the author, Frank LoMonte, former director of the Student Press Law Center, described Poynter as "a freestanding nonprofit that offers continuing ed for journalists. They have no partisan or ideological identity." With respect to the Koch grant, he added, "The journalism programs they started with (Iowa State, Virginia Tech, Howard) are all good-quality programs that certainly aren't captive to any libertarian ideology."

35. Quoted in Paul Basken, "Think You Know What Type of College Would Accept Charles Koch Foundation Money? Think Again," *Chronicle of*

Higher Education, Dec. 20, 2017, www.chronicle.com/article/Think-You-Know
-What-Type-of/242103.

36. Becky Johnson, "WCU Faculty Set New Precedent for Standing Up to Political Influence of Big Donors," *Smoky Mountain News*, Sept. 21, 2016, http://smokymountainnews.com/news/item/18456-wcu-faculty-set-new
-precedent-for-standing-up-to-political-influence-of-big-donors.

37. Marjorie Cortez, "U. Faculty: Koch Foundation Gift 'Raises Serious Concerns' about Academic Freedom," *Deseret News*, Aug. 1, 2017, www
.deseretnews.com/article/865685934/U-faculty-Koch-Foundation-gift-raises
-serious-concerns-about-academic-freedom.amp.

38. Colleen Flaherty, "Strings Attached," *Inside Higher Ed*, Oct. 12, 2016, www.insidehighered.com/news/2016/10/12/kentuckys-university-senate
-opposes-terms-10m-deal-free-enterprise-center.

39. Scott Jaschik, "Donor's Slur Raises Questions for Colleges," *Inside Higher Ed*, July 12, 2018, www.insidehighered.com/quicktakes/2018/07/12
/donors-slur-raises-questions-colleges.

40. Margo Roosevelt, "$5 Million to California University from Billionaire Charles Koch Sparks an Uproar," *Mercury News*, June 11, 2018, www
.mercurynews.com/2018/06/11/5-million-to-california-university-from
-billionaire-charles-koch-sparks-an-uproar/amp/.

41. Jay Ford and Doug Beets, "Why the WFU Faculty Senate Opposes Koch Funding," *Winston-Salem Journal*, Apr. 19, 2017, www.journalnow.com
/opinion/columnists/jay-ford-and-doug-beets-why-the-wfu-faculty-senate
/article_29b70a29-257c-5722-83bf-2f9be6e49011.html; emphasis in the original.

42. Johnson, "Academe on the Auction Block."

43. American Academy of Arts and Sciences, *Public Research Universities: Changes in State Funding*, 2015, www.amacad.org/multimedia/pdfs
/publications/researchpapersmonographs/PublicResearchUniv
_ChangesInStateFunding.pdf.

44. Council for Aid to Education, "Press Release: Colleges and Universities Raise Record $40.30 Billion in 2015," Jan. 27, 2016, http://cae.org/images
/uploads/pdf/VSE_2015_Press_Release.pdf.

45. Christopher Newfield, *The Great Mistake: How We Wrecked Public Universities and How We Can Fix Them* (Baltimore: Johns Hopkins University Press, 2016), 86, 115; emphasis in the original.

46. Michael Mitchell and Michael Leachman, "Years of Cuts Threaten to Put College Out of Reach for More Students," Center on Budget and Policy Priorities, May 13, 2015, www.cbpp.org/research/state-budget-and-tax/years
-of-cuts-threaten-to-put-college-out-of-reach-for-more-students.

47. Colleen Flaherty, "$5 Million for 'Freedom Centers,'" *Inside Higher Ed*, Apr. 25, 2016, www.insidehighered.com/news/2016/04/25/arizona-amid-cuts-higher-ed-may-help-centers-supported-charles-koch.

48. Valerie Strauss, "Professor: A Disturbing Story about the Influence of the Koch Network in Higher Education," *Washington Post*, Apr. 22, 2018, www.washingtonpost.com/news/answer-sheet/wp/2018/04/22/professor-a-disturbing-story-about-the-influence-of-the-koch-network-in-higher-education/.

49. Stephanie Saul, "Arizona Republicans Inject Schools of Conservative Thought into State Universities," *New York Times*, Feb. 26, 2018, www.nytimes.com/2018/02/26/us/arizona-state-conservatives.html. In May 2018, a Republican member of the UNC Board of Governors proposed creation of an "honors college" devoted to the glorification of Western civilization, totally exempt from ordinary university policies. See John K. Wilson, "The Republican War on Academic Freedom in North Carolina," *Academe* (blog), May 27, 2018, https://academeblog.org/2018/05/27/the-republican-war-on-academic-freedom-in-north-carolina/.

50. Jim Small, "GOP Legislature Sending More Money to 'Freedom Schools,' Despite Existing Surplus," Arizona Center for Investigative Reporting, May 2, 2018, https://azcir.org/news/2018/05/02/gop-legislature-sending-more-money-to-freedom-schools-despite-existing-surplus/amp/.

51. Naveena Sadasivam, "Hostile Takeover," *Texas Observer*, Sept. 26, 2016, www.texasobserver.org/koch-free-market-institute-texas-tech/.

52. Gene Nichol, "Lessons on Political Speech, Academic Freedom, and University Governance from the New North Carolina," *First Amendment Law Review* 16 (2018): 68.

53. See http://students.yaf.org/young-americans-for-freedom/start-a-chapter/.

54. Amy Binder, "There's a Well-Funded Campus Industry behind the Ann Coulter Incident," *Washington Post*, May 1, 2017, www.washingtonpost.com/news/monkey-cage/wp/2017/05/01/theres-a-well-funded-campus-outrage-industry-behind-the-ann-coulter-incident/; Alex Kotch, "How the Right-Wing Koch and DeVos Families Are Funding Hate Speech on College Campuses across the U.S.," *Alternet*, Apr. 18, 2017, www.alternet.org/right-wing/rightwing-billionaires-are-intentionally-funding-hate-speech-college-campuses.

55. Alex Kotch, "Who Funds Conservative Campus Group Turning Point USA? Donors Revealed," *International Business Times*, Nov. 28, 2017, www.ibtimes.com/political-capital/who-funds-conservative-campus-group-turning-point-usa-donors-revealed-2620325.

56. Valerie Strauss, "Charles Koch Foundation's Unique Definition of 'Academic Freedom,'" *Washington Post*, Nov. 7, 2014, www.washingtonpost

.com/news/answer-sheet/wp/2014/11/07/charles-koch-foundations-unique-definition-of-academic-freedom/.

57. Colleen Flaherty, "A Shift for Koch, but How Much of a Shift?," *Inside Higher Ed*, July 25, 2018, www.insidehighered.com/news/2018/07/25/koch-foundation-pledges-make-future-grant-terms-public-critics-want-know-more-about.

58. Tankersley, "Inside Charles Koch's $200 Million Quest."

59. Stripling, "How George Mason Became Koch's Academic Darling"; Larimer, "George Mason President."

60. Stripling, "How George Mason Became Koch's Academic Darling."

61. Tankersley, "Inside Charles Koch's $200 Million Quest."

62. Jim Dwyer, "What Happened to Jane Mayer When She Wrote about the Koch Brothers," *New York Times*, Jan. 26, 2016, www.nytimes.com/2016/01/27/nyregion/what-happened-to-jane-mayer-when-she-wrote-about-the-koch-brothers.html.

63. Hank Reichman, "On Blacklists, Harassment, and Outside Funders: A Response to Phil Magness," *Academe* (blog), Apr. 11, 2017, https://academeblog.org/2017/04/11/on-blacklists-harassment-and-outside-funders-a-response-to-phil-magness/.

64. Gene Nichol, "Lessons on Political Speech," 39–72.

65. "Statement on the Proposed Closure of the University of North Carolina Law School Poverty Center," Feb. 2015, www.aaup.org/povertycenter. In 2017, the UNC Board of Governors once again took politically motivated action against the law school's Civil Rights Center. Despite objections from students, faculty, campus leaders, alumni, hundreds of deans and law professors, the AAUP, and the university's accrediting agency, the center was barred by a 24–3 vote from engaging in litigation. See Nichol, "Lessons on Political Speech," 60–64.

66. Ford and Beets, "Why the WFU Faculty Senate Opposes Koch Funding."

67. Mary Burgan, "Faculty Governance and Special-Interest Centers," *Academe* 95 (Nov.–Dec. 2009).

68. Jennifer Washburn, *University, Inc.: The Corporate Corruption of Higher Education* (New York: Basic Books, 2005).

69. AAUP, *Recommended Principles to Guide Academy-Industry Relationships* (Urbana-Champaign: University of Illinois Press, 2014).

70. Johnson, "Academe on the Auction Block."

71. AAUP, *Recommended Principles*, 43–44.

72. Johnson, "Academe on the Auction Block." On the privatization of scientific research, see Philip Mirowski, *Science Mart: Privatizing American Science* (Cambridge, MA: Harvard University Press, 2011).

73. Bryan Bender, "Choice for Energy Secretary Has Ties to Oil, Gas Examined," *Boston Globe*, Mar. 23, 2013, www.bostonglobe.com/news/nation/2013/03/22/industry-ties-scrutinized-mit-professor-picked-for-top-energy-post/lPgTD3FfXYf7FKbZKvpoDL/story.html.

74. Johnson, "Academe on the Auction Block."

75. L. D. Burnett, "Some Thoughts on the Kochlings at GMU," *Saved by History* (blog), May 1, 2018, http://savedbyhistory.blogspot.nl/2018/05/some-thoughts-on-kochlings-at-gmu.html.

76. "Statement on Corporate Funding of Academic Research," in American Association of University Professors, *Policy Documents and Reports*, 11th ed. (Baltimore: Johns Hopkins University Press, 2015), 275–76.

77. AAUP, *Recommended Principles*, 29.

78. AAUP, *Recommended Principles*, 4.

79. "On Partnerships with Foreign Governments: The Case of Confucius Institutes," June 2014, www.aaup.org/file/Confucius_Institutes_0.pdf.

80. Rudy Fichtenbaum, "Here's Why Politically Motivated Philanthropy Is Dangerous," *Chronicle of Higher Education*, May 10, 2018, www.chronicle.com/article/Here-s-Why-Politically/243389.

Chapter 6. Will Online Education Cure the "Cost Disease"?

1. See California Community Colleges Online Education Initiative, http://ccconlineed.org/.

2. Quoted in George Skelton, "Is Gov. Brown's Proposal for a Public Online Community College a Good Idea? Some Educators Say No," *Los Angeles Times*, Jan. 15, 2018, www.latimes.com/politics/la-pol-sac-skelton-jerry-brown-online-community-college-20180115-story.html.

3. The proposal may be found at http://doingwhatmatters.cccco.edu/FullyOnlineCommunityCollege.aspx.

4. Karin Fischer, "Can a Huge Online College Solve California's Work-Force Problems?," *Chronicle of Higher Education*, July 29, 2018, www.chronicle.com/article/Can-a-Huge-Online-College/244054. See also Felicia Mello, "A Community College Online? Gov. Brown's Plan Re-imagines Cyber Learning, but Faces Skeptics," *Calmatters*, Feb. 8, 2018, https://calmatters.org/articles/community-college-online-gov-browns-plan-re-imagines-cyber-learning-faces-skeptics/. On faculty union opposition, see Adolfo Guzman-Lopez, "Faculty Union Says They Don't Want a New Online Community College," Southern California Public Radio, Apr. 12, 2018, www.scpr.org/news/2018/04/12/82235/faculty-say-they-don-t-want-a-new-online-community/. For a defense of the plan, see Eloy Ortiz Oakley, "Forging New Territory Online," *Inside Higher Ed*, Mar. 20, 2018, www.insidehighered.com/views/2018/03/20

/californias-online-community-college-better-alternative-profit-colleges
-opinion.

5. Toby Higbie, "The Governor's Thinking Has Become Very Uptight," *Remaking the University* (blog), Nov. 25, 2012, https://utotherescue.blogspot .com/2012/11/the-governors-thinking-has-become-very_25.html. Writes Higbie, "When [Brown] thinks about the digital revolution in education, he sees only online courses. When he reads an old out of print book on his iPhone, he sees only Google Books and not the library that contributed the book. When he Googles 'university education online' he just reads the hits, and doesn't see the educational infrastructure that trained the computer scientists who wrote algorithms and designed his iPhone."

6. Ry Rivard, "Udacity Project on 'Pause,'" *Inside Higher Ed*, July 18, 2013, www.insidehighered.com/news/2013/07/18/citing-disappointing-student -outcomes-san-jose-state-pauses-work-udacity. See also Anya Kamenetz, "San Jose State's MOOC Missteps Easy to See," *Diverse Issues in Higher Education*, July 29, 2013, diverseeducation.com/article/54903/.

7. Christopher Newfield, "Where Are the Savings?," *Inside Higher Ed*, June 24, 2013, www.insidehighered.com/views/2013/06/24/essay-sees -missing-savings-georgia-techs-much-discussed-mooc-based-program.

8. Christopher Newfield, "Online and the Color Line," *Remaking the University* (blog), Jan. 18, 2018, http://utotherescue.blogspot.com/2018/01 /online-and-color-line.html.

9. William G. Bowen in collaboration with Kelly A. Lack, *Higher Education in the Digital Age* (Princeton, NJ: Princeton University Press, 2013).

10. William Baumol and William Bowen, *Performing Arts, the Economic Dilemma: A Study of Problems Common to Theater, Opera, Music, and Dance* (New York: Twentieth Century Fund, 1966).

11. Bowen, *Higher Education in the Digital Age*, 3–4.

12. William J. Baumol, "Macroeconomics of Unbalanced Growth: The Anatomy of Urban Crisis," *American Economic Review* 57, no. 3 (1967): 421. Baumol served as AAUP first vice president from 1968 to 1970 and as chair of the association's Committee on the Economic Status of the Profession from 1961 to 1970.

13. Robert E. Martin and R. Carter Hill, "Measuring Baumol and Bowen Effects in Public Research Universities," Dec. 29, 2012, www.pdx.edu/sites /www.pdx.edu.econ/files/Measuring_Baumol_and_Bowen_Effects_in _Public_Research_Universities__NewDataFinal.pdf. For a recent survey of the issue, see Preston Cooper, "The Exaggerated Role of 'Cost Disease' in Soaring College Tuition," *Forbes*, May 10, 2017, www.forbes.com/sites /prestoncooper2/2017/05/10/the-exaggerated-role-of-cost-disease-in-soaring -college-tuition/#33bd60cf2b4e.

14. Dennis Jones and Jane Wellman, "Rethinking Conventional Wisdom about Higher Ed Finance," www.deltacostproject.org/sites/default/files /products/advisory_10_Myths_0.pdf.

15. CSU Audited Financial Statements, www.calstate.edu/financialservices /resources/auditedstatements/systemwide/2016-2017_SystemwideFS.PDF. For 2017 enrollment, see www.calstate.edu/as/cyr/cyr17-18/table03.shtml. For 1990 enrollment, see www.calstate.edu/as/stat_abstract/stat0910/pdf/z2a10 .pdf (p. 42 of document). See also CSU Management Personnel Plan Database, analyzed by California Faculty Association (CFA), www.calfac.org/sites/main /files/file-attachments/mpp_hc_longitudinal_93_to_16.pdf. I am indebted to Aimee Schreck and Vincent Cevasco of CFA for this information.

16. John Seery, "Somewhere between a Jeremiad and a Eulogy," *Modern Age* 59, no. 3 (2017), https://home.isi.org/somewhere-between-jeremiad-and -eulogy.

17. "Discussion by John Hennessy," in Bowen, *Higher Education in the Digital Age*, 115.

18. "Here's the News: The Annual Report on the Economic Status of the Profession, 2012–13," www.aaup.org/report/heres-news-annual-report -economic-status-profession-2012-13.

19. "Here's the News."

20. Bowen, *Higher Education in the Digital Age*, 45.

21. Chuck Rybak, *UW Struggle: When a State Attacks Its University* (Minneapolis: University of Minnesota Press, 2017), 49.

22. For a thoughtful treatment of the challenges posed by online education, see Mary Burgan, *What Ever Happened to the Faculty? Drift and Decision in Higher Education* (Baltimore: Johns Hopkins University Press, 2006), chap. 4.

23. For the instructors' own initial evaluation of the edX partnership sections, see www.edx.org/sites/default/files/upload/ed-tech-paper.pdf.

24. Shanna Smith Jaggars and Di Xu, "Online Learning in the Virginia Community College System," Sept. 2010, https://ccrc.tc.columbia.edu /publications/online-learning-virginia.html; Di Xu and Shanna Smith Jaggars, "Online and Hybrid Course Enrollment and Performance in Washington State Community and Technical Colleges," Mar. 2011, https://ccrc.tc .columbia.edu/publications/online-hybrid-courses-washington.html. See also Shanna Smith Jaggars, "Online Learning in the Community Colleges," in *Handbook of Distance Education* (New York: Routledge, 2012).

25. Jill Barshay, "Five Studies Find Online Courses Are Not Working Well at Community Colleges," *Hechinger Report*, Apr. 27, 2015, https:// hechingerreport.org/five-studies-find-online-courses-are-not-working-at -community-colleges/.

26. Hans Johnson and Marisol Cuellar Mejia, "Online Learning and Student Outcomes in California's Community Colleges," Public Policy Institute of California, May 2014, www.ppic.org/content/pubs/report/R _514HJR.pdf.

27. John Kenny and Andrew Edward Fluck, "Towards a Methodology to Determine Standard Time Allocations for Academic Work," *Journal of Higher Education Policy and Management* 39, no. 5 (2017): 503–23.

28. Robin Eberhardt, "Former Students File Class Action Lawsuit over Quality of Online Program," *GW Hatchet*, Apr. 13, 2016, www.gwhatchet.com /2016/04/13/former-students-file-class-action-lawsuit-over-quality-of-online -program/; Beth McMurtrie, "Controversy at George Washington U. Highlights Challenges of Diving Deeply into Online Education," *Chronicle of Higher Education*, Oct. 23, 2017, www.chronicle.com/article/Controversy-at -George/241528.

29. Margaret Mattes, "The Private Side of Public Higher Education," Century Foundation, Aug. 7, 2017, https://tcf.org/content/report/private -side-public-higher-education/.

30. Allison Bailey et al., *Making Digital Learning Work: Success Strategies from Six Leading Universities and Community Colleges*, Boston Consulting Group, Mar. 2018, https://edplus.asu.edu/sites/default/files/BCG-Making -Digital-Learning-Work-Apr-2018%20.pdf.

31. Phil Hill, "Rio Salado College as Exemplar: A Critical Internal View," *e-Literate* (blog), Apr. 22, 2018, https://mfeldstein.com/rio-salado-college-as -exemplar-a-critical-internal-view/; Phil Hill, "Rio Salado College as Exemplar: A Critical External View," *e-Literate* (blog), Apr. 23, 2018, https://mfeldstein .com/rio-salado-college-as-exemplar-a-critical-external-view/. See also Paul Fain, "Defining What's 'Good Enough' on Completion," *Inside Higher Ed*, May 9, 2018, www.insidehighered.com/digital-learning/article/2018/05/09 /debate-over-graduation-rates-rio-salado-largely-online-community.

32. Derek Newton, "Study: Online College Classes Cost Less to Deliver Because They Are Larger, Hire Cheaper Teachers," *Forbes*, May 23, 2018, www .forbes.com/sites/dereknewton/2018/05/23/study-online-college-classes-cost -less-to-deliver-because-they-are-larger-hire-cheaper-teachers/.

33. Newton, "Study"; Mark Liebman, "Dissecting a Glowing Report on Online Learning," *Inside Higher Ed*, Apr. 18, 2018, www.insidehighered.com /digital-learning/article/2018/04/18/online-education-observers-see -glowing-report-intriguing.

34. Quoted in Liebman, "Dissecting a Glowing Report."

35. Teresa Watanabe, "Gov. Brown Proposes California's First Fully Online Public Community Colleges," *Los Angeles Times*, Jan. 10, 2018, www.latimes .com/local/education/la-me-online-community-college-20170110-story.html.

36. California Community Colleges Chancellor's Office, "California Community Colleges Key Facts," http://californiacommunitycolleges.cccco .edu/PolicyInAction/KeyFacts.aspx.

37. Christopher Newfield and Cameron Sublett, "Does Online Reinforce the Color Line?," *Inside Higher Ed*, Mar. 20, 2018, www.insidehighered.com /views/2018/03/20/racial-implications-californias-proposed-online -university-opinion.

38. Rachel Baker et al., "Bias in Online Classes: Evidence from a Field Experiment," Stanford Center for Education Policy Analysis Working Paper 18-03, Mar. 2018, http://cepa.stanford.edu/sites/default/files/wp18-03-201803 .pdf; Scott Jaschik, "Race and Gender Bias in Online Courses," *Inside Higher Ed*, Mar. 8, 2018, www.insidehighered.com/news/2018/03/08/study-finds -evidence-racial-and-gender-bias-online-education.

39. Newfield and Sublett, "Does Online Reinforce the Color Line?"

40. Kentaro Toyama, *Geek Heresy: Rescuing Social Change from the Cult of Technology* (New York: Public Affairs, 2015), 7–8.

41. For a blistering survey of the demise of the "MOOC revolution," see Audrey Watters, "Education's Online Futures," *hackeducation* (blog), Dec. 13, 2017, http://hackeducation.com/2017/12/13/top-ed-tech-trends-online -education.

42. Bowen, *Higher Education in the Digital Age*, 65.

43. "Discussion by Daphne Koller," in Bowen, *Higher Education in the Digital Age*, 151.

44. Jonathan Rees, "I Have Run Out of Interesting Things to Write about Edtech," *More or Less Bunk* (blog), n.d., http://moreorlessbunk.net /technology/i-have-run-out-of-interesting-things-to-write-about-edtech/.

Chapter 7. Do Students Have Academic Freedom?

1. "Academic Freedom and Tenure: University of Missouri (Columbia)," *AAUP Bulletin* 102 (2016): 25–43. For an assessment of the crisis by the then chair of the university's Faculty Council, see Ben Trachtenberg, "The 2015 University of Missouri Protests and Their Lessons for Higher Education Policy and Administration," University of Missouri School of Law Legal Studies Research Paper no. 2018-27, July 24, 2018, https://papers.ssrn.com /sol3/papers.cfm?abstract_id=3217199##. It now appears that racial tensions at the university were also fueled by false information circulated by Russian bots. Lt. Col. Jarred Prier, USAF, "Commanding the Trend: Social Media as Information Warfare," *Strategic Studies Quarterly*, Winter 2017, 50–85, reported in Scott Jaschik, "How Russian Bots Spread Fear at University in the U.S.," *Inside Higher Ed*, Feb. 15, 2018, www.insidehighered.com/news/2018/02/15 /journal-article-explains-how-russian-bots-created-fear-university-missouri.

2. Hank Reichman, "Racism and Academic Freedom at Yale," *Academe* (blog), Nov. 10, 2015, https://academeblog.org/2015/11/10/racism-and -academic-freedom-at-yale/.

3. David Bromwich, "The New Campus Censors," *Chronicle of Higher Education*, Nov. 5, 2017, www.chronicle.com/article/The-New-Campus -Censors/241637. See also Jonathan Cole, "The Chilling Effect of Fear at America's Colleges," *Atlantic*, June 9, 2016, www.theatlantic.com/education /archive/2016/06/the-chilling-effect-of-fear/486338/.

4. See Greg Lukianoff, *Unlearning Liberty: Campus Censorship and the End of American Debate* (New York: Encounter, 2012); and Jon B. Gould, *Speak No Evil: The Triumph of Hate Speech Regulation* (Chicago: University of Chicago Press, 2005).

5. On student media censorship, see "Threats to the Independence of Student Media," *AAUP Bulletin* 103 (2017): 25–33. See also Frank LoMonte, "Beyond the Hashtag: Saving Student Newsrooms," *Medium*, Apr. 25, 2018, https://medium.com/@FrankLoMonte/beyond-the-hashtag-saving-student -newsrooms-ad5060d34bf8.

6. John Villasenor, "Views among College Students regarding the First Amendment: Results from a New Survey," Brookings Institution, Sept. 18, 2017, www.brookings.edu/blog/fixgov/2017/09/18/views-among-college -students-regarding-the-first-amendment-results-from-a-new-survey/. The study received major coverage in the *Washington Post* (see Catherine Rampell, "A Chilling Study Shows How Hostile College Students Are toward Free Speech," *Washington Post*, Sept. 18, 2017, www.washingtonpost.com/opinions /a-chilling-study-shows-how-hostile-college-students-are-toward-free-speech /2017/09/18/cbb1a234-9ca8-11e7-9083-fbfddf6804c2_story.html) and was touted by the editorial board of the *Wall Street Journal* and other conservative outlets.

7. Hank Reichman, "Debunking a 'Junk Science' Survey of Student Views on Free Speech," *Academe* (blog), Sept. 23, 2017, https://academeblog.org /2017/09/23/debunking-a-junk-science-survey-of-student-views-on-free -speech/.

8. Gallup, Inc., *Free Expression on Campus: A Survey of U.S. College Students and U.S. Adults*, www.knightfoundation.org/media/uploads/publication _pdfs/FreeSpeech_campus.pdf.

9. Vann R. Newkirk, "A Free-Speech Debate Devoid of Facts," *Atlantic*, Apr. 7, 2016, www.theatlantic.com/politics/archive/2016/04/first-amendment -college-campus-millennials/477171/. The survey was conducted again in 2017 and arguably revealed moderately less sympathy for free expression, although the differences were not large. The tone of media coverage also remained mostly unchanged. The survey also asked about social media. Those surveyed

reported that social media tended to stifle free speech. About 60% indicated that too many people block others online with whom they disagree—up 12 percentage points from 2016. About 59% said that they feared being attacked online for their views, an increase of 10 percentage points from 2016. Jeremy Bauer-Wolf, "Students Say Diversity Is More Important Than Free Speech," *Inside Higher Ed*, Mar. 12, 2018, www.insidehighered.com /news/2018/03/12/students-value-diversity-inclusion-more-free-expression -study-says.

10. Nick Anderson, "Survey: College Students Seek Balance on Free Speech and Hate Speech," *Washington Post*, Apr. 4, 2016, www.washingtonpost .com/news/grade-point/wp/2016/04/04/survey-college-students-seek -balance-on-free-speech-and-hate-speech/.

11. Cole, "Chilling Effect of Fear at America's Colleges."

12. Matthew Yglesias, "Everything We Think about the Political Correct-ness Debate Is Wrong," *Vox*, Mar. 12, 2018, www.vox.com/policy-and-politics /2018/3/12/17100496/political-correctness-data; Jeffrey Adam Sachs, "The 'Campus Free Speech Crisis' Is a Myth. Here are the Facts," *Washington Post*, Mar. 16, 2018, www.washingtonpost.com/news/monkey-cage/wp/2018/03/16 /the-campus-free-speech-crisis-is-a-myth-here-are-the-facts/. See also Jennifer Rubin, "The First Amendment Is Better Off Than You Might Think," *Washington Post*, Apr. 23, 2018, www.washingtonpost.com/blogs/right-turn /wp/2018/04/23/the-first-amendment-is-better-off-than-you-might-think/. For a thoughtful, if unpersuasive, retort to these views, see Sean Stevens, "The Skeptics Are Wrong: Attitudes about Free Speech on Campus Are Changing," Heterodox Academy, Mar. 19, 2018, https://heterodoxacademy.org/skeptics -are-wrong-about-campus-speech/. For Sachs's response, see "There Is No Campus Free Speech Crisis: A Close Look at the Evidence," Niskanen Center, Apr. 27, 2018, https://niskanencenter.org/blog/there-is-no-campus-free -speech-crisis-a-close-look-at-the-evidence/.

13. Foundation for Individual Rights In Education, "Speaking Freely: What Students Think about Expression at American Colleges," Oct. 2017, www .thefire.org/publications/student-surveys/student-attitudes-free-speech -survey/student-attitudes-free-speech-survey-full-text/. For an informative survey of attitudes toward diversity, discrimination, and political engagement of Americans aged 15–24, see Robert P. Jones et al., "Diversity, Division, Discrimination: The State of Young America," MTV-PRRI Report, Jan. 10, 2018, www.prri.org/research/mtv-culture-and-religion/.

14. "On Trigger Warnings," Aug. 2014, www.aaup.org/file/2014-Trigger _Warnings.pdf. For a useful discussion of trigger warnings, see Keith Whittington, *Speak Freely: Why Universities Must Defend Free Speech* (Prince-ton, NJ: Princeton University Press, 2018), 57–66.

15. Jacob T. Levy, "The Defense of Liberty Can't Do without Identity Politics," Niskanen Center, Dec. 13, 2016, https://niskanencenter.org/blog /defense-liberty-cant-without-identity-politics/.

16. "U of Chicago Faculty Letter to the Students," *Academe* (blog), Sept. 14, 2016, https://academeblog.org/2016/09/14/u-of-chicago-faculty-letter-to -the-students/.

17. "Academic Freedom at the University of Pittsburgh," *AAUP Bulletin* 15, no. 8 (Dec. 1929): 580–81. To my knowledge, the AAUP has not subsequently investigated alleged violations of student rights and has only twice investigated cases involving graduate student instructors—the 1929 Pittsburgh case and a 2018 case at the University of Nebraska–Lincoln.

18. Ralph F. Fuchs, "Academic Freedom—Its Basic Philosophy, Function, and History," *Law and Contemporary Problems* 28 (1963): 432.

19. "Joint Statement on Rights and Freedoms of Students," in American Association of University Professors, *Policy Documents and Reports*, 11th ed. (Baltimore: Johns Hopkins University Press, 2015), 381–86. For the history of the *Joint Statement*, see Richard H. Mullendore, "The 'Joint Statement on Rights and Freedoms of Students': Twenty-Five Years Later," *New Directions for Student Services*, Fall 1992, 5–23.

20. Recent treatments of campus free speech issues include Erwin Chemerinsky and Howard Gillman, *Free Speech on Campus* (New Haven, CT: Yale University Press, 2017); Sigal Ben-Porath, *Free Speech on Campus* (Philadelphia: University of Pennsylvania Press, 2017); Whittington, *Speak Freely*; "Symposium: Balancing First Amendment Rights with an Inclusive Environment on Public University Campuses," *Minnesota Law Review* 101, no. 5 (Mar. 2017); and Catherine J. Ross, "Campus Discourse and Democracy: Free Speech Principles Provide Sound Guidance Even after the Tumult of 2017," *University of Pennsylvania Journal of Constitutional Law*, Mar. 2018, 101–30. In 2017, the Association of Governing Boards of Universities and Colleges issued a report, *Freedom of Speech on Campus: Guidelines for Governing Boards and Institutional Leaders* (Washington, DC: AGB Press, 2017). For a perceptive treatment of contemporary student protest in the context of post-WWII student movements, see Roderick A. Ferguson, *We Demand: The University and Student Protests* (Oakland: University of California Press, 2017).

21. Hank Reichman, "A Troubling Assault on Student Rights at Fordham," *Academe* (blog), Feb. 16, 2017, https://academeblog.org/2017/02/16/a -troubling-assault-on-student-rights-at-fordham/.

22. "Threats to the Independence of Student Media."

23. "Draft Statement on Student Participation in College and University Government," *AAUP Bulletin* 56 (1970): 33–35.

24. "Yale's Little Robespierres," *Wall Street Journal*, Nov. 9, 2015, www.wsj .com/articles/yales-little-robespierres-1447115476.

25. Chemerinsky and Gillman, *Free Speech on Campus*, 73–74, 125.

26. Bruce Shapiro, "Don't Tell the Student Protesters at Yale to 'Grow Up,'" *Nation*, Nov. 13, 2015, www.thenation.com/article/dont-tell-the-student -protestors-at-yale-to-grow-up/.

27. Ben-Porath, *Free Speech on Campus*, 2–3.

28. See especially University of Chicago, "Statement on Principles of Free Expression," July 2012, https://freeexpression.uchicago.edu/page/statement -principles-free-expression. As of early 2018, the statement had been endorsed by thirty-five universities, and FIRE has begun a national campaign to gather more. For a skeptical take, see Osita Nwanevu, "When 'Free Speech' Is a Marketing Ploy," *Slate*, Mar. 23, 2018, https://slate.com/news-and-politics /2018/03/when-campus-free-speech-is-a-marketing-ploy.html.

29. "University to Freshmen: Don't Expect Safe Spaces or Trigger Warnings," *Chicago Maroon*, Aug. 24, 2016, www.chicagomaroon.com/2016/08 /24/university-to-freshmen-dont-expect-safe-spaces-or-trigger-warnings/.

30. See www.facebook.com/heritagefoundation/posts /10154446081184481.

31. John K. Wilson, "Does the University of Chicago Really Protect Free Expression?," *Academe* (blog), Aug. 25, 2016, https://academeblog.org/2016 /08/25/does-the-university-of-chicago-really-protect-free-expression/.

32. Jacob Levy, "Safe Spaces, Academic Freedom, and the University as a Complex Association," *Bleeding Heart Libertarians* (blog), Mar. 28, 2016, http://bleedingheartlibertarians.com/2016/03/safe-spaces-academic -freedom-and-the-university-as-a-complex-association/.

33. Brad DeLong, "A University Is Supposed to Be a Safe Space for Ideas . . . ," *Berkeley* (blog), Jan. 10, 2016, http://blogs.berkeley.edu/2016/01/10 /a-university-is-supposed-to-be-a-safe-space-for-ideas/.

34. Keith Whittington, *Speak Freely*, 71–73. Whittington's full discussion of "safe spaces" (65–74) is especially nuanced and persuasive.

35. "Tucker Carlson: On College Campuses 'Everybody Gets a Safe Space except White Men. They Are Hated and Despised,'" *Media Matters*, Feb. 10, 2017, www.mediamatters.org/video/2017/02/10/tucker-carlson-everybody -gets-safe-space-except-white-men-they-are-hated-and-despised/215316.

36. For a more extensive response to Carlson's stupidity, see Hank Reichman, "The Idiocy of Tucker Carlson," *Academe* (blog), Feb. 11, 2017, https://academeblog.org/2017/02/11/the-idiocy-of-tucker-carlson/.

37. "U of Chicago Faculty Letter to the Students."

38. John K. Wilson, "Disruptive Conduct and the University of Chicago," *Academe* (blog), Mar. 19, 2017, https://academeblog.org/2017/03/19

/disruptive-conduct-and-the-university-of-chicago/. See also Hank Reichman, "More on the Hypocrisy of the University of Chicago Administration," *Academe* (blog), Aug. 27, 2016, https://academeblog.org/2016/08/27 /more-on-the-hypocrisy-of-the-university-of-chicago-administration/.

39. Wilson, "Disruptive Conduct and the University of Chicago."

40. Malloy Owen, "What U. of Chicago Activists Are Complaining About," *American Conservative*, Aug. 26, 2016, www.theamericanconservative .com/articles/what-campus-activists-are-complaining-about/.

41. "Revised Final Report of the Committee on University Discipline for Disruptive Conduct," June 2, 2017, https://provost.uchicago.edu/sites/default /files/DCCRevisedFinal%20%286-2-2017%29_0.pdf.

42. Jeannie Suk Gersen, "How Trump Has Stoked the Campus Debate on Speech and Violence," *New Yorker*, June 4, 2017, www.newyorker.com/news /news-desk/how-trump-has-stoked-the-campus-debate-on-speech-and -violence.

43. "Hatch Introduces Bill to Protect Free Speech on College Campuses," press release, Feb. 7, 2018, www.hatch.senate.gov/public/index.cfm/2018/2 /hatch-introduces-bill-to-protect-free-speech-on-college-campuses. In July 2018, John Hardin, director of university relations for the Charles Koch Foundation, expressed criticism of such legislation, especially provisions that mandate suspension of students for "interfering with the rights of others." However, the Koch Foundation is a major funder of the Goldwater Institute. See James Hohmann, "The Daily 202: Koch Network Warns of 'McCarthyism 2.0' in Conservative Efforts to Harass Professors," *Washington Post*, Aug. 1, 2018, www.washingtonpost.com/news/powerpost/paloma/daily-202/2018 /08/01/daily-202-koch-network-warns-of-mccarthyism-2-0-in-conservative -efforts-to-harass-professors/5b611a871b326b0207955e90/.

44. PEN America, "Wrong Answer: How Good Faith Attempts to Address Free Speech and Anti-Semitism on Campus Could Backfire," Nov. 7, 2017, https://pen.org/wp-content/uploads/2017/11/2017-wrong-answer_11.9.pdf; "Campus Free-Speech Legislation: History, Progress, and Problems," *AAUP Bulletin* 104 (July–Aug. 2018): 38–47.

45. "Legislation on Free Speech," May 11, 2017, www.aaup.org/file/2017 -free_speech_legislation.pdf.

46. Pat Schneider, "Gagging the UW: Critics Worry Campus Speech Bill Is Another Attack on Academic Freedom," *Madison Capital Times*, June 7, 2017, http://host.madison.com/ct/news/local/education/university/gagging-the -uw-critics-worry-campus-speech-bill-is-another/article_cc7e994b-e6f2-5d16 -8ff2-11513bc03033.html.

47. North Carolina H.B. 527, Gen. Assemb., Reg. Sess. (N.C. 2017). See also Sam Killenberg, "Does the Campus Free Speech Bill Protect First

Amendment Rights—or Restrict Them?," *Raleigh News and Observer*, July 28, 2017, www.newsobserver.com/news/local/article164138247.html.

48. Gene Nichol, "Lessons on Political Speech, Academic Freedom, and University Governance from the New North Carolina," *First Amendment Law Review* 16 (2018): 56.

49. "Some Thoughts and Advice for Our Students and All Students," James Madison Program in American Ideals and Institutions at Princeton University, Aug. 29, 2017, https://jmp.princeton.edu/announcements/some -thoughts-and-advice-our-students-and-all-students.

50. Robert Quinn, "Free Speech Is Not Enough," *Diversity and Democracy* 20, nos. 2–3 (2017), www.aacu.org/diversitydemocracy/2017/spring-summer /quinn.

51. Aaron Hanlon, assistant professor of English at Colby College, has pointed out how "when students speak for themselves—as opposed to when media outlets disingenuously frame their concerns as matters of 'offense'— they don't usually speak of being offended. . . . If we actually listen to the students present at and behind some of the highest-profile campus controversies over the past few years, we find them articulating concerns that go well beyond being 'offended.'" Aaron R. Hanlon, "The Problem with 'Taking Offense,'" *Academe* (blog), Oct. 29, 2017, https://academeblog.org/2017/10 /29/the-problem-with-taking-offense/.

52. Geoffrey R. Stone, "Understanding the Free Speech Issues at Missouri and Yale," *Huffington Post*, Nov. 11, 2016, www.huffingtonpost.com/geoffrey-r -stone/understanding-the-free-sp_b_8535304.html.

Chapter 8. Are Invited Speakers Entitled to a Platform?

Epigraph: Timothy Garton Ash, *Free Speech: Ten Principles for a Connected World* (New Haven, CT: Yale University Press, 2016), 155.

1. Hank Reichman, "On Milo's Right to Speak," *Academe* (blog), Feb. 2, 2017, https://academeblog.org/2017/02/02/on-milos-right-to-speak/.

2. Jeremy Bauer-Wolf, "White Nationalist Defies Auburn," *Inside Higher Ed*, Apr. 19, 2017, www.insidehighered.com/news/2017/04/19/white -nationalist-backed-court-order-appears-auburn; Scott Jaschik, "Shouting Down a Lecture," *Inside Higher Ed*, Mar. 3, 2017, www.insidehighered.com /news/2017/03/03/middlebury-students-shout-down-lecture-charles -murray; Scott Jaschik, "Another Speech Shut Down," *Inside Higher Ed*, Apr. 10, 2017, www.insidehighered.com/news/2017/04/10/protest-over -speakers-views-race-and-crime-prevents-event-taking-place-planned.

3. On Milo's "Free Speech Week" fiasco, see Andrew Marantz, "How Social-Media Trolls Turned U.C. Berkeley into a Free-Speech Circus," *New*

Yorker, July 2, 2018, www.newyorker.com/magazine/2018/07/02/how-social
-media-trolls-turned-uc-berkeley-into-a-free-speech-circus. For Berkeley's
own summation of these events, with recommendations for future policy, see
"Report of the Chancellor's Commission on Free Speech," Apr. 9, 2018,
https://chancellor.berkeley.edu/sites/default/files/report_of_the
_commission_on_free_speech.pdf.

4. Jeremy Bauer-Wolf, "Coulter Changes Course," *Inside Higher Ed*, Apr. 27,
2017, www.insidehighered.com/news/2017/04/27/ann-coulter-will-back-out
-berkeley-talk; "UC Berkeley Spent $4 Million for Free Speech Event
Security," *Los Angeles Times*, Feb. 5, 2018, www.latimes.com/local/lanow/la
-me-berkeley-security-20180205-story.html; Diana Kampa, "Conservative
Pundit Ben Shapiro Lectures to Turbulent Crowd on Safe Spaces, Freedom of
Speech," *Badger Herald*, Nov. 17, 2016, https://badgerherald.com/news/2016
/11/17/conservative-pundit-ben-shapiro-lectures-to-turbulent-crowd-on-safe
-spaces-freedom-of-speech/; Kamal Kelkar, "Inside the 'Free Speech' Debate
That Rocked a Wisconsin Campus, with Ripples across the Country," *PBS
NewsHour*, May 13, 2018, www.pbs.org/newshour/nation/inside-the-free
-speech-debate-that-rocked-a-wisconsin-campus-with-ripples-across-the
-country.

5. Stanley Kurtz, "Understanding the Campus Free-Speech Crisis,"
National Review, Apr. 12, 2017, www.nationalreview.com/corner/campus-free
-speech-crisis/; "Tucker Carlson: On College Campuses 'Everybody Gets a
Safe Space except White Men. They Are Hated and Despised,' " *Media
Matters*, Feb. 10, 2017, www.mediamatters.org/video/2017/02/10/tucker
-carlson-everybody-gets-safe-space-except-white-men-they-are-hated-and
-despised/215316; "Attorney General Jeff Sessions Delivers Remarks to
Turning Point USA's High School Leadership Summit," US Department of
Justice, July 24, 2018, www.justice.gov/opa/speech/attorney-general-jeff
-sessions-delivers-remarks-turning-point-usas-high-school-leadership;
Donald Downs, "Free Speech Is More Threatened Than Ever and We Must
Respond," James G. Martin Center for Academic Renewal, May 3, 2017, www
.jamesgmartin.center/2017/05/free-speech-threatened-ever-must-respond/;
Jonathan Haidt, "Intimidation Is the New Normal on Campus," *Chronicle of
Higher Education*, Apr. 26, 2017, www.chronicle.com/article/Intimidation-Is
-the-New-Normal/239890.

6. "When Flamethrowers like Ann Coulter Come to Campus: Six
Students Weigh In," *New York Times*, May 2, 2017, www.nytimes.com/2017/05
/02/opinion/a-controversial-speaker-comes-to-campus-what-do-you-do
.html.

7. Corey Robin, "On Liberals, the Left, and Free Speech: Something Has
Changed, and It's Not What You Think It Is," *Corey Robin* (blog), Apr. 27,

2017, http://coreyrobin.com/2017/04/27/on-liberals-the-left-and-free-speech
-something-has-changed-and-its-not-what-you-think-it-is/.

8. "On Freedom of Expression and Campus Speech Codes," in American
Association of University Professors, *Policy Documents and Reports*, 11th ed.
(Baltimore: Johns Hopkins University Press, 2015), 361.

9. Ulrich Baer, "What 'Snowflakes' Get Right about Free Speech," *New
York Times*, Apr. 24, 2017, www.nytimes.com/2017/04/24/opinion/what
-liberal-snowflakes-get-right-about-free-speech.html.

10. Alan Ryan, *On Politics: A History of Political Thought: From Herodotus to
the Present* (New York: Liveright, 2012), 938.

11. Alyssa Rosenberg, "Ignore Ann Coulter. She's a Boring Performance
Artist, and She's Gaming Us All," *Washington Post*, Apr. 26, 2017, www
.washingtonpost.com/news/act-four/wp/2017/04/26/ignore-ann-coulter
-shes-a-boring-performance-artist-and-shes-gaming-us-all/.

12. David Faris, "Coultergate and the Truth about Campus Speech,"
Informed Comment (blog), May 2, 2017, www.juancole.com/2017/05
/coultergate-campus-speech.html.

13. Stanley Fish, "Free Speech Is Not an Academic Value," *Chronicle of
Higher Education*, Mar. 20, 2017, www.chronicle.com/article/Free-Speech-Is
-Not-an-Academic/239536. Sigal Ben-Porath writes, "Free speech is not in fact
a core value of the university. *Academic freedom* is a core value, and it does
both more and less than free speech." *Free Speech on Campus* (Philadelphia:
University of Pennsylvania Press, 2017), 20.

14. "Academic Freedom and Outside Speakers," in AAUP, *Policy Documents
and Reports*, 37–38.

15. Jordan Kurland, "Ban Outside Speakers? Not on Our Watch," *Academe*
93 (Sept.–Oct. 2007): 26–29. Subsequent quotes in this section are taken from
this article.

16. Feiner v. New York, 340 U.S. 315 (1951).

17. Hill v. Colorado, 530 U.S. 703 (2000). For a provocative treatment of
the legal standard governing the rights of speakers and hecklers alike, see
Frederick Schauer, "The Hostile Audience Revisited," Knight First Amendment Institute, 2017, and responses by David Pozen, Jelani Cobb, Mark
Edmundson, Suzanne Goldberg, and Rachel Harmon, https://knightcolumbia
.org/content/hostile-audience-revisited.

18. Quoted in Allan C. Brownfeld, "Heckler's Veto and Speech Codes
Threaten Free Speech at Universities," *Salem News*, Apr. 15, 2013, www.salem
-news.com/articles/april152013/free-speech-ab.php.

19. Thomas I. Emerson, *The System of Freedom of Expression* (New York:
Vintage, 1970), 338.

20. "Too PC or Not PC? The Debate over Free Speech on Campus," the1a .org, Apr. 25, 2017, https://the1a.org/shows/2017-04-25/too-pc-or-not-pc-the -debate-over-free-speech-on-campus.

21. The charges were ultimately dropped. Laurel Wamsley, "DOJ Drops Case against Woman Who Laughed during Sessions Hearing," National Public Radio, Nov. 8, 2017, www.npr.org/sections/thetwo-way/2017/11/08 /562823691/charges-dropped-against-woman-who-laughed-during-sessions -hearing.

22. David Pozen, "From the Heckler's Veto to the Provocateur's Privilege," Knight First Amendment Institute, 2017, https://knightcolumbia.org/content /hecklers-veto-provocateurs-privilege.

23. Jelani Cobb, "Unsafe Spaces," Knight First Amendment Institute, 2017, https://knightcolumbia.org/content/unsafe-spaces.

24. Jeremy Bauer-Wolf, "A Limit on Paying for Controversial Speakers," *Inside Higher Ed*, May 24, 2018, www.insidehighered.com/news/2018/05/24 /ucla-will-limit-how-much-it-will-pay-security-outside-speakers.

25. Erwin Chemerinsky, "UC Irvine's Free Speech Debate," *Los Angeles Times*, Feb. 18, 2010, http://articles.latimes.com/2010/feb/18/opinion/la-oe -chemerinsky18-2010feb18.

26. Erwin Chemerinsky, "Prosecuting UCI Students Unjust," *Orange County Register*, Oct. 5, 2011, www.ocregister.com/2011/10/05/erwin -chemerinsky-prosecuting-uci-students-unjust/.

27. Kurtz, "Understanding the Campus Free-Speech Crisis."

28. David Brooks, "The Crisis of Western Civ," *New York Times*, Apr. 21, 2017, www.nytimes.com/2017/04/21/opinion/the-crisis-of-western-civ.html; "Campus Mobs Muzzle Free Speech: Our View," *USA Today*, May 1, 2017, www.usatoday.com/story/opinion/2017/05/01/campus-protesters-free -speech-editorials-debates/100885962/; Adam Johnson, "N.Y. Times Focuses on Rights of Campus Conservatives, Slights Liberals," *Truthdig*, Jan. 22, 2018, www.truthdig.com/articles/new-york-times-campus-free-speech-coverage -focuses-7-1-plight-right/.

29. Jonathan Chait, "The 'Shut It Down!' Left and the War on the Liberal Mind," *New York*, Apr. 26, 2017, http://nymag.com/daily/intelligencer/2017 /04/the-shut-it-down-left-and-the-war-on-the-liberal-mind.html; Joe Concha, "CNN's Zakaria: Conservative Voices 'Are Being Silenced Entirely' on Campus," *Hill*, May 30, 2017, http://thehill.com/homenews/media/335586 -cnns-zakaria-conservative-voices-are-being-silenced-entirely-on-campus.

30. Hank Reichman, "Graduates Boo DeVos at HBCU Commencement," *Academe* (blog), May 10, 2017, https://academeblog.org/2017/05/10 /graduates-boo-devos-at-hbcu-commencement/.

31. See https://twitter.com/aaronrhanlon/status/1023900959976697856.

32. Adam Serwer, "A Nation of Snowflakes," *Atlantic*, Sept. 26, 2017, www.theatlantic.com/politics/archive/2017/09/it-takes-a-nation-of-snowflakes/541050/.

33. "Couple Charged in Shooting of Protester at Milo Yiannopoulos Event in Seattle," *Guardian*, Apr. 25, 2017, www.theguardian.com/us-news/2017/apr/25/milo-yiannopoulos-event-shooting-couple-charged-seattle.

34. Matt Pearce, "White Nationalist Shot at Protesters after Richard Spencer Speech in Florida, Police Say," *Los Angeles Times*, Oct. 20, 2017, www.latimes.com/nation/la-na-richard-spencer-speech-20171020-story.html.

35. Nick Coltrain, "Protests Turn Violent at CSU after Charlie Kirk Speech," *Coloradan*, Feb. 2, 2018, www.coloradoan.com/story/news/2018/02/02/violence-erupts-csu-protest-conservative-speaker-led/301496002/.

36. Adam Steinbaugh, "Hecklers Shout Down California Attorney General, Assembly Majority Leader at Whittier College," Foundation for Individual Rights in Education, Oct. 13, 2017, www.thefire.org/hecklers-shout-down-california-attorney-general-assembly-majority-leader-at-whittier-college/.

37. David Snyder, "How Trump's War on Free Speech Threatens the Republic," *Mother Jones*, June 2, 2017, www.motherjones.com/politics/2017/06/donald-trump-war-free-speech-attacks-news-media/; Bernard Weissberger, "Red Alert: The First Amendment Is in Danger," *Moyers and Company*, June 2, 2017, http://billmoyers.com/story/red-alert-first-amendment-danger/.

38. "Threats to the Independence of Student Media," *AAUP Bulletin* 103 (2017): 25–33.

39. Eddie S. Glaude Jr., "The Real 'Special Snowflakes' in Campus Free-Speech Debates," *Time*, Sept. 29, 2017, http://time.com/4958261/eddie-glaude-special-snowflakes/.

40. Sarah Jones, "The Invisible Free Speech Crisis," *New Republic*, Apr. 10, 2018, https://newrepublic.com/article/147908/invisible-free-speech-crisis.

41. Brandon Ambrosino, "How Trump Is Dividing Jerry Falwell's University," *Politico*, Oct. 27, 2016, www.politico.com/magazine/story/2016/10/trump-evangelical-falwell-liberty-university-christian-conservatives-214394.

42. Jones, "Invisible Free Speech Crisis."

43. Dave Vanness, "Professor Joel Berkowitz on the Exchange of Ideas in the University Classroom," storify.com, June 2017.

44. Jon A. Shields and Joshua M. Dunn Sr., "Forget What the Right Says: Academia Isn't So Bad for Conservative Professors," *Washington Post*, Mar. 11, 2016, www.washingtonpost.com/posteverything/wp/2016/03/11/forget-what-the-right-says-academia-isnt-so-bad-for-conservative-professors; Peter

Augustine Lawler, "The Standardization of Higher Education," *National Review*, Apr. 14, 2016, www.nationalreview.com/postmodern-conservative /434078/beyond-competency-and-diversity; Matthew Woessner, "Rethinking the Plight of Conservatives in Higher Education," *Academe* 98 (Jan.– Feb. 2012), www.aaup.org/article/rethinking-plight-conservatives-higher -education#.WoXeuXxG1Ag. See also Neil Gross and Solon Simmons, "The Social and Political Views of American College and University Professors," in *Professors and Their Politics*, ed. Neil Gross and Solon Simmons (Baltimore: Johns Hopkins University Press, 2014), 19–52; and Jason Blakely, "Deconstructing the 'Liberal Campus' Cliche," *Atlantic*, Feb. 13, 2017, www.theatlantic .com/education/archive/2017/02/deconstructing-the-liberal-campus-cliche /516336/.

45. "Does College Turn People into Liberals?," *Conversation*, Feb. 2, 2018, http://theconversation.com/does-college-turn-people-into-liberals-90905. See also Neil Gross, "The Indoctrination Myth," *New York Times*, Mar. 3, 2012, www.nytimes.com/2012/03/04/opinion/sunday/college-doesnt-make-you -liberal.html; and Christopher Newfield, "On Sympathy and Professionalism," *Remaking the University* (blog), Oct. 14, 2014, http://utotherescue.blogspot .com/2014/10/on-sympathy-and-professionalism.html.

46. Hank Reichman, "Are Campus Conservatives Besieged? Not in Wisconsin," *Academe* (blog), Nov. 6, 2017, https://academeblog.org/2017/11 /06/are-campus-conservatives-besieged-not-in-wisconsin/.

47. Serwer, "Nation of Snowflakes."

48. Stephen L. Carter, "The Ideology behind Intolerant College Students," Bloomberg News, Mar. 6, 2017, www.bloomberg.com/view/articles/2017-03 -06/the-ideology-behind-intolerant-college-students.

49. Paul Campos, "The New Hysteria over Campus Speech," *Lawyers, Guns, & Money* (blog), Mar. 12, 2017, www.lawyersgunsmoneyblog.com/2017 /03/new-hysteria-campus-speech.

50. Michael Hiltzik, "Are College Campuses Growing More Intolerant of Free Speech? The Numbers Say No," *Los Angeles Times*, Mar. 13, 2017, www .latimes.com/business/hiltzik/la-fi-hiltzik-campus-speech-20170313-story .html.

51. Charles G. Häberl, "Commentary: Obama Gets It Wrong on Rutgers' Speaker Protest," *Philadelphia Inquirer*, May 20, 2016, www.philly.com/philly /opinion/20160520_Commentary__Obama_gets_it_wrong_on_Rutgers __speaker_protest.html.

52. Ari Cohn, "Is FIRE's Disinvitation Database 'Shallow'? Hardly," Mar. 14, 2017, www.thefire.org/is-fires-disinvitation-database-shallow-hardly/.

53. Michael Hiltzik, " 'Political Correctness' on Campus: A Free-Speech Watchdog Defends Its Questionable Evidence," *Los Angeles Times*, Mar. 15,

2017, www.latimes.com/business/hiltzik/la-fi-hiltzik-fire-free-speech-20170315
-story.html.

54. Donald P. Moynihan, "Who's Really Placing Limits on Free Speech?,"
New York Times, Jan. 9, 2017, www.nytimes.com/2017/01/09/opinion/whos
-really-placing-limits-on-free-speech.html.

55. Samantha Harris, "Censorship Is a Bipartisan Issue," Jan. 9, 2017, www
.thefire.org/censorship-is-a-bipartisan-issue/.

56. Hiltzik, " 'Political Correctness' on Campus."

57. Moynihan, "Who's Really Placing Limits on Free Speech?"

58. See https://twitter.com/studentactivism/status/858073125761802242.

59. Hank Reichman, "Another Speaker Disinvited; This Time It's a Priest,"
Academe (blog), Sept. 16, 2017, https://academeblog.org/2017/09/16/another
-speaker-disinvited-this-time-its-a-priest/.

60. See www.facebook.com/haymarketbooks/posts/1494045207312386.

61. Sarah Jones, "Where Is the Outrage for Keeanga-Yamahtta Taylor?,"
New Republic, n.d., https://newrepublic.com/minutes/143064/outrage
-keeanga-yamahtta-taylor.

62. Quoted in Eli Rosenberg, "A Muslim-American Activist's Speech Raises
Ire Even Before It's Delivered," *New York Times*, May 26, 2017, www.nytimes
.com/2017/05/26/nyregion/linda-sarsour-cuny-speech-protests.html.

63. Baer, "What 'Snowflakes' Get Right."

64. Conor Friedersdorf, "What an NYU Administrator Got Wrong about
Campus Speech," *Atlantic*, Apr. 27, 2017, www.theatlantic.com/politics/archive
/2017/04/what-an-nyu-administrator-got-wrong-about-campus-speech
/524442/.

65. Friedersdorf, "What an NYU Administrator Got Wrong."

66. Friedersdorf, "What an NYU Administrator Got Wrong."

67. Traci Yoder, "Free Speech on Campus: A Critical Analysis," National
Lawyers Guild, May 25, 2017, www.nlg.org/free-speech-on-campus-a-critical
-analysis/

68. Yoder, "Free Speech on Campus."

69. Yoder, "Free Speech on Campus."

70. Frederick M. Lawrence, "The Contours of Free Expression on
Campus: Free Speech, Academic Freedom, and Civility," *Liberal Education* 103
(Spring 2017).

71. Yoder, "Free Speech on Campus."

72. Lawrence, "Contours of Free Expression on Campus."

73. Jim Sleeper, "First Amendment's Slippery Slope: Why Are Civil
Liberties Advocates Joining Forces with the Right?," *Salon*, Aug. 3, 2018, www
.salon.com/2018/08/03/free-speech-on-a-slippery-slope-why-are-civil

-liberties-advocates-joining-forces-with-the-right/. See also Jim Sleeper, "Speech Defects: How Consumer Marketing Distorts Democracy," *Baffler* 40 (Summer 2018).

74. Louis Michael Seidman, "Can Free Speech Be Progressive?," *Columbia Law Review* (forthcoming), available at https://scholarship.law.georgetown.edu/facpub/2038/.

75. Laura Weinrib, "The ACLU's Free Speech Stance Should Be about Social Justice, Not 'Timeless' Principles," *Los Angeles Times*, Aug. 30, 2017, www.latimes.com/opinion/op-ed/la-oe-weinrib-aclu-speech-history-20170830-story.html. See also Laura Weinrib, *The Taming of Free Speech: America's Civil Liberties Compromise* (Cambridge, MA: Harvard University Press, 2016). Seidman and Weinrib have been challenged by *Reason* editor J. D. Tucille in "Trump's Anti-Speech Agenda Gets a Boost from Lefty Lawyers and Academics," *Reason*, Mar. 19, 2018.

76. Walt Hunter, "The New Intellectuals," *Atlantic*, May 8, 2017, www.theatlantic.com/education/archive/2017/05/the-new-intellectuals/525660/.

77. Robert Paul Wolff, *The Ideal of the University* (Boston: Beacon, 1969), 53.

78. Wolff, *Ideal of the University*, 56.

79. Lisi Schoenbach, "Enough with the Crisis Talk!," *Chronicle of Higher Education*, May 16, 2018, www.chronicle.com/article/Enough-With-the-Crisis-Talk-/243423.

80. Fish, "Free Speech Is Not an Academic Value."

81. Fish, "Free Speech Is Not an Academic Value."

82. Jacob Levy, *Rationalism, Pluralism, and Freedom* (New York: Oxford University Press, 2015), 274.

83. Joan W. Scott, "On Free Speech and Academic Freedom," *Journal of Academic Freedom* 8 (2017).

84. Robert C. Post, "The Classic First Amendment Tradition under Stress: Freedom of Speech and the University," Yale Law School, Public Law Research Paper no. 619 (Oct. 2017).

85. *Report of the Committee on Freedom of Expression at Yale*, Dec. 1974, https://yalecollege.yale.edu/deans-office/reports/report-committee-freedom-expression-yale. The report has been republished as a small book with a new laudatory preface, introduction, and commentaries—but not with the powerful dissenting statement offered at the time by the panel's law student member. *Campus Speech in Crisis: What the Yale Experience Can Teach America* (New York: Encounter Books, 2016).

86. "An Open Letter from the AAUP to the Yale Community," www.aaup.org/news/2012/open-letter-aaup-yale-community; Scott Jaschik, "Black-balled at Yale," *Inside Higher Ed*, June 5, 2006, www.insidehighered.com/news

/2006/06/05/blackballed-yale; Colleen Flaherty, "Writing Bad Code?," *Inside Higher Ed*, Feb. 24, 2015, www.insidehighered.com/news/2015/02/24/yale-professors-object-vague-new-faculty-conduct-policy.

87. Fish, "Free Speech Is Not an Academic Value."

88. Fish, "Free Speech Is Not an Academic Value."

89. Aaron R. Hanlon, "Why Colleges Have a Right to Reject Hateful Speakers like Ann Coulter," *New Republic*, Apr. 24, 2017, https://newrepublic.com/article/142218/colleges-right-reject-hateful-speakers-like-ann-coulter.

90. Post, "Classic First Amendment Tradition under Stress."

91. Levy, *Rationalism, Pluralism, and Freedom*, 275–76.

92. See, e.g., his presentation at a forum at the University of California, Davis, in 2015, available at www.youtube.com/watch?v=bt4tYFlFOCQ.

93. Scott, "On Free Speech and Academic Freedom."

94. "1915 Declaration of Principles on Academic Freedom and Academic Tenure," in AAUP, *Policy Documents and Reports*, 5.

95. Carter, "Ideology behind Intolerant College Students."

96. Herbert Marcuse, "Repressive Tolerance," in *A Critique of Pure Tolerance*, ed. Robert Paul Wolff, Barrington Moore Jr., and Herbert Marcuse (Boston: Beacon, 1969), 81–123.

97. Carter, "Ideology behind Intolerant College Students."

98. Rainer Forst, *Toleration in Conflict: Past and Present* (Cambridge: Cambridge University Press, 2013).

99. Wendy Brown, *Regulating Aversion: Tolerance in the Age of Identity and Empire* (Princeton, NJ: Princeton University Press, 2008). Space is lacking for a more thorough consideration of this literature, but those interested may find helpful a short book, *The Power of Tolerance* (New York: Columbia University Press, 2014), which includes a debate between Brown and Forst.

100. Marcuse, "Repressive Tolerance," 84–85.

101. Marcuse, "Repressive Tolerance," 95.

102. Marcuse, "Repressive Tolerance," 90.

103. Marcuse, "Repressive Tolerance," 81.

104. Barrington Moore Jr., "Tolerance and the Scientific Outlook," in Wolff, Moore, and Marcuse, *Critique of Pure Tolerance*, 63.

105. Robert Paul Wolff, "Beyond Tolerance," in Wolff, Moore, and Marcuse, *Critique of Pure Tolerance*, 41, 43.

106. Wolff, "Beyond Tolerance," 47, 48–49.

107. Marcuse, "Repressive Tolerance," 123.

108. Wolff, *Ideal of the University*, 56; emphasis in the original.

109. Brown, *Regulating Aversion*, 11, 16.

110. Wolff, *Ideal of the University*, 148.

Chapter 9. Can Unions Defend Academic Freedom?

1. An early version of this chapter was presented at the panel "The AAUP at 100: A Century of Activity in Support of Academic Freedom" at the annual meeting of the American Historical Association (AHA) in New York on January 2, 2015. I am grateful for the support of my fellow panelists, Hans-Joerg Tiede, Ellen Schrecker, and Joan Scott, and especially for the insightful commentary of Clyde Barrow at that session.

2. "The Professors' Union," editorial, *New York Times*, Jan. 21, 1916; Frank Thilly, "Address of the President to the Members of the Association," *AAUP Bulletin* 3, no. 2 (1917): 7–10; "The Association Not a 'Union,'" *AAUP Bulletin* 3, no. 3 (1917): 3. In his comments at the AHA annual meeting in 2015, Clyde Barrow, referring to the letter writer's statement, noted, "Can one imagine the president of the U.S. Chamber of Commerce lamenting that his organization has become identified in the public mind with the fortunes of business? Can one imagine the president of the American Medical Association lamenting that his organization has become identified in the public mind with the fortunes of the medical profession? Only a professor would be embarrassed by the prospect of joining an organization that collectively represents his/her economic and occupational interest!"

3. Walter P. Metzger, *Academic Freedom in the Age of the University* (New York: Columbia University Press, 1955), 196, 203; Upton Sinclair, *The Goose-Step: A Study of American Education* (Pasadena, CA: self-pub., 1923), 455.

4. "Mission," http://aaup.org/about/mission-1.

5. Hans-Joerg Tiede, "'To Make Collective Action Possible': The Founding of the AAUP," *Journal of Academic Freedom* 5 (2014): 1, 24.

6. "1915 Declaration of Principles on Academic Freedom and Academic Tenure," in American Association of University Professors, *Policy Documents and Reports*, 11th ed. (Baltimore: Johns Hopkins University Press, 2015), 11; emphasis added.

7. Hans-Joerg Tiede, *University Reform: The Founding of the American Association of University Professors* (Baltimore: Johns Hopkins University Press, 2015), 201–9.

8. "1915 Declaration," 6.

9. See Timothy Reese Cain, "The First Attempts to Unionize the Faculty," *Teachers College Record* 112, no. 3 (Mar. 2010): 876–913.

10. Cain, "First Attempts to Unionize," 898–900.

11. Cain, "First Attempts to Unionize," 902.

12. Cain, "First Attempts to Unionize," 905.

13. Philo Hutcheson, *A Professional Professoriate: Unionization, Bureaucratization, and the AAUP* (Nashville: Vanderbilt University Press, 2000), 10.

14. Earl E. Cummins and Harold A. Larrabee, "Individual versus Collective Bargaining for Professors," *AAUP Bulletin* 24, no. 6 (Oct. 1938): 489.

15. Cummins and Larrabee, "Individual versus Collective Bargaining," 492.

16. Arthur O. Lovejoy, "Professional Association or Trade Union?," *AAUP Bulletin* 24, no. 5 (May 1938): 417, 410; emphasis in the original.

17. George A. Coe and Arthur O. Lovejoy, "Communications: Professional Association or Trade Union?," *AAUP Bulletin* 25, no. 3 (June 1939): 346. Lovejoy responded at length in the same issue, arguing that adoption of trade unionism would be equivalent to the adoption of a specific political creed and thereby concluding that "the real question at issue is whether we want academic freedom within the Association" (355).

18. William A. Herbert, "The History Books Tell It? Collective Bargaining in Higher Education in the 1940s," *Journal of Collective Bargaining in the Academy* 9 (2017): 21–37.

19. Hutcheson, *Professional Professoriate*, 36–37.

20. Hutcheson, *Professional Professoriate*, 84.

21. Hutcheson, *Professional Professoriate*, 82.

22. Hutcheson, *Professional Professoriate*, 60.

23. Hutcheson, *Professional Professoriate*, 61. Kugler would soon leave the AAUP for the AFT and go on to lead the 1966 strike of faculty at St. John's University and the formation of what would in 1972 become the Professional Staff Congress at the City University of New York. His son Phil became national organizing director for the AFT and played a key role in the development and implementation of the current joint organizing agreement between the AFT and the AAUP.

24. Hutcheson, *Professional Professoriate*, 69.

25. Hutcheson, *Professional Professoriate*, 70.

26. Hutcheson, *Professional Professoriate*, 74. See also Ralph S. Brown Jr., "Representation of Economic Interests: Report of a Conference," *AAUP Bulletin* 51, no. 4 (Sept. 1965): 374–77.

27. "Academic Freedom and Tenure: St. John's University," *AAUP Bulletin* 52, no. 1 (Mar. 1966). The AAUP investigating team would find no evidence of such a "rebellion."

28. "Faculty Participation in Strikes," *AAUP Bulletin* 54, no. 2 (June 1968): 155–59.

29. Hutcheson, *Professional Professoriate*, 79. Reviewing Hutcheson's book in *Academe*, Ernst Benjamin noted that Hutcheson "omits the AAUP's subsequent successes: its direct role in negotiating a collective bargaining agreement at St. John's incorporating AAUP standards, the successful resolution of the faculty cases as a precondition for censure removal, and the salutary effect of these actions on other Catholic colleges and universities."

Ernst Benjamin, review of *A Professional Professoriate: Unionization, Bureaucratization, and the AAUP*, by Philo A. Hutcheson, *Academe* 86, no. 6 (Nov.–Dec. 2000): 69.

30. "Representation of Economic Interests," *AAUP Bulletin* 52, no. 2 (June 1966): 229–34. Two members of the Special Committee, Robert Bierstedt and Fritz Machlup, dissented from the report, arguing that "the notion of collective bargaining, supported by most of us in the industrial context, is wholly inappropriate in the academic situation" and further that "the differences between the union approach and our own is fundamental" (34).

31. Hutcheson, *Professional Professoriate*, 100.

32. The Catholic University strike involved the denial of tenure to liberal theologian Charles Curran, who was reinstated but finally removed from the teaching of theology by order of the Vatican in 1988, resulting in the university's placement on the AAUP censure list. On the 1967 strike and subsequent events, see "Academic Freedom and Tenure: The Catholic University of America," *Academe* 75, no. 5 (Sept.–Oct. 1989): 27–40.

33. "Statement on Faculty Participation in Strikes," *AAUP Bulletin* 54, no. 2 (June 1968): 157.

34. "Policy on Representation of Economic and Professional Interests," *AAUP Bulletin* 55, no. 6 (Dec. 1969): 490.

35. "Council Position on Collective Bargaining," *AAUP Bulletin* 58, no. 1 (Mar. 1972): 46–61. On January 1, 2013, the association, with the encouragement of the Internal Revenue Service, divided into three legally distinct entities: the AAUP, a professional association; the AAUP Collective Bargaining Congress, a union federation of collective bargaining chapters; and a charitable foundation. Formally similar to the Gorman report's second alternative, the new arrangement, however, maintains a common staff and office headquarters for the three entities, with interlocking governance and leadership structures that retain the essence of the first alternative while conforming to legal requirements. All individual members of collective bargaining chapters automatically become members of the AAUP professional association.

36. During these years, the AAUP also participated in joint organizing efforts with the NEA, most notably at California State University, and with the AFT, most notably in the Professional Staff Congress at CUNY. The association, however, rejected overtures from the NEA for a merger.

37. Hutcheson, *Professional Professoriate*, 170–71.

38. On the *Yeshiva* decision, see Robert A. Gorman, "The Yeshiva Decision," *Academe* 66, no. 4 (May 1980): 188–97, which includes both the majority and minority opinions and an analysis of the case.

39. Ernst Benjamin, "How Did We Get Here?," *Academe* 101, no. 1 (Jan.–Feb. 2015): 43.

40. Matthew Finkin, "Report of Committee A 1983–84," *Academe* 70, no. 4 (Sept.–Oct. 1984): 21a–28a.

41. Reflecting on this report in an email to the author, Finkin wrote, "The rhetoric strikes me as much too shrill."

42. "Academic Freedom and Tenure: Temple University," *Academe* 71, no. 3 (May–June 1985): 16–27. A similar situation emerged at Northeastern Illinois University in 2013, where the AAUP again censured an administration for violating AAUP principles of academic due process and tenure, even though a state agency governing public employee labor relations had ruled that the case did not violate the university's contract with the AFT local representing the faculty, and the union had ceased to pursue the matter. Similarly, at the University of Southern Maine in 2015, a union contract made it difficult to adhere to AAUP standards, but the association placed the administration on its censure list nonetheless. See "Academic Freedom and Tenure: Northeastern Illinois University (December 2013)," *AAUP Bulletin* 100, no. 4 (July–Aug. 2014), www.aaup.org/sites/default/files/files/NEIU%20Bulletin_AcademeJulyAugust14full-2.pdf; "Academic Freedom and Tenure: The University of Southern Maine (May 2015)," *AAUP Bulletin* 102, no. 4 (July–Aug. 2015), www.aaup.org/sites/default/files/files/SME.pdf.

43. Benjamin, "How Did We Get Here?," 44–45.

44. Stephen R. Porter and Clinton M. Stephens, "The Causal Effect of Faculty Unions on Institutional Decision-Making," *ILR Review* 66, no. 5 (Oct. 2013).

45. Erik Olin Wright, "Class Boundaries in Advanced Capitalist Societies," *New Left Review* 98 (1976): 3–41. The quote from Barrow is from his commentary at the AHA session referenced in note 1. In these comments Barrow noted an additional ideological dimension of the tensions:

A lingering problem is that most university faculty have never made an ideological transition from the medieval to the industrial era in the sense that their self-consciousness and collective identity is still permeated by the religious and clerical origins of the Western university. Faculty have never relinquished the religious idea that "the material" is debased and degraded, that worldly politics is "dirty and corrupt," and that faculty are in the service of a "higher moral good," whose nobility is somehow enhanced by vows of poverty. Thus, as much as some faculty may declare their demand for professional status, what they really want is the wealth, prerogatives, and immunity of a priesthood that outwardly (if hypocritically) conveys the appearance of disdain for money and power, while simultaneously craving it. This is a contradiction at the core of the ideology of the intellectuals that has not yet been expunged by either professional associations or faculty unions, but the absence of "seculariza-tion" remains a major obstacle to collective action of any kind by university faculty.

46. Ernst Benjamin, review of *Professional Professoriate*, 70.

47. On the railwaymen's union, see Henry Reichman, *Railwaymen and Revolution: Russia, 1905* (Berkeley: University of California Press, 1987), especially chap. 6. On the pharmacists, see the wonderfully titled piece by Jonathan Sanders, "Drugs and Revolution: Moscow Pharmacists in the First Russian Revolution," *Russian Review* 44, no. 4 (Oct. 1985): 351–77. On the Union of Unions, see Jonathan Sanders, "The Union of Unions: Political, Economic, Civil, and Human Rights Organizations in the 1905 Russian Revolution" (PhD diss., Columbia University, 1993).

48. "Academic Unionism," Nov. 2005, www.aaupcbc.org/academic-unionism.

49. Mary Burgan, *What Ever Happened to the Faculty? Drift and Decision in Higher Education* (Baltimore: Johns Hopkins University Press, 2006), 121, 120.

Chapter 10. What Is the Future of Academic Freedom under the Trump Regime?

1. "Higher Education after the 2016 Election," Nov. 9, 2016, www.aaup.org/file/2016-HigherEd_Election_0.pdf.

2. Sheila Slaughter and Gary Rhoades, *Academic Capitalism and the New Economy: Markets, State, and Higher Education* (Baltimore: Johns Hopkins University Press, 2004).

3. Christopher Newfield, *The Great Mistake: How We Wrecked Public Universities and How We Can Fix Them* (Baltimore: Johns Hopkins University Press, 2016), 4. See also Christopher Newfield, *Unmaking the Public University: The Forty-Year Assault on the Middle Class* (Cambridge, MA: Harvard University Press, 2008).

4. "The responsibility of the university as a whole is to the community at large, and any restriction upon the freedom of the instructor is bound to react injuriously upon the efficiency and the morale of the institution, and therefore ultimately upon the interests of the community." "1915 Declaration of Principles on Academic Freedom and Academic Tenure," in American Association of University Professors, *Policy Documents and Reports*, 11th ed. (Baltimore: Johns Hopkins University Press, 2015), 8. "Institutions of higher education are conducted for the common good and not to further the interest of either the individual teacher or the institution as a whole. The common good depends upon the free search for truth and its free exposition."

338 Notes to Pages 245–247

"1940 Statement of Principles on Academic Freedom and Tenure," in AAUP,
Policy Documents and Reports, 14.

5. Comments made at opening plenary of annual meeting of the American Association of Colleges and Universities, San Francisco, Jan. 25, 2017, available at https://youtu.be/6POUpphHzudA. See also Sara Goldrick-Rab, *Paying the Price: College Costs, Financial Aid, and the Betrayal of the American Dream* (Chicago: University of Chicago Press, 2016); "It's Hard to Study If You're Hungry," *New York Times*, Jan. 14, 2018, www.nytimes.com/2018/01/14 /opinion/hunger-college-food-insecurity.html; "Poverty Is Largely Invisible among College Students," *Talk Poverty*, Nov. 7, 2017, https://talkpoverty.org /2017/11/07/poverty-largely-invisible-among-college-students/; "This Is #RealCollege: Some Students Struggle to Pay for Food, Housing," *Washington Post*, May 10, 2016, www.washingtonpost.com/news/grade-point/wp/2016/05 /10/this-is-realcollege-students-facing-food-and-housing-insecurity/; and Goldrick-Rab and Katherine M. Broton, "Hungry, Homeless and in College," *New York Times*, Dec. 4, 2015, www.nytimes.com/2015/12/04/opinion/hungry -homeless-and-in-college.html.

6. Jillian Berman, "Public Colleges Are Becoming Less Public, Fueling Inequality," *Market Watch*, Feb. 22, 2018, www.marketwatch.com/story/public -colleges-are-becoming-less-public-fueling-inequality-2018-02-22.

7. Danielle Douglas-Gabriel, "Trump and DeVos Call for Massive Cuts to College Student Aid Programs," *Washington Post*, Feb. 13, 2018, www.washington post.com/news/grade-point/wp/2018/02/13/trump-and-devos-call-for -massive-cuts-to-college-student-aid-programs/.

8. Michael Stratford, "Trump and DeVos Fuel a For-Profit College Comeback," *Politico*, Aug. 31, 2017, www.politico.com/story/2017/08/31 /devos-trump-forprofit-college-education-242193.

9. Spiros Protopsaltis and Clare McCann, "Misguided Effort to Dismantle Federal Protections," *Inside Higher Ed*, Apr. 16, 2018, www.insidehighered.com /views/2018/04/16/risks-trump-administrations-next-push-deregulate -higher-education-opinion; Erica L. Green, "DeVos Proposes to Curtail Debt Relief for Defrauded Students," *New York Times*, July 25, 2018, www.nytimes .com/2018/07/25/us/politics/betsy-devos-debt-relief-for-profit-colleges .html; Erica L. Green, "DeVos to Eliminate Rules Aimed at Abuses by For-Profit Colleges," *New York Times*, July 26, 2018, www.nytimes.com/2018 /07/26/us/politics/betsy-devos-for-profit-colleges.html.

10. Protopsaltis and McCann, "Misguided Effort."

11. Eric Kelderman, "Issues of Accreditation Predominate in New Rulemaking Announced by Education Dept.," *Chronicle of Higher Education*, July 30, 2018, www.chronicle.com/article/Issues-of-Accreditation/244097.

12. Andrew Kreighbaum, "DeVos to Announce New Push for Deregulation, Innovation," *Inside Higher Ed*, July 30, 2018, www.insidehighered.com /news/2018/07/30/trump-administration-official-describes-plan-rethink -higher-education-through. Soon after the department's announcement, the special White House office headed by Jared Kushner, senior adviser to and son-in-law of President Trump, held a meeting with officials from the department and conservative organizations to discuss accreditation issues. Kreighbaum, "White House, and Kushner, Dig Into Higher Ed," *Inside Higher Ed*, August 10, 2018, www.insidehighered.com/news/2018/08/10/kushner -team-convened-higher-ed-meeting-white-house-focused-accreditation.

13. Anya Kamenetz and Cory Turner, "DeVos Seeks to Rewrite the Rules on Higher Ed," National Public Radio, Aug. 2, 2018, www.npr.org/2018/08/02 /634398751/devos-seeks-to-rewrite-the-rules-on-higher-ed.

14. Anya Kamentetz, "Who Is a College Teacher, Anyway? Audit of Online University Raises Questions," National Public Radio, Sept. 28, 2017, www.npr .org/sections/ed/2017/09/28/553753020/who-is-a-college-teacher-anyway -audit-of-online-university-raises-questions; Paul Fain, "Federal Audit Challenges Faculty Role at WGU," *Inside Higher Ed*, Sept. 22, 2017, www .insidehighered.com/news/2017/09/22/education-depts-inspector-general -calls-western-governors-repay-713-million-federal.

15. Kreighbaum, "DeVos to Announce New Push"; Kelderman, "Issues of Accreditation Predominate in New Rulemaking."

16. Mark Potok, "The Year in Hate and Extremism," *SPLC Intelligence Report*, Feb. 15, 2017, www.splcenter.org/fighting-hate/intelligence-report /2017/year-hate-and-extremism; Aaron Williams, "Hate Crimes Rose the Day After Trump Was Elected, FBI Data Show," *Washington Post*, Mar. 23, 2018, www.washingtonpost.com/news/post-nation/wp/2018/03/23/hate-crimes -rose-the-day-after-trump-was-elected-fbi-data-show/; "The Year in Hate: Trump Buoyed White Supremacists in 2017, Sparking Backlash among Black Nationalist Groups," *SPLC Intelligence Report*, Feb. 21, 2018, www.splcenter.org /news/2018/02/21/year-hate-trump-buoyed-white-supremacists-2017 -sparking-backlash-among-black-nationalist.

17. SPLC, *The Alt-Right Is Killing People*, Feb. 5, 2018, www.splcenter.org /20180205/alt-right-killing-people; ADL, *Murder and Extremism in the United States in 2017*, Jan. 2018, www.adl.org/sites/default/files/documents/adl-murder -and-extremism-report-2017.pdf; J. M. Berger, *Nazis vs. ISIS on Twitter: A Comparative Study of White Nationalist and ISIS Online Social Media Networks*, George Washington University Program on Extremism, Sept. 2016, https://cchs .gwu.edu/files/downloads/Nazis%2520v.%2520ISIS%2520Final_0.pdf. See also Jonathan Greenblatt, "The Resurgent Threat of White-Supremacist Violence,"

Atlantic, Jan. 17, 2018, www.theatlantic.com/politics/archive/2018/01/the
-resurgent-threat-of-white-supremacist-violence/550634/.

18. Dan Bauman, "After 2016 Election, Campus Hate Crimes Seemed to
Jump. Here's What the Data Tell Us," *Chronicle of Higher Education*, Feb. 16,
2018, www.chronicle.com/article/After-2016-Election-Campus/242577. Need
it be noted that the numbers of such crimes far exceed the small number of
reported incidents in which invited speakers have been denied a platform,
although the latter receive far greater attention in media reporting?

19. Hank Reichman, "The Debate over 'Safe Spaces' Has Taken on New
Significance," *Academe* (blog), Nov. 13, 2016, https://academeblog.org/2016
/11/13/the-debate-over-safe-spaces-has-taken-on-new-significance/.

20. "The Atmosphere on Campus in the Wake of the Elections," Nov. 22,
2016, www.aaup.org/file/2016-PostElection-Atmosphere_0.pdf.

21. Andrew Kreighbaum, "As Civil Rights Office Gets More Money, It
Limits Investigations," *Inside Higher Ed,* March 30, 2018, www.insidehighered
.com/news/2018/03/30/more-money-civil-rights-office-comes-it-narrows-its
-investigative-work; Erica L. Green, "DeVos Education Dept. Begins
Dismissing Civil Rights Cases in Name of Efficiency," *New York Times*,
April 20, 2018, www.nytimes.com/2018/04/20/us/politics/devos-education
-department-civil-rights.html; National Federation of the Blind et al., v.
Department of Education, http://live-naacp-site.pantheonsite.io/wp-content
/uploads/2018/06/NFB-et-al-v-Dept-of-Education2c-et-al-Complaint
-Accessible-version-5-31-18.pdf.

22. "Atmosphere on Campus."

23. "AAUP Joins ACE Letter Urging Congress to Pass DACA Legislation,"
Sept. 14, 2017, www.aaup.org/news/aaup-joins-ace-letter-urging-congress-pass
-daca-legislation.

24. "AAUP Denounces Decision to End DACA Program," Sept. 5, 2017,
www.aaup.org/news/aaup-denounces-decision-end-daca-program.

25. "New Ban, Same Discrimination," Mar. 6, 2017, www.aaup.org/file/2017
-March_ban.pdf.

26. See www.aaup.org/sites/default/files/travel_ban_amicus_Sept2017.pdf.

27. See "Trump v. Hawaii, 138 S. Ct. 2392 (2018)," www.aaup.org/brief
/trump-v-hawaii-199-led2d-620-us-2018.

28. Aaron Nisenson, "Border Patrol Searches of Electronic Devices,"
Academe 103, no. 5 (Sept.–Oct. 2017).

29. Trump v. Hawaii, 585 U.S.___(2018), www.supremecourt.gov/opinions
/17pdf/17-965_h315.pdf.

30. On the *Yeshiva* decision, see Robert A. Gorman, "The Yeshiva
Decision," *Academe* 66, no. 4 (May 1980): 188–97, which includes both the
majority and minority opinions and an analysis of the case.

31. Kristen Edwards and Kim Tolley, "Do Unions Help Adjuncts?," *Chronicle of Higher Education*, June 3, 2018, www.chronicle.com/article/Do -Unions-Help-Adjuncts-/243566; Kim Tolley, ed., *Professors in the Gig Economy: Unionizing Adjunct Faculty in America* (Baltimore: Johns Hopkins University Press, 2018).

32. National Labor Relations Board, "The Trustees of Columbia University in the City of New York," case no. 02-RC-143012, Aug. 23, 2016, www.nlrb .gov/news-outreach/news-story/board-student-assistants-covered-nlra-0. See also Risa L. Lieberwitz, "Legal Watch: Reconsidering (Again) Graduate Assistants' Rights to Unionize," *Academe* 102, no. 3 (May–June 2016); "Improving the Legal Landscape for Unionization at Private Colleges and Universities," *Academe* 101, no. 6 (Nov.–Dec. 2015).

33. See www.aaup.org/sites/default/files/Janus_AFSCME_AAUP_NEA _Jan2018_0.pdf. See also Hank Reichman, "AAUP, NEA File Amicus Brief with Supreme Court in Agency Fee Case," *Academe* (blog), Jan. 22, 2018; and Hank Reichman, "Janus, Agency Fees, and the First Amendment," *Academe* (blog), Feb. 4, 2018, https://academeblog.org/2018/02/04/janus-agency-fees -and-the-first-amendment/.

34. Janus v. AFSCME, Council 31, 585 U.S.___(2018), www.scotusblog.com /case-files/cases/janus-v-american-federation-state-county-municipal -employees-council-31/.

35. "Brief for Amici Curiae Charles Fried and Robert C. Post in Support of Neither Party," www.supremecourt.gov/DocketPDF/16/16-1466/22874 /20171206174457493_16-1466%20ac%20Charles%20Fried%20and%20 Robert%20C.%20Post.pdf. See also Reichman, "Janus, Agency Fees, and the First Amendment."

36. "Protecting an Independent Faculty Voice: Academic Freedom after *Garcetti v. Ceballos* (Nov.–Dec. 2009)," *Academe* 96 (July–Aug. 2010): 64–88.

37. John K. Wilson, "The Right to Freeload Threatens Free Speech," *Inside Higher Ed*, Aug. 16, 2018, www.insidehighered.com/views/2018/08/16 /problems-janus-decision-union-dues-opinion; "Board of Regents of the University of Wisconsin System v. Southworth," 529 U.S. 217 (2000), https://supreme.justia.com/cases/federal/us/529/217/case.pdf.

38. "Columbia University, 364 NLRB No. 90 (August 23, 2016)," www.aaup .org/brief/columbia-university-364-nlrb-no-90-august-23-2016.

39. Eli Lee, "Graduate Student Strike Ends on Schedule, Union Organizers Threaten More Disruption Next Year," *Columbia Spectator*, May 4, 2018, www .columbiaspectator.com/news/2018/04/30/graduate-student-strike-ends-on -schedule-union-organizers-threaten-more-disruption-next-year/.

40. "Brown University Graduate Employees Sign Landmark Union Agreement with Administration," *Uprise RI*, June 21, 2018, https://upriseri

.com/news/labor/2018-06-21-brown-university-sugse/. See also Josh Eidelson, "Trump's Labor Board Turns Ivy League Schools against Each Other," *Bloomberg News*, June 21, 2018, www.bloomberg.com/amp/news/articles/2018 -06-21/trump-s-labor-board-turns-ivy-league-schools-against-each-other.

41. "University of Southern California v. National Labor Relations Board, No. 17-1149 (D.C. Cir. 2017)," www.aaup.org/sites/default/files/USC_amicus _Dec2017.pdf.

42. Chuck Rybak, *UW Struggle: When a State Attacks Its University* (Minneapolis: University of Minnesota Press, 2017), 5.

43. John McNay, "The Ohio AAUP and the Repeal of Senate Bill 5," *Academe* 101, no. 3 (May–June 2015).

44. Jacob Carter et al., *Sidelining Science since Day One: How the Trump Administration Has Harmed Public Health and Safety in Its First Six Months*, Union of Concerned Scientists, July 2017, www.ucsusa.org/sites/default/files /attach/2017/07/sidelining-science-report-ucs-7-20-2017.pdf.

45. Hank Reichman, "Proposed Visa Restrictions on Chinese Scholars Threaten Scientific Exchange, Academic Freedom," *Academe* (blog), May 18, 2018, https://academeblog.org/2018/05/18/proposed-visa-restrictions-on -chinese-scholars-threaten-scientific-exchange-academic-freedom/; Fernanda Zamudio-Suaréz, "Higher-Ed Groups Warn against Visa Restrictions for Chinese Students," *Chronicle of Higher Education*, May 30, 2018, www.chronicle .com/article/Higher-Ed-Groups-Warn-Against/243534.

46. "National Security, the Assault on Science, and Academic Freedom," *AAUP Bulletin* 104 (July–Aug. 2018): 25–37.

47. Energy & Env't Legal Inst. v. Ariz. Bd. of Regents, no. 2 CA-CV 2017-0002, 2017 Ariz. App. Unpub. LEXIS 1342 (Ct. App. Sept. 14, 2017).

48. "Win for Climate Science and the AAUP," Sept. 15, 2017, www.aaup.org /news/win-climate-science-and-aaup#.

49. "A Concerted Attack on Academic Freedom," Jan. 13, 2017, www.aaup .org/news/concerted attack academic freedom#.WodrCHɪC1Ag).

50. Hank Reichman, "AAUP Statement on Developments in the University of Wisconsin System," *Academe* (blog), Nov. 6, 2015, https://academeblog.org /2015/11/06/aaup-statement-on-developments-in-the-university-of -wisconsin-system/; and Hank Reichman, "Wisconsin Regents Committee Approves Tenure Changes without Discussion," *Academe* (blog), Feb. 6, 2016, https://academeblog.org/2016/02/06/wisconsin-regents-committee -approves-tenure-changes-without-discussion/.

51. Hank Reichman, "No Longer Superior?," *Academe* (blog), Nov. 4, 2017, https://academeblog.org/2017/11/04/no-longer-superior/; AFT Wisconsin, "UW-Superior Faculty Cast Unprecedented Vote of 'No Confidence' in Chancellor Wachter and UWS Administration after Program Suspensions

Announcement," n.d., http://wi.aft.org/press/uw-superior-faculty-cast
-unprecedented-vote-%E2%80%9Cno-confidence%E2%80%9D-chancellor
-wachter-and-uws; Fernanda Zamudio-Suaréz, "Wisconsin-Superior Leaders
Mulled Their Ability to Skirt Shared Governance in Cutting Programs,"
Chronicle of Higher Education, Feb. 27, 2018, www.chronicle.com/article
/Wisconsin-Superior-Leaders/242649.

52. Jennifer Martin-Romme, "Mad as a Yellow Jacket: Cuts and Changes
Continue to Roil the University of Wisconsin–Superior," *Zenith City News*,
May 17, 2018, www.zenithcitynews.com/single-post/051518-feature.

53. Valerie Strauss, "A University of Wisconsin Campus Pushes Plan to
Drop 13 Majors—Including English, History and Philosophy," *Washington
Post*, Mar. 21, 2018, www.washingtonpost.com/news/answer-sheet/wp/2018
/03/21/university-of-wisconsin-campus-pushes-plan-to-drop-13-majors
-including-english-history-and-philosophy/.

54. "Statement on Proposed Program Cuts at the University of Wisconsin
Stevens Point," Mar. 15, 2018, https://c.ymcdn.com/sites/www.apaonline.org
/resource/resmgr/docs/UWSP_Statement.pdf.

55. Christopher Newfield, "Newfield on the Proposed Cuts at Stevens
Point," *Academe* (blog), Mar. 26, 2018, https://academeblog.org/2018/03/26
/newfield-on-the-proposed-cuts-at-stevens-point/.

56. Anonymous, "Ghosting the Region: How UWSP's Abandonment of
the Liberal Arts Hurts Central Wisconsin," *Academe* (blog), Mar. 12, 2018,
https://academeblog.org/2018/03/12/ghosting-the-region-how-uwsps
-abandonment-of-the-liberal-arts-hurts-central-wisconsin/.

57. Paula Krebs, "Wisconsin Is Trying to Segregate Higher Education into
the Haves and Have-Nots," *Washington Post*, Mar. 21, 2018, www.washingtonpost
.com/opinions/wisconsin-is-trying-to-segregate-higher-education-into-the
-haves-and-have-nots/2018/03/21/8cd67ac0-2886-11e8-b79d-f3d931db7f68
_story.html.

58. Willard Dix, "The 'Wisconsin Idea' Is More Important Than Ever in
Higher Education," *Forbes*, Mar. 19, 2018, www.forbes.com/sites/willarddix
/2018/03/19/the-wisconsin-idea-is-more-important-than-ever-in-higher
-education/#15249e327f9b; Christine Evans, "Save the Wisconsin Idea," *New
York Times*, Feb. 16, 2015, www.nytimes.com/2015/02/16/opinion/save-the
-wisconsin-idea.html.

59. George Anders, "The Unexpected Value of the Liberal Arts," *Atlantic*,
Aug. 1, 2017, www.theatlantic.com/education/archive/2017/08/the
-unexpected-value-of-the-liberal-arts/535482/. See also George Anders, "That
'Useless' Liberal Arts Degree Has Become Tech's Hottest Ticket," *Forbes*,
July 29, 2015, www.forbes.com/sites/georgeanders/2015/07/29/liberal-arts
-degree-tech/#2bae1a6e745d.

60. Scott Jaschik, "Shocker: Humanities Grads Gainfully Employed and Happy," *Inside Higher Ed*, Feb. 7, 2018, www.insidehighered.com/news/2018 /02/07/study-finds-humanities-majors-land-jobs-and-are-happy-them. See also Derek Newton, "It's Not Liberal Arts and Literature Majors Who Are Most Underemployed," *Forbes*, May 31, 2018, www.forbes.com/sites /dereknewton/2018/05/31/its-not-liberal-arts-and-literature-majors-who-are -most-underemployed/#5cf281a11de5; Willard Dix, "A Liberal Arts Degree Is More Important Than Ever," *Forbes*, Nov. 16, 2016, www.forbes.com/sites /willarddix/2016/11/16/a-liberal-arts-degree-is-more-important-than-ever /#1fbdf0ef339f.

61. Newfield, "Newfield on the Proposed Cuts."

62. Christopher Newfield, "Newfield on the Proposed Cuts at Stevens Point, Part II," *Academe* (blog), Apr. 21, 2018, https://academeblog.org/2018 /04/21/newfield-on-the-proposed-cuts-at-stevens-point-part-ii/.

63. "Joint Statement with AAC&U on the Liberal Arts," May 31, 2018, www .aaup.org/news/joint-statement-aacu-liberal-arts#.WxgzoYoh1Ag. For a classic defense of liberal education's pursuit of knowledge for its own sake, see Abraham Flexner, "The Usefulness of Useless Knowledge," *Harpers*, Oct. 1939, 544–52, republished as Abraham Flexner, *The Usefulness of Useless Knowledge*, with a companion essay by Robert Dijkgraaf (Princeton, NJ: Princeton University Press, 2017).

64. Jon Loomis, "Guest Post: Jon Loomis on the Changing Idea in Wisconsin Higher Ed," *Inside Higher Ed*, Mar. 13, 2018, www.insidehighered .com/blogs/education-oronte-churm/guest-post-jon-loomis-changing-idea -wisconsin-higher-ed.

65. "Statement on Government of Colleges and Universities," in AAUP, *Policy Documents and Reports*, 117–22.

66. "On the Relationship of Faculty Governance to Academic Freedom," in AAUP, *Policy Documents and Reports*, 123.

67. "Why are people who drone on about 'accountability' for others allowed to act without any accountability to the institutions they are supposed to represent?" Rybak, *UW Struggle*, 75.

68. "College and University Governance: Idaho State University," *AAUP Bulletin* 97 (2011): 67–80.

69. "College and University Governance: Union County College (New Jersey)," *AAUP Bulletin* 102 (2016): 44–51.

70. Academic Senate of the California State University, "On the Development and Implementation of Executive Orders 1100 (Revised) and 1110," resolution approved Sept. 14–15, 2017, www.calstate.edu/acadsen/Records /Resolutions/2017-2018/Documents/3304.shtml.

71. "Statement on Government of Colleges and Universities," in AAUP, *Policy Documents and Reports*, 120–21.

72. "AAUP Urges CSU Chancellor to Suspend Executive Orders," Mar. 1, 2018, www.aaup.org/news/aaup-urges-csu-chancellor-suspend-executive-orders#.WxW-sIoh1Ag.

73. Colleen Flaherty, "Wisconsin in Wyoming?," *Inside Higher Ed*, May 15, 2018, www.insidehighered.com/news/2018/05/15/proposed-changes-shared-governance-university-wyoming-recall-those-passed-wisconsin.

74. "Unilateral Governance Changes at Maricopa," Apr. 26, 2018, www.aaup.org/news/unilateral-governance-changes-maricopa#.WxW-pYoh1Ag.

75. "Statement on Presidential Searches," Nov. 3, 2015, www.aaup.org/sites/default/files/AAUP_Statement_on_Presidential_Searches_0.pdf.

76. Ryan J. Foley, "Regents Detail Secret Harreld Meetings during U. Iowa Search," *Associated Press*, Sept. 25, 2017, https://apnews.com/1d9b339a344843c6ab731ec2f5aeb534.

77. "College and University Governance: The University of Iowa Governing Board's Selection of a President," *AAUP Bulletin* 102 (2016): 52–68.

78. John Seery, "Somewhere between a Jeremiad and a Eulogy," *Modern Age* 59, no. 3 (2017), https://home.isi.org/somewhere-between-jeremiad-and-eulogy.

79. Granville Hicks, "The Timid Profession," *New Masses*, June 18, 1935, 15. For the AAUP's investigation, see "Academic Freedom and Tenure: Rensselaer Polytechnic Institute," *AAUP Bulletin* 22, no. 1 (1936): 15–24.

80. Rybak, *UW Struggle*, 87.

81. "2010 Alexander Meiklejohn Award for Academic Freedom," *AAUP Bulletin* 96 (2010): 137.

Index

American Association of University
  Professors (AAUP) (cont'd.)
  sanctuary campuses, 252; on social
  media policies, 65–67; on student
  academic freedom, 156–58, 170; on
  targeted harassment, 23, 77; on tenure,
  4, 6–8, 255, 262. See also academic
  freedom; Declaration of Principles on
  Academic Freedom and Academic Tenure
  (1915); shared governance; Statement of
  Principles on Academic Freedom and
  Tenure (1940); Statement on Government
  of Colleges and Universities; tenure
American Civil Liberties Union (ACLU),
  65, 202, 205, 237
American Council on Education, 179, 253.
  See also Statement on Government of
  Colleges and Universities
American Enterprise Institute, 124
American Federation of Teachers (AFT):
  on concealed carry, 19; early AAUP and,
  223, 227; embrace of 1940 Statement by,
  3; graduate student organizing, 258; on
  targeted harassment, 23, 77
American University, 82, 251
Anders, George, 266
Anglin, Andrew, 82
Anna Maria College, 197
Anti-Defamation League, 249
Arizona State University (ASU), 119–21,
  144–46
Ash, Timothy Garton, 171, 283n34, 297n9
Association of American Colleges and
  Universities (AAC&U), 107; on
  concealed carry, 19; on extramural
  expression, 53–55; on humanities,
  267–68; on targeted harassment, 23, 77.
  See also Statement of Principles on
  Academic Freedom and Tenure (1940)
Association of Governing Boards of
  Universities and Colleges: on campus
  free speech, 321n20; on concealed
  carry, 19. See also Statement on
  Government of Colleges and Universities
Auburn University, 114, 172

Baer, Ulrich, 201–2, 220
Balkin, Jack, 66
Ball State University, 117
Barrow, Clyde, 239, 333n2, 336n45
Baumol, William, 138–39, 315n12
Bayh-Dole Act, 11, 284n41
Baylor University, 250
Becerra, Xavier, 188–89
Belleville College, 233
Bemis, Edward, 51
Benjamin, Ernst, 235, 238–39, 334n29
Ben-Porath, Sigal, 159, 292n25, 326n13
Berger, Phil, 123
Berkowitz, Joel, 191–92
Bérubé, Michael, 7, 46
Bethune-Cookman University, 187
Bond, Sarah, 79–80
Bork, Nathaniel, 1
Boston Consulting Group (BCG), 144–46
Botstein, Leon, 108
Bowen, William, 137–42, 148–50
Boycott, Divestment, Sanctions (BDS)
  movement. See Israeli-Palestinian
  conflict
Brandeis, Louis, 203–4
Bray, Mark, 80
Breitbart News, 78, 80, 171
Bridgewater State University, 300n34
Broad, Molly, 127
Bromwich, David, 28–29, 37–38, 152
Brookings Institution, 153
Brooklyn College, 80
Brooks, David, 106
Brown, Jerry, 136–37, 146–47, 150, 226,
  315n5
Brown, Wendy, 218, 221
Burgan, Mary, 26, 128–29, 241, 316n22
Burnett, L. D., 73
Butler, Henry, 112
Butler, Judith, 41–42, 62, 292n18, 292n23
Butz, Arthur, 60
Byse, Clark, 233

Cabrera, Angel, 109–10
Cain, Timothy Reese, 20, 225